America's
TEST KITCHEN

"Ideal as a reference for the bookshelf and as a book to curl up and get lost in, this volume will be turned to time and again for definitive instruction on just about any food-related matter."
PUBLISHERS WEEKLY ON THE SCIENCE OF GOOD COOKING

"A one-volume kitchen seminar, addressing in one smart chapter after another the sometimes surprising whys behind a cook's best practices . . . You get the myth, the theory, the science and the proof, all rigorously interrogated as only America's Test Kitchen can do."
NPR ON THE SCIENCE OF GOOD COOKING

"The Cook's Illustrated Cookbook is the perfect kitchen home companion."
THE WALL STREET JOURNAL ON THE COOK'S ILLUSTRATED COOKBOOK

"A wonderfully comprehensive guide for budding chefs . . . Throughout are the helpful tips and exacting illustrations that make ATK a peerless source for culinary wisdom."
PUBLISHERS WEEKLY ON THE COOK'S ILLUSTRATED COOKBOOK

"For a practical, encyclopedic approach to baking— holiday and otherwise—the ultimate reference volume has to be The Cook's Illustrated Baking Book."
THE WALL STREET JOURNAL ON THE COOK'S ILLUSTRATED BAKING BOOK

"If this were the only cookbook you owned, you would cook well, be everyone's favorite host, have a well-run kitchen, and eat happily every day."
THECITYCOOK.COM ON THE AMERICA'S TEST KITCHEN MENU COOKBOOK

"This book upgrades slow cooking for discriminating, 21st-century palates—that is indeed revolutionary."
THE DALLAS MORNING NEWS ON SLOW COOKER REVOLUTION

"America's Test Kitchen spent two years reimagining cooking for the 21st century. The result is an exhaustive collection offering a fresh approach to quick cooking."
THE DETROIT NEWS ON THE AMERICA'S TEST KITCHEN QUICK FAMILY COOKBOOK

"This comprehensive collection of 800-plus family and global favorites helps put healthy eating in an everyday context, from meatloaf to Indian curry with chicken."
COOKING LIGHT ON THE AMERICA'S TEST KITCHEN HEALTHY FAMILY COOKBOOK

"Expert bakers and novices scared of baking's requisite exactitude can all learn something from this hefty, all-purpose home baking volume."
PUBLISHERS WEEKLY ON THE AMERICA'S TEST KITCHEN FAMILY BAKING BOOK

"This tome definitely raises the bar for all-in-one, basic, must-have cookbooks . . . Kimball and his company have scored another hit."
PORTLAND OREGONIAN ON THE AMERICA'S TEST KITCHEN FAMILY COOKBOOK

"A foolproof, go-to resource for everyday cooking."
PUBLISHERS WEEKLY ON THE AMERICA'S TEST KITCHEN FAMILY COOKBOOK

"Forget about marketing hype, designer labels, and pretentious entrées: This is an unblinking, unbedazzled guide to the Beardian good-cooking ideal."
THE WALL STREET JOURNAL ON THE BEST OF AMERICA'S TEST KITCHEN 2009

"Worth its weight in gold for the practical cook who wants to feel confident about putting good food on the table."
THE DETROIT NEWS ON THE COMPLETE AMERICA'S TEST KITCHEN TV SHOW COOKBOOK

"Even ultra-experienced gluten-free cooks and bakers will learn something from this thoroughly researched, thoughtfully presented volume."
PUBLISHERS WEEKLY ON THE HOW CAN IT BE GLUTEN FREE COOKBOOK

"Further proof that practice makes perfect, if not transcendent . . . If an intermediate cook follows the directions exactly, the results will be better than takeout or Mom's."
THE NEW YORK TIMES ON THE NEW BEST RECIPE

THE TV COMPANION
COOKBOOK

2015

America's TEST KITCHEN

THE TV COMPANION COOKBOOK

2015

BY THE EDITORS AT
AMERICA'S TEST KITCHEN

PHOTOGRAPHY BY
CARL TREMBLAY
DANIEL J. VAN ACKERE
STEVE KLISE

AMERICA'S TEST KITCHEN
BROOKLINE, MASSACHUSETTS

AMERICA'S TEST KITCHEN
17 Station Street, Brookline, MA 02445

AMERICA'S TEST KITCHEN: THE TV
COMPANION COOKBOOK 2015
1st Edition

ISBN-13: 978-1-936493-94-4
ISBN-10: 1-936493-94-2
ISSN 2161-6671
Hardcover: $34.95 US

Manufactured in the United States of
America

10 9 8 7 6 5 4 3 2 1

Distributed by America's Test Kitchen
17 Station Street, Brookline, MA 02445

EDITORIAL DIRECTOR: Jack Bishop
EDITORIAL DIRECTOR, BOOKS: Elizabeth Carduff
EXECUTIVE EDITOR: Lori Galvin
SENIOR EDITOR: Debra Hudak
ASSISTANT EDITOR: Melissa Herrick
EDITORIAL ASSISTANTS: Rachel Greenhaus and Samantha Ronan
DESIGN DIRECTOR: Amy Klee
ART DIRECTOR, BOOKS: Greg Galvan
ASSOCIATE ART DIRECTOR, BOOKS: Taylor Argenzio
DESIGNERS: Allison Boales and Jen Kanavos Hoffman
PHOTOGRAPHY DIRECTOR: Julie Cote
STAFF PHOTOGRAPHER: Daniel J. van Ackere
ASSOCIATE ART DIRECTOR, PHOTOGRAPHY: Steve Klise
ADDITIONAL PHOTOGRAPHY: Keller + Keller, Steve Klise, and Carl Tremblay
FOOD STYLISTS: Catrine Kelty and Marie Piraino
PRODUCTION DIRECTOR: Guy Rochford
SENIOR PRODUCTION MANAGER: Jessica Lindheimer Quirk
PROJECT MANAGEMENT DIRECTOR: Alice Carpenter
PROJECT MANAGER: Britt Dresser
WORKFLOW AND DIGITAL ASSET MANAGER: Andrew Mannone
PRODUCTION AND IMAGING SPECIALISTS: Heather Dube, Dennis Noble, and Lauren Robbins
COPY EDITOR: Cheryl Redmond
PROOFREADER: Christine Corcoran Cox
INDEXER: Elizabeth Parson

CONTENTS

PREFACE

I AM OFTEN ASKED IF FILMING OUR PUBLIC TELEVISION show, *America's Test Kitchen*, is as much fun as it looks and the answer is yes. I have worked with Bridget, Julia, Jack, and Adam for 20 years and we really do enjoy each other's company. Plus, I get fed pretty well and someone else does all of the cooking and cleaning. Not bad work if you can get it.

The other reason I love our TV show is that I am reminded of the thousands of hours of kitchen testing and development that have gone into our recipes. Some of the recipes on this season of the show have truly changed how I cook at home. Perfect Poached Chicken Breasts, for example, solves the problem of dried out, flavorless chicken with a simple recipe that uses a soy sauce/water brine and then cooks the chicken directly in the brine itself. Simple and, if I may say so, brilliant. We took a page from Yotam Ottolenghi, the famous author of *Plenty* and *Jerusalem*, and made Roasted Butternut Squash, roasted slices of peeled butternut squash served with savory toppings. The Southern Shrimp Burgers are a revelation—both simple and delicious. Our Best Almond Cake (a one-layer torte) is to die for—lighter than traditional recipes but still full of almond flavor. Oddly enough, we made Gluten-Free Chocolate Chip Cookies that really are as good as the original. And, for fancy occasions, our French Apple Tart is a winner as well—thinly sliced parcooked apples on top of a concentrated base of applesauce with a bit of apricot preserves thrown in for good measure.

I also learned which stand mixer can handle small batches as well as big and which freezer storage bags are easy to seal while keeping food both fresh and dry. Of course, the show is not complete without the tasting challenges with Jack Bishop—this year the high points were prosciutto and Swiss cheese (an American company makes better Swiss cheese than the Swiss). We even tasted gluten-free spaghetti. (Yes, there is a gluten-free product—Jovial—that is actually pretty good.)

This year, I got to dress up as a strawberry, an eggplant, a Deadhead (that was not a stretch), and the Earl of Grantham from *Downton Abbey* (that wasn't a stretch either!) to name a few of my favorite costumes. If you are confused why I do this on a cooking show, well, so am I. It is a long-standing tradition and that's that. (And kids who watch the show like it, too.)

After more than 30 years in this business, I am very proud of our work, represented by the type of recipes that you will find in this book. Good recipes and good cooking really can change lives for the better. Being known among friends and family as a good cook builds self-confidence and provides immense pleasure.

Of course, in Vermont being a good trader is a virtue right up there with cooking. This story is about a man who went to town to get his horse shod; he brought an egg along with him to trade for a knitting needle for his wife. At the general store he inquired as to the price of knitting needles and eggs—both cost one cent apiece. When he suggested a swap, the storekeeper indicated that the one-cent price for the egg was a retail price, not wholesale, but, since he knew the man and his father as well, he would do the swap. The farmer, however, did not pick up the needle. He was asked what was wrong and the farmer replied, "Well, I heard that when you get a new customer, you offer him a noggin of rum." The storekeeper hesitated but then gave him a shot of rum. The farmer didn't take the rum and said, "I also heard that sometimes you drop a raw egg in it." Again the storekeeper hesitated but finally cracked the farmer's egg into the rum. The farmer noticed that it had two yolks and looked straight at the storekeeper and said, "Well, I guess that you owe me another knitting needle!"

If you love cooking as much as Vermonters love trading, well, you'll be in great shape!

Christopher Kimball
Founder and Editor, *Cook's Illustrated* and *Cook's Country*
Host, *America's Test Kitchen* and
Cook's Country from America's Test Kitchen

WELCOME TO AMERICA'S TEST KITCHEN

THIS BOOK HAS BEEN TESTED, WRITTEN, AND EDITED BY the folks at America's Test Kitchen, a very real 2,500-square-foot kitchen located just outside of Boston. It is the home of *Cook's Illustrated* and *Cook's Country* magazines and is the Monday-through-Friday destination for more than four dozen test cooks, editors, food scientists, tasters, and cookware specialists. Our mission is to test recipes over and over again until we understand how and why they work and until we arrive at the "best" version.

Our television show highlights the best recipes developed in the test kitchen during the past year—those recipes that our test kitchen staff makes at home time and time again. These recipes are accompanied by our most exhaustive equipment tests and our most interesting food tastings.

Christopher Kimball, the founder and editor of *Cook's Illustrated* magazine, is host of the show and asks the questions you might ask. It's the job of our chefs, Julia Collin Davison, Bridget Lancaster, Becky Hays, Bryan Roof, and Dan Souza to demonstrate our recipes. The chefs show Chris what works and what doesn't, and they explain why. In the process, they discuss (and show you) the best examples from our development process as well as the worst.

Adam Ried, our equipment expert, and Lisa McManus, our gadget guru, share the highlights from our detailed testing process in equipment corner segments. They bring with them our favorite (and least favorite) gadgets and tools. Jack Bishop is our ingredient expert. He has Chris taste our favorite (and least favorite) brands of common food products. Chris may not always enjoy these exercises (hot sauce isn't exactly as fun to taste as mozzarella or dark chocolate), but he usually learns something as Jack explains what makes one brand superior to another.

Although just 10 cooks and editors appear on the television show, another 50 people worked to make the show a reality. Executive Producer Melissa Baldino conceived and developed each episode with help from Co-Executive Producer Stephanie Stender and Associate Producer Kaitlin Hammond. Debby Paddock assisted with all the photo research. Guy Crosby, our science expert, researched the science behind the recipes. Along with the on-air crew, executive chefs Erin McMurrer and Keith Dresser helped plan and organize the 26 television episodes shot in May 2014 and ran the "back kitchen," where all the food that appeared on camera originated. Hannah Crowley, Kate Shannon, and Lauren Savoie organized the tasting and equipment segments.

During filming, chefs Morgan Bolling, Aaron Furmanek, Andrea Geary, Andrew Janjigian, Cecelia Jenkins, Lan Lam, Suzannah McFerran, Ashley Moore, Christie Morrison, Chris O'Connor, Diane Unger, and Cristin Walsh cooked all the food needed on set. Interns Jared Hughes, Abby Miller, Amy Siblik, and Robin Swayze worked on-set developing recipes for our magazines and books. Assistant Test Kitchen Director

Leah Rovner and Senior Kitchen Assistants Michelle Blodget and Alexxa Grattan were charged with making sure all the ingredients and kitchen equipment we needed were on hand. Kitchen assistants Maria Elena Delgado, Ena Gudiel, Eliot Carduff, and Jason Roman also worked long hours. Chefs Daniel Cellucci, Danielle DeSiato-Hallman, Sara Mayer, Sebastian Nava, Stephanie Pixley, Russell Selander, Meaghen Walsh, and Anne Wolf helped coordinate the efforts of the kitchen with the television set by readying props, equipment, and food. Shannon Hatch, Kate Zebrowski, and Christine Gordon led all tours of the test kitchen during filming.

Special thanks to director and editor Herb Sevush and director of photography Jan Maliszewski.

We also appreciate the hard work of the video production team, including Stephen Hussar, Michael McEachern, Peter Dingle, Roger Macie, Gilles Morin, Brenda Coffey, Ken Fraser, Joe Christofori, James Hirsch, Bob Hirsch, Jeremy Bond, Eric Joslin, Cara McCabe, Phoebe Melnick, Wes Palmer, and Matt Stavropoulos. Thanks also to Nick Dakoulas, the second unit videographer.

We also would like to thank Nancy Bocchino, Bara Levin, and Victoria Yuen at WGBH Station Relations, and the team at American Public Television that presents the show: Cynthia Fenneman, Chris Funkhouser, Judy Barlow, and Tom Davison. Thanks also for production support from Elena Battista Malcolm and DGA Productions, Boston, and Zebra Productions, New York.

DCS by Fisher & Paykel, SieMatic, Kohler, Diamond Crystal Salt, Cooking.com, and Wente Vineyards helped underwrite the show, and we thank them for their support. We also thank Michael Burton, Anne Traficante, Kate Zebrowski, and Morgan Mannino for handling underwriter relations and Deborah Broide for managing publicity.

Meat was provided by Kinnealey Meats of Brockton, Massachusetts. Fish was supplied by Ian Davison of Constitution Seafoods of Boston, Massachusetts. Live plants and garden items for the show were furnished by Mahoney's Garden Center of Brighton, Massachusetts. Aprons for Christopher Kimball were made by Nicole Romano and staff aprons were made by Crooked Brook.

AMERICA'S TEST KITCHEN

THE TV COMPANION COOKBOOK 2015

Get a Rise Out of Your Eggs

*Parmesan cheese boosts the
flavor of traditional Gruyère
in our perfectly risen soufflé.*

EGGS FOR SUPPER ISN'T EXACTLY A NEW CONCEPT. SURE, YOU CAN FRY up a couple of eggs and call it dinner, but go just one or two steps further and you've got a dish that you might want to pull out the linen napkins for and pour a glass of wine. We're talking two classic egg dishes: pasta frittata and cheese soufflé. We'll show you how to use eggs to their full potential—with delicious results.

Pasta frittata can be a perfect way to use up leftover pasta—but that's rarely a problem we have. Instead, we aimed to find a way to use dried pasta to perfect this dish of lightly scrambled eggs enveloped in a web of tender pasta. And we didn't want to hide our creamy, rich egg base under a mask of heavy dairy. A few flavorful meat and vegetable additions made our frittata into a one-dish meal.

Cheese soufflé is an elegant French classic, but most recipes seem so finicky. We discovered that you don't have to tiptoe around the whipped egg whites—in fact, roughing them up a little gave our soufflé the perfect structure. With its ample cheese flavor and impressive presentation, we think this soufflé will have you rethinking eggs for the better.

PASTA FRITTATA WITH SAUSAGE AND HOT PEPPERS

PASTA FRITTATA

✔ **WHY THIS RECIPE WORKS:** This classic Neapolitan dish usually starts with leftover sauced pasta, which is mixed with beaten eggs for a simple one-dish dinner. But here in the test kitchen, we're rarely faced with leftover pasta. We wanted a streamlined recipe for pasta frittata that used dried pasta. Angel hair turned out to be the ideal pasta shape, providing a good balance of pasta and egg in each bite. Cooking the pasta in a small amount of water in a skillet allowed us to make the entire dish using only one pan. Adding some oil to the pasta as it was cooking helped it to "fry" lightly once the water had evaporated, making a crispy noodle crust. Once we added the eggs, we let the frittata finish cooking over gentle heat. A bit of extra-virgin olive oil added to the eggs provided richness, and boldly flavored additions like sausage and hot peppers or broccoli rabe and pepper flakes boosted flavor without breaking up the creamy texture.

LEFTOVERS GET A BAD RAP. IT'S A SHAME, BECAUSE they're the foundation of some of the best dishes out there. For us, one of the most underrated made-from-leftovers preparations is pasta frittata, in which leftover pasta is transformed into a thick, creamy, golden-brown omelet laced with noodles. The dish got its start in Naples, Italy. The classic Neapolitan pasta frittata starts with leftover cooked and sauced pasta (most often a long noodle shape) and half a dozen or so eggs beaten with salt, pepper, melted lard or butter, and grated Parmigiano-Reggiano cheese. In our opinion, the best versions are those that also feature small bites of meat or vegetables that contribute flavor without overly disrupting the creamy texture of the dish.

Of course, here in the test kitchen, we rarely find ourselves with leftover pasta. But why should that stand in the way of a great pasta frittata? Cooking dried pasta would require a little more effort, but maybe we could streamline the process and find a way to make a good dish even better.

Since we weren't dealing with leftovers, we had the whole world of pasta open to us. To see which particular type might work best, we boiled up a variety of shapes and sizes and tested them in a bare-bones recipe of eight beaten eggs, ½ cup of Parmesan cheese, and some salt and pepper. It was clear right off the bat that long noodles like spaghetti, linguine, and fettuccine were superior to short and tubular types. While the strands effortlessly blended with the eggs, chunky and tubular pastas created gaps and led to frittatas that broke apart during slicing. Among the long noodles, spaghetti was the winner, ensuring a more balanced ratio of pasta to egg in each bite compared with the wider linguine and fettuccine. If skinny was good, perhaps skinnier would be even better, so we made one more frittata, this time using angel hair pasta. These delicate strands proved ideal, bringing a satisfying web of pasta to every bite without marring the tender egg texture.

While most Italians will claim that there is only one way to cook pasta—in a large quantity of boiling water—we've actually found that the process is far more flexible. While a full pot of water does help keep pasta from sticking together, it turns out that a little water works just fine, provided you stir often. Perhaps even more surprising is that you can start pasta directly in cold water that is then brought to a boil and get results identical to those you'd get from throwing it into already boiling water. We decided to put these discoveries into practice in the name of convenience. Instead of pulling out a large Dutch oven, filling it with 4 quarts of water, and bringing it to a full boil, we tossed 6 ounces of angel hair pasta (broken in half) into a 10-inch nonstick skillet along with 3 cups of water and some salt. We placed the skillet over high heat and stirred occasionally as it came to a boil. Then we let it simmer, again stirring occasionally, until the pasta was tender and the water had evaporated. All told it took about 15 minutes, and by cooking off the water, we could even skip dirtying a strainer. On to the egg mixture.

Beating together eight eggs (the number that provided the right balance and structure for 6 ounces of dried pasta) with salt, pepper, and Parmesan and tossing in cooked angel hair was about as easy as it gets—but

few strands of angel hair that had settled at the bottom or sides of the hot pan, turning brown and crispy. The contrast between the creamy eggs and these crispy strands was actually one of the best parts. Was there any way to get even more of these browned strands?

To this end, we started fiddling with how we layered the egg and the noodles, thinking that we could purposely leave some of the pasta on the bottom of the frittata to ensure contact with the pan. We got mixed results—sometimes the pasta would stay put and other times the egg would just seep under it and prevent crisping. Up to this point we'd been boiling the pasta in the skillet and then pouring in the egg mixture. But what we really needed to do was fry the pasta before incorporating the eggs. Why not just add a little oil to the skillet with the pasta and water and let it start frying once the water evaporated? This is the same technique that is used with potstickers and, to our delight, it worked just as well here. As soon as the last bit of water evaporated, the pasta started sizzling. We cooked it, swirling and shaking the pan to prevent sticking, until the strands at the bottom of the pan turned lightly crispy. Then we simply poured the egg mixture over the pasta and used tongs to mix the egg throughout the uncrisped strands, leaving the bottom layer as undisturbed as possible. Sure enough, the time that it took to cook the egg through resulted in a substantial, lacy layer of crispy, browned pasta that almost served as a crust, delivering satisfying crunch in every bite. Meanwhile, the rest of the pasta stayed tender, melding into the creamy eggs.

The frittata was ready to be flavored with some bold ingredients. We knew that the key to adding vegetables and meat was cutting everything into small pieces (which didn't disturb the interior texture). The add-ins also needed to precook in the skillet since they would just warm through in the frittata. Our favorite combination was a mix of savory-sweet Italian sausage and chopped hot cherry peppers. It offered richness and plenty of acidity and heat to balance. We also whipped up a version featuring broccoli rabe and a pinch of red pepper flakes. No matter the flavor, this pasta frittata never lasted long in the kitchen. A shame—we like leftovers.

ensuring that this mixture cooked up creamy and tender took a bit more thought. We knew that the final texture of the frittata would be determined by how gently it was cooked and the amount of fat in the mix. Gently cooking any egg preparation ensures that the exterior portions don't overcook and turn rubbery while the interior comes up to temperature. Turning the stove dial to medium, covering the frittata during cooking, and flipping it halfway through proved a winning formula. The top and bottom took on a burnished appearance while the inside stayed moist and relatively tender.

But we wanted it to be even more tender, so we turned our attention to fat. Fat keeps eggs tender by coating their proteins and preventing them from bonding together too firmly. Neapolitans would likely reach for lard, butter, or cream when making this dish, but after a series of tests, we preferred extra-virgin olive oil since it produced a frittata that tasted more of egg and less of rich dairy. For eight eggs, 3 tablespoons of oil provided good richness and plenty of protection against toughness.

We were feeling pretty pleased and nearly ready to close the file on the recipe but for one thing: All along, tasters had raved when they encountered the inevitable

Pasta Frittata with Sausage and Hot Peppers

SERVES 4 TO 6

To ensure the proper texture, it's important to use angel hair pasta. We like to serve the frittata warm or at room temperature, with a green salad.

- 8 large eggs
- 1 ounce Parmesan cheese, grated (½ cup)
- 3 tablespoons extra-virgin olive oil
- 3 tablespoons coarsely chopped jarred hot cherry peppers
- 2 tablespoons chopped fresh parsley
  Salt and pepper
- 8 ounces sweet Italian sausage, casings removed, crumbled
- 2 garlic cloves, sliced thin
- 3 cups water
- 6 ounces angel hair pasta, broken in half
- 3 tablespoons vegetable oil

1. Whisk eggs, Parmesan, olive oil, cherry peppers, parsley, ½ teaspoon salt, and ½ teaspoon pepper in large bowl until egg is even yellow color; set aside.

2. Cook sausage in 10-inch nonstick skillet over medium heat, breaking up sausage with wooden spoon, until fat renders and sausage is about half cooked, 3 to 5 minutes. Stir in garlic and cook for 30 seconds. Remove skillet from heat. Transfer sausage mixture (some sausage will still be raw) to bowl with egg mixture and wipe out skillet.

3. Bring water, pasta, vegetable oil, and ¾ teaspoon salt to boil in now-empty skillet over high heat, stirring occasionally. Cook, stirring occasionally, until pasta is tender, water has evaporated, and pasta starts to sizzle in oil, 8 to 12 minutes. Reduce heat to medium and continue to cook pasta, swirling pan and scraping under edge of pasta with rubber spatula frequently to prevent sticking (do not stir), until bottom turns golden and starts to crisp, 5 to 7 minutes (lift up edge of pasta to check progress).

4. Using spatula, push some pasta up sides of skillet so entire pan surface is covered with pasta. Pour egg mixture over pasta. Using tongs, lift up loose strands of

NOTES FROM THE TEST KITCHEN

PASTA FRITTATA MADE WITHOUT LEFTOVERS
Though it's usually whipped up with last night's noodles, pasta frittata can be just as simple using our one-skillet approach.

1. USE A SKILLET: Add water, broken angel hair, and oil to skillet.

2. COOK OFF LIQUID: Once pasta is tender, keep cooking until water evaporates and pasta starts sizzling in oil.

3. LET IT CRISP: After about 5 minutes, pasta will start to crisp (check progress by lifting up edge).

4. LIFT LOOSE STRANDS: Pour eggs over pasta, then gently pull up top strands to allow eggs to flow into center.

5. SLIDE AND INVERT: To brown second side, slide frittata onto plate, invert onto second plate, and return to skillet.

pasta to allow egg to flow toward pan, being careful not to pull up crispy bottom crust. Cover skillet and continue to cook over medium heat until bottom crust turns golden brown and top of frittata is just set (egg below very top will still be raw), 5 to 8 minutes. Slide frittata onto large plate. Invert frittata onto second large plate and slide it browned side up back into skillet. Tuck edges of frittata into skillet with rubber spatula. Continue to cook second side of frittata until light brown, 2 to 4 minutes longer.

5. Remove skillet from heat and let stand for 5 minutes. Using your hand or pan lid, invert frittata onto cutting board. Cut into wedges and serve.

VARIATION

Pasta Frittata with Broccoli Rabe

Omit cherry peppers, parsley, and sausage. Heat 2 teaspoons vegetable oil in 10-inch nonstick skillet over medium heat until shimmering. Add garlic and ⅛ teaspoon red pepper flakes and cook for 1 minute. Stir in 8 ounces broccoli rabe, trimmed and cut into ½-inch pieces, 1 tablespoon water, and ¼ teaspoon salt; cover skillet and cook until broccoli rabe is crisp-tender, 2 to 3 minutes. Remove skillet from heat and add 1 tablespoon white wine vinegar. Transfer broccoli rabe to bowl with egg mixture. Proceed with recipe from step 3, cooking pasta with remaining 7 teaspoons vegetable oil.

NOTES FROM THE TEST KITCHEN

A TOASTY BOTTOM

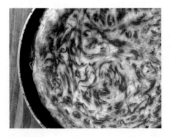

A layer of crispy golden pasta on the bottom of the frittata (shown here after we flipped it to brown the top and before we reinverted it for serving) distinguishes our version.

CHEESE SOUFFLÉ

✔ WHY THIS RECIPE WORKS: Making a truly great cheese soufflé is like finding the Holy Grail for most cooks—unattainable. But this classic French dish doesn't have to be relegated to the realm of professional chefs. We wanted a cheese soufflé with bold cheese flavor, good stature, and a light but not-too-airy texture—all without the fussiness of most recipes. To bump up the cheese flavor without weighing down the soufflé, we added lightweight-but-flavorful Parmesan cheese to the traditional Gruyère. Reducing the amount of butter and flour also amplified the cheese flavor. Filling the soufflé dish to an inch below the rim allowed ample room for the soufflé to rise high. To get the texture just right while keeping the preparation simple, we beat egg whites to stiff peaks, and then—rather than carefully folding them into the cheese sauce—added the sauce right to the stand mixer, and beat everything until uniform. When the center reached 170 degrees after baking for about half an hour, our soufflé had a perfect luscious creamy center and lightly bronzed edges.

SOUFFLÉ AU FROMAGE—ETHEREALLY LIGHT EGGS AND nutty, tangy Gruyère cheese combined and lifted to startlingly tall heights   can't help but impress. So why don't many people make it anymore?

Maybe because most people assume that it's a dish fraught with disaster, ready to collapse with the slightest disturbance. Classic French cookbooks intimidate with pages upon pages devoted to how to perfectly whip and fold in egg whites and precisely time the dish for your guests. ("A soufflé can be waited for, but it can never wait," declares *La Bonne Cuisine de Madame E. Saint-Ange: The Original Companion for French Home Cooking*.) Then there's the matter of fashioning a parchment collar around the dish to contain the batter as it rises, not to mention the mystery of determining when the soufflé is done—more concerns that make soufflé seem like a dish best left to the experts.

As we tried out a few recipes, we realized the truth: Soufflés are neither complicated nor finicky. In fact, a cheese soufflé is nothing more than a sauce that's transformed into dinner through the addition of egg whites and air. The sauce, typically a béchamel made of milk thickened with a paste (or roux) of equal parts butter and flour, provides the soufflé with stability. Grated cheese is added for flavor, and egg yolks introduce richness and a silky texture. Stop here and you'd have something that might dress up steamed broccoli or poached chicken. But fold in stiffly beaten egg whites and the dish stands on its own, literally and figuratively. After this batter is poured into a round, straight-sided soufflé dish and baked in a hot oven, the water in the mixture rapidly turns to steam, inflating air bubbles and raising the soufflé to high heights.

But that doesn't mean all recipes for soufflés lead to optimal results. Some of the recipes we tried turned out soufflés that were overly heavy and dense; others were so light and ethereal that they were hardly substantial enough for a meal. Still others had negligible cheese flavor. We wanted a cheese soufflé boasting not only stature but also enough substance to serve as a main

course. It needed a balanced but distinctive cheese flavor and contrasting textures in the form of a crispy, nicely browned crust and a moist, almost custardy center.

We cobbled together a basic recipe—six eggs, 6 tablespoons each of butter and flour, a little more than a cup of milk, and 4 ounces of grated Gruyère (the classic choice)—and got down to testing. The resulting soufflé wasn't terrible, but it had a long way to go. It didn't have loads of cheese flavor; its texture was closer to that of a quiche than that of a soufflé; and it rose only about an inch or so above the lip of the dish.

We wondered if the béchamel might be the cause of multiple problems. Flour has a tendency to mute flavors, and its thickening power, while essential to providing the soufflé with stability, can also weigh things down. When we dialed back the amounts of butter and flour to 4 tablespoons each (anything less than that and the soufflé verged on soupy), the flavor of the cheese came through more clearly and the texture lightened up. This gave us enough wiggle room to add more cheese. But beyond a certain point (6 ounces) the texture began to suffer and the soufflé turned out squat. To increase the cheese flavor without causing damage, we turned to more

SOUFFLÉ MYTHS DEBUNKED

MYTH: The soufflé will collapse from loud noises or sudden movements.
REALITY: Steam will keep a hot soufflé fully inflated. No loud noise or slamming of the oven door can change that.

MYTH: The egg whites must be gently folded into the base.
REALITY: Egg whites whipped to stiff peaks will have ample structure to handle aggressive beating, even in a stand mixer.

MYTH: Prodding to check doneness will make it collapse.
REALITY: A soufflé is not a balloon; it's a matrix of very fine bubbles. No tool can pop enough of them to cause it to fall.

MYTH: You can't make a fallen soufflé rise again.
REALITY: Yes, your soufflé will fall after it's been out of the oven for about 5 minutes. But returning it to a 350-degree oven will convert the water back into steam and reinflate it (it will lose about ½ inch of height).

FALLEN FROM GRACE   **RETURNED TO GLORY**

AVOID A SOUFFLÉ MELTDOWN

Soufflé recipes traditionally require attaching a greased parchment collar around the lip of the soufflé dish. Extending the collar several inches above the dish keeps the soufflé contained so that it rises up rather than spills over. But we found that the old-fashioned approach isn't necessary. The key is giving the fluid batter enough room to set up before it rises above the dish's lip. It takes about 20 minutes for the batter to reach the rim, at which point it's set and will continue to rise up, rather than spill over. In our Cheese Soufflé recipe, we call for leaving an inch of space between the top of the batter and the rim of the dish. Because soufflé dishes vary a bit in capacity, you may not need all the batter in our recipe, so discard any left over after filling your dish to the proper level. (For more information about soufflé dishes, see our testing on page 13.)

intensely flavored yet feathery grated Parmesan. Adding 5 tablespoons, along with the 6 ounces of Gruyère, gave the soufflé the cheese flavor that it needed without the weight. We also dusted the sides and bottom of the soufflé dish and the top of the batter with a few more tablespoons of Parmesan.

As for baking temperature, recipes that we consulted varied from 300 degrees to 400 degrees. We wanted a soufflé with a crispy mahogany crust, nicely set edges, and a moist, barely set core. When the soufflé was cooked at too-low temperatures, the crust resisted browning and the interior set too evenly. Excessively high temperatures, on the other hand, cooked it too fast: When the crust was nicely browned, the interior was still soupy. We found that 350 degrees worked best. Another key discovery: Rather than deal with the fussy step of greasing a parchment collar and securing it around the lip of the dish to create a taller soufflé and also prevent overflow as the soufflé rises, we simply left about 1 inch of headspace between the top of the batter and the lip of the dish.

Knowing when the soufflé was done turned out to be very straightforward. Some recipes tell you that it should be "slightly jiggly" at the center, while others say to insert a skewer (or knitting needle) and look for a moist but not wet batter. We liked using two spoons to pry open the middle of the soufflé to check that it looked barely set but not soupy. Even better, though, was using an instant-read thermometer. We found that when inserted into the soufflé's core, the thermometer should reach about 170 degrees.

We were making progress, but the interior consistency of the soufflé was still not exactly where we wanted it to be. The soufflé was rising nearly 3 inches when cooked, making it a bit too light and delicate. We already knew that more cheese wasn't the answer (plus we already had the cheese flavor down), so what could we do to create a soufflé that was light but not featherweight?

Up until now we'd been following soufflé convention and whipping the egg whites to stiff peaks in order to

CHEESE SOUFFLÉ

time around, we whipped the whites to stiff peaks and then stirred them vigorously rather than folded them into the cheese mixture. In doing this, we hoped that we could break down some of the structure by whipping out just enough air from the whites. We worried that such manhandling might be overkill and ruin the soufflé completely, but it seemed to have plenty of volume going into the oven. And it baked up better than ever. The soufflé had risen beautifully (if not quite as high as before), and its consistency was perfect: light and airy but with the extra heft that it had been missing. We did one more test to see if we could streamline things even further and found that we could simply whip the cheese mixture into the whites right in the stand mixer.

Before wrapping things up, we wanted to find out if other cheeses could stand in for the Gruyère. Softer or milder cheeses, like goat, blue, and mild cheddar, were not good alternatives, since they either added too much moisture to the soufflé or were simply not potent enough. But cheeses with a similar depth of flavor, consistency, and meltability, like Comté, sharp cheddar, and gouda, made equally great-tasting soufflés.

At last, we had a richly flavored, entrée-worthy cheese soufflé that was as easy to prepare as it was impressive.

create maximum volume. We wondered whether we could dial back the lightness by not working them so hard. For the next test, we whipped the whites to soft peaks instead. While the resulting soufflé had a denser consistency, it was a little too dense and squat. Here was the Goldilocks moment: Stiff peaks provided a bit too much lift and airiness, and soft peaks provided not quite enough. "Medium" peaks would probably be perfect—if we only knew of a way to call for such a thing. Soft peaks retain some shape but droop slowly from the end of a whisk, while stiff peaks are glossy and firm and hold their shape entirely. But the midway point between the two is a nebulous thing; there just isn't a good visual indicator for such a stage.

But maybe there was another way. Most recipes insist that you fold the whites gradually and gently into the cheese-béchamel mixture to ensure that the soufflé rises properly. We wondered if that was really important. Next

Cheese Soufflé

SERVES 4 TO 6

Serve this soufflé with a green salad for a light dinner. Comté, sharp cheddar, or gouda cheese can be substituted for the Gruyère. To prevent the soufflé from overflowing the soufflé dish, leave at least 1 inch of space between the top of the batter and the rim of the dish; any excess batter should be discarded. The most foolproof way to test for doneness is with an instant-read thermometer. To judge doneness without an instant-read thermometer, use two large spoons to pry open the soufflé so that you can peer inside it; the center should appear thick and creamy but not soupy.

1 ounce Parmesan cheese, grated (½ cup)

¼ cup (1¼ ounces) all-purpose flour

¼ teaspoon paprika

¼ teaspoon salt

⅛ teaspoon cayenne pepper

⅛ teaspoon white pepper

Pinch ground nutmeg

4 tablespoons unsalted butter

1⅓ cups whole milk

6 ounces Gruyère cheese, shredded (1½ cups)

6 large eggs, separated

2 teaspoons minced fresh parsley

¼ teaspoon cream of tartar

1. Adjust oven rack to middle position and heat oven to 350 degrees. Spray 8-inch round (2-quart) soufflé dish with vegetable oil spray, then sprinkle with 2 tablespoons Parmesan.

2. Combine flour, paprika, salt, cayenne, white pepper, and nutmeg in bowl. Melt butter in small saucepan over medium heat. Stir in flour mixture and cook for 1 minute. Slowly whisk in milk and bring to simmer. Cook, whisking constantly, until mixture is thickened and smooth, about 1 minute. Remove pan from heat and whisk in Gruyère and 5 tablespoons Parmesan until melted and smooth. Let cool for 10 minutes, then whisk in egg yolks and 1½ teaspoons parsley.

3. Using stand mixer fitted with whisk, whip egg whites and cream of tartar on medium-low speed until foamy, about 1 minute. Increase speed to medium-high and whip until stiff peaks form, 3 to 4 minutes. Add cheese mixture and continue to whip until fully combined, about 15 seconds.

4. Pour mixture into prepared dish and sprinkle with remaining 1 tablespoon Parmesan. Bake until risen above rim, top is deep golden brown, and interior registers 170 degrees, 30 to 35 minutes. Sprinkle with remaining ½ teaspoon parsley and serve immediately.

RATING SOUFFLÉ DISHES

A round, straight-sided ceramic soufflé dish elegantly launches a soufflé—that's its raison d'être. Sweet as well as savory soufflés rose reliably in each of the three classic soufflé dishes that we tested. Their differences came down to two factors: the actual (versus stated) capacity of each dish and the thickness of each dish's walls. One thick-walled dish insulated the contents enough for slow baking, but this same dish, with the largest capacity in the lineup at 2.5 quarts, dwarfed our soufflé's elegant rise. Another dish couldn't accommodate all the batter, requiring that we discard about ⅓ cup. With its straight, not-too-thick sides and just the right capacity to hold the batter, the HIC 64 Ounce Soufflé dish—our winner and Best Buy—produced evenly cooked soufflés that rose high above the rim without spilling over. Products are listed in order of preference. See AmericasTestKitchen.com for updates and complete testing results.

RECOMMENDED

HIC 64 Ounce Soufflé
PRICE: $15.12
PERFORMANCE: ★★★
COMMENTS: This dish has walls with just the right thickness to ensure even cooking. It has a shelf-like indentation all the way around the inside rim and a decent capacity (2 quarts plus ¼ cup). It gave soufflés just enough room to rise without going over the edge—but it was close.

PILLIVUYT Pleated Deep Soufflé Dish, Extra Large
PRICE: $42.10
PERFORMANCE: ★★★
COMMENTS: With a scant 2-quart capacity, this tall, narrow dish didn't hold all the batter for our soufflé recipe, though when we added a parchment collar to the dish the soufflé rose well and cooked evenly. Keeping the batter a good inch from the rim of the dish also produced good results.

RECOMMENDED WITH RESERVATIONS

BIA CORDON BLEU 2 Quart Soufflé
PRICE: $9.99
PERFORMANCE: ★★½
COMMENTS: This dish's large capacity (2 quarts plus 1¾ cups) more than accommodated the contents. In fact it accommodated them a little too well: Soufflés never rose above the rim and looked a bit lost, and because of the dish's thick walls, baking our soufflés took 5 to 7 minutes longer than it did in our favorite dish.

Pasta Rustica

Vigorously stirring potatoes into pasta breaks down some of the potatoes' starch, creating a rich, silky "sauce."

THERE'S SOMETHING ABOUT PASTA—WE JUST CAN'T SEEM TO GET enough of it. This simple Italian pantry ingredient is the base of many a meal, and we're always on the hunt for new (to us) ways to serve it. Lucky for us, the Italian culinary imagination never disappoints, creating sauces that are as unique as the Italian provinces themselves. We came across two recipes with deep histories and intense flavors, and set out to bring these regional classics back to life using modern ingredients (and modern palates) as our guides.

In 16th-century Naples, thrift was the driving force behind *La Genovese*, or beef and onion ragu. Historically, this dish made one inexpensive beef roast into two meals. We updated the classic recipe to create a single dish of warm, hearty pasta sauce chock-full of tender beef and savory onions—and we learned a few surprising tricks along the way.

The original Ligurian pesto sauce was served not only over pasta, but pasta with potatoes. Two starches in one dish? We were skeptical at first, but all our doubts dissolved when we were able to come up with a creamy, rich pasta dish unlike anything else in our repertoire.

RIGATONI WITH BEEF AND ONION RAGU

✔ **WHY THIS RECIPE WORKS:** This rich, supple meat sauce was born out of thrift in 16th-century Naples. *La Genovese* began as a combination of beef and aromatic vegetables that were cooked down to make two meals: a savory sauce for pasta and another, separate meal of cooked beef. Later, most of the vegetables took a backseat to the onions, which became the foundation of this deeply flavorful sauce. To make the ultrasavory recipe work in a modern context, we decided to turn all the elements into one substantial sauce by shredding the meat into the sauce. To eliminate the need for intermittent stirring and monitoring during cooking, we moved the process from the stovetop to the even heat of the oven. A surprising ingredient—water—proved essential to extracting maximum flavor from the onions. We also added tomato paste for an extra boost of flavor and color. To encourage the sauce to cling to the pasta, we vigorously stirred them together so that the starch from the pasta added body to the sauce. A bit of grated Pecorino Romano brought the flavors together and added a mild tang.

THERE ARE THOSE WHO HAVE THE BEST OF EVERYTHING, and there are those who make the best of everything. The residents of 16th-century Naples fell into the latter category. Faced with a population explosion that caused severe food shortages, they created a thrifty yet supremely satisfying gravy of beef and aromatic vegetables known, ironically, as *la Genovese*. (The provenance of the name is unclear: Some theorize that Genovese cooks brought it to Naples; others believe that the name references the reputed frugality of the people of Genoa.) Later in the 19th century, onions took center stage, and the dish became one of the region's most beloved. The classic preparation is straightforward: A piece of beef, usually from the round, is placed in a pot and covered with approximately twice its weight in sliced onions,

along with chopped aromatic vegetables, salt, and perhaps some herbs. Then several cups of water and a bit of wine go into the pot, and the mixture is simmered for anywhere from 3 to 6 hours, until the liquid has evaporated, the beef is tender, and the onions have cooked down into a soft, pulpy mass.

Traditionally, frugal cooks served the beef-flavored onion gravy—notice that we didn't mention tomatoes; the dish predates the introduction of tomatoes to European kitchens—as a sauce for sturdy tubular pasta like rigatoni. (Incidentally, the sauce doesn't include garlic either.) The meat itself was typically reserved for a second meal, or at least a second course, with a vegetable. But in today's comparatively prosperous times, the beef is more likely to be shredded and incorporated into the sauce for a substantial single dish—a perfect pasta sauce to make in cold-weather months.

We started with a very traditional recipe, but since we were making just one meal, not two, we immediately cut down the amount of beef and onions to a more practical size—1 pound of trimmed beef round and 2½ pounds of thinly sliced onions, which we hoped would produce six to eight servings. To those key players we added a finely chopped carrot and rib of celery, plus some minced marjoram and salt, all of which we put in a Dutch oven with 8 cups of water and 1 cup of white wine (the meat is not usually seared). We let the pot bubble away for a good 2½ hours, giving it an occasional stir to keep the contents cooking evenly. By that point, the beef was fully cooked; we removed it to let it cool before chopping it (its texture was too tight to shred) and adding it back to the sauce. In the meantime we reduced the oniony cooking liquid.

Perhaps not surprisingly, this early version did not produce the succulent, deeply flavorful ragu we had envisioned. The lean round was not the best cut to use in a moist heat environment; it lacks fat and collagen, which keep meat tasting tender and juicy, so it cooked up dry and tight. Also, reducing the sauce itself took too long—almost 40 minutes. Lastly, the color of the sauce was an unappealing beige.

What did impress us was the deeply savory flavor of the onions. They weren't sharp and sulfurous like fresh

RIGATONI WITH BEEF AND ONION RAGU

onions, nor did they have the sweetness of the caramel-ized kind. They were just plain beefy-tasting. In fact, one taster observed that the onions tasted beefier than the actual beef. We'd come back to this discovery once we'd nailed down the basics of the sauce—for starters, the meat.

Beef round's tight grain makes this cut a good candidate for slicing, but since we were in pursuit of more tender meat that we could shred and return to the sauce, we moved to our favorite braising cuts: short ribs, blade steaks, and chuck-eye roast. The latter won for its beefy flavor, tenderness, and (in homage to the thrifty nature of this dish) relatively low price tag. The only glitch? Cooked whole, it took upwards of 3½ hours to turn tender. Cutting it into four chunks reduced the cooking time to 2½ hours and allowed us to trim away intramuscular fat pockets. We also seasoned the roast with salt and pepper before cooking and moved the braising to a low (300-degree) oven, where the meat would cook more evenly.

And we cut way back on the water—down to 3 cups—hoping to drastically shorten the reduction time. But even with that little amount, it still took about a half-hour of stovetop reduction to turn the onions and cooking liquid saucy. We wondered: Did we have to add water at all?

In the next batch we omitted the water and simply nestled the beef in the onion mixture and sealed the pot tightly with foil (to lock in steam) and then the lid. This worked well; the meat braised to perfect tenderness in the released juices, and the sauce required less stovetop reduction time—just 10 minutes. But strangely, this version tasted less savory.

To ramp up meatiness, we turned to innovations that started to show up in later Genovese recipes: pancetta and salami (which we finely chopped in the food processor) and tomato paste. They all made the ragu more savory, particularly the umami-rich tomato paste when we browned it in the pot before adding the onions. The tomato paste also warmed up the color of the formerly drab-looking finished sauce. But while this batch tasted meatier than the previous one, it still was not as savory as the first version. We were baffled. We had not only

added meaty ingredients but also taken away the world's most neutral ingredient: water.

A consultation with our science editor solved the mystery. Astonishingly, it was the water that was the key to extracting the meaty flavor that was locked inside the onions. That meatiness is due to a water-soluble compound known as 3-mercapto-2-methylpentan-1-ol (MMP), the byproduct of a reaction that occurs when onions are cut and then heated in water.

By eliminating the water, we were severely limiting the development of savory flavors, so we added back 2 cups—just enough to cover the onions but not so much that the sauce's reduction time would be lengthy. We also switched from slicing the onions to chopping them in the food processor—a timesaving technique that would also lead to the creation of more MMP. This time the sauce regained the meatiness of the original batch, and then some, with the pancetta, salami, and tomato paste. Even better, we found that we could cook it in the oven with the lid off, which encouraged evaporation and saved some reducing time at the end. The sauce was a bit sweet, so we reserved half of the wine for adding at the end for extra brightness.

One last tweak: We found that when we vigorously mixed—instead of just lightly tossed—together the cooked pasta and sauce and a bit of cheese, the starch on the surface of the pasta pulled the components together, helping keep the liquid from separating out from the solids.

We had to hand it to those thrifty 16th-century Neapolitans. This was a true ragu—humble at its roots but as savory and satisfying as the meat-and-tomato-heavy versions that would follow. Our 21st-century tweaks would make it a staple in our wintertime pasta sauce rotation.

Rigatoni with Beef and Onion Ragu

SERVES 6 TO 8

If marjoram is unavailable, substitute an equal amount of oregano. Pair this dish with a lightly dressed salad of assertively flavored greens.

1 (1- to 1¼-pound) boneless beef chuck-eye roast,
   cut into 4 pieces and trimmed of large pieces of fat
   Kosher salt and pepper
2 ounces pancetta, cut into ½-inch pieces
2 ounces salami, cut into ½-inch pieces
1 small carrot, peeled and cut into ½-inch pieces
1 small celery rib, cut into ½-inch pieces
2½ pounds onions, halved and cut into 1-inch pieces
2 tablespoons tomato paste
1 cup dry white wine
2 tablespoons minced fresh marjoram
1 pound rigatoni
1 ounce Pecorino Romano cheese, grated (½ cup),
   plus extra for serving

1. Sprinkle beef with 1 teaspoon salt and ½ teaspoon pepper and set aside. Adjust oven rack to lower-middle position and heat oven to 300 degrees.

2. Process pancetta and salami in food processor until ground to paste, about 30 seconds, scraping down sides of bowl as needed. Add carrot and celery and process 30 seconds longer, scraping down sides of bowl as needed. Transfer paste to Dutch oven and set aside; do not clean out processor bowl. Pulse onions in processor in 2 batches, until ⅛- to ¼-inch pieces form, 8 to 10 pulses per batch.

SCIENCE DESK

A SURPRISING FORMULA FOR MEATY FLAVOR

Believe it or not, much of the meaty flavor in our Genovese ragu actually comes from the 2½ pounds of onions in our recipe. Specifically, the flavor stems from a compound in onions called 3-mercapto-2-methylpentan-1-ol, or MMP for short. When an onion is cut, some of its sulfur compounds combine to form a new compound: propanethial-S-oxide—the stuff that makes your eyes tear. When heated, this compound turns into MMP. And what does MMP taste like? Meat broth.

To harness MMP's full savory power, we switched from slicing to finely chopping the onions in a food processor to create even more opportunities for sulfur compounds to be released and transformed into MMP. But there's a hitch: MMP's flavor is water-soluble, which means that to create it, water must be present. And the more water, the more beefy flavor that's extracted. By cooking the onions and meat in 2 cups of water (rather than allowing them to simmer in their own juices), we were able to create a marked increase in meaty flavor.

3. Cook pancetta mixture over medium heat, stirring frequently, until fat is rendered and fond begins to form on bottom of pot, about 5 minutes. Add tomato paste and cook, stirring constantly, until browned, about 90 seconds. Stir in 2 cups water, scraping up any browned bits. Stir in onions and bring to boil. Stir in ½ cup wine and 1 tablespoon marjoram. Add beef and push into onions to ensure that it is submerged. Transfer to oven and cook, uncovered, until beef is fully tender, 2 to 2½ hours.

4. Transfer beef to carving board. Place pot over medium heat and cook, stirring frequently, until mixture is almost completely dry. Stir in remaining ½ cup wine and cook for 2 minutes, stirring occasionally. Using 2 forks, shred beef into bite-size pieces. Stir beef and remaining 1 tablespoon marjoram into sauce and season with salt and pepper to taste. Remove from heat, cover, and keep warm.

5. Bring 4 quarts water to boil in large pot. Add rigatoni and 2 tablespoons salt and cook, stirring often, until just al dente. Drain rigatoni and add to warm sauce. Add Pecorino and stir vigorously over low heat until sauce is slightly thickened and rigatoni is fully tender, 1 to 2 minutes. Serve, passing extra Pecorino separately.

RATING COLANDERS

Though logic would dictate that larger holes mean a faster-draining colander, we found that tiny perforations perform better while also preventing pastas like orzo and angel hair from escaping into the sink. Our favored colander—the RSVP International Endurance Precision Pierced 5 Qt. Colander—boasts an excellent combination of small, all-over perforations, a wide base for great stability, and a decent amount—1⅛ inches—of ground clearance, which helped avoid backsplash from the sink. All these features add up to class-leading performance. Products are listed in order of preference. See AmericasTestKitchen.com for updates and complete testing results.

HIGHLY RECOMMENDED

RSVP INTERNATIONAL Endurance Precision Pierced 5 Qt. Colander
DESIGN: ★★★ CLEANUP: ★★★
PERFORMANCE: ★★★   PRICE: $25.99
COMMENTS: With all-over tiny perforations that don't allow small foods to escape, our longtime favorite colander has a draining performance that remains unmatched. Its 1⅛ inches of ground clearance was enough to keep nearly all the drained pasta from getting hit with backwash. The model cleans up nicely in the dishwasher, and its handles are slim but still substantial enough to grip easily.

RECOMMENDED

OXO Good Grips 5-Quart Stainless Steel Colander
DESIGN: ★★½ CLEANUP: ★★★
PERFORMANCE: ★★★   PRICE: $29.99
COMMENTS: Testers appreciated this colander's beefy rim, its point at the center of the base to drive liquid down and out the bottom perforations, and its nonskid feet, though we wish they raised the bowl more than ⅜ inch off the sink floor to combat the backwash effect.

CUISINOX 24 Cm Footed Colander
DESIGN: ★★½ CLEANUP: ★★★
PERFORMANCE: ★★½   PRICE: $19.90
COMMENTS: Though its larger perforations allowed a few strands of angel hair and 1½ teaspoons of orzo to escape, this reasonably priced colander had other redeeming traits—namely, a deep bowl and large, easy-to-grip handles. But it felt lightweight and a bit chintzy, which made us worry about long-term durability.

RECOMMENDED WITH RESERVATIONS

EXCEL Steel Cook Pro Stainless Steel Mesh Colanders with Silicone Handles, Set of 3
DESIGN: ★★ CLEANUP: ★★
PERFORMANCE: ★★★   PRICE: $39.95
COMMENTS: Each of the fine-mesh colanders in this set of three drained efficiently but lacked a sturdy frame: The delicate walls dented easily. Orzo grains became lodged between the mesh and the frame.

RECOMMENDED WITH RESERVATIONS (cont.)

NORPRO Krona Stainless Steel 9.5" Deep Colander
DESIGN: ★★½ CLEANUP: ★★
PERFORMANCE: ★★½   PRICE: $32.27
COMMENTS: No strand pasta slipped through the larger holes on this deep colander, but 2 tablespoons of orzo did. Its patchy clusters of holes didn't allow water to drain as easily as did top-performing models. The deep bowl cleaned up readily with a soapy sponge—though we'd really prefer it if the model were dishwasher-safe.

NOT RECOMMENDED

SQUISH 4-Quart Collapsible Colander
DESIGN: ★★ CLEANUP: ★★
PERFORMANCE: ★½ PRICE: $19.99
COMMENTS: With some holes in this colander measuring almost ¼ inch, it's no wonder that a full 5 tablespoons of orzo escaped. This collapsible model has no base and, therefore, practically no elevation from the bottom of the sink. Its silicone body became faded and dingy after the dishwasher cycles.

SQUISH Expanding Over-the-Sink Colander
DESIGN: ★★ CLEANUP: ★★
PERFORMANCE: ★½ PRICE: $24.99
COMMENTS: While there's plenty of clearance when this model is anchored over the sink, there's almost none when it sits on the sink floor. Several tablespoons of orzo slipped through its large holes. Its oblong frame was awkward to maneuver and didn't fit over the draining bowl. The colorful silicone looked faded after being run through the dishwasher.

RESTON LLOYD Calypso Basics 5-Quart Colander
DESIGN: ★★ CLEANUP: ★★
PERFORMANCE: ★ PRICE: $25.99
COMMENTS: This model's only perk: its 1¾-inch base, which raised it high off the sink floor. But since it allowed a whopping ½ cup of orzo to escape, was not dishwasher-safe, and required vigorous scrubbing to remove stuck-on bits of pasta, we'll pass.

PASTA WITH PESTO, POTATOES, AND GREEN BEANS

✔ WHY THIS RECIPE WORKS: The idea of serving two starches together might seem unusual, but this dish from Liguria is the traditional way to serve classic basil pesto. The starch from red potatoes enriched the pesto, transforming it into a creamy sauce with good body. Tender green beans added color, flavor, and just enough contrasting texture. Although some traditional recipes called for cooking the potatoes, green beans, and pasta together in the same pot, we found that cooking them separately was the only way to ensure that every element was cooked perfectly.

WE DON'T USUALLY FOLLOW TRENDS IN THE TEST kitchen, but even we know that carbohydrates are out of fashion. That's why the notion of putting pasta and potatoes in the same dish initially struck us as just plain wrong. But we were intrigued to learn that the preferred way to serve pesto in Liguria, Italy—the birthplace of the basil sauce—involved just that combination. Wondering what the Italians knew that we didn't, we found a handful of recipes and gave them a whirl.

The Ligurian cook has two pasta options for this dish: trenette, a fettuccine-like strand, or trofie, a shorter, thicker twist. Neither was available at the local supermarket, so we chose short, thick double helix–shaped gemelli. We ground one batch of basil leaves, garlic, and toasted pine nuts with a mortar and pestle as tradition dictated and, for comparison, buzzed another in a food processor before stirring in olive oil and grated Parmesan cheese. We then cooked batches of pasta, potatoes (peeled and cut into a variety of shapes), and green beans (cut into bite-size lengths) together in single pots of boiling salted water, staggering the addition of ingredients and hoping they would all finish cooking simultaneously. Finally, we tossed each dish's ingredients with pesto and some cooking water.

Some variations were dull and heavy, but we were surprised that many boasted a creamy lightness. Why? It all came down to how the potatoes were treated. The most successful recipes called for cutting the potatoes into chunks and then, once cooked, vigorously mixing them with the pesto, pasta, and green beans. The agitation sloughed off their corners, which dissolved into the dish, pulling the pesto and cooking water together to form a simple sauce.

But the recipe still needed work. The sauce was slightly grainy and the sharp, raw garlic dominated. Timing was another issue: The green beans could be jarringly crisp and the pasta way too soft—or vice versa. And that mortar and pestle? No thanks. We'd opt for the convenience of the food processor.

We knew that the potatoes were the key to the sauce, and we wondered if the choice of russets was the reason for the slightly rough texture. Sure enough, when we subbed waxy red potatoes for russets, the graininess disappeared. Why? Waxy red potatoes contain about 25 percent less starch than russet potatoes do. When waxy

PASTA WITH PESTO, POTATOES, AND GREEN BEANS

potatoes are boiled, they absorb less water and their cells swell less and do not separate and burst as those in russet potatoes do. As a result, waxy potatoes produce a smooth, creamy texture, while russets can be mealy and grainy.

Now to address the timing problem. The traditional method of staggering the addition of the ingredients to the pot doesn't allow for much variation in the size or quality of each, making it difficult to cook each element perfectly. But cooking each ingredient sequentially took too long, and boiling them simultaneously in separate pots dirtied too many dishes. By recycling the pine nut–toasting skillet to steam the beans and by fully cooking the potatoes in the water before the pasta went in, we were able to cook everything separately using only two pots. While the potatoes bubbled, we made the pesto.

To mellow the garlic cloves, we toasted them skin-on with the pine nuts before making the pesto. We cooked and drained the pasta and then returned everything to the pot, along with the pesto and 1¼ cups of cooking water. That sounds like a lot of cooking water (we usually call for about ⅓ cup), but the potato starch needs more water in which to disperse.

Finally, we stirred with a rubber spatula until the magic sauce formed. Two tablespoons of butter made it even silkier, and a splash of lemon juice brought all the flavors into focus. This simple classic confirmed what the Ligurians have known all along: Fashion has its place, and the dinner plate isn't it.

Pasta with Pesto, Potatoes, and Green Beans

SERVES 6

If gemelli is unavailable, penne or rigatoni make good substitutes. Use large red potatoes measuring 3 inches or more in diameter.

¼ cup pine nuts

3 garlic cloves, unpeeled

1 pound large red potatoes, peeled and cut into ½-inch pieces

Salt and pepper

12 ounces green beans, trimmed and cut into 1½-inch lengths

2 cups fresh basil leaves

1 ounce Parmesan cheese, grated (½ cup)

7 tablespoons extra-virgin olive oil

1 pound gemelli

2 tablespoons unsalted butter, cut into ½-inch pieces and chilled

1 tablespoon lemon juice

1. Toast pine nuts and garlic in 10-inch skillet over medium heat, stirring frequently, until pine nuts are golden and fragrant and garlic darkens slightly, 3 to 5 minutes. Transfer to bowl and let cool. Peel garlic and chop coarse.

2. Bring 3 quarts water to boil in large pot. Add potatoes and 1 tablespoon salt and cook until potatoes are tender but still hold their shape, 9 to 12 minutes. Using slotted spoon, transfer potatoes to rimmed baking sheet. (Do not discard water.)

NOTES FROM THE TEST KITCHEN

KEEPING PASTA WARMER LONGER

Pasta cools off quickly. Here's a tip to keep it warmer for longer.

Drain the cooked pasta in a colander set in a large serving bowl. In addition to heating the bowl, the starchy pasta water can easily be reserved for use in the sauce.

GRATING HARD CHEESE

When grating Parmesan and other hard cheeses, we use a rasp-style grater because it produces lighter, fluffier shreds of cheese that melt seamlessly into pasta dishes and sauces.

3. Meanwhile, bring ½ cup water and ¼ teaspoon salt to boil in now-empty skillet over medium heat. Add green beans, cover, and cook until tender, 5 to 8 minutes. Drain green beans and transfer to sheet with potatoes.

4. Process basil, Parmesan, oil, pine nuts, garlic, and ½ teaspoon salt in food processor until smooth, about 1 minute.

5. Add gemelli to water in large pot and cook, stirring often, until al dente. Set colander in large bowl. Drain gemelli in colander, reserving cooking water in bowl. Return gemelli to pot. Add butter, lemon juice, potatoes and green beans, pesto, 1¼ cups reserved cooking water, and ½ teaspoon pepper and stir vigorously with rubber spatula until sauce takes on creamy appearance. Add additional cooking water as needed to adjust consistency and season with salt and pepper to taste. Serve immediately.

RATING WHITE BEANS

The creamy texture and mildly nutty flavor of cannellini beans rounds out soups, casseroles, pasta dishes, and salads, and they make appealing dips. We've always appreciated the convenience of canned beans for use in quick recipes, but we've also always been a little prejudiced in favor of dried beans, considering their flavor and texture superior. We included five brands each of canned and dried beans, including two dried "heirloom" varieties. We held six blind tastings, serving two rounds each of the beans plain, in dip, and in soup. Surprisingly, top scores for our favorite canned beans, Goya Cannellini, actually edged out top scores for the best dried beans, Rancho Gordo Classic Cassoulet Beans. In both canned and dried varieties, tasters liked beans that were firm and intact, with meltingly tender skins, creamy texture, and clean bean flavor. In dried beans, calcium levels determined how well the beans held their shape during cooking, and moisture content (indicative of storage techniques) between 10 percent and 18 percent made for the best flavor and most even cooking. Products are listed in order of preference. See AmericasTestKitchen.com for updates and complete tasting results.

CANNED WHITE BEANS

RECOMMENDED

GOYA Cannellini
PRICE: $1.49 for 15.5 oz ($0.10 per oz)
SODIUM: 416 mg per ½-cup serving
COMMENTS: Tasters' favorite canned beans were "well seasoned" (they had the highest sodium level of the lineup) and "big and meaty," with both "earthy sweetness" and "savory flavor." Their texture was consistently firm and "ultracreamy."

BUSH'S BEST Cannellini Beans White Kidney Beans
PRICE: $1.19 for 15.5 oz ($0.08 per oz)
SODIUM: 270 mg per ½-cup serving
COMMENTS: "Creamy and firm," these beans were "smooth and intact," with a nutty, clean flavor. In soup, the beans kept their creamy texture and "hearty" flavor. But these beans lost a few points because they tasted less seasoned than our winner did and had a slightly chalkier texture in the dip.

RECOMMENDED WITH RESERVATIONS

PROGRESSO Cannellini White Kidney Beans
PRICE: $1.59 for 19 oz ($0.08 per oz)
SODIUM: 340 mg per ½-cup serving
COMMENTS: These beans had a "bland" flavor and were also "a bit mealy." "Almost every bean is broken, with tough skins and grainy flesh," noted one taster. Their softness helped make the dip "richer and creamier," but "bits of skin" got in the way.

NOT RECOMMENDED

EDEN ORGANIC Cannellini White Kidney Beans, No Salt Added
PRICE: $2.19 for 15 oz ($0.15 per oz)
SODIUM: 40 mg per ½-cup serving
COMMENTS: Tasters hated these beans, which have no added salt, calcium chloride for firmness, or preservatives, rejecting them in every tasting. We found them "very sour," "watery," and "rank," with "grainy interiors" and "tough skins." At best, they were "inedibly bland." Even with fresh lemon, parsley, garlic, and olive oil, the dip tasted like "chalk dip."

DRIED WHITE BEANS

RECOMMENDED

RANCHO GORDO Classic Cassoulet Bean
PRICE: $5.95 for 1 lb ($0.37 per oz), plus shipping
MOISTURE: 10.5%   **CALCIUM:** 362 mg per 100 g
COMMENTS: Although this purveyor was sold out of cannellini beans, the company suggested a variety grown in California from French Tarbais beans. Our tasters found them "creamy and smooth, nutty and sweet," with a "fresh, clean" taste and a "lovely texture and appearance."

RECOMMENDED WITH RESERVATIONS

ZÜRSUN IDAHO Heirloom Beans, Cannellini
PRICE: $8 for 1½ lb ($0.33 per oz), plus shipping
MOISTURE: 8.67%   **CALCIUM:** 204 mg per 100 g
COMMENTS: An heirloom variety grown in Idaho's Snake River Canyon region, tasters found these beans "fresh," with a texture that "melts in the mouth but still has a slight bite." They lost points in soup for "tough skins" and "lots of blowouts."

BOB'S RED MILL Cannellini Beans, Premium Quality
PRICE: $8.08 for 1½ lb ($0.34 per oz)
MOISTURE: 9.25%   **CALCIUM:** 176 mg per 100 g
COMMENTS: These were "big, intact, smooth beans; all identical; sweet and nutty," with a "slightly grassy" taste. They lost points for textural issues, with tasters noting that they were a bit "grainy" and "dry," both plain and in dip.

GOYA White Kidney Beans Cannellini, No. 1 Grade
PRICE: $1.99 for 1 lb ($0.12 per oz)
MOISTURE: 9.36%   **CALCIUM:** 168 mg per 100 g
COMMENTS: The dried version of our winning canned bean was disappointing. Goya said the identical variety of beans is sold in both canned and dried form. But the dried beans cooked up "uneven" with "tough skins" and "lots of blowouts." In dip, the skins remained "too chewy." Still, tasters appreciated their "solid," "earthy" flavor.

Spa Cuisine Gets a Makeover

Our poaching liquid doubles as a gentle brine, infusing the chicken with lots of flavor while also keeping it moist and tender.

HERE IN THE TEST KITCHEN, WE TASTE-TEST BUTTERY CONFECTIONS and creamy sauces every day. But sometimes we long for a lighter meal that still has plenty of flavor. The challenge is that getting food to taste great without using much fat can be tricky—and even the recipes that do turn out terrific boast overcomplicated processes. Here, we'll show you simple, foolproof ways to get maximum flavor into two spa cuisine classics: tender poached chicken and silky carrot-ginger soup.

The two main ingredients in carrot-ginger soup (you guessed it: carrots and ginger) are too often buried under layers of conflicting flavors. We wanted a simple soup that highlighted the star ingredients, so we used plenty of each (and little else). A secret ingredient made for the smoothest soup we'd ever had, no tedious straining necessary.

Poached chicken suffers from two major setbacks: a fussy procedure and bland flavor. But what better way to cook delicate chicken breasts than by gently poaching them? We improved on the traditional poaching method with a few pantry ingredients, with the goal of infusing the chicken with lots of flavor and producing moist and tender meat.

CARROT-GINGER SOUP

✔ WHY THIS RECIPE WORKS: Sometimes the simplest recipes get overcomplicated as more and more versions appear. Case in point: carrot-ginger soup, whose flavors often get elbowed out with the addition of other vegetables, fruits, or dairy. For a fresh, clean-tasting soup, we decided to go back to the basics. With a combination of cooked carrots and carrot juice, we were able to get well-rounded, fresh carrot flavor. Using a mixture of grated fresh ginger and crystallized ginger gave us a bright, refreshing ginger flavor with a moderate kick of heat. Finally, for a smooth texture without the fuss of straining, we added a touch of baking soda to help break down the carrots and ginger, producing a perfectly silky, creamy result. To keep the flavors straightforward and simple, we finished with some basic garnishes that provided texture and tang.

THE COUPLING OF SWEET CARROTS AND PUNGENT ginger has the potential to produce an elegant, flavorful soup. It's troubling, then, that it's difficult to truly taste either ingredient in most versions. That's due primarily to the hapless addition of other vegetables, fruits, or dairy—all of which mask the starring flavors. Another irritating problem is a grainy consistency; we like our pureed soups to be perfectly smooth and creamy. Could we bring this soup to its full potential, producing a version with a smooth, silken texture and pure, clean flavors?

We started by making a bare-bones soup, sweating minced onion and garlic in butter and then adding peeled, sliced carrots, fresh grated ginger, and vegetable broth. We simmered the mixture until the carrots were tender and then gave it a whirl in the blender. Unfortunately, the carrot flavor seemed muddled. And while the soup had a fiery kick, it had not even a hint of the fresh, bright flavor associated with ginger. What's more, even though they'd been cooking for 20 minutes and seemed sufficiently tender, the carrots hadn't

completely broken down, so the soup was riddled with fibrous bits. Not a promising start.

First up for repair: flavor. For unadulterated carrot flavor, it made sense to ditch the broth in favor of plain water, which we augmented with a couple of complementary sprigs of fresh thyme. This was a vast improvement, eliminating the blurred vegetable background of the first batch. Next, trying for an even more concentrated, caramelized taste, we whipped up two more soups—one with roasted carrots and another with slices sautéed in butter until caramelized. Unfortunately, neither method added quite the right flavor. Roasting brought an undesirable earthiness and sautéing yielded a soup that tasted like sweet potatoes.

But these tests made us realize that what was really missing in this soup was ultrafresh carrot flavor. That in turn made the solution seem obvious: Just use raw carrots—in the form of carrot juice. After a few tries, we settled on swapping in ¾ cup of carrot juice for some of the water and stirring in another ¾ cup (along with a tablespoon of cider vinegar for sweet tang) right before serving. Between the earthy, sweet cooked carrots and the bright, raw carrot juice, this was a well-balanced soup.

On to the ginger. The soup had the peppery heat associated with the root but almost none of its vibrant fruitiness. We rounded up the different forms of ginger—fresh juice, fresh grated, ground, and crystallized—and started sampling. Ginger juice offered plenty of heat but little flavor. Ground ginger simply tasted bitter. A combo of fresh and crystallized ginger was the best of the bunch, with the former supplying spiciness and the latter delivering the almost citrusy freshness that ginger is prized for.

We sautéed 1 tablespoon of finely grated fresh ginger and ¼ cup of minced crystallized ginger (plus 1 teaspoon of sugar to counter their spiciness) with the other aromatics and then continued with the recipe. In the finished soup, the duo struck an ideal balance of flavor and heat.

For the silkiest possible consistency, we tried cooking the carrots longer, until they were mushy and breaking

CARROT-GINGER SOUP

apart. After we pureed it, the soup was better but still not smooth enough. We wanted to avoid straining, so it only made sense to turn to one of the test kitchen's secret weapons: baking soda. We have used it on numerous occasions to break down the cell walls of a vegetable as it cooks in water. Sure enough, with just ½ teaspoon of baking soda and 20 minutes of simmering, the soup was smoother than any we'd ever had. In fact, it was downright velvety—all without the need for lengthy cooking or fussy straining.

As finishing touches, a sprinkle of fresh chives and a swirl of sour cream provided subtle onion flavor and mild tang. With a few crispy, buttery croutons for textural contrast, our retooled classic was complete.

Carrot-Ginger Soup

SERVES 6

A food processor can be used to slice the carrots. In addition to sour cream and chives, serve the soup with Buttery Croutons (recipe follows).

2	tablespoons unsalted butter
2	onions, chopped fine
¼	cup minced crystallized ginger
1	tablespoon grated fresh ginger
2	garlic cloves, peeled and smashed
	Salt and pepper
1	teaspoon sugar
2	pounds carrots, peeled and sliced ¼ inch thick
4	cups water
1½	cups carrot juice
2	sprigs fresh thyme
½	teaspoon baking soda
1	tablespoon cider vinegar
	Chopped chives
	Sour cream

1. Melt butter in large saucepan over medium heat. Add onions, crystallized ginger, fresh ginger, garlic, 2 teaspoons salt, and sugar; cook, stirring frequently, until onions are softened but not browned, about 5 minutes.

2. Increase heat to high; add carrots, water, ¾ cup carrot juice, thyme sprigs, and baking soda and bring to simmer. Reduce heat to medium-low and simmer, covered, until carrots are very tender, 20 to 25 minutes.

3. Discard thyme sprigs. Working in batches, process soup in blender until smooth, 1 to 2 minutes. Return soup to clean pot and stir in vinegar and remaining ¾ cup carrot juice. Return to simmer over medium heat and season with salt and pepper to taste. Serve with sprinkle of chives and dollop of sour cream.

Buttery Croutons

MAKES ABOUT 2 CUPS

3	tablespoons unsalted butter
1	tablespoon olive oil
3	large slices hearty white sandwich bread, cut into ½-inch cubes
	Salt

Heat butter and oil in 12-inch skillet over medium heat. When foaming subsides, add bread cubes and cook, stirring frequently, until golden brown, about 10 minutes. Transfer croutons to paper towel–lined plate and season with salt to taste.

RATING MANDOLINES

A good mandoline can thin-slice, julienne, and (in some cases) waffle-cut produce far faster than a skilled cook wielding a sharp knife can, and with utter precision. That uniformity is at least as valuable as the time savings—and not just for cosmetic reasons. When cuts are uneven, so is cooking. But for a mandoline to be truly useful in a home kitchen, it must be easy to set up, clean, and store. And given that you're working with sharp blades, it must also be as safe to use as it is efficient. We selected seven models under $50 each and cut firm russet potatoes and soft ripe tomatoes with all available slice thicknesses. We julienned potatoes and carrots, sliced zucchini lengthwise, and made wavy/waffle slices when available. Our winning mandoline, the Swissmar Börner Original V-Slicer Plus Mandoline, is one of the few models with a long, unobstructed platform, which enabled us to produce long, graceful zucchini planks and full-length French fries. We found that this simple device made cuts effortlessly and its hat-shaped guard kept our fingertips safe while slicing. Products are listed in order of preference. See AmericasTestKitchen.com for updates and complete testing results.

HIGHLY RECOMMENDED

SWISSMAR BÖRNER Original V-Slicer Plus Mandoline
SAFETY: ★★★   CLEANUP: ★★★   EASE OF USE: ★★★
PERFORMANCE: ★★★   PRICE: $29.99
COMMENTS: This simple device made cuts effortlessly with stunningly precise results. Its hat-shaped guard protects fingers well; cleanup and storage are a breeze, thanks to its compact vertical caddy. Even with just four cutting options, all this adds up to a slicer that we'll use every day.

KYOCERA Adjustable Slicer with Handguard
SAFETY: ★★   CLEANUP: ★★★   EASE OF USE: ★★★
PERFORMANCE: ★★★   PRICE: $24.95
COMMENTS: This paddle continues to be a terrific choice for cooks looking only for fast, precise slicing (it doesn't julienne). Changing the thickness setting requires no blade handling, and it stows in a drawer. We'd prefer a more secure hand guard.

RECOMMENDED

PROGRESSIVE Prepworks Julienne and Slicer
SAFETY: ★★   CLEANUP: ★★★   EASE OF USE: ★★½
PERFORMANCE: ★★½   PRICE: $22.25
COMMENTS: A built-in julienne blade and slice adjustment settings make this paddle efficient, compact, and supereasy to use. One quibble: The thinnest slice setting was almost flush with the platform and worked best with firm foods that could push down on the platform.

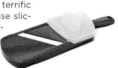

OXO Good Grips V-Blade Mandoline Slicer
SAFETY: ★★★   CLEANUP: ★½   EASE OF USE: ★★
PERFORMANCE: ★★★   PRICE: $39.99
COMMENTS: Our former favorite adjusts slice thickness with a dial, includes a broad hand guard, and makes crisp cuts. But blades stored beneath its platform get dirty during cutting, forcing us to clean and reassemble them—a tricky task akin to playing with a Transformers toy.

RECOMMENDED WITH RESERVATIONS

NORPRO Mandoline Slicer/Grater with Guard
SAFETY: ★★½   CLEANUP: ★★   EASE OF USE: ★★
PERFORMANCE: ★★½   PRICE: $24.25
COMMENTS: A dial adjusts slice thickness—no blade handling required—but gauging thickness requires a ruler. Though it slices and juliennes well, other nonessential "bonus" attachments proved disappointing, and there is no place to store them. The lock switch to change blades also jams when the slicer is wet.

NOT RECOMMENDED

KUHN RIKON Thick & Thin Mandoline
SAFETY: ★★½   CLEANUP: ★★   EASE OF USE: ★
PERFORMANCE: ★   PRICE: $25.00
COMMENTS: Two blades—one thick, one thin—built into this slicer's platform were set too close together to allow for long slices. The skinny platform forced us to trim down a potato and squeeze in a tomato. Its mini hat-shaped hand guard imitated the OXO hand guard's larger design but was less effective.

MICROPLANE Adjustable Slicer with Julienne Blade
SAFETY: ★   CLEANUP: ★½   EASE OF USE: ★
PERFORMANCE: ★   PRICE: $29.95
COMMENTS: Handling this paddle's julienne blade felt dicey. An ill-placed support bar broke long slices. Long spikes on the guard mangled food. Slicing firm potatoes was fine, but softer tomatoes turned to mush.

PERFECT POACHED CHICKEN BREASTS WITH WARM TOMATO-GINGER VINAIGRETTE

PERFECT POACHED CHICKEN BREASTS

✔ **WHY THIS RECIPE WORKS:** Poaching can be a perfect way to gently cook delicate chicken breasts, but the standard approach can be fussy and it offers little in the way of flavor or pizzazz. To up the ante on flavor, we added salt, soy sauce, garlic, and a small amount of sugar to the poaching liquid for meaty, rich-tasting chicken. We found that our salty poaching liquid could double as a quick brine, simplifying the recipe and infusing the chicken with flavor all the way through. To ensure that the chicken cooked evenly, we used plenty of water and raised the chicken off the bottom of the pot in a steamer basket. Taking the pot off the heat partway through cooking allowed the delicate meat to cook through using gentle, residual heat and prevented overcooking. A few simple, flavorful sauces made the perfect accompaniment to our tender, moist chicken.

PEOPLE SAY IT ALL THE TIME: BONELESS, SKINLESS chicken breasts are dry and stringy. But we know it's not the chickens' fault. Sure, modern chicken breasts are lean and mild. But the same can be said for most fish, and we don't pass the buck to our finned friends. Instead, we adjust our cooking techniques. Yet we throw delicate chicken breasts onto a white-hot grill, sear them hard in a skillet, and even toss them under the broiler—all potential paths to leathery flesh. Meanwhile we ignore one of the most obvious methods for delivering tender, moist chicken: poaching.

This old-school technique has a reputation for being fussy—and it is. The traditional method calls for maintaining a pot of water just below a simmer (between 160 and 180 degrees); it's not exactly hands-free or foolproof since you have to be vigilant about keeping the heat level just so. Furthermore, it rarely does much for flavor.

That said, it has the potential to deliver meat that's exceptionally moist and succulent. If we could take away some of the fussiness and figure out how to use the method to boost flavor, we might just be able to kick-start a poaching renaissance.

We already had a head start: When we developed a chicken salad recipe a few years ago, we came up with an easier, more hands-free poaching method. Instead of heating water in a pot and then tossing in cold chicken breasts and fiddling constantly with the burner until the breasts are done, we combine the water and chicken from the beginning. Four boneless, skinless chicken breasts go into a Dutch oven with 6 cups of salted cold water; we heat the pot over medium heat until the water temperature reaches 170 degrees; and then we remove the pot from the heat and allow it to sit, covered, until the breasts are cooked through.

The beauty of this technique is that it's incredibly gentle and mostly hands-off. It results in moist meat that's ready to be cubed and tossed with mayonnaise and seasonings for chicken salad. We adopted this basic approach as our starting point, hoping that a few adjustments would produce breasts with meatier, richer flavor and that were even more moist, if possible. We were after chicken breasts that could stand alone on a dinner plate with nothing more than a simple sauce.

The first change we made was increasing the water to 4 quarts. More water translates to a larger reserve of heat and thus better assurance that the breasts will hit the desired internal temperature of 160 degrees, even if you are using a thin pot or a poorly calibrated thermometer. And since the sides of the breasts in contact with the bottom of the pan could potentially cook faster, we also raised the breasts off the bottom of the pot—the additional liquid allowed us to put them in a steamer basket while still keeping them fully submerged. And finally, we used a meat mallet to lightly pound the thicker end of the breasts to promote more even cooking. These adjustments worked well, so we moved on to amping up flavor.

Our primary goal was to add richer, more complex flavor to the breasts during cooking, but keep the flavors neutral enough that the chicken could still pair with a range of sauces for a versatile main course. Over the years we've learned that it's difficult for most flavorings to penetrate very far into a piece of poultry or meat. During marinating, brining, and even cooking, most flavors travel only a few millimeters into meat. There are, luckily, some exceptions. Many recipes, including our working one here, testify to the fact that given sufficient concentration and time, salt can penetrate much farther into the interior of a chicken breast. Sugar also works in this way, so we added a few tablespoons to the salted poaching water. Tasters approved; the chicken didn't taste sweet—just a bit rounder and fuller.

We then looked to two other categories of ingredients for more flavor: alliums and foods rich in glutamate. A common amino acid, glutamate gives food a savory, meaty flavor. In addition to being found in ingredients like tomatoes, Parmesan cheese, and mushrooms, glutamates are in many fermented seasonings, such as miso, soy sauce, and fish sauce. We tried adding quantities of all three seasonings to the poaching liquid. Used in a relatively dilute concentration, the soy sauce won out, adding meatiness and depth without giving itself away.

Alliums, such as onions, scallions, shallots, and garlic, contain potent flavor compounds that are water-soluble, which meant we could use the cooking water to transfer their flavor into the meat. We tried adding each of the aforementioned alliums to separate pots of poached chicken and asked tasters to pick a favorite. Garlic took first for the complex, sweet background flavor that it added; we smashed six cloves with the side of a knife, peeled away the skins, and tossed the cloves into the pot.

We were making good progress in the flavor department, and the salt was penetrating decently into each chicken breast, though not as much as we would have liked. Quantity and time are the key players in how far the salt could get, and the poaching time wasn't all that long. This got us thinking about brining and salting, two techniques that give salt time to diffuse deeper into pieces of meat or poultry. Salting is a longer process than brining, and it's a technique that we typically use when we want to develop browning and crispy skin on meat—not something that we were going for here. But we'd just finished crafting the perfect salty, flavorful poaching liquid. Could it also serve as a brine? Our standard brine for boneless, skinless chicken breasts is ¼ cup salt to 2 quarts water. With ¼ cup salt and ½ cup soy sauce to 4 quarts water, our poaching solution was just below that ratio. We thought that it could possibly serve as a gentle brine and double as the poaching liquid without making the chicken overly salty.

We gave it a shot, adding the chicken breasts to the poaching liquid and letting them sit for 30 minutes at room temperature, which allowed the breasts' internal temperature to slowly start to rise. Then we turned on the heat and proceeded with the recipe. Tasters declared this batch the most evenly seasoned and flavorful thus far, as well as the most juicy and tender. Those 30 minutes had given the salt time to dissolve some proteins in the chicken, resulting in a tenderizing effect. At the same time, the water, glutamate, and garlic flavor compounds had time to make their way deeper into the flesh. Even our skeptical "anti–white meat" colleagues had to admit that this was really good, flavorful chicken.

Now all we needed was a couple of simple sauces that would complement the chicken's mild, meaty flavor and juicy, tender texture. The first was a yogurt-based sauce with cumin, garlic, and fresh cilantro. For the second sauce we took inspiration from an Indian chutney and made a warm vinaigrette with tomato, ginger, fennel, and brown sugar. And finally, we put together a salsa verde–inspired parsley sauce with briny capers and cornichons.

With a technique so easy, foolproof, and good, even the most skeptical of cooks will never again doubt the power of poaching.

NOTES FROM THE TEST KITCHEN

TENDER, JUICY POACHED CHICKEN THAT TASTES GOOD, TOO

Traditional poaching is a fussy procedure that requires constant monitoring of the cooking liquid and fiddling with the stove to ensure that it stays at a subsimmer—the main hallmark of this method. Our approach is gentler, requires no monitoring, and even adds flavor to mild chicken.

1. USE LOTS OF FLAVORFUL WATER: In traditional poaching, only an inch or two of plain water is used. We use a full 4 quarts and add water-soluble flavorings like soy sauce, salt, sugar, and garlic to thoroughly season the meat.

2. PROP UP CHICKEN: Elevating the chicken on a steamer basket ensures that none of the meat will be in contact with the bottom of the pot and all sides will cook evenly.

3. COOK COVERED, OFF HEAT: Bringing the cooking liquid to 175 degrees, covering the pot, and cooking the chicken in residual heat is foolproof and hands-off.

POACHING LIQUID THAT DOUBLES AS A BRINE

We use our well-seasoned poaching liquid not only to impart flavor to the chicken as it cooks but also as a solution in which to brine the meat before turning on the heat. Letting the breasts sit in this liquid for 30 minutes at room temperature has its benefits: The salt (along with the sugar and flavorings) gets a jump start on seasoning the meat and breaking down proteins to create more-tender chicken. Furthermore, the chicken loses its chill, so it needs less exposure to the heat to come up to temperature.

Perfect Poached Chicken Breasts

SERVES 4

To ensure that the chicken cooks through, don't use breasts that weigh more than 8 ounces each. If desired, serve the chicken with one of our sauces (recipes follow) or in a salad or sandwiches.

- **4 (6- to 8-ounce) boneless, skinless chicken breasts, trimmed**
- **½ cup soy sauce**
- **¼ cup salt**
- **2 tablespoons sugar**
- **6 garlic cloves, smashed and peeled**

1. Cover chicken breasts with plastic wrap and pound thick ends gently with meat pounder until ¾ inch thick. Whisk 4 quarts water, soy sauce, salt, sugar, and garlic in Dutch oven until salt and sugar are dissolved. Arrange breasts, skinned side up, in steamer basket, making sure not to overlap them. Submerge steamer basket in brine and let sit at room temperature for 30 minutes.

2. Heat pot over medium heat, stirring liquid occasionally to even out hot spots, until water registers 175 degrees, 15 to 20 minutes. Turn off heat, cover pot, remove from burner, and let stand until meat registers 160 degrees, 17 to 22 minutes.

3. Transfer breasts to cutting board, cover tightly with aluminum foil, and let rest for 5 minutes. Slice each breast on bias into ¼-inch-thick slices, transfer to serving platter or individual plates, and serve.

Cumin-Cilantro Yogurt Sauce

MAKES ABOUT 1 CUP

Mint may be substituted for the cilantro. This sauce is prone to curdling and thus does not reheat well; prepare it just before serving.

- **2 tablespoons extra-virgin olive oil**
- **1 shallot, minced**
- **1 garlic clove, minced**
- **1 teaspoon ground cumin**
- **⅛ teaspoon red pepper flakes**
- **½ cup plain whole-milk yogurt**
- **⅓ cup water**
- **1 teaspoon lime juice**
- **Salt and pepper**
- **2 tablespoons chopped fresh cilantro**

Heat 1 tablespoon oil in small skillet over medium heat until shimmering. Add shallot and cook until softened, about 2 minutes. Stir in garlic, cumin, and pepper flakes and cook until fragrant, about 30 seconds. Remove from heat and whisk in yogurt, water, lime juice, and remaining 1 tablespoon oil. Season with salt and pepper to taste, and cover to keep warm. Stir in cilantro just before serving.

Warm Tomato-Ginger Vinaigrette

MAKES ABOUT 2 CUPS

Parsley may be substituted for the cilantro.

¼ cup extra-virgin olive oil

1 shallot, minced

1½ teaspoons grated fresh ginger

⅛ teaspoon ground cumin

⅛ teaspoon ground fennel

12 ounces cherry tomatoes, halved

Salt and pepper

1 tablespoon red wine vinegar

1 teaspoon packed light brown sugar

2 tablespoons chopped fresh cilantro

Heat 2 tablespoons oil in 10-inch nonstick skillet over medium heat until shimmering. Add shallot, ginger, cumin, and fennel and cook until fragrant, about 15 seconds. Stir in tomatoes and ¼ teaspoon salt and cook, stirring frequently, until tomatoes have softened, 3 to 5 minutes. Off heat, stir in vinegar and sugar and season with salt and pepper to taste; cover to keep warm. Stir in cilantro and remaining 2 tablespoons oil just before serving.

Parsley Sauce with Cornichons and Capers

MAKES ABOUT 1¼ CUPS

Use a good-quality extra-virgin olive oil in this sauce.

6 tablespoons minced cornichons plus 1 teaspoon brine

¾ cup minced fresh parsley

½ cup extra-virgin olive oil

2 scallions, minced

¼ cup capers, rinsed and chopped coarse

¼ teaspoon pepper

Pinch salt

Mix all ingredients together in bowl.

Chicken and Rice Get an Upgrade

Giving the rice a quick presoak ensures that every grain cooks evenly.

THINK ABOUT THE AVERAGE DINNER PLATE FOR A MOMENT. THERE'S probably some protein on there, maybe a run-of-the-mill pan-seared chicken breast. A starch like rice or pasta. It seems mundane, right? But it's not the ingredients—it's how the ingredients are treated. With some small adjustments, weeknight dinners don't have to be lackluster. We'll show you how to take standby base ingredients and make them into something truly noteworthy. And don't worry: You can still put dinner on the table in no time.

The problem we most often run into with rice and pasta pilaf is that the two starches cook unevenly. It took us a few tries to perfect our version of the "San Francisco Treat," but once we did, we had a recipe so easy and tasty, we were able to come up with several variations to suit a variety of meals.

Perfectly crispy chicken skin is one of those elusive culinary tricks that seem to be relegated to restaurant chefs with expert butchering skills and searing hot flat-top griddles. Not so: With our recipe, shatteringly crisp, bronzed chicken skin and a bright, tangy sauce are within arm's reach. All you need is a little bit of confidence—and a heavy pot.

RICE AND PASTA PILAF WITH GOLDEN RAISINS AND ALMONDS

RICE AND PASTA PILAF

✔ WHY THIS RECIPE WORKS: Typically, rice pilaf combines rice with pieces of vermicelli that have been toasted in butter to add richness and a nutty flavor. To produce rice that was as tender and fluffy as the pasta, we needed both elements to cook at the same rate. Jump-starting the rice by soaking it in hot water for a mere 15 minutes softened its outer coating and let it absorb water quickly. Once the pasta and rice were cooked perfectly, we let the pilaf stand for 10 minutes with a towel under the lid to absorb steam. A handful of fresh parsley lent brightness to the finished pilaf.

FOR SOME, RICE AND PASTA PILAF CONJURES UP IMAGES of streetcars ascending steep hills to the tune of that familiar TV jingle. But in fact, Rice-A-Roni has its origins in a traditional Armenian dish. The "San Francisco Treat" owes its existence to a fateful meeting in 1940s San Francisco. Lois DeDomenico, daughter of Italian immigrants, learned to make rice and pasta pilaf from her Armenian landlady, Pailadzo Captanian. The dish became a staple of the DeDomenico household and would eventually inspire Lois's husband, Tom, whose family owned a pasta factory, to develop a commercial version. They named the product after its two main ingredients—rice and macaroni (pasta)—and the rest is history.

The original dish is a simple affair: A fistful of pasta (usually vermicelli) is broken into short pieces and toasted in butter. Finely chopped onion and/or minced garlic is added next, followed by basmati rice. Once the grains are coated in fat, chicken broth is poured in. After simmering, the pilaf is often allowed to sit covered with a dish towel under the lid to absorb steam—a trick that yields superfluffy results. In a well-executed version, the rice and pasta are tender and separate, boasting rich depth from the butter and nuttiness from the toasted noodles.

But the cookbook versions we tried fell short. Some featured mushy, overcooked vermicelli; in others, the rice was the problem, either sticking together in a mass or cooking up too firm. Using both garlic and onion (shredded on a box grater so that it would add flavor but not a distracting texture), we patched together a recipe and mostly resolved the under- or overcooked rice problem simply by nailing the appropriate amount of liquid: 2½ cups to 1½ cups rice and ½ cup pasta.

But even with this ratio, the pilaf was plagued by a thin layer of somewhat raw, crunchy rice just beneath the pasta, which always floated to the top of the pot during simmering. What's more, the pasta was too soft and mushy. The quicker-cooking vermicelli seemed to absorb broth more rapidly than the rice, thereby denying the rice that surrounded it sufficient liquid to cook through. Our theory was confirmed when we reduced the liquid by ¼ cup and deliberately left the pasta out of a batch: The rice cooked up tender as could be.

Adding more broth would make the dish soggy. Stirring during cooking helped, but it wasn't a reliable fix: Plenty of grains still emerged underdone.

We needed every last grain of rice to absorb the broth at the same rate as the pasta did. We considered removing the toasted vermicelli from the pot, starting the rice, and then adding back the pasta when the rice was nearly tender, but that seemed unwieldy. Then we came up with a more viable solution: soaking. Starches absorb water at relatively low temperatures, so we guessed that we could hydrate, or sort of parcook, the rice in hot tap water ahead of time. Sure enough, when we saturated the grains in hot water for 15 minutes before continuing with the recipe, the finished rice and pasta both had an ideal tender texture.

With a foolproof approach in hand, we developed a classic herbed variation as well as versions incorporating spices, sweet ingredients, and nuts. We now had a nutty, buttery, perfectly cooked side dish that would make Pailadzo Captanian and the DeDomenico family proud.

Rice and Pasta Pilaf

SERVES 4 TO 6 AS A SIDE DISH

Use long, straight vermicelli or vermicelli nests. Grate the onion on the large holes of a box grater.

1½	cups basmati or other long-grain white rice
3	tablespoons unsalted butter
2	ounces vermicelli, broken into 1-inch pieces
1	onion, grated
1	garlic clove, minced
2½	cups chicken broth
1¼	teaspoons salt
3	tablespoons minced fresh parsley

1. Place rice in medium bowl and cover with hot tap water by 2 inches; let stand for 15 minutes.

2. Using your hands, gently swish grains to release excess starch. Carefully pour off water, leaving rice in bowl. Add cold tap water to rice and pour off water. Repeat adding and pouring off cold water 4 to 5 times, until water runs almost clear. Drain rice in fine-mesh strainer.

3. Melt butter in large saucepan over medium heat. Add pasta and cook, stirring occasionally, until browned, about 3 minutes. Add onion and garlic and cook, stirring occasionally, until onion is softened but not browned, about 4 minutes. Add rice and cook, stirring occasionally, until edges of rice begin to turn translucent, about 3 minutes. Add broth and salt and bring to boil. Reduce heat to low, cover, and cook until all liquid is absorbed, about 10 minutes. Off heat, remove lid, fold dish towel in half, and place over pan; replace lid. Let stand for 10 minutes. Fluff rice with fork, stir in parsley, and serve.

VARIATIONS

Herbed Rice and Pasta Pilaf

Stir ¼ cup plain whole-milk yogurt, ¼ cup minced fresh dill, and ¼ cup minced fresh chives into pilaf with parsley.

Rice and Pasta Pilaf with Golden Raisins and Almonds

Place ½ cup golden raisins in bowl and cover with boiling water. Let stand until plump, about 5 minutes. Drain and set aside. Stir 2 bay leaves and 1 teaspoon ground cardamom into rice with chicken broth. Discard bay leaves and stir raisins and ½ cup slivered almonds, toasted and chopped coarse, into rice with parsley.

Rice and Pasta Pilaf with Pomegranate and Walnuts

Omit onion and garlic. Add 2 tablespoons grated fresh ginger to pan with rice. Stir ½ teaspoon ground cumin into rice with chicken broth. Omit parsley and stir ½ cup walnuts, toasted and chopped coarse; ½ cup pomegranate seeds; ½ cup chopped fresh cilantro; and 1 tablespoon lemon juice into fluffed rice.

CRISPY-SKINNED CHICKEN BREASTS

✔ WHY THIS RECIPE WORKS: Perfectly cooked chicken with shatteringly crispy, flavorful skin is a rare find, so we set out to develop a foolproof recipe that would work every time. Boning and pounding the chicken breasts was essential to creating a flat, even surface to maximize the skin's contact with the hot pan. We salted the chicken to both season the meat and dry out the skin; poking holes in the skin and the meat allowed the salt to penetrate deeply. Starting the chicken in a cold pan allowed time for the skin to crisp without overcooking the meat. Weighing the chicken down for part of the cooking time with a heavy Dutch oven encouraged even contact with the hot pan for all-over crunchy skin. Finally, we created a silky, flavorful sauce with a bright, acidic finish, which provided the perfect foil to the skin's richness.

WE'RE ALWAYS ON THE LOOKOUT FOR WAYS TO GET great skin on chicken. By that we mean skin that's paper-thin, deep golden brown, and so well crisped that it crackles when you take a bite. Such perfectly cooked skin, however, is actually a rarity. A good roast chicken may have patches of it, but the rotund shape of the bird means that uneven cooking is inevitable and that some of the skin will also cook up flabby and pale. And even on relatively flat chicken parts, there's the layer of fat beneath the skin to contend with: By the time it melts away during searing, the exterior often chars and the meat itself overcooks.

We wanted tender meat with a sheath of skin so gorgeously bronzed and shatteringly crunchy that you'd swear it was deep-fried.

There were a number of hurdles to achieving chicken-skin nirvana at home, not the least of which was the cut of meat itself. At some restaurants, the kitchen serves half of a chicken per person, removing all but the wing bones from the meat before searing it.

The point of all that butchery is to flatten out the bird so that its entire surface makes direct, even contact with the pan—a must for producing thoroughly rendered, deeply crisped skin. But since few home cooks can do that kind of knife work confidently and quickly, we decided to keep things simple and work with only breast meat, which would eliminate more than half of the butchering. Removing the breast bones required just a few quick strokes of a sharp knife. Moreover, switching from half chickens to split breasts made for more reasonable portions. We would serve a pair of breasts—enough for two people—and keep things simple so that the dish would work as a weeknight meal.

Of course, the drawback to working with breast meat would be its tendency to overcook, particularly once we'd removed the bones—poor conductors of heat and, therefore, good insulators. Our very basic initial cooking technique was placing the boned breasts skin side down in a hot, oiled skillet to crisp up their surface and then flipping the meat to let it color briefly on the other side. This gave us fairly crispy skin but meat that was dry and chalky. When we tried a slightly gentler approach, briefly pan-searing the chicken skin side down and then transferring the pan to the more even heat of a 450-degree oven until the breasts were cooked through, the meat was only somewhat more moist and tender. Clearly, some form of pretreatment was essential if we wanted the meat to be as succulent as the skin was crispy.

Brining was out, since it introduces additional water to the meat and inevitably leaves the skin slightly water-logged. Salting would be the way to go. Besides seasoning the meat deeply and helping it retain moisture as it cooked, salt would assist in drying out the skin. To further encourage the skin's dehydration (as well as the salt's penetration), we used one of the test kitchen's favorite techniques for chicken: poking holes in both the skin and meat with a sharp knife before applying the salt. (We have also had great success drying out the skin with a dusting of baking powder, but that trick requires an overnight stay in the fridge—too much to ask for a weeknight dish.)

Salting and slashing helped, but they got us only so far with the skin, which indicated that our simple searing technique needed further tweaking. Thus far, the best we'd accomplished was unevenly cooked skin, as we'd anticipated early on: patches that were gorgeously crispy and brown and adjacent patches that were inedibly pale and flabby. What's more, the skin tended to shrink away from the edges of the breast as it cooked, which, apart from the unsightly appearance, also caused the now-exposed meat to brown and turn dry and leathery in the process. Finally, the thin end of the breast still cooked up a bit dry by the time the thick end had fully cooked.

Evening out the thickness of the meat was easy: we simply pounded the thick end of the breast gently so that the entire piece cooked at the same rate. As for evening out the browning of the skin, we adapted a classic Italian technique: pinning the bird to the cooking surface with bricks. We figured that we could mimic that technique by weighing down the chicken breasts with a heavy Dutch oven. (Since we had no interest in transferring the weighty duo of pans to the oven, we'd switch to cooking the breasts entirely on the stovetop and see if we could manage without the oven's more even heat.) After cooking the breasts for 10 minutes over medium heat, we removed the pot and surveyed the chicken skin, which, for the most part, was far crispier than ever before and not at all shrunken. But maddeningly, pockets of fat persisted under the surface at the center and along the edges. And the meat? It was way overcooked now that the lean meat was pressed hard against the hot surface.

Amid our frustration, we had noticed something curious: When we removed the Dutch oven, a puff of steam arose from the pan—moisture from the chicken that had been trapped beneath the pot. That moisture was thwarting our skin-crisping efforts, so we wondered if the weight was necessary for the entire duration of the cooking time or if we could remove it partway through to prevent moisture buildup.

We prepared another batch, this time letting the breasts cook in the preheated oiled skillet under the pot for just 5 minutes before uncovering them. At this stage the skin was only just beginning to brown, and we feared that it might shrink without the weight, but we needn't have worried. As it continued to cook for another 2 to 4 minutes, the skin remained flat against the pan, crisping up nicely without contracting in the least. Removing the pot early also allowed the meat to cook a bit more gently, as the heat that had been trapped around the chicken was released. But it wasn't quite gentle enough; dry meat still persisted.

The core problem—that it takes longer to render and crisp chicken skin than it does to cook the meat beneath it—had us feeling defeated until we realized a way to give the skin a head start: a "cold" pan. The idea wasn't our invention; it's a classic French technique for cooking duck breasts—the ultimate example of delicate meat covered with a layer of fatty skin. Putting the meat skin side down in the oiled pan before turning on the heat allows more time for the skin to render out its fat layer before the temperature of the meat reaches its doneness point. We hoped this approach would apply to chicken.

Initially, we thought we'd hit a roadblock: The breasts were sticking to the skillet—a nonissue when adding proteins to a hot pan, which usually prevents sticking.

CRISPY-SKINNED CHICKEN BREASTS

Fortunately, by the time the skin had rendered and fully crisped up, the breasts came away from the surface with just a gentle tug. Once the skin had achieved shattering crispness, all it took was a few short minutes on the second side to finish cooking the meat.

NOTES FROM THE TEST KITCHEN

BONING A SPLIT CHICKEN BREAST

Why would you want to bone chicken breasts when they're available in every supermarket already boned? Answer: Because you want to cook boneless breasts with skin (which are far harder to find). In our recipe for crispy-skinned chicken breasts, removing the bones allows the entire surface of the meat to lie flat and even against the pan—a must for perfectly crispy skin.

1. With chicken breast skin side down, run tip of boning or sharp paring knife between breastbone and meat, working from thick end of breast toward thin end.

2. Angling blade slightly and following rib cage, repeat cutting motion several times to remove ribs and breastbone from breast.

3. Find short remnant of wishbone along top edge of breast and run tip of knife along both sides of bone to separate it from meat.

Chicken with skin this bronzed and brittle was tasty enough as is, but to dress things up a bit, we set our sights on developing a few sauces.

For a tangy, bright counterpart to the rich chicken skin, we first developed a simple version of a classic *alla diavola* sauce. This sauce needed nothing more than a reduction of pickled-pepper vinegar and chicken broth, thickened with a little flour and butter and garnished with a few chopped pickled peppers. Since it's the tanginess of this sauce that makes it the perfect accompaniment to the skin's ultrameaty flavor, we also came up with a pair of variations on the same acid-based theme: lemon-rosemary and maple–sherry vinegar.

Achieving chicken skin perfection was gratifying in and of itself. But coming up with a quick and elegant way to dress up ordinary old chicken breasts? That was even better.

Crispy-Skinned Chicken Breasts with Vinegar-Pepper Pan Sauce

SERVES 2

This recipe requires refrigerating the salted meat for at least 1 hour before cooking. Two 10- to 12-ounce chicken breasts are ideal, but three smaller ones can fit in the same pan; the skin will be slightly less crispy. A boning knife or sharp paring knife works best to remove the bones from the breasts. To maintain the crispy skin, spoon the sauce around, not over, the breasts when serving.

CHICKEN
- 2 (10- to 12-ounce) bone-in split chicken breasts
   Kosher salt and pepper
- 2 tablespoons vegetable oil

PAN SAUCE
- 1 shallot, minced
- 1 teaspoon all-purpose flour
- ½ cup chicken broth

¼ **cup chopped pickled hot cherry peppers,**
   plus ¼ cup brine
1 **tablespoon unsalted butter, chilled**
1 **teaspoon minced fresh thyme**
   Salt and pepper

1. FOR THE CHICKEN: Place 1 chicken breast, skin side down, on cutting board, with ribs facing away from knife hand. Run tip of knife between breastbone and meat, working from thick end of breast toward thin end. Angling blade slightly and following rib cage, repeat cutting motion several times to remove ribs and breastbone from breast. Find short remnant of wishbone along top edge of breast and run tip of knife along both sides of bone to separate it from meat. Remove tenderloin (reserve for another use) and trim excess fat, taking care not to cut into skin. Repeat with second breast.

2. Using tip of paring knife, poke skin on each breast evenly 30 to 40 times. Turn breasts over and poke thickest half of each breast 5 to 6 times. Cover breasts with plastic wrap and pound thick ends gently with meat pounder until ½ inch thick. Evenly sprinkle each breast with ½ teaspoon kosher salt. Place breasts, skin side up, on wire rack set in rimmed baking sheet, cover loosely with plastic, and refrigerate for 1 hour or up to 8 hours.

3. Pat breasts dry with paper towels and sprinkle each breast with ¼ teaspoon pepper. Pour oil into 12-inch skillet and swirl to coat. Place breasts skin side down in oil and place skillet over medium heat. Place Dutch oven or heavy skillet on top of breasts. Cook breasts until skin is beginning to brown and meat is beginning to turn opaque along edges, 7 to 9 minutes.

4. Remove weight and continue to cook until skin is well browned and very crispy, 6 to 8 minutes. Flip breasts, reduce heat to medium-low, and cook until second side is lightly browned and meat registers 160 to 165 degrees, 2 to 3 minutes. Transfer breasts to individual plates and let rest while preparing pan sauce.

5. FOR THE PAN SAUCE: Pour off all but 2 teaspoons oil from skillet. Return skillet to medium heat and add shallot; cook, stirring occasionally, until shallot is softened, about 2 minutes. Add flour and cook, stirring constantly, for 30 seconds. Increase heat to medium-high, add broth and brine, and bring to simmer, scraping up any

SECRETS TO STUNNINGLY CRISPY SKIN

We did a little knife work and borrowed a pair of cooking techniques (one French and one Italian) to produce skin that's so crispy it crackles.

1. REMOVE BONE; FLATTEN: Boning and flattening the chicken ensures that it makes even contact with the pan's surface—a must for rendering the fat and crisping the skin.

2. START "COLD": Placing the chicken breasts skin side down in a "cold" (not preheated) skillet, a classic French technique for pan-searing duck breasts, gives the skin enough time to render its fat before the meat overcooks.

3. ADD WEIGHT: Using bricks to weigh down chicken so that every inch of skin stays flat and crisps up evenly is a common Italian technique. We achieved equally good results by pinning down the breasts with a Dutch oven.

browned bits. Simmer until thickened, 2 to 3 minutes. Stir in any accumulated chicken juices; return to simmer and cook for 30 seconds. Remove skillet from heat and whisk in butter, thyme, and peppers; season with salt and pepper to taste. Spoon sauce around breasts and serve.

VARIATIONS

Crispy-Skinned Chicken Breasts with Lemon-Rosemary Pan Sauce

In step 5, increase broth to ¾ cup and substitute 2 tablespoons lemon juice for brine. Omit peppers and substitute rosemary for thyme.

Crispy-Skinned Chicken Breasts with Maple–Sherry Vinegar Pan Sauce

In step 5, substitute 2 tablespoons sherry vinegar for brine, 1 tablespoon maple syrup for peppers, and sage for thyme.

RATING JASMINE RICE

A staple in Southeast Asian cuisine, jasmine rice is becoming a favorite in America, too: Its consumption shot up by 15 percent in the United States between 2011 and 2012, according to the USA Rice Federation. Unlike ordinary white rice, it carries a delicate scent that's not a byproduct of jasmine flowers but the result of an elevated level of the flavor compound 2-acetyl-1-pyrroline. The scent is detectable even when the rice is covered with bold sauces. When it comes to texture, jasmine rice is lower in amylose—a starch that resists water—than other long-grain varieties, so it tends to cook up softer and stickier than rice with a higher amylose content, such as basmati, though it still maintains a slightly firm chew. Of the six jasmine rice products that we tasted, both plain and with Thai-style curry, the lone microwavable contender ranked dead last for tasting like "plastic," while a pricey mail-order brand lost points for disintegrating in the curry. Top honors went to a supermarket product, for its floral fragrance and separate, firm yet tender grains. Products are listed in order of preference. See AmericasTestKitchen.com for updates and complete tasting results.

RECOMMENDED

DYNASTY Jasmine Rice
PRICE: $4.59 for 2 lb ($0.14 per oz)
ORIGIN: Thailand
COMMENTS: Its "clean" flavor with a "great finishing hit of jasmine" and "tender, distinct grains" earned this rice our highest praise, even when it was covered with rich curry.

CAROLINA Jasmine Rice (also sold as Mahatma Jasmine Rice)
PRICE: $4.19 for 2 lb ($0.13 per oz)
ORIGIN: Thailand
COMMENTS: This particularly floral rice with a "slight sweetness" finished a close second. Served with curry, the grains remained "distinct" and "firm," with a "smooth" texture.

A TASTE OF THAI Jasmine Enriched Thai Fragrant Long Grain Rice
PRICE: $4.94 for 17.6 oz ($0.28 per oz)
ORIGIN: Thailand
COMMENTS: Most tasters described this rice as "very aromatic," with "minor floral notes," though some found the flavor "neutral" and "too subtle." Its "slightly firmer texture" meant that it "held its integrity with the curry."

RECOMMENDED (*cont.*)

GOYA Thai Jasmine Rice
PRICE: $2.89 for 2 lb ($0.09 per oz)
ORIGIN: Thailand
COMMENTS: While this rice had a "floral" aroma, its flavor was still described as "bland." However, its texture was good, with "very distinct" and "firm" but "sticky" grains that "absorb sauce nicely."

RECOMMENDED WITH RESERVATIONS

LOTUS FOODS Organic Mekong Flower Jasmine Rice
PRICE: $4.69 for 15 oz ($0.31 per oz), plus shipping
ORIGIN: Cambodia
COMMENTS: This mail-order, organic, heirloom strain drew mixed reviews: Some thought it was "a bit toasty" and even like "butter and flowers," while others called it "plain." Its downfall: a "mushy" texture that "got lost" with curry.

NOT RECOMMENDED

UNCLE BEN'S Ready Rice, Jasmine
PRICE: $2.94 for 8.5 oz ($0.35 per oz; includes water content)
ORIGIN: Thailand
COMMENTS: The microwavable pouch delivered rice in 90 seconds; too bad it tasted like "plastic," was a "weird color" (it's predressed with canola or sunflower oil, soy lecithin, and natural flavor, which tints it a yellowish brown), and had a "waxy," "wet sponge" texture.

Comfort Food Revisited

For a cream cheese swirl that can hold its own next to our rich, chocolate brownie batter, we add sour cream for tang and a bit of flour to absorb excess moisture.

WHEN THE WEATHER GETS COLD, FEW THINGS WARM US UP BETTER than a steaming bowl of stew. Most often, of course, stew brings to mind pieces of tender beef in a dark, velvety sauce, but we wondered if we could create a chicken stew that would be just as good as its beef brethren. But we were up against a serious challenge: Chicken doesn't behave like beef. While beef relies on long cooking to turn tender, chicken needs only a short amount of time to cook through—not enough time to build rich flavor. But our determination paid off: With a little bit of creativity (and a pound of chicken wings), our stew had all the depth and comforting richness of even the best beef versions. On chilly evenings, we'll be glad to have this stew in our repertoire.

Comfort food doesn't have to be savory. When we really want to indulge, we turn to cream cheese brownies. But many versions can be disappointing: The two batters are unevenly distributed, and most recipes are plagued with gritty cream cheese filling or a dry, overbaked texture. We wanted to find a way to make both elements work together, with lightly sweet cream cheese and chocolaty brownie in every bite. Here, we'll show you how to make these two batters work in perfect harmony, using a novel technique of spreading and swirling. And you can take comfort in the fact that these brownies will turn out perfectly every time.

BEST CHICKEN STEW

✔ **WHY THIS RECIPE WORKS:** To make a chicken stew that could satisfy like its beef brethren, we looked to two different chicken parts: We seared collagen-rich wings to provide full chicken flavor and plenty of thickening gelatin and then we gently simmered small chunks of boneless chicken thighs for tender bites throughout the stew. To boost meatiness, we used a combination of bacon, soy sauce, and anchovy paste (whose fishy character was imperceptible in our stew). Finally, we took full advantage of the concentrating effect of reduction by cooking down wine, broth, and aromatics at the start and simmering the stew uncovered during its stay in the oven.

LIVING IN A NATION OF CHICKEN LOVERS, WE'RE ALWAYS surprised at how rarely we find chicken stew on a menu or in a cookbook. We have great chicken pot pies, plenty of chicken casseroles, and some of the best chicken noodle soups going, but in the stew category we seem almost exclusively drawn to beef. The few chicken stews we have seen are either too fussy or too fancy, derivatives of French fricassee or coq au vin, or seem more soup than stew, with none of the complexity and depth we expect from the latter. It was time to make an adjustment to the American canon. We wanted to develop a chicken stew recipe that would satisfy like the beef kind—one with succulent bites of chicken, tender vegetables, and a truly robust gravy.

Since the clear goal was to develop a beef stew–caliber chicken stew, that's exactly where we started. Beef is practically designed for stew. Chuck roast (cut from the shoulder) can be easily cubed into even pieces, seared hard to develop a rich-tasting crust, and simmered for hours until fall-apart tender, all the while remaining juicy. This treatment is made possible by the meat's tough network of connective tissue, which slowly converts into lubricating gelatin during cooking. This turns the beef tender while the gravy is infused with rich beefiness and body—a culinary win-win.

How could we make chicken behave like beef? Well, we couldn't—not really: Today's chicken is butchered very young so even its thighs and drumsticks have little time to develop much connective tissue. But obviously the fattier, richer-tasting dark meat was the best choice. We could start by subbing boneless, skinless thighs for the meat in a basic beef stew recipe, shortening the cooking time drastically for the quicker-cooking chicken. We didn't expect perfection, but perhaps we'd have a good jumping-off point from which we could tweak and adjust as needed.

We heated a couple of tablespoons of oil in a large Dutch oven and seared 2 pounds of halved thighs. After they browned, we transferred them to a bowl. In the now-empty pot we softened some basic aromatics in butter and then sprinkled in flour to create a roux for thickening. Next we stirred in store-bought chicken broth, the browned chicken, and chunks of red potatoes and carrots. After an hour of gentle simmering, the vegetables were soft and the chicken was tender. The stew looked pretty good. But its appearance was deceiving: One bite revealed a weak-flavored gravy. Not to mention that the chicken, though not desiccated, showed a disappointing lack of juiciness. In fact, the vegetables were just about the only redeeming things in the pot.

But what if, instead of trying to preserve some of its flavor and juiciness—which didn't work anyway—we cooked the life out of the chicken so that at least it would enrich the gravy? After the chicken had given it all up to the pot, we would discard it and cook more chicken in the stewing liquid just until tender. It didn't make sense to treat thighs or even drumsticks this way. But wings would be another story. They actually have a decent amount of collagen, and because they're more about skin and bones than about meat, discarding them after they'd enriched the gravy wouldn't seem wasteful. (Wings are fun to pick at during a football game, but shredding them

BEST CHICKEN STEW

individually after cooking and stirring the meat into a stew is a hassle that most cooks would prefer to avoid.)

We split a pound of wings at their joints to ensure that they'd lie flat and brown evenly, allowing us to maximize the flavorful Maillard reaction. After browning the wings on both sides, we removed them and built a gravy with aromatics, a roux, and chicken broth just as we had before. We then added the browned wings back to the pot along with potato and carrot pieces. We covered the pot and let everything simmer in a 325-degree oven for about 30 minutes.

Next we stirred in the halved boneless, skinless chicken thighs (We skipped searing this time to prevent them from drying out) and returned the pot to the oven until they were fork-tender, about 45 minutes longer. When we removed the wings from the pot, they literally fell apart in the tongs, a sure sign that much of their connective tissue had been converted into gelatin. We also tasted the meat to see what flavor it might have left to give. The answer: not very much, meaning that we'd effectively extracted it into the gravy. Indeed, the stew had improved dramatically. The thighs were tender and juicy and the gravy was more chicken-y and velvety. It wasn't beef-stew good, but we were making progress.

Next we focused on really ramping up flavor. While good chicken soup is all about attaining pure chicken flavor, stew requires more depth and complexity—the kind of richness that can stave off winter's harshest chill. Browning the wings was a step in the right direction, but we needed a lot more reinforcement. Our first move was to the fridge, where we rounded up some big flavor boosters: bacon, soy sauce, and anchovy paste. A few strips of bacon, crisped in the pot before we browned the wings in the rendered fat, lent porky depth and just a hint of smoke. Soy sauce and anchovy paste may sound like strange additions to an all-American chicken stew, but their inclusion was strategically sound. When ingredients rich in glutamates (such as soy sauce) are combined with those rich in free nucleotides (like anchovies), flavor-boosting synergy is achieved. The nucleotides affect our tastebuds so that our perception of meaty-tasting glutamates is amplified by up to 30 times.

We added 2 teaspoons of anchovy paste with the aromatics—minced onion, celery, garlic, and thyme—and a tablespoon of soy sauce along with the broth. Just as we'd hoped, things took an immediate turn to the more savory—without tasting salty or fishy. Tasters were finally going for seconds and admitting that they'd consider eating a bowl of chicken stew over beef stew. We were feeling pretty good, but we knew that we could take things further.

In restaurants, one of the most important flavor-creating tools is the technique of reduction. Whether you are dealing with a stock, broth, sauce, or stew, reduction evaporates water and concentrates flavors. In that vein, we tried cooking the stew uncovered to gain a bit more intensity. The flavors concentrated, plus we got an extra boost of browning on the surface of the stew and around the rim of the pot. Deglazing the sides of the pot by wetting them with a bit of gravy and scraping it into the stew with a spatula produced a considerable flavor boost. Reduction was proving its value and we wondered if we could put it to even better use.

We started another batch. This time after the aromatics turned a fragrant golden brown, we stirred in a cup of the broth along with the soy sauce and a cup of white wine and brought everything to a boil. It took about 12 minutes for the liquid to fully evaporate, at which point the aromatics started to sizzle again and we proceeded to prepare the roux, add the rest of the broth, and continue with the recipe. A little over an hour later, we proudly presented tasters with the results. The reduction had not only concentrated flavors but also mellowed everything for a rounder-tasting, soul-satisfying stew.

Having done essentially all the work upfront, all we had to do to finish the stew was remove the wings, add a splash of white wine for some bright acidity, and sprinkle the pot with some chopped fresh parsley. This was truly a stew worthy of the name; the proof was in the pot, no beef necessary.

Best Chicken Stew

SERVES 6 TO 8

Two anchovy fillets, minced, dried, and mashed, can be used instead of anchovy paste. Use small red potatoes measuring 1½ inches in diameter.

- 2 pounds boneless, skinless chicken thighs, halved crosswise and trimmed
  Kosher salt and pepper
- 3 slices bacon, chopped
- 1 pound chicken wings, halved at joint
- 1 onion, chopped fine
- 1 celery rib, minced
- 2 garlic cloves, minced
- 2 teaspoons anchovy paste
- 1 teaspoon minced fresh thyme
- 5 cups chicken broth
- 1 cup dry white wine, plus extra for seasoning
- 1 tablespoon soy sauce
- 3 tablespoons unsalted butter, cut into 3 pieces
- ⅓ cup all-purpose flour
- 1 pound small red potatoes, unpeeled, quartered
- 4 carrots, peeled and cut into ½-inch pieces
- 2 tablespoons chopped fresh parsley

NOTES FROM THE TEST KITCHEN

BUILDING A RICH, FLAVORFUL GRAVY

1. START WITH BACON AND WINGS: Brown chopped bacon, then sear halved wings in rendered fat to develop meaty depth. Set bacon and wings aside.

2. ENHANCE FLAVOR BASE: Sauté aromatics, thyme, and anchovy paste in fat to create rich fond. Add chicken broth, wine, and soy sauce, then boil until liquid evaporates.

3. COOK GRAVY: Cook reserved bacon and wings (with potatoes and carrots) in more broth. This extracts flavor from meats and body-enhancing collagen from wings (later discarded).

THIS IS FOND, TOO

We often use liquid to release the browned bits, or fond, that remain on the bottom of the pan after meat has been sautéed or pan-seared; this enables us to easily stir the fond into the dish. These bits are packed with the complex flavors that are created by the Maillard reaction and can greatly enhance the flavor of a braise or a sauce. We found that leaving the lid off our chicken stew as it cooked in the oven led to the development of fond on the sides of the Dutch oven as well. To take advantage of this flavor-packed substance, we deglazed the sides by wetting them with a bit of gravy and scraping it into the stew with a spatula. The result? A considerable flavor boost.

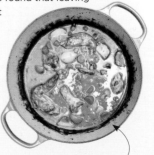

Scrape the dark ring into the stew.

1. Adjust oven rack to lower-middle position and heat oven to 325 degrees. Arrange chicken thighs on baking sheet and lightly season both sides with salt and pepper; cover with plastic wrap and set aside.

2. Cook bacon in large Dutch oven over medium-low heat, stirring occasionally, until fat renders and bacon browns, 6 to 8 minutes. Using slotted spoon, transfer bacon to medium bowl. Add chicken wings to pot, increase heat to medium, and cook until well browned on both sides, 10 to 12 minutes; transfer wings to bowl with bacon.

3. Add onion, celery, garlic, anchovy paste, and thyme to fat in pot; cook, stirring occasionally, until dark fond forms on pan bottom, 2 to 4 minutes. Increase heat to high; stir in 1 cup broth, wine, and soy sauce, scraping up any browned bits; and bring to boil. Cook, stirring occasionally, until liquid evaporates and vegetables begin to sizzle, 12 to 15 minutes. Add butter and stir to melt; sprinkle flour over vegetables and stir to combine. Gradually whisk in remaining 4 cups broth until smooth. Stir in wings and bacon, potatoes, and carrots; bring to simmer. Transfer to oven and cook, uncovered, for 30 minutes, stirring once halfway through cooking.

4. Remove pot from oven. Use wooden spoon to draw gravy up sides of pot and scrape browned fond into stew. Place over high heat, add thighs, and bring to simmer. Return pot to oven, uncovered, and continue to cook, stirring occasionally, until chicken offers no resistance when poked with fork and vegetables are tender, about 45 minutes longer. (Stew can be refrigerated for up to 2 days.)

5. Discard wings and season stew with up to 2 tablespoons extra wine. Season with salt and pepper to taste, sprinkle with parsley, and serve.

CREAM CHEESE BROWNIES

✓ WHY THIS RECIPE WORKS: Rich, decadent cream cheese brownies are hard to get just right: They are plagued by chalky cream cheese, dry brownie, and uneven distribution of each element. To fix these issues, we started with a cakey brownie, which would absorb some of the moisture from the cream cheese. Unsweetened chocolate gave us the most intense chocolate flavor, and a bit of extra sugar eliminated bitter notes. For the cream cheese swirl, we mixed in some sour cream for tang and richness. Dolloping the cream cheese into the brownie batter made for unevenly dispersed swirls; we fixed this problem by layering some of the brownie batter, then the cream cheese, then dolloping more brownie batter on top and giving the whole construction a few quick swirls with a knife.

THOUGH THE IDEA OF CREAM CHEESE BROWNIES IS undeniably appealing, every one we've encountered has had serious flaws. In some, the cream cheese swirl is chalky and flavorless, overwhelmed by the chocolate brownie. In others, the cream cheese is properly creamy and moist but the brownie portion is wet and dense. And often the swirl is so uneven, one bite is all cream cheese and the next is all chocolate. It's enough to make anyone stick with a standard-issue brownie.

Still, the potential nagged at us: In one dessert, we could have moist, chocolaty richness balanced by a tangy, creamy cheesecake-like swirl. For a cream cheese brownie that lived up to that ideal, the key would be to develop a brownie batter and a cream cheese swirl that worked with, not against, each other.

For an ideal moist, chocolaty brownie component, we started with a test kitchen recipe that relies on a combination of 2 ounces of unsweetened chocolate and 4 ounces of bittersweet for deep and complex chocolate flavor, plus just ¾ cup of flour and 1 cup of sugar—enough to tame any bitterness without making the dessert candy-like. As for the cream cheese portion, recipes we'd found called for anywhere from 8 to 16 ounces of cream cheese, so we split the difference, mixing 12 ounces of softened cream cheese with ¼ cup of granulated sugar and an egg (for both moisture and structure). We spread the brownie batter in the pan, dropped spoonfuls of the cream cheese mixture on top, and then swirled them together with a knife and baked it off.

Once cooled and cut, these brownies revealed a problem common to so many of the bad versions we'd tried: They were too wet. The cream cheese swirl was leaching liquid into the brownie portion. We needed to start with a cakier style of brownie so that once the brownies absorbed moisture from the cream cheese swirl, they would land just where we wanted them. So we switched to another test kitchen recipe, one that delivers cakier brownies by using proportionally more flour and less chocolate (just 3 ounces of unsweetened), as well as a little baking powder for lift.

This was a definite step in the right direction, but the brownies were still baking up too wet, and the chocolate flavor was a bit muted. Dropping the cream cheese down to 8 ounces helped with the moisture issue and also moved the chocolate flavor more to the front—but not enough. When we upped the unsweetened chocolate from 3 to 4 ounces, the brownies were more chocolaty, but they also turned overly bitter.

We wondered if another variety of chocolate would be a better choice. We made three pans of brownies, comparing batches made with cocoa powder and bittersweet chocolate with our working recipe. The two made with bittersweet chocolate definitely weren't bitter but they also lacked the assertive chocolate punch that the brownies needed for contrast with the cream cheese swirl. Cocoa powder produced a flat chocolate flavor and also went too far texturally, making the brownies way too dry. We thought briefly about reexamining the combination of bittersweet and unsweetened chocolate from our initial test, but buying two bars of chocolate only to use 2 ounces from each seemed beyond the pale.

The best approach turned out to be simple: We stuck with the 4 ounces of unsweetened chocolate for depth of flavor and increased the sugar from 1 cup to 1¼ cups to tame the bitterness. A teaspoon of vanilla extract helped round out the flavors.

With the brownie portion where we wanted it, we moved on to the cream cheese swirl. Its texture was spot-on—perfectly creamy and not at all chalky—but the flavor was wan and it got lost in the rich chocolate. Cutting the sugar in the swirl mixture in half, down from ¼ cup to just 2 tablespoons, allowed the swirl's dairy profile to come out a bit more, but it needed more tang. Adding lemon juice made it more tart than tangy, so we tried substituting increasing amounts of sour cream for a portion of the cream cheese. We could tell we were on the right track, and eventually we settled on ½ cup of sour cream with 4 ounces of cream cheese. This gave the swirl enough refreshing tanginess to stand out against the chocolate (any more and it tasted sour). Of course, adding sour cream had reintroduced an old enemy: moisture. So

CREAM CHEESE BROWNIES

we took out the egg and added 1 tablespoon of flour to return the body that the mixture had just lost. (The flour also helped absorb a tad more moisture.)

Finally, we were getting really close to the ideal—the two batters had the right texture and flavor—but the cream cheese swirl wasn't evenly distributed. It was more concentrated toward the center, which meant that almost every brownie had either too little or too much of the cream cheese. And beyond the aesthetics, this was causing structural problems. The brownies were sinking in the center because of the heavier, moister cream cheese batter, while the edges where the brownie batter dominated were puffed and overly dry. The cause, we realized, was the swirling approach—spreading the brownie batter in the pan, dolloping the cream cheese mixture on top, and then swirling them together. Only wisps of the swirl were getting to the very edges.

For the next test, we spread most but not all of the brownie batter evenly in the pan, and then topped it with the cream cheese mixture, this time spreading it into an even layer all the way to the edges of the pan. Then we dolloped the small amount of remaining brownie batter (microwaved briefly to loosen it up) on top and swirled it together with a knife. These brownies not only had a more uniformly distributed layer of the cream cheese filling but also baked more evenly. The final tweak was to lower the oven temperature from 350 to 325 degrees, allowing the brownies to bake more slowly and gently to guarantee that the edges wouldn't dry out by the time the center had cooked through.

Finally we had a moist, chocolaty brownie with a rich, tangy cheesecake swirl—and now, old-fashioned brownies seemed a bit boring.

Cream Cheese Brownies

MAKES SIXTEEN 2-INCH BROWNIES

To accurately test the doneness of the brownies, be sure to stick the toothpick into the brownie portion, not the cream cheese. Leftover brownies should be stored in the refrigerator. Let leftovers stand at room temperature for 1 hour before serving.

WHY THE SWIRLING TECHNIQUE MATTERS

CREAM CHEESE COLLAPSE
Most cream cheese brownies suffer from a wet center weighed down by too much cream cheese.

SWIRLED CHAMPION
Our version is well balanced and fudgy through and through.

CREAM CHEESE FILLING

- 4 ounces cream cheese, cut into 8 pieces
- ½ cup sour cream
- 2 tablespoons sugar
- 1 tablespoon all-purpose flour

BROWNIE BATTER

- ⅔ cup (3⅓ ounces) all-purpose flour
- ½ teaspoon baking powder
- ½ teaspoon salt
- 4 ounces unsweetened chocolate, chopped fine
- 8 tablespoons unsalted butter
- 1¼ cups (8¾ ounces) sugar
- 2 large eggs
- 1 teaspoon vanilla extract

1. FOR THE CREAM CHEESE FILLING: Microwave cream cheese until soft, 20 to 30 seconds. Add sour cream, sugar, and flour and whisk to combine. Set aside.

MAKING CREAM CHEESE BROWNIE SWIRLS

By rethinking the standard swirling process, we get a perfectly marbled pan of brownies that bakes evenly from edge to center.

1. Spread all but ½ cup of brownie batter in prepared pan. Spread cream cheese mixture evenly over top.

2. Microwave remaining brownie batter until warm and pourable, 10 to 20 seconds.

3. Using spoon, dollop softened batter over cream cheese filling (6 to 8 dollops).

4. Using knife, swirl brownie batter through cream cheese topping, making marbled pattern, leaving ½-inch border around edges.

2. Adjust oven rack to middle position and heat oven to 325 degrees. Make foil sling for 8-inch square baking pan by folding 2 long sheets of aluminum foil so each is 8 inches wide. Lay sheets of foil in pan perpendicular to each other, with extra foil hanging over edges of pan. Push foil into corners and up sides of pan, smoothing foil flush to pan. Grease foil.

3. FOR THE BROWNIE BATTER: Whisk flour, baking powder, and salt together in bowl and set aside. Microwave chocolate and butter in bowl at 50 percent power, stirring occasionally, until melted, 1 to 2 minutes.

4. Whisk sugar, eggs, and vanilla together in medium bowl. Add melted chocolate mixture (do not clean bowl) and whisk until incorporated. Add flour mixture and fold to combine.

5. Transfer ½ cup batter to bowl used to melt chocolate. Spread remaining batter in prepared pan. Spread cream cheese filling evenly over batter.

6. Microwave bowl of reserved batter until warm and pourable, 10 to 20 seconds. Using spoon, dollop softened batter over cream cheese filling, 6 to 8 dollops. Using knife, swirl batter through cream cheese filling, making marbled pattern, 10 to 12 strokes, leaving ½-inch border around edges.

7. Bake until toothpick inserted in center comes out with a few moist crumbs attached, 35 to 40 minutes, rotating pan halfway through baking. Let cool in pan on wire rack for 1 hour.

8. Using foil overhang, lift brownies out of pan. Return brownies to wire rack and let cool completely, about 1 hour. Cut into 2-inch squares and serve.

RATING 13 BY 9-INCH METAL BAKING PANS

We can't think of a piece of cookware that's more basic than the 13 by 9-inch metal baking pan, but we also can't think of one that's more essential. We tested eight pans with straight sides and 90-degree corners, since this shape provides the most even cooking surface, and used them to make brownies, sticky buns, and cornbread. We assessed each pan on its performance, design, cleanup, and ability to withstand scratches. Pans that were too dark left some of our baked goods nearly burnt, while lighter finishes produced more even browning. We also preferred pans with a nonstick coating, as they released baked goods easily (even gooey sticky buns) and cleaned up nicely. Our winning pan—the Williams-Sonoma Goldtouch Nonstick Rectangular Cake Pan—has a durable finish and produces perfect results every time. Products are listed in order of preference. See AmericasTestKitchen.com for updates and complete testing results.

HIGHLY RECOMMENDED

WILLIAMS-SONOMA Goldtouch Nonstick Rectangular Cake Pan, 9" x 13"
DESIGN: ★★★   CLEANUP: ★★★   SCRATCHING: ★★
PERFORMANCE: ★★★   PRICE: $32.95
COMMENTS: Producing the most evenly cooked, professional-looking baked goods of all the pans we tested, this model made brownies that were level and moist from center to edge and cornbread that was deeply golden and uniformly browned. Not even sticky bun glaze stuck to the pan. Despite becoming slightly scratched in abuse tests, its surface released perfectly and was easy to clean.

RECOMMENDED

USA PAN Rectangular Cake Pan
DESIGN: ★★   CLEANUP: ★★★   SCRATCHING: ★★½
PERFORMANCE: ★★★   PRICE: $19.99
COMMENTS: This pan was a strong performer in all tests, though its corrugated-looking bottom ridges were controversial: They left marks that some testers found unappealing on baked goods, but the ridges helped minimize scratches. The pan's nonstick coating released flawlessly. (Note: USA Pan is also the maker of our top-rated Goldtouch pan, though the two have different nonstick finishes.)

RECOMMENDED WITH RESERVATIONS

FAT DADDIO'S 9- by 13- by 2-Inch Sheet Cake Pan
DESIGN: ★★★   CLEANUP: ★½   SCRATCHING: ★½
PERFORMANCE: ★★   PRICE: $12.94
COMMENTS: The large rolled lip on this pan made it extra-easy to handle. It baked evenly, but the lack of nonstick coating was problematic for gooey sticky bun recipes. The surface showed every scratch, and the pan is not dishwasher-safe.

NOT RECOMMENDED

CHICAGO Metallic Non-Stick Bake & Roast Pan
DESIGN: ★★   CLEANUP: ★★★   SCRATCHING: ★
PERFORMANCE: ★★   PRICE: $13.49
COMMENTS: The darkest pan in the testing produced the deepest browning, which gave us a flavorful crust on cornbread but created a challenge with other recipes. We learned to check for doneness early: Brownies had tougher, drier edges; sticky bun glaze hardened into candy. The pan's coating released well, but the knife scratched it deeply, and tiny pieces of coating chipped off.

FAT DADDIO'S Anodized Aluminum Sheet Cheesecake Pan with Removable Bottom
DESIGN: ★★   CLEANUP: ★   SCRATCHING: ★
PERFORMANCE: ★   PRICE: $23.79
COMMENTS: We had high hopes for this pan with a removable bottom (like a tart pan), looking forward to not having to flip out a cake. But sticky bun glaze leaked and burned, and cornbread batter oozed under and baked the removable bottom right into the bread. The surface scratched deeply.

FOCUS FOODSERVICE Aluminum Sheet Pan Extender, Quarter Size
DESIGN: ★   CLEANUP: ★   SCRATCHING: N/A
PERFORMANCE: ★   PRICE: $9.99
COMMENTS: For bakeries, this product may be a great way to get another use out of a rimmed baking sheet, but it was a flop for us: Sticky bun glaze leaked all over the oven and burned, and cornbread rose on both sides of the extender and glued it to the sheet. Brownie batter stayed put because of the aluminum sling we'd made to lift the bars from the pan.

Mahogany Chicken and Asparagus Stir-Fry

A soy sauce–based braising liquid gains complexity and depth from sherry, vinegar, ginger, sugar, and molasses, and the moist environment helps to melt away pockets of fat from our meaty chicken thighs.

SOME SEEMINGLY INNOCUOUS DISHES ARE SURPRISINGLY TRICKY TO get just right, and sometimes getting perfect results means breaking a few kitchen rules. Take the rich, dark meat of chicken thighs. Their generous amount of fat gives them lots of flavor. But while their fat content is part of their appeal, it is also one of the reasons that thighs are so difficult to cook well: Pesky pockets of stubborn connective tissue can blemish the meat even after cooking. While braising does a decent job of melting the fat into tender gelatin, some fat inevitably remains; plus, the moist environment prevents any crispy skin from forming. To achieve perfectly cooked, tender meat and plenty of crunchy, crackly skin, we had to break a couple of cardinal rules of cooking.

Stir-frying asparagus with a flavorful sauce sounds simple, right? Wrong. Unevenly cooked asparagus and lack of browning can plague asparagus stir-fries. And sauces often slide right off, rather than clinging to the spears. We set out to correct these issues and add color and textural interest to this classic side.

MAHOGANY CHICKEN THIGHS

✓ **WHY THIS RECIPE WORKS:** The dark meat of chicken thighs may be flavorful, but too often it's riddled with pockets of fat. Braising can help, but we wanted crispy skin, too. We developed a hybrid cooking method that helped us to achieve all of our goals. Gently simmering the thighs in a potent mixture of soy sauce, sherry, ginger, and garlic rendered the fat, melted the tough connective tissues into rich gelatin, and boosted the flavor. Although the meat ended up "overcooked" by usual standards, the plentiful gelatin ensured that it was moist and tender. A brief flash under the broiler crisped the skin and enhanced the rich mahogany color.

IN THE TEST KITCHEN, WE LOVE TO WORK WITH CHICKEN thighs, but we're aware that not everyone shares our enthusiasm. Even those who admit that a roasted thigh delivers more flavorful meat than a roasted breast might steer clear of the dark meat, lest they encounter the pockets of fat and chewy connective tissue that tend to hide beneath the crispy skin.

There is a cooking method that directly addresses those flaws: braising, which melts the fat and breaks down the connective tissue into soft, rich gelatin. Both coat the muscle fibers and leave the meat moist and silky. But braised chicken thighs have one big drawback: flabby, pale, waterlogged skin. To tempt white meat devotees to the dark side, we'd have to develop a method that delivered the best of both worlds: the moist meat of braising—with no pockets of fat or connective tissue—and the crispy skin of roasting.

A hybrid approach seemed like the best bet. First we'd braise the chicken to render the skin's fat and melt down the sinew—and we'd do so in a flavorful liquid that would season the meat. Then we'd blast the chicken with dry heat to crisp that rendered skin.

In a Dutch oven we stirred together 1 cup of soy sauce and six smashed cloves of garlic, as both contain water-soluble flavor compounds that would penetrate the surface of the meat. We nestled eight chicken thighs into the pot, skin side down to encourage the fatty layer under the skin to render, and added 1½ cups of water—enough to just cover them. We brought it all to a simmer on the stove and then transferred the pot to a 350-degree oven for its gentler, more even heat.

After 40 minutes, the chicken had reached 175 degrees, the temperature at which we usually pull roasted chicken thighs from the oven. We transferred the pieces skin side up to a wire rack set in a rimmed baking sheet before returning them to the oven, this time setting them just below the fierce heat of the broiler.

The moist heat had melted most, though not all, of the fat and connective tissue, so the meat wasn't as tender as we'd like. Its flavor was also one-dimensional. As for the skin, it wasn't quite crispy, but it was attractive; the soy sauce had dyed it (and the meat) a deep mahogany color that intensified under the broiler.

To add complexity to the soy flavor, we whisked in sherry, white vinegar, a big piece of smashed ginger, and sugar and molasses for sweetness (both would also caramelize and boost that mahogany hue). Turning the chicken skin side up halfway through braising allowed the rendered skin to dry before broiling, which helped

MAHOGANY CHICKEN THIGHS

THE PARCHMENT TEST: FINDING THE BROILER SWEET SPOT

As we learned with our Broiled Pork Tenderloin (page 91) and our Mahogany Chicken Thighs, the intense heat of the broiler can be great for deep browning. The key to success is finding the rack position where even cooking and even browning are achieved simultaneously. This spot will vary from recipe to recipe, but the general principle will always apply.

Finding the zone that produces even browning can be particularly tricky with electric broilers, which heat food via multiple rods that have gaps between them. This setup can create hot spots. To find the zone in your oven that delivers the most even browning, you can broil parchment paper on a baking sheet at each position. There are likely two or three rack positions that will evenly brown the parchment (and your food); which one you should use will depend on the food you are cooking.

TOO CLOSE

The radiant heat is too narrowly focused, so the browning on the parchment is concentrated in spots. By the time there is some browning, the areas directly under the rods will have burned.

JUST RIGHT

The radiant heat waves spread evenly over the entire width of the parchment, delivering even browning.

TOO FAR

The heat is so diffuse that it will take food so long to brown that it will likely overcook. And because of the longer time frame, reflected rays have a more noticeable impact, leading to uneven browning.

it crisp a little more. We also swapped the Dutch oven for a 12-inch skillet, which we could use for both braising and broiling.

On to the bigger question: how to rid the meat of the fatty, chewy bits once and for all and make it more tender. Clearly, 40 minutes was ample time for the thighs to cook through, but their connective tissue was another matter. This portion starts breaking down at 140 degrees, does so slowly, and—if these tests had taught us anything—can't be rushed.

Realizing that we needed to hold the meat in the collagen breakdown sweet spot—above 140 degrees but below the temperature at which the meat would be overcooked—for longer, we lowered the oven temperature by 50 degrees and increased the braising time to an hour. We thought that the lower heat would prevent the meat's temperature from climbing too rapidly, but alarmingly, the braised pieces registered 195 degrees—and we still had the broiling step to go. We were sure we'd way overshot the mark, but finished the batch anyway.

But this mistake turned out to be a happy accident. These thighs were by far the best yet: beautifully moist and tender. Yes, the meat was overcooked according to our usual standards, but the extended braising time had broken down the connective tissue so thoroughly that there was loads of gelatin to bathe the muscle fibers, resulting in meat that was supple and juicy.

Now it was time to go back to the skin, which was still less than perfectly crispy. It was an easy fix, though: We simply lowered the oven rack to the middle position, which put more distance between the broiler element and the meat and gave the skin more time to brown and crisp.

We celebrated the victory by using a portion of the leftover braising liquid to make a quick sauce (thickened with a little cornstarch for body).

Now that we know how to get the best out of chicken thighs, we're planning on spending a lot more time on the dark side.

Mahogany Chicken Thighs

SERVES 4 TO 6

For best results, trim all visible fat and skin from the underside of the thighs. Serve with steamed rice and vegetables.

1½ cups water
 1 cup soy sauce
 ¼ cup dry sherry
 2 tablespoons sugar
 2 tablespoons molasses
 1 tablespoon distilled white vinegar
 8 (5- to 7-ounce) bone-in chicken thighs, trimmed
 1 (2-inch) piece ginger, peeled, halved, and smashed
 6 garlic cloves, peeled and smashed
 1 tablespoon cornstarch

1. Adjust oven rack to lower-middle position and heat oven to 300 degrees. Whisk 1 cup water, soy sauce, sherry, sugar, molasses, and vinegar together in ovensafe 12-inch skillet until sugar is dissolved. Arrange chicken, skin side down, in soy mixture and nestle ginger and garlic between pieces of chicken.

2. Bring soy mixture to simmer over medium heat and simmer for 5 minutes. Transfer skillet to oven and cook, uncovered, for 30 minutes.

3. Flip chicken skin side up and continue to cook, uncovered, until chicken registers 195 degrees, 20 to 30 minutes longer. Transfer chicken to platter, taking care not to tear skin. Pour cooking liquid through fine-mesh strainer into fat separator and let settle for 5 minutes. Heat broiler.

4. Whisk cornstarch and remaining ½ cup water together in bowl. Pour 1 cup defatted cooking liquid into now-empty skillet and bring to simmer over medium heat. Whisk cornstarch mixture into cooking liquid and simmer until thickened, about 1 minute. Pour sauce into bowl and set aside for serving.

5. Return chicken skin side up to now-empty skillet and broil until well browned, about 4 minutes. Return chicken to platter, and let rest for 5 minutes. Serve, passing reserved sauce separately.

ASPARAGUS STIR-FRY

✔ **WHY THIS RECIPE WORKS:** To achieve stir-fried asparagus with a flavorful browned exterior and a crisp-tender texture, we had to start with a hot pan and only stir the asparagus occasionally. This allowed the vegetables to char and caramelize. To ensure that the vegetables cooked evenly, we diluted the sauce with water. This diluted sauce created a small amount of steam, cooking the spears through, before evaporating and leaving behind a flavorful glaze.

IT'S NO SECRET THAT STIR-FRYING BRINGS A LOT TO THE table: Intense heat has the potential to beautifully caramelize ingredients, creating a natural sweetness that pairs perfectly with a potent, Asian-inspired sauce. We particularly like to stir-fry vegetables; since they cook in a flash, their crisp-tender bite is preserved. But things can go awry when a delicate, quick-cooking choice like asparagus hits the pan. Many recipes produce both overdone and underdone spears in a single batch, and the pieces often lack sufficient browning or flavor from the sauce.

Gorgeously browned, deeply flavorful, evenly cooked spears were the goal, so we got our bearings by following a basic stir-fry technique. We snapped the tough ends from a bunch of asparagus, cut them on the bias into bite-size lengths, and tossed them into an oil-slicked nonstick skillet (our choice over a wok since its flat-bottomed design allows more of its surface area to come in direct contact with the flat burner of a Western stove). We stirred the pieces almost constantly for a couple of minutes, until they were nearly crisp-tender, and then sprinkled in some grated fresh ginger. As soon as its pungent aroma was released (this took about 30 seconds), we poured in a sauce of dry sherry, sesame oil, soy sauce, and brown sugar and let the asparagus cook for a minute longer before scattering some sliced scallions on top for a fresh finish.

Sure enough, the browning in the dish was spotty. So was the cooking: Mushy and crunchy pieces converged

in the same bite. The problem of pale spears was easy to fix. We simply used a takeaway from past stir-fry recipes: Stir less—much less. Indeed, when we only occasionally stirred as the asparagus cooked, the longer periods of contact with the hot pan caramelized the spears nicely, boosting their inherent sweetness. But this step did nothing to even out the inconsistent cooking—in fact, it seemed to only exacerbate it.

For that problem we turned to a method we've used for hardy vegetable stir-fries: adding ¼ cup of water to the hot skillet and then covering it to trap the steam. The moist environment evenly cooked the asparagus, but by the time we added the aromatics and sauce, the frail spears were all but mush. Plus, all that water had diluted the taste of the flavorful browning we had worked so hard to achieve.

We tinkered with the steaming time, the amount of water, and whether to leave the cover on. Ditching the lid and using very little water—just 1 or 2 tablespoons, depending on the other liquids in the sauces—created a burst of steam that evenly cooked the spears without ruining their texture or browning. We also found that when we combined the water with the sauce, the mixture reduced quickly, glazing the asparagus and infusing it with the flavors of the sauce.

Next, we addressed the serving size. We wanted to serve four, but a single bunch of asparagus weighs about a pound—enough to serve only two or three. Instead of using 1½ bunches, we wondered whether we could increase the yield with a second, complementary vegetable. As it turned out, this was a very good idea. We created variations using shiitake mushrooms, red bell pepper, and red onion, which added contrasting flavor and color and cooked up nicely, provided that we cut each vegetable so that its stir-fry time aligned with that of the asparagus. Finally, to complete our mastery of asparagus stir-fries, we used a few common Asian pantry ingredients to create intense sauces to match up with each variation.

NOTES FROM THE TEST KITCHEN

TRIMMING ASPARAGUS

1. Remove one spear of asparagus from bunch and bend it at thicker end until it snaps.

2. With broken asparagus spear as guide, trim tough ends from remaining asparagus bunch using chef's knife.

STIR-FRIED ASPARAGUS WITH RED BELL PEPPER

Stir-Fried Asparagus with Shiitake Mushrooms

SERVES 4

To allow it to brown, stir the asparagus only occasionally. Look for spears that are no thicker than ½ inch.

- 2 tablespoons water
- 1 tablespoon soy sauce
- 1 tablespoon dry sherry
- 2 teaspoons packed brown sugar
- 2 teaspoons grated fresh ginger
- 1 teaspoon toasted sesame oil
- 1 tablespoon vegetable oil
- 1 pound asparagus, trimmed and cut on bias into 2-inch lengths
- 4 ounces shiitake mushrooms, stemmed and sliced thin
- 2 scallions, green parts only, sliced thin on bias

1. Combine water, soy sauce, sherry, sugar, ginger, and sesame oil in bowl.

2. Heat vegetable oil in 12-inch nonstick skillet over high heat until smoking. Add asparagus and mushrooms and cook, stirring occasionally, until asparagus is spotty brown, 3 to 4 minutes. Add soy sauce mixture and cook, stirring once or twice, until pan is almost dry and asparagus is crisp-tender, 1 to 2 minutes. Transfer to serving platter, sprinkle with scallion greens, and serve.

VARIATIONS

Stir-Fried Asparagus with Red Bell Pepper

Omit soy sauce, sherry, brown sugar, ginger, and sesame oil. Reduce water to 1 tablespoon. Whisk 1 tablespoon orange juice, 1 tablespoon rice vinegar, 1 tablespoon granulated sugar, 1 teaspoon ketchup, and ½ teaspoon salt into water. Substitute 1 red bell pepper cut into 2-inch-long matchsticks for shiitakes.

Stir-Fried Asparagus with Red Onion

Omit soy sauce, sherry, ginger, and sesame oil. Whisk 4 teaspoons fish sauce, 1 tablespoon lime juice, 2 teaspoons minced fresh lemon grass, and ⅛ teaspoon red pepper flakes into water, along with sugar. Substitute ½ red onion sliced through root end into ¼-inch-thick pieces for shiitakes and 2 tablespoons chopped fresh mint for scallion greens.

Stir-Fried Asparagus with Carrots

Omit soy sauce, brown sugar, sesame oil, and ginger. Reduce water to 1 tablespoon. Whisk 5 teaspoons lemon juice, 2 thinly sliced garlic cloves, 1 teaspoon granulated sugar, 1 teaspoon red curry paste, and ½ teaspoon salt into water, along with sherry. Substitute 1 large peeled carrot sliced ⅛ inch thick on bias for shiitakes and 2 tablespoons chopped fresh basil for scallions.

RATING TABLET STANDS AND COVERS

Bringing slim, portable tablets into the kitchen puts online recipes at your fingertips—but also places the pricey gadgets within range of splatters and sticky hands. Tablet stands promise to protect and prop up the flat computers for easy reference. There are also plastic covers and bags that act as protective sleeves. We fitted various tablets (including the iPad, iPad mini, and multiple Kindles) with five products—stands, covers, or a combo of both (priced from $10.16 to $67.99)—to see how well they stood up to the challenges of a busy kitchen. And because the covers resembled the plastic zipper-lock bags we already keep on hand, we added those to the mix, too. We pounded pork chops to see if the stands would rattle; stuffed the plastic covers with paper cut to tablet size, sealed them, and submerged them in water for 5 minutes, noting any leaks; and simply used the stands and covers as directed as we read recipes. Our favorite turned out to be the combination of the Arkon Portable Fold-Up Stand for Tablets and a plain old zipper-lock bag. The stand featured well-placed grips that secured every device we tried, a small footprint, and a neat foldable design, and the bag shielded the screen at least as well as tablet-specific covers (we taped back excess plastic to create a snug fit and punched holes for charger wires). Note: Because we did not evaluate every product under the same standards—for instance, plastic bags were not rated for stability—we indicated in the chart where rating categories did not apply with "N/A." Products are listed in order of preference. See AmericasTestKitchen.com for updates and complete testing results.

RECOMMENDED

ARKON Portable Fold-Up Stand for Tablets
PRICE: $10.16
VALUE: ★★★ **STABILITY:** ★★½
USABILITY: ★★★ **PROTECTION:** N/A
COMMENTS: This inexpensive stand folds up smaller than a remote control yet expands to fit everything from an iPad mini to a notebook-size tablet. Its lightweight plastic body wasn't completely sturdy, though pounding a pork cutlet right next to it didn't rock our tablet out of the stand. Our winning combination was pairing this tablet stand with a plastic zipper-lock storage bag.

Plastic Zipper-Lock Storage Bags
PRICE: $0.04 to $0.22 per bag, sandwich to gallon-size
VALUE: ★★★ **STABILITY:** N/A
USABILITY: ★★½ **PROTECTION:** ★★★
COMMENTS: Everyday plastic storage bags offer at least as much protection as tablet-specific covers for a fraction of the price—they cost up to 20 times less. The downside: Zipper-lock bags don't hug devices quite as tightly, but they are still watertight and can be taped back for a snugger fit. Our winning solution was pairing a zipper-lock bag with the Arkon Portable Fold-Up Stand for Tablets.

BELKIN Chef Stand + Stylus
PRICE: $19.99
VALUE: ★★½ **STABILITY:** ★★½
USABILITY: ★★★ **PROTECTION:** ★★½
COMMENTS: This model is stable and compatible with many devices, and its narrow, ultraresponsive stylus clicked exactly where we pointed it. One design flaw: Exposed buttons could get grimy.

RECOMMENDED WITH RESERVATIONS

BOOS IBLOCK Cutting Board and Stand
PRICE: $67.99
VALUE: ★ **STABILITY:** ★★★
USABILITY: ★★½ **PROTECTION:** ★★★
COMMENTS: This sturdy stand was by far the handsomest we tested—but also the biggest, heaviest (8 pounds), and most expensive, thanks to an odd-size cutting board that rests behind it. It's practical only for cooks with money and counter space to spare.

CHEF SLEEVE Disposable iPad/Kindle Sleeves, 25 Pack
PRICE: $19.99 for 25 ($0.80 per sleeve)
VALUE: ★ **STABILITY:** N/A
USABILITY: ★★ **PROTECTION:** ★★★
COMMENTS: Because these plastic sheaths are tailored to specific tablets, there's nary a baggy spot in sight. That's a nice perk, but not one that's worth the money when regular zipper-lock bags offer just as much protection for much less money. Also notable: While the iPad sleeve fit all iPad models, the Kindle version didn't fit newer, wider HD tablets.

NOT RECOMMENDED

OXO Good Grips Pop-Up Cookbook Holder
PRICE: $24.99
VALUE: ★★ **STABILITY:** ★★★
USABILITY: ★ **PROTECTION:** ★½
COMMENTS: This cookbook holder supposedly doubles as a tablet stand and protector—except that the touch screen doesn't work through the clear plastic splatter guard, which requires two hands to flip down to access the device. Plus, the guard is short; only tablets less than 8 inches tall are fully covered.

Classic Fare with Flair

Parcooking the sliced apples makes them pliable enough to bend into our rosette design, and it also ensures that the apples are fully tender when the tart is finished baking.

IT'S HARD TO GO WRONG WITH ALL-AMERICAN ROASTED CHICKEN AND apple pie. But some nights call for something a bit out of the ordinary. Without straying from the essential simplicity of this classic meal, we wanted to up the ante for a dinner with a little bit of panache.

Cornish game hens' diminutive size means they cook quickly, which can be a good thing—but it makes achieving perfectly crispy, rendered skin an outsize challenge. We borrowed a few techniques from roasted chicken, but these little birds needed some extra special treatment. A bit of butchering was half the battle—and just part of the secret. For the crispiest skin and moistest meat possible, we needed to take a multi-pronged approach. Here, we'll show you how a few extra steps can lead to a big flavor payoff.

Some home cooks find fruit tarts intimidating, but they can actually be easier than pie. For a showstopping take on apple tart, we looked to France for inspiration. We wanted a simple pat-in-pan crust with all the buttery flavor and crisp texture of traditional pastry, and a stunning but easy-to-execute presentation. Tall orders, we know, but we think our solutions make this dessert a new go-to.

ROASTED CORNISH GAME HENS

✔ **WHY THIS RECIPE WORKS:** Quick-cooking roasted Cornish game hens are an easy, elegant dinner option, but achieving crispy skin and tender meat in the short cooking time can be a challenge. Poking holes in the skin helped the fat to render quickly. To help the skin crisp up and brown, we used a baking powder rub and let the hens air-dry in the refrigerator overnight. To guarantee evenly golden skin, we butterflied the hens and started cooking them skin side down on a preheated baking sheet. Finally, we flipped them over for a final stint under the broiler. To season the meat inside and out, we added a light coating of kosher salt and fragrant spices on the undersides of the birds.

SINCE THEY FIRST APPEARED ON AMERICAN TABLES in the 1950s, Cornish game hens have typically been more of a special-occasion meal than a weeknight family dinner. But these Lilliputian birds have attributes that make them appealing to serve any night of the week. For starters, they typically weigh between 1¼ and 1½ pounds, so they cook quickly—in less than 30 minutes. What's more, the exteriors of their smaller breasts aren't prone to drying out before the interiors cook through, a perennial hurdle when roasting regular chickens. The hens also boast a higher skin-to-meat ratio than regular chickens, which makes them both more forgiving and more flavorful. The skin shields the meat from the oven's heat, and its fatty underbelly bastes the meat throughout cooking, leaving not just the dark portions but the white meat juicy and rich in a way that the breast on a chicken rarely is. Finally, hens offer the benefit of elegant presentation: Everyone at the table gets an entire bird on his or her plate.

That's not to say that Cornish game hens don't come with challenges. In fact, their combination of small size and abundant skin makes getting the exterior crispy and golden at the same time that the meat comes up to temperature even trickier than when working with a larger bird. Why? Because in order for the skin to brown and crisp, it must first render its fat and moisture, a process that takes more time than the meat beneath it takes to cook through. With a regular chicken, the bird spends the better part of an hour in the oven (so it's doable, though still a challenge); with a Cornish game hen, you're working with less than half of that time, which barely gives the skin a chance to render, much less brown and crisp.

With that in mind, we set our sights on roasting moist, juicy Cornish game hens with the same beautifully browned, crackling-crisp skin that we expect on larger birds.

The good news: When we developed our recipe for Crisp Roast Chicken, we devised a few tricks that hasten the skin-crisping process and guarantee a bird with moist meat. First, we attack the layer of fat under the skin before cooking, since fat can thwart crisping as much as moisture can. By loosening the skin and poking holes in the thickest pockets of fat, we essentially create channels through which the fat can drain.

Then we go after the skin's moisture: We rub the surface with a mixture of kosher salt and baking powder. Salt helps pull moisture to the skin's surface so that it can evaporate more quickly. And baking powder is slightly alkaline, which helps it break down the proteins in the skin to further promote crisping and browning. (For the hens, we also added a little vegetable oil to the salt before mixing in the powder, which helped the latter cling to the salt grains and, in turn, to the skin.) Finally, we air-dry the salt-rubbed chicken uncovered in the fridge for a number of hours. It's a step that requires some forethought, but the results are worth it, as the naturally dry environment evaporates moisture from the skin.

We applied this three-pronged pretreatment to four hens, air-drying them for 4 hours, and compared them with another batch of birds that went straight from

ROASTED CORNISH GAME HENS

the package to the oven. The cooking method for both (which we adapted from that same roast chicken recipe) was simple: Roast the hens, breast side down on a wire rack set in a rimmed baking sheet, in a 450-degree oven for 10 minutes; flip them and roast them 10 minutes longer; and then crank the heat to 500 degrees for the final 5 to 10 minutes of cooking, until the white and dark meat hit 160 and 175 degrees, respectively.

To our disappointment, the skin on the pretreated poultry, while improved, was still far from ideal. Extending the air-drying time all the way to 24 hours (so that more moisture would evaporate) helped, but not enough, so we moved on to the cooking method. We thought that roasting the birds low and slow might give the skin time to render its fat, at which point we could blast them under high heat to develop color. But when we dropped the heat to 300 degrees, not enough moisture evaporated from the skin and it didn't crisp. And at that rate the birds took an hour to cook.

Next we took it to the opposite extreme. We tried roasting the hens really high, at 500 degrees, the entire time—and when that still didn't even out the skin color, we tried pushing things even further. We left the birds in the oven past when the meat was up to temperature. Our logic was that if there was all that extra fat and moisture, the meat might not suffer much if it was a

little overcooked. That turned out to be true—to a point. The meat, including the breast, was still relatively juicy and tender at 180 degrees, but even then the skin was unimpressive. We continued to roast the hens until the skin was finally evenly browned, but by that point the meat was compromised.

What did get us closer was a blast under the broiler after the birds' initial 10-minute stint at 500 degrees. After about 5 minutes, their white and dark portions were up to temperature, the meat was juicy, and the skin was evenly burnished. Well, almost. The problem was the birds' rotund shape, which was keeping some of the surface at a greater distance from the heating element. A little knife work was in order.

Before pretreating the next batch, we removed the hens' backbones so that they could lie flat, giving their skin even exposure to the heating element. They looked really good now—golden from edge to edge. But the flattened birds spanned an entire dinner plate—not the elegant presentation we had in mind. Splitting them in half after removing the backbones made them more manageable to serve.

Admittedly, we have high standards for crackly-crisp skin, so as a last-ditch move we went for the extreme and seared a couple of the halves skin side down in a skillet before transferring the pan to a 500-degree oven to finish cooking. At last, the skin was gorgeously brown and crispy. Of course, cooking four hens, two halves at a time, in a skillet was impractical, so we switched to using a baking sheet preheated in the oven. We spritzed the skin of each bird with vegetable oil spray and sprinkled it with pepper. Then we placed all the halves skin side down on the hot sheet and slid it into the oven. When we flipped the halves 10 minutes later, the skin looked almost as good as that on the batch we'd seared in the skillet. Blasting the birds skin side up under the broiler for 5 minutes easily finished the job.

All that remained to consider was flavor. The overnight salt rub was seasoning the tops of the birds; rubbing a bit more kosher salt on their undersides evened it out. We also realized that we could dress up the salt rub by adding dried herbs and spices. After a few flavor experiments, we settled on combinations of cumin, coriander, and paprika; thyme, marjoram, and rosemary; and oregano, anise, and hot smoked paprika.

Now that we had a recipe for roasted poultry that guaranteed great meat and skin and, once pretreated, could be on the table in well under half an hour, Cornish game hens were looking more appealing than ever for any day of the week.

Roasted Cornish Game Hens

SERVES 4

This recipe requires refrigerating the salted meat for at least 4 hours or up to 24 hours before cooking (a longer salting time is preferable). If your hens weigh 1½ to 2 pounds, cook three instead of four, and extend the initial cooking time in step 5 to 15 minutes. We prefer Bell & Evans Cornish Game Hens.

  4 (1¼- to 1½-pound) Cornish game hens,
     giblets discarded
     Kosher salt and pepper
  ¼ teaspoon vegetable oil
  1 teaspoon baking powder
     Vegetable oil spray

NOTES FROM THE TEST KITCHEN

NOT JUST A LITTLE CHICKEN

Cornish game hens are neither from Cornwall nor wild game, and they can be hens or roosters. They were reportedly first bred in the 1950s by a Connecticut couple, Jacques and Alphonsine Makowsky, who crossed breeds of domestic chickens with a Cornish gamecock and sold the hybrid when it was very young. As a result, Cornish game hens typically weigh less than 2 pounds, so they cook faster than larger chickens and look nice on a plate—traits that make them popular with consumers. They also feature small breasts and a high ratio of fatty skin to meat. The fatty underside bastes the meat as it cooks, which might explain why we found both their white and dark portions more tender, juicy, and flavorful than those on regular chickens. We prefer **Bell & Evans Cornish Game Hens**, which have a pleasant, clean flavor and tender meat.

ADD OIL FOR AN EVENLY DISTRIBUTED RUB

To give our Roasted Cornish Game Hens shatteringly crispy skin, we rub them with a mixture of two ingredients: kosher salt, which removes moisture, and baking powder, which promotes browning and crisping. Combining the baking powder and salt in a bowl before applying the rub works OK, but it isn't ideal. That's because the finer grains of baking powder settle out from the coarser salt, which makes even distribution tricky. To prevent them from separating, we mix the salt with a little oil and then add the baking powder. The oil creates a moist, tacky surface on the salt, giving the baking powder something to cling to, thus ensuring that it distributes evenly and our game hens have evenly crispy skin.

1. Using kitchen shears and working with 1 hen at a time, with hen breast side down, cut through bones on either side of backbone; discard backbone. Lay hens breast side up on counter. Using sharp chef's knife, cut through center of breast to make 2 halves.

2. Using your fingers, carefully separate skin from breasts and thighs. Using metal skewer or tip of paring knife, poke 10 to 15 holes in fat deposits on top of breasts and thighs. Tuck wingtips underneath hens. Pat hens dry with paper towels.

3. Sprinkle 1 tablespoon salt on underside (bone side) of hens. Combine 1 tablespoon salt and oil in small bowl

GETTING CORNISH GAME HENS TO CRISP QUICKLY AND EVENLY

For evenly crisp skin on Cornish game hens, we use a few tricks.

1. SPATCHCOCK: For each bird, cut through the bones on either side of the backbone; discard the backbone.

2. SPLIT: Cutting through the center of the breast makes two halves that lie flat for better browning.

3. SEPARATE AND POKE: Loosening and poking holes in the skin allows the fat to drain during cooking, aiding crisping.

4. SALT AND AIR-DRY: Rubbing the birds with salt and baking powder and then chilling them evaporates moisture.

5. SEAR: Starting the birds skin side down on a preheated baking sheet effectively (and efficiently) crisps their skin.

and stir until salt is evenly coated with oil. Add baking powder and stir until well combined. Turn hens skin side up and rub salt–baking powder mixture evenly over surface. Arrange hens skin side up and in single layer on large platter or plates and refrigerate, uncovered, for at least 4 hours or up to 24 hours.

4. Adjust oven racks to upper-middle and lower positions, place rimmed baking sheet on lower rack, and heat oven to 500 degrees.

5. Once oven is fully heated, spray skin side of hens with oil spray and season with pepper. Carefully transfer hens, skin side down, to preheated sheet and cook for 10 minutes.

6. Remove hens from oven and heat broiler. Flip hens skin side up. Transfer sheet to upper rack and broil until well browned and breasts register 160 degrees and drumsticks/thighs register 175 degrees, about 5 minutes, rotating sheet as needed to promote even browning. Transfer to platter or individual plates and serve.

VARIATIONS

Herb-Roasted Cornish Game Hens

In step 3, combine 2 tablespoons kosher salt with 1 teaspoon dried thyme, 1 teaspoon dried marjoram, and 1 teaspoon dried crushed rosemary. Sprinkle half of salt mixture on underside of hens; stir oil into remaining salt-herb mixture until mixture is evenly coated with oil. Add baking powder to oil-salt mixture and proceed with recipe.

Cumin-Coriander Roasted Cornish Game Hens

In step 3, combine 2 tablespoons kosher salt with 2 teaspoons ground cumin, 2 teaspoons ground coriander, 1 teaspoon paprika, and ¼ teaspoon cayenne pepper. Sprinkle half of salt mixture on underside of hens; stir oil into remaining salt mixture until mixture is evenly coated with oil. Add baking powder to oil-salt mixture and proceed with recipe.

Oregano-Anise Roasted Cornish Game Hens

In step 3, combine 2 tablespoons kosher salt with 1 teaspoon dried oregano, ½ teaspoon anise seeds, and ½ teaspoon hot smoked paprika. Sprinkle half of salt mixture on underside of hens; stir oil into remaining salt mixture until mixture is evenly coated with oil. Add baking powder to oil-salt mixture and proceed with recipe.

FRENCH APPLE TART

✔ **WHY THIS RECIPE WORKS:** Classically elegant French apple tart is little more than apples and pastry, but such simplicity means that imperfections like tough or mushy apples, unbalanced flavor, and a sodden crust are hard to hide. We wanted a foolproof way to achieve tender apples and a flavorful, buttery crust. We parbaked our quick pat-in-pan dough for a cookie-like texture that gave the tart a sturdy base. For intense fruit flavor, we packed the tart with a whopping 5 pounds of Golden Delicious apples. We cooked half into a concentrated puree, which we made more luxurious with butter and apricot preserves. For textural contrast, we sliced and parcooked the remaining apples and used them to adorn the top. A thin coat of preserves and a final stint under the broiler provided an attractively caramelized finish.

THE WORD "ELEGANT" IS USUALLY USED TO DESCRIBE something that's exquisite and special occasion–worthy, like hand-cut crystal. But it can also refer to something that's ingeniously simple yet effective, like a mathematical proof. Both applications of the word fit the classic French apple tart, a visually stunning dessert that has intense fruit flavor and diverse textures, yet is made with just a few basic ingredients.

Some variations feature extras like almonds or custard, but in its simplest form *tarte aux pommes* has a crisp pastry shell that's filled with a concentrated apple puree and then topped with a spiraling fan of paper-thin apple slices. It's usually finished with a delicate glaze, which caramelizes during baking, providing an extra layer of flavor and a distinctly European flair.

But dazzling looks quickly lose their appeal when there's no integrity backing them up, and poor structure is the fatal flaw of many a handsome apple tart. If the apple slices on top are tough, they resist the knife and

FRENCH APPLE TART

the soft puree beneath squirts out under the pressure. That layer of puree also tends to make the crust sodden and mushy. And the dessert's overall flavor can be a bit one-dimensional.

Still, we were drawn to the idea of a showstopper dessert that could be made with a short list of pantry staples. Our challenge would be perfecting each component to produce a tart with lively, intense apple flavor and a crust that stayed crisp. And we were unwilling to sacrifice integrity for beauty; we wanted both.

For a dough that would hold its shape and maintain a crisp texture even after being filled with the apple puree, we started by preparing the three classic French pastry options and filling them with a placeholder puree: five peeled and cored Golden Delicious apples (widely available, and good quality year round), cooked with a splash of water until soft, mashed with a potato masher, and reduced until thick. (We'd deal with the apple slices on top later).

Our first attempt was with puff pastry (frozen, since making puff pastry is a feat in and of itself), which is essentially many alternating layers of lean dough and butter. We lined the 10-inch tart pan with a sheet of the dough that had been rolled very thin, parbaked it to dry it out and firm it up, and then filled it with the puree. But it was a flop—literally. Despite parbaking it, the dough shrank. Its initially crisp texture also softened beneath the wet puree. On to the next crust option.

Following a classic recipe for *pâte brisée* (essentially the French equivalent of flaky American pie dough), we buzzed 1⅓ cups of flour in the food processor with a touch each of salt and sugar and then pulsed in 11 tablespoons of cold butter until the mixture formed a coarse meal dotted with lumps of butter. We drizzled in 5 tablespoons of water, pulsed the mixture until the dough formed a solid mass, chilled it, and then moved through a series of prebaking steps known as blind-baking: we rolled out the chilled dough, fitted it into the tart pan, chilled it again, lined the dough with parchment, weighed it down with pie weights, parbaked it,

removed the parchment and weights, and baked it until it was crisp.

The purpose of all that upfront work is to keep the dough from shrinking—and it paid off, as this shell held its shape nicely. The problem came when we introduced the puree, which turned the pastry soggy.

Lastly, we tried a *pâte sucrée* (also called *pâte sablée*). This pastry typically contains more sugar than the previous doughs, but the most significant difference is the degree to which the butter gets incorporated. Whereas most of the butter in pâte brisée is left in small chunks, here the butter is thoroughly worked into the flour, which limits the development of gluten—the strong elastic network that forms when flour proteins are moistened with water. Less gluten translates to pastry that is less prone to shrinking and that bakes up with a finer, "shorter" crumb.

We worked the butter into the dry ingredients until the mixture looked like sand, and then bound it with an egg (typical in pâte sucrée recipes). We chilled, rolled, chilled, and baked as before—but we skipped the pie weights, since the dough wasn't likely to shrink.

Indeed, this crust baked up plenty sturdy without the weights. Even better, it didn't sog out when we filled it with the puree. Its texture was, however, a tad puffy, like a sugar cookie. And, frankly, all that chilling and rolling was tiresome. Maybe there was an easier way to get the dough into the pan.

We suspected that the cookie-like lift had something to do with the egg, so we eliminated it. But without the egg's moisture, how would we bind the dry ingredients with the cold butter?

We needed a liquid component but didn't want to add water, since that would create gluten. That ruled out milk and cream, too. But what if we turned the butter (which contains very little water) into a liquid by melting it?

Stirring melted butter into the dry ingredients produced a cohesive, Play Doh–like mass—so far so good. We considered rolling out this dough, but its consistency was so malleable that we could simply press it into the pan. Then we chilled it and baked it.

This was by far the easiest pastry we'd ever made, but we reserved any celebration until we saw the final result. To our delight, the crust baked up perfectly sturdy and, without the egg, was no longer puffed up like a sugar cookie, but crisp and delicate like shortbread. When we filled it with the puree, cut a slice, and heard a promising crunch as the knife passed through the still-crisp crust, we knew that this ultrasimple pastry was a game changer.

But it got even better: Subsequent streamlining tests showed that we didn't even have to chill this modified pâte sucrée before baking; the sides of the tart pan were shallow enough that the pastry didn't slump. Now to improve that placeholder puree.

The apple filling had to meet two criteria: concentrated fruit flavor and enough body to not require a spoon. The latter goal we'd almost met by cooking down the puree

until it measured about 2 cups. The texture, and actually the flavor, was something of a cross between applesauce and more-concentrated apple butter. The only change we made was to move this operation from a saucepan to a covered skillet, the wide surface of which helped water from the fruit evaporate faster.

But for that European flair, we wanted the flavor to be more distinctive. We found the answer in Julia Child's recipe for tarte aux pommes, in which she adds butter and apricot preserves to her puree. We did the same and found that adding a few tablespoons of butter and ½ cup of the tangy fruit preserves to the pot along with the apples yielded a richer, brighter-tasting puree. (A dash of salt boosted that flavor.) The preserves also contributed pectin, which helped the filling firm up.

Next, we moved on to the decorative top. Painstakingly shingling thin-sliced apples (for ease, we'd stick with Golden Delicious on the top as well) over the entire surface was time-consuming and fussy. The outer ring looked uniform, but making the slices lie flat became more difficult and the design looked increasingly amateurish as we proceeded toward the center.

Hoping the tart would look better in its fully baked state, we turned our attention to making a glaze. The apricot preserves we were already using would add bright flavor and a dazzling sheen, so we microwaved them to make them fluid, sieved them, gingerly painted a few tablespoons over the tart's surface (tricky, because the slightest drag of the brush could dislodge the delicate apples), and baked it.

What we pulled out of the oven 30 minutes later looked OK, if a bit pale. The bigger problem was that the apple slices never became tender enough to cut the tart without them resisting and becoming dislodged. We made a series of attempts to soften the fruit—baking the tart longer, brushing the slices with water or melted butter, covering the tart with foil for part of the baking time so the slices might soften in the trapped steam—none of which made much of a difference.

In the end, we swapped the wafer-thin apple slices for more generous slices and (since we were already using a skillet to make the apple puree) sautéed them briefly to jump-start the softening before placing them on the tart. As for the spiral shingling, we decided to forgo this fussy tradition and devise a more easygoing, but still elegant, alternative. Rather than lie the slices flat, we opted to arrange them in a rosette pattern made by bending the apple slices into concentric circles. The parcooking had made the slices conveniently pliable, so there was no awkwardness toward the center of the arrangement; we simply bent the pieces and slipped them into place.

Encouragingly, these sturdier pieces stayed put when we brushed them with the glaze, leaving us hopeful as we placed the tart in the oven. Then we briefly ran the tart under the broiler to get that burnished finish that characterizes this French showpiece.

The rosette-like design of this tart made it look a bit different from the classic French apple tart, but it was every bit as elegant. And thanks to the now-tender apple slices, the rich puree, and the crisp—not to mention utterly simple and foolproof—crust, every slice of the tart that we cut was picture-perfect, too.

French Apple Tart

SERVES 8

You may have extra apple slices after topping the tart in step 6. If you don't have a potato masher, you can puree the applesauce in a food processor. For the best flavor and texture, be sure to bake the crust thoroughly. The tart is best served the day it is assembled. To ensure that the outer ring of the pan releases easily from the tart, avoid getting apple puree and apricot glaze on the crust.

CRUST

1⅓ cups (6⅔ ounces) all-purpose flour
5 tablespoons (2¼ ounces) sugar
½ teaspoon salt
10 tablespoons unsalted butter, melted

FILLING

- 10 Golden Delicious apples (8 ounces each), peeled and cored
- 3 tablespoons unsalted butter
- 1 tablespoon water
- ½ cup apricot preserves
- ¼ teaspoon salt

1. FOR THE CRUST: Adjust 1 oven rack to lowest position and second rack 5 to 6 inches from broiler element. Heat oven to 350 degrees. Whisk flour, sugar, and salt together in bowl. Add melted butter and stir until dough forms. Using your hands, press two-thirds of dough into bottom of 9-inch tart pan with removable bottom. Press remaining dough into fluted sides of pan. Press and smooth dough with your hands to even thickness. Place pan on wire rack set in rimmed baking sheet and bake on lowest rack, until crust is deep golden brown and firm to touch, 30 to 35 minutes, rotating pan halfway through baking. Set aside until ready to fill.

2. FOR THE FILLING: Cut 5 apples lengthwise into quarters and cut each quarter lengthwise into 4 slices. Melt 1 tablespoon butter in 12-inch skillet over medium heat. Add apple slices and water and toss to combine. Cover and cook, stirring occasionally, until apples begin to turn translucent and are slightly pliable, 3 to 5 minutes. Transfer apples to large plate, spread into single layer, and set aside to cool.

3. While apples cook, microwave apricot preserves until fluid, about 30 seconds. Strain preserves through fine-mesh strainer into small bowl, reserving solids. Set aside 3 tablespoons strained preserves for brushing tart.

4. Cut remaining 5 apples into ½-inch-thick wedges. Melt remaining 2 tablespoons butter in now-empty skillet over medium heat. Add remaining strained apricot preserves, reserved apricot solids, apples, and salt. Cover and cook, stirring occasionally, until apples are very soft, about 10 minutes.

5. Mash apples to puree with potato masher. Continue to cook, stirring occasionally, until puree is reduced to 2 cups, about 5 minutes.

6. Transfer apple puree to baked tart shell and smooth surface. Select 5 thinnest slices of sautéed apple and set aside. Starting at outer edge of tart, arrange remaining slices, tightly overlapping in concentric circles. Bend reserved slices to fit in center. Bake tart, still on wire rack in sheet, on lowest rack, for 30 minutes. Remove tart from oven and heat broiler.

7. While broiler heats, warm reserved preserves in microwave until fluid, about 20 seconds. Brush evenly over surface of apples, avoiding tart crust. Broil tart, checking every 30 seconds and turning as necessary, until apples are attractively caramelized, 1 to 3 minutes. Let tart cool for at least 1½ hours. Remove outer metal ring of tart pan, slide thin metal spatula between tart and pan bottom, and carefully slide tart onto serving platter. Cut into wedges and serve.

TO MAKE AHEAD: Baked crust, apple slices, and apple puree can be made up to 24 hours in advance. Apple slices and puree should be refrigerated separately. Assemble tart with refrigerated apple slices and puree and bake as directed, adding 5 minutes to baking time.

NOTES FROM THE TEST KITCHEN

ARRANGING APPLES IN A ROSETTE

1. Starting at edges and working toward center, arrange most of the cooled sautéed apple slices in tightly overlapping concentric circles.

2. Bend remaining slices to fit in center.

RATING FRENCH PRESSES

French press coffee makers are not only elegant, but they also can potentially deliver a thicker, more full-bodied cup of coffee. But this brewing method does have its drawbacks: The filter can be difficult to plunge through the brew, heat escapes glass pots quickly, and some people dislike suspended coffee particles in their cups. Spent grounds are messy, wet, and hard to dislodge from the bottom of the pot when it's time to clean up. Recently, we've seen a number of French presses that promise to address these issues. We judged each pot based on its brew, the pot's heat retention, and the ease of cleanup. Our top pick, the Bodum Columbia French Press Coffee Maker, is simple to use, brews great coffee that stays piping hot, and is a snap to clean up. Products are listed in order of preference. See AmericasTestKitchen.com for updates and complete testing results.

HIGHLY RECOMMENDED

BODUM Columbia French Press Coffee Maker, Double Wall, 8 Cup
PRICE: $79.95
HEAT RETENTION: ★★★   QUALITY OF COFFEE: ★★★
EASE OF USE/CLEANUP: ★★★
COMMENTS: This thick, insulated pot was as simple to use as a traditional glass press, but it kept coffee hotter much longer. It's also sturdier, with a round, comfortable handle. It took top honors in our tasting, producing coffee that tasters called "rich," "rounded," "nutty," and "full-bodied."

RECOMMENDED

ESPRO PRESS Coffee Maker, Large
PRICE: $119.95
HEAT RETENTION: ★★★   QUALITY OF COFFEE: ★★★
EASE OF USE/CLEANUP: ★★
COMMENTS: Some tasters found the texture of this coffee "a little thin" for French-press coffee: "Seems lighter, less full-bodied, less viscous." That's a result of its unique double filter, which prevents sediment from passing into the coffee, producing a "clean cup [with] no grit." The big basket-like double filter, ringed by a grippy silicone gasket, was harder and slower than usual to press, and it was a bit more time-consuming to clean up around its nooks and crannies. But the solidly built, insulated steel pot kept coffee piping hot.

BODUM Chambord French Press, 8-Cup
PRICE: $39.95
HEAT RETENTION: ★   QUALITY OF COFFEE: ★★★
EASE OF USE/CLEANUP: ★★★
COMMENTS: Tasters praised the coffee from this classic pot: "good flavor, lots of sediment," with a "pleasant" taste and a "slightly richer," "not-too-thin texture." It's easy and straightforward to set up and clean. But the thin glass walls of this traditional press lost heat faster than insulated pots did. It does a great job if you're drinking the coffee right away, but it cools off quickly.

RECOMMENDED (cont.)

FRIELING French Press Brushed Stainless Steel, 8 Cup
PRICE: $94.95
HEAT RETENTION: ★★★   QUALITY OF COFFEE: ★★
EASE OF USE/CLEANUP: ★★★
COMMENTS: This handsome, sturdy, insulated pot kept coffee hot and was easy to use. Nevertheless, tasters rated the coffee as slightly more bitter than that of other top-rated pots, though still "very smooth" and "balanced," with "a decent thickness." Its filter was able to tip slightly as we pressed, letting more grounds into the brew; it also lacked a grille over the spout to hold back larger particles. The pot was especially easy to clean, due to its smooth, simple surfaces, which didn't trap grounds or water.

RECOMMENDED WITH RESERVATIONS

OXO Good Grips French Press 8-Cup with GroundsKeeper
PRICE: $39.99
HEAT RETENTION: ★   QUALITY OF COFFEE: ★★★
EASE OF USE/CLEANUP: ★★
COMMENTS: While we liked the coffee made from this pot, its claim to fame is the innovative GroundsKeeper, which helps you pull spent grounds from the bottom of the carafe. However, this can still make a mess when the grounds are wet and slushy (tip: pull out the GroundsKeeper over the trash can). A steel sleeve over the glass pot does little to insulate; the temperature of the coffee dropped as quickly as that of other thin glass pots. The sleeve also trapped stray grounds and water, necessitating removal from the fragile glass pot for washing.

LA CAFETIÈRE Classic Chrome 8-Cup Cafetière
PRICE: $26.43
HEAT RETENTION: ★   QUALITY OF COFFEE: ★★
EASE OF USE/CLEANUP: ★★
COMMENTS: This traditional-style press works fine but feels a little cheap compared with others in the lineup. The glass pot is very tightly fitted into the stainless-steel cage, making it hard to remove, although this usually isn't necessary for routine cleaning. Its filter was able to wiggle and tip slightly as we pressed, letting more grounds through into the brew and making the coffee slightly bitter; it also lacked a grille over the spout to hold back larger particles. The thin glass pot cooled off fastest of the lineup; its lid has no deep collar or spout cover to help trap heat.

Pork Tenderloin Dinner

While developing our recipe for broiled pork tenderloin, we learned that broilers cook food using radiant heat, which means that, rather than surrounding the food, heat comes from only one direction.

EVERY BROILER, LIKE EVERY COOK, IS DIFFERENT, WHICH IS WHY USING the broiler to cook can be tricky. A recipe that works perfectly in one oven may produce dramatically different results in another. But the appeal of the broiler is undeniable—its intense heat (and speed) can, in the case of pork tenderloin, produce a browned, crusty roast with moist meat, stat. To avoid a desiccated roast, we'd need to tread carefully and develop a foolproof method for optimal results every time. In addition, we wanted to make this main course recipe so simple that we'd be able to devote extra time to a side worthy of more attention than usual.

One such side is the Levantine classic *mujaddara*, or rice and lentil pilaf—a dish that can pull double duty as star side dish or vegetarian main. The pilaf is topped with supercrispy deep-fried onions, which provide the dish with irresistibly savory crunch. But cooking both the rice and the lentils to perfection in one pot was challenging, and the onions—which could make or break the dish—needed to be spot-on. Plus, we wanted to streamline the cumbersome recipe. We found a way to achieve all of our goals, and even infuse the pilaf with extra savory flavor for a dish that would steal the show.

BROILED PORK TENDERLOIN

BROILED PORK TENDERLOIN

✓ **WHY THIS RECIPE WORKS:** Although broiling quick-cooking pork tenderloin sounds like a good idea, the results can be unpredictable. Differences between broilers make achieving even browning and tender meat simply a matter of luck. We wanted a recipe that would produce perfectly cooked pork tenderloins in any oven. We started by putting the tenderloins in a high-sided disposable aluminum roasting pan, which directed more of the broiler's heat directly toward the meat. Preheating the oven and then turning on the broiler eliminated variations in different ovens. Finally, we developed a couple of flavorful sauces to complement the deeply browned pork.

WHAT COULD BE AN EASIER WAY TO PREPARE QUICK-cooking cuts like pork tenderloin than to stick them under the broiler? Instead of the two-step approach of searing the roast on the stove and then transferring it to the oven, the intense heat of the broiler promises to deeply brown the exterior and cook the roast through in one fell swoop. But having worked with dozens of broilers in the test kitchen, we know that using them isn't quite that straightforward.

The problem is that recipes calling for the broiler rely on a one-size-fits-all approach, when in reality no two behave exactly the same way. This was made clear when we took a typical recipe for broiled pork tenderloin and made it in different ovens in the test kitchen. The results were all over the map—and none was perfect. One was beautifully browned but overcooked within; another was burned in patches; a third came out tender and juicy inside but with an unappetizing drab gray exterior.

Our goal was twofold: to create a recipe for richly browned, juicy pork tenderloin—and to figure out a way to minimize differences among broilers so every oven would produce the same results.

We began with a pair of 1-pound tenderloins to serve four. We wanted the simplest possible weeknight dinner, so we decided to forgo brining or salting. To ensure even cooking, we folded the thinner tail end underneath the middle, and tied the meat at 2-inch intervals to give it a uniform rounded shape. After brushing the roasts with oil and seasoning them with salt and pepper, we placed them on a baking sheet.

Though many recipes instruct to get the meat as close to the element as possible, we knew from experience that closer was not necessarily better. Too close a position can not only exacerbate uneven browning but also leave the middle of the meat raw. The key would be to find the position where the exterior browned evenly and the interior cooked through at roughly the same pace.

Indeed, when we roasted the tenderloins about 3 inches from the heat source, by the time the meat cooked through, the top of each roast was partly pale and partly scorched. Roasts cooked close to the center of the oven browned somewhat more evenly, but they took so long to get deeply browned that the interiors overcooked. The best results came from cooking the roasts 4 to 5 inches from the broiler element; tenderloins cooked here were lightly but evenly browned. And because the broiler's intense heat was causing the roasts' internal temperature to rise 15 to 25 degrees after cooking, we pulled them from the oven when they registered 125 to 130 degrees to ensure they would be at the ideal serving temperature after a 10-minute rest.

On to the next challenge: producing not only even browning, but deep browning. We often use baking soda to help in this department. By creating an alkaline environment, the soda accelerates the Maillard reaction, which browns food and creates numerous flavor and aroma compounds in the process. For even distribution, we made a paste with just ¼ teaspoon of baking soda, salt, and a little oil that was easy to spread over the roasts. This treatment boosted browning, but it was still not enough. We couldn't get the broiler any hotter, so what else could we do?

We took a break to think about how broilers actually work. Unlike roasting or baking, in which the walls of the oven heat the air within, which in turn heats the food (a phenomenon called convection), broiling cooks food directly with infrared light in the form of waves, or radiant heat. We realized that the broiler's heat waves weren't hitting just the pork but also the baking sheet, the oven racks, and the oven walls. What if we were able to direct more of those waves toward the meat?

With that in mind, we ditched the baking sheet for the taller sides of a 13 by 9-inch metal baking pan, which we lined with foil to reflect as much of the heat as possible. The roasts were definitely deeper in color, but we figured we could do better still.

We found our answer in a disposable aluminum roasting pan. With even taller 3-inch sides and a shiny surface that didn't require lining with foil, it was a winner. Tenderloins broiled in it came out with beautiful browning on the top and sides facing the reflective surface. For browning all the way around, we tried flipping the roasts halfway through, but they overcooked. In the end, we found that deeply browning half of each roast achieved the best flavor without negatively affecting the interior.

At this point, the tenderloins were actually coming out a bit underdone, but instead of making small tweaks to fix this, it seemed like the right time to try the recipe out under some other broilers.

Not at all surprisingly, while some tenderloins came out just as the working recipe had, many had subpar browning by the time they were cooked through. After poring over a stack of oven manuals, it didn't take long to pinpoint the source of the problem. Every manual had a different recommendation for preheating the broiler, from as long as 8 minutes (the length of time we'd been following) to as few as 2 minutes. Therein lay the issue.

Broilers that were preheated for too long were likely shutting off midway through cooking. This is because most ovens these days are designed with a built-in maximum temperature (typically around 500 degrees). Once the air temperature rises beyond that point, the oven (and broiler) will automatically turn off, wait for the temperature to drop, and then turn back on again. Because the broiler was also heating up the air in the oven, this would mean that the meat could continue to cook in the

residual heat (by convection)—but it wouldn't continue to brown under radiant heat from the broiler.

We could err on the side of caution and preheat the broiler for only a minute or two—but slower-to-heat broilers would still produce roasts that weren't browned enough. What if we preheated the oven first and then switched on the broiler and slid in the meat? This would not only heat the air and walls inside the oven, but also—and most important for this recipe—the broiler element, which would narrow the jump it had to make to fully come up to temperature. We settled on 325 degrees (any higher, and the ovens might still cycle on and off during broiling).

We preheated several ovens in the test kitchen as we prepped more tenderloins and then popped the meat into the ovens and switched on the broilers. After 5 minutes, we flipped the roasts to ensure that their bottoms got exposure to the broiler and then pulled each tenderloin once it reached 125 to 130 degrees. We were overjoyed to find that every roast boasted a rich brown color—and even more gratified once we sliced into them to find that they were all equally tender and juicy.

We not only nailed a recipe for broiled pork tenderloin that would truly work in any oven but also walked away with a deeper knowledge of broilers in general—sure to make us better cooks down the road.

Broiled Pork Tenderloin
SERVES 4 TO 6

We prefer natural pork, but if you use enhanced pork (injected with a salt solution), reduce the salt in step 2 to 1½ teaspoons. A 3-inch-deep aluminum roasting pan is essential. Do not attempt this recipe with a drawer broiler. If you like, serve the pork with Mustard–Crème Fraîche Sauce or Sun-Dried Tomato and Basil Salsa (recipes follow).

- 2 (1-pound) pork tenderloins, trimmed
- 2 teaspoons kosher salt
- 1¼ teaspoons vegetable oil
- ½ teaspoon pepper

NOTES FROM THE TEST KITCHEN

AVOID OVERCOOKING
As the roasts rest, their internal temperature rises 10 to 15 degrees more than it would in a typical roasting recipe. For the ideal 145-degree serving temperature, take them out of the oven when they hit 125 degrees.

UNDERSTANDING BROILERS
While roasting relies on convective heat (air molecules surround the food), a broiler cooks food primarily with radiant heat, a form of invisible infrared light waves. The broiler element can reach 2,000 degrees. There are several challenges unique to broiling, so to use a broiler effectively, it's important to understand how it differs from regular oven cooking.

HEAT WAVES HAVE TO HIT THE FOOD TO COOK IT
Rather than surrounding the food, heat waves from the broiler come from only one direction. The waves must directly hit the food in order to brown it effectively. Food should be just far enough away from the element that the heat is intense but also evenly hitting the food.

PREHEATING THE BROILER IS UNRELIABLE
Most broilers have no ready signal, so you're left guessing when (and if) the broiler element is preheated. Those that heat quickly may cycle off during cooking, while slow-to-heat broilers will be too cool and won't cook the food in the given time.

IF A BROILER CYCLES OFF, BROWNING SUFFERS
If the broiler is on for too long, most ovens will exceed a maximum air temperature and the broiler will temporarily switch off. The food will continue to cook by convection but, without the radiant heat, browning will slow dramatically.

- ¼ teaspoon baking soda
- 1 (13 by 9-inch) disposable aluminum roasting pan

1. Adjust oven rack 4 to 5 inches from broiler element and heat oven to 325 degrees. Fold thin tip of each tenderloin under about 2 inches to create uniformly shaped roast. Tie tenderloins crosswise with kitchen twine at 2-inch intervals, making sure folded tip is secured underneath. Trim excess twine close to meat to prevent it from scorching under broiler.

2. Mix salt, oil, and pepper in small bowl until salt is evenly coated with oil. Add baking soda and stir until

well combined. Rub mixture evenly over pork. Place tenderloins in disposable pan, evenly spaced between sides of pan and each other.

3. Turn oven to broil. Immediately place meat in oven and broil tenderloins for 5 minutes. Flip tenderloins and continue to broil until golden brown and meat registers 125 to 130 degrees, 8 to 14 minutes. Remove disposable pan from oven, tent loosely with aluminum foil, and let rest for 10 minutes. Remove twine, slice tenderloins into ½-inch-thick slices, and serve.

Mustard–Crème Fraîche Sauce
MAKES ABOUT 1 CUP

Crème fraîche can be found in the specialty cheese section of most supermarkets.

- ½ **cup crème fraîche**
- 3 **tablespoons Dijon mustard**
- 3 **tablespoons chopped fresh parsley**
   Salt and pepper

Whisk crème fraîche, mustard, and parsley together in bowl. Season with salt and pepper to taste.

NOTES FROM THE TEST KITCHEN

GETTING A BROILER TO WORK FOR PORK TENDERLOIN
For well-browned, perfectly cooked pork tenderloin, the key is eliminating the variables and catching more heat. Our solution works with every broiler.

RACK POSITION MATTERS
Rack position terms like "upper-middle" can be interpreted differently from oven to oven. We set the rack 4 to 5 inches from the element for the best results in this recipe.

USE A DEEP DISPOSABLE ALUMINUM ROASTING PAN
The high 3-inch sides of the pan reflect more radiant heat from the broiler toward the pork, maximizing browning.

PREHEAT THE OVEN, NOT THE BROILER
Preheating the oven brings not just the air in the oven but also the broiler element up to 325 degrees, narrowing the jump before the broiler element is fully preheated. Broilers that run hot won't cycle off, and broilers that run cool will be fully preheated.

Sun-Dried Tomato and Basil Salsa
MAKES ABOUT 1 CUP

We like the sweet flavor and pliable texture of oil-cured sun-dried tomatoes.

- ¼ **cup oil-packed sun-dried tomatoes, rinsed and chopped fine**
- ¼ **cup chopped fresh basil**
- ¼ **cup chopped fresh parsley**
- ¼ **cup extra-virgin olive oil**
- 2 **tablespoons balsamic vinegar**
- 1 **small shallot, minced**
   Salt and pepper

Combine all ingredients in bowl and season with salt and pepper to taste.

RICE AND LENTILS WITH CRISPY ONIONS

✔ **WHY THIS RECIPE WORKS:** *Mujaddara*, the rice and beans of the Middle East, is a hearty, warm-spiced rice and lentil pilaf containing large brown or green lentils and crispy fried onion strings. We wanted a version of this dish in which all of the elements were cooked perfectly. For the pilaf, we found that precooking the lentils and soaking the rice in hot water before combining them ensured that both components cooked evenly. For the crispiest possible onions, we removed some moisture from the onions by salting and microwaving them before frying. This allowed us to pare down the typically fussy process of batch-frying in several cups of oil to a single batch fried in just 1½ cups of oil. And using some of the oil from the onions to dress our pilaf gave it ultrasavory depth.

IN *A BOOK OF MIDDLE EASTERN FOOD*, COOKBOOK author Claudia Roden recounts an anecdote about the Levantine rice and lentil pilaf known as *mujaddara* (pronounced "MOO-ha-druh"). When her Egyptian aunt presented guests with this dish, she would ask them to excuse this food of the poor. To which they would reply: "Keep your food of kings and give us mujaddara every day!"

Essentially the "rice and beans" of the Middle East, this might be the most spectacular example of how a few humble ingredients can add up to a dish that's satisfying, complex, and deeply savory. Though every household and restaurant differs in its approach, it's simple to throw together. Basically: Boil basmati rice and lentils until each component is tender but intact, then work in warm spices such as coriander, cumin, cinnamon, allspice, and pepper, as well as a good measure of minced garlic. But the real showpiece of the dish is the onions—either fried or caramelized—which get stirred into and sprinkled over the pilaf just before serving. Their flavor is as deep as their mahogany color suggests, and they break up the starchy components. Finished with a bracing garlicky yogurt sauce, this pilaf is comfort food at its best.

But the recipes we'd tried thus far had been disappointing. They all could do a better job cooking the lentils and rice, which we've found either too firm or overcooked and mushy. And while the onions should be the best part, the ones we made were either leathery, cloyingly sweet, or crunchy. We could—and would—do better.

For any other lentil recipe, the first test might be to figure out which variety was best for the job, but in this case we knew that brown or green lentils were the way to go. When cooked properly, they become tender while just holding their shape—a consistency that ensures that they meld well with the tender-chewy rice. The other plausible choice, French *lentilles du Puy*, would remain too firm and distinct.

So we moved on to the cooking method. Lentil cookery is simple: Bring 4 cups of water to a boil with 1¼ cups of lentils and a dash of salt, reduce the heat to low and simmer until they're just tender, and drain.

But cooking lentils with rice was another matter, since we needed both components, which cook at different rates, to emerge evenly tender and also form a cohesive pilaf. The options were many: Cook the rice and lentils in separate pots and fold them together; simmer them together in one pot; stagger their start times by parcooking the lentils until they were just tender, draining them, adding them to raw rice with a measured amount of water, and simmering until the liquid was absorbed; or try a variation on the absorption approach, in which the rice and parcooked lentils were cooked pilaf-style—that is, toasted in fat before liquid was added.

After a battery of tests, it was clear that a combination of staggered and pilaf-style cooking was the way to go. Giving the lentils a 15-minute head start ensured that they finished cooking on pace with the rice. This step also allowed us to drain away their muddy cooking liquid before combining them with the rice, which made for a

cleaner-looking dish. Toasting the rice in oil brought out its nutty flavor and let us deepen the flavor of the spices and garlic by cooking them in the fat, too.

The one snag: Even after we parcooked the lentils, they still absorbed quite a bit of water, robbing the rice of the liquid it needed to cook through. Adding more water didn't help; the lentils simply soaked it up faster than the rice and turned mushy. Fortunately, we had a quick fix—one that we'd used in previous pilaf recipes. We soaked the raw rice in hot water for 15 minutes (while the lentils simmered), which softened the grains' exteriors so that they could absorb water more easily. Plus, this step loosened and washed away some of the excess starches, helping the rice cook up fluffy, not sticky.

On to those onions. We decided to go the deep-fried route; the onions' crispy-chewy texture would be the perfect contrast to the soft pilaf. And given that we'd be both stirring the fried onions into the dish and using them as a garnish (and, let's be honest, snacking on a

few here and there), we'd start with a generous 2 pounds. That way, we'd have plenty even after the onions shrank way down during cooking.

The downsides of frying are the time it takes (multiple batches cooked for upwards of 30 minutes apiece) and the large amount of oil (typically about 3 cups), so we made it a goal to cut down on both. Most of the cooking time is spent waiting for the water in the onions to boil away, so we thought about ways to rid the onions of some liquid before they hit the oil. The obvious answer: salt, the thirsty mineral we regularly use to pull water from vegetables.

So, after cutting the onions into thin half-moons, we coated them with a couple of teaspoons of salt and let them sit. After 10 minutes, they'd shed a few tablespoons of water—encouraging results. We rinsed them to remove excess salt, dried them thoroughly, and fried them in two batches in a Dutch oven.

Frankly, the time savings was disappointing—just 5 minutes from each batch—so we took more drastic

RICE AND LENTILS WITH CRISPY ONIONS (MUJADDARA)

draining measures. After tossing the onions with the salt, we popped the bowl into the microwave for 5 minutes. Now we were getting somewhere, as the two-part approach pulled more moisture from the slices and jump-started the cooking process. Still, batch frying was fussy and long; we were hovering over that pot of oil for more than 40 minutes, waiting for the heaps of onions to shrink and crisp.

That's when we had an idea. The onions were initially piled high in the pot, but there was room to spare once they really started to cook down. Did we even need to bother with batch frying?

We sliced, salted, and microwaved another batch, this time piling all the onions into the pot at once, and turned the burner to high. Most of the onion slices started out well above the surface of the oil, but sure enough they collapsed quickly and everything was soon fully

submerged. About 25 minutes later, every last morsel was deeply golden and crispy with just a hint of chew. Not only that, but they were so far below the oil's surface that we made another batch with just 1½ cups of oil—half the amount we'd been using. Happily, these were every bit as crispy and golden as the onions cooked in 3 cups of oil. We strained them and packed the onion-infused oil into a container to save, as it adds savory depth to salad dressings, sautés, and sauces.

In fact, why not swap the 3 tablespoons of oil that we were using for the pilaf for an equal amount of the reserved onion oil, boosting the savory flavor of the pilaf right from the start? We also added a touch of sugar to the rice and lentils to complement the warmth of the spices—a tweak we'd seen in a few mujaddara recipes. Many versions also suggested stirring in fresh herbs; we chose cilantro for its fresh, faintly citrusy flavor and bright color.

As we scooped bowls of the fragrant pilaf; scattered a handful of crispy, supersavory onions on top; and dolloped on a few spoonfuls of our quick-to-make garlicky yogurt sauce, we couldn't help thinking that this was in fact food fit for a king.

Rice and Lentils with Crispy Onions (Mujaddara)
SERVES 4 TO 6

Do not substitute smaller French lentils for the green or brown lentils. When preparing the Crispy Onions, be sure to reserve 3 tablespoons of the onion cooking oil for cooking the rice and lentils.

YOGURT SAUCE
- 1 cup plain whole-milk yogurt
- 2 tablespoons lemon juice
- ½ teaspoon minced garlic
- ½ teaspoon salt

RICE AND LENTILS

8½ ounces (1¼ cups) green or brown lentils,
      picked over and rinsed
      Salt and pepper
1¼ cups basmati rice
1   recipe Crispy Onions, plus 3 tablespoons
      reserved oil (recipe follows)
3   garlic cloves, minced
1   teaspoon ground coriander
1   teaspoon ground cumin
½   teaspoon ground cinnamon
½   teaspoon ground allspice
⅛   teaspoon cayenne pepper
1   teaspoon sugar
3   tablespoons minced fresh cilantro

1. FOR THE YOGURT SAUCE: Whisk all ingredients together in bowl. Refrigerate while preparing rice and lentils.

2. FOR THE RICE AND LENTILS: Bring lentils, 4 cups water, and 1 teaspoon salt to boil in medium saucepan over high heat. Reduce heat to low and cook until lentils are tender, 15 to 17 minutes. Drain and set aside. While lentils cook, place rice in medium bowl and add hot tap water to cover by 2 inches; let stand for 15 minutes.

3. Using your hands, gently swish rice grains to release excess starch. Carefully pour off water, leaving rice in bowl. Add cold tap water to rice and pour off water. Repeat adding and pouring off cold tap water 4 or 5 times, until water runs almost clear. Drain rice in fine-mesh strainer.

4. Heat reserved onion oil, garlic, coriander, cumin, cinnamon, allspice, ¼ teaspoon pepper, and cayenne in Dutch oven over medium heat until fragrant, about 2 minutes. Add rice and cook, stirring occasionally, until edges of rice begin to turn translucent, about 3 minutes. Add 2¼ cups water, sugar, and 1 teaspoon salt and bring

to boil. Stir in lentils, reduce heat to low, cover, and cook until all liquid is absorbed, about 12 minutes.

5. Off heat, remove lid, fold dish towel in half, and place over pot; replace lid. Let stand for 10 minutes. Fluff rice and lentils with fork and stir in cilantro and half of crispy onions. Transfer to serving platter, top with remaining crispy onions, and serve, passing yogurt sauce separately.

Crispy Onions

MAKES 1½ CUPS

Reserve 3 tablespoons of oil when draining the onions to use in Rice and Lentils with Crispy Onions. It is crucial to thoroughly dry the microwaved onions after rinsing. The best way to accomplish this is to use a salad spinner. Remaining oil may be stored in an airtight container and refrigerated for up to 4 weeks.

- 2 **pounds onions, halved and sliced crosswise into ¼-inch-thick pieces**
- 2 **teaspoons salt**
- 1½ **cups vegetable oil**

1. Toss onions and salt together in large bowl. Microwave for 5 minutes. Rinse thoroughly, transfer to paper towel–lined baking sheet, and dry well.

2. Heat onions and oil in Dutch oven over high heat, stirring frequently, until onions are golden brown, 25 to 30 minutes. Drain onions in colander set in large bowl. Transfer onions to clean paper towel–lined baking sheet to drain. Serve.

RATING WINE SAVERS

For years we've preserved open bottles of wine either by using the Vacu Vin Wine Saver, an inexpensive ($9.29) pair of rubber stoppers with a pump that sucks the air out of the bottle, or by pouring leftover wine into a smaller bottle or Mason jar to stave off oxidation. But innovative new gadgets promise to keep wine drinkable longer. We tested five tools, including the Vacu Vin, on half-empty bottles of red and white wine, comparing and evaluating the wines' flavors and drinkability at various time intervals. Three models were either ineffective or fussy or both. Our old favorite worked reliably and kept wine drinkable for a week, but a new model bested it. Our winner, Air Cork: The Wine Preserver, forms a barricade against air when its balloon is lowered into the bottle and inflated just above the surface of the leftover wine. It preserved wine for at least a month. Products are listed in order of preference. See AmericasTestKitchen.com for updates and complete testing results.

RECOMMENDED

AIR CORK The Wine Preserver
EASE OF USE: ★★ EFFECTIVENESS: ★★★
COST: $24.95 (replacement balloons: about $5 each) **BEST BUY**
COMMENTS: Once you get the hang of lowering the food-safe latex balloon into the bottle and inflating it just above the leftover wine's surface, this budget-friendly device effectively seals off air, preserving wine's drinkability for at least one month (we are continuing to test). A downside: You can seal only one bottle at a time. Balloons are guaranteed for 80 uses; replacement balloons cost about $5.

RECOMMENDED WITH RESERVATIONS

VACU VIN Wine Saver
EASE OF USE: ★★★ EFFECTIVENESS: ★★
COST: $9.29
COMMENTS: After discovering new, more effective products that raised the bar for wine preservation, we developed some reservations about recommending our former favorite tool. We still value it for its compact design, ease of use, and budget-friendly price, but since it keeps wine drinkable for only about a week, we'll use it just for short-term storage.

NOT RECOMMENDED

SAVINO Wine Saving Carafe
EASE OF USE: ★★ EFFECTIVENESS: ★
COST: $59.95
COMMENTS: This separate carafe features a hollow plastic insert that floats on top of the wine, supposedly protecting its surface from air exposure, as well as a glass-and-plastic stopper to keep the vessel sealed. But it simply wasn't effective: After one week, tasters found that both white and red wines stored in the Savino lost too much of their character and flavor.

NOT RECOMMENDED (cont.)

PRIVATE PRESERVE Wine Preserver
EASE OF USE: ★½ EFFECTIVENESS: ★
COST: $8.99
COMMENTS: Spraying the surface of the leftover wine with a mixture of inert gases (argon, nitrogen, and carbon dioxide) chases out the air—if done properly. On our first attempt, the straw inside the canister flew off the sprayer head and into the wine. But even when we successfully sprayed and then sealed the bottles with the original corks and (for extra protection) plastic wrap, the results were unimpressive: After one week, tasters found both the red and white wines unsatisfactory.

RABBIT Wine Preserver with V-Gauge Technology by Metrokane
EASE OF USE: ★ EFFECTIVENESS: ★
COST: $15
COMMENTS: This vacuum-sealing hand pump and stopper supposedly lets the user see how much pressure is applied via the built-in gauge, but we pumped and pumped without any movement from the gauge needle until we figured out the trick: You have to pull up on a small knob on top of the sealer to start (the directions don't say this). It didn't matter much, though. Even when we did get the gauge to register, the stopper often lost suction overnight, requiring resealing, and taste tests confirmed that the wine had gone downhill after two days.

A Meal to Celebrate Fall

FALL, ESPECIALLY HERE IN NEW ENGLAND, BOASTS A DAZZLING cornucopia of foods and flavors. But unlike summer's bounty, which needs only minimal treatment (like fresh blueberries, crisp greens, plump tomatoes, and sweet corn), the fall harvest holds considerable potential for cooking up a feast. As the cooler weather approaches, we find ourselves itching to turn on our ovens and get roasting.

Ever roasted a pork rib roast? Many haven't, thinking it's a complicated cut of meat to cook. So we set out to demystify this versatile cut. For a centerpiece-worthy roast, we knew that we would be up against two problems common to pork: dry meat and lack of flavor. We found ways to combat both by treating our pig more like a cow. And to make the roast extra special, we wanted nuanced sauces, rife with rich fall flavors, to accompany it.

Butternut squash shows up everywhere in the fall, but our go-to cooking methods simply weren't doing justice to this vibrant vegetable. We wanted perfectly caramelized squash with meltingly tender flesh, and we wanted it to be extraordinary. For extra pizzazz, we turned to a variety of surprising toppings that perfectly complemented the sweet squash in new and unexpected ways.

Bones help insulate the roast during cooking and prevent the meat from drying out.

SLOW-ROASTED BONE-IN PORK RIB ROAST

✔ **WHY THIS RECIPE WORKS:** Pork rib roast can be an impressive cut when it's done right, so we set out to create a celebration-worthy rib roast with big flavor and tender, moist meat. We cured the pork overnight with a salt and brown sugar rub, which had the double benefit of seasoning the meat and promoting flavorful browning, allowing us to skip tedious searing. Removing the bones before seasoning ensured that the meat was flavorful throughout, and tying the meat back onto the bones before roasting protected it from overcooking. Using a low oven ensured that the roast was evenly cooked from edge to center, and a final stint under the broiler crisped the fat nicely. To dress it up for a holiday feast, we paired the pork with one of several elegant sauces with concentrated flavors.

A CENTER-CUT PORK RIB ROAST HAS A LOT OF POTENTIAL. Its cylindrical, uniform loin muscle and long bones make this cut so appealing for serving that some butchers call it the "pork equivalent of prime rib." Treated in a way that makes up for its slight shortcomings in the flavor department, it can be truly impressive: moist, tender, and full of rich, meaty taste. All this—and for far less money than a prime rib costs. We wanted to develop a recipe that would make this cut worthy of being the focal point of a holiday spread.

To get our bearings, we cooked an initial roast following a standard approach: We sprinkled the meat with salt and pepper and seared it on all sides in a hot skillet. Next we placed the roast on a wire rack set in a baking sheet (to prevent the meat from steaming in its juices) and transferred it to a 375-degree oven. After about 90 minutes, it reached 145 degrees (the ideal doneness temperature for pork). We let the roast rest for 30 minutes and then sliced it up for evaluation. Not too surprisingly, tasters found its flavor so-so.

Pretreating the meat before cooking was definitely in order. Pork almost always benefits from the application of salt, whether the meat is soaked in a saltwater solution or rubbed with a coating of salt and left to sit in the refrigerator. Both techniques season the meat, which boosts flavor, and draw moisture into the flesh, helping keep it juicy.

Indeed, when we put the ideas into action, a simple salt brine produced a more flavorful roast that was very moist—but almost to a fault: It had a wet, almost spongy consistency, especially toward the exterior. The salt rub, which we left on for at least 6 hours, was far superior. It helped the meat hold on to just the right amount of moisture.

For the next go-round, we added brown sugar to the salt rub, hoping that its mild molasses notes would pair nicely with the pork. (We also sprinkled black pepper onto the meat right before roasting.) With sugar in the mix, the meat took on not just deeper flavor but also a gorgeous mahogany color, thanks to the Maillard reaction. In fact, the method worked so beautifully that we made a bold decision: we would skip the tedious task of searing the meat before roasting. Happily, tasters didn't miss the searing since the meat browned nicely in the oven. The only problem was that the oven wasn't hot enough to render the dense fat cap. But we had an easy fix for that: we simply scored deep crosshatch marks into the fat with a sharp knife to help it melt and baste the meat during roasting.

And yet in spite of these efforts, the roast wasn't quite centerpiece-worthy. Salting had improved its texture considerably, but the meat still had a tendency to overcook and dry out toward the exterior. What's more, the meat closest to the bones wasn't nearly as well seasoned as the rest of the roast.

It seemed likely that bones were preventing the salt and sugar from penetrating into the meat. For the next test, we gave a boneless rib roast the usual application of salt and sugar. As we had expected, this meat was far better seasoned than a bone-in roast treated the same way, but we could hardly call the result an

SLOW-ROASTED BONE-IN PORK RIB ROAST

improvement: Without the bones to insulate the meat, much of the roast ended up dry. We scrapped the boneless roast idea, and instead turned our attention to other ways to improve a bone-in roast.

Then it hit us: If this roast really was the pork equivalent of prime rib, why not cook it like prime rib? In the test kitchen's recent recipe for prime rib, we removed the bones from the beef in order to salt the meat on all sides, and then we nestled the meat back up against the bones and secured it with kitchen twine before transferring the assembly to the oven for roasting. We applied this idea to the pork roast and it worked perfectly: The meat was now seasoned throughout, and since heat travels more slowly through bone than through flesh, the bones helped keep the center of the roast moist. Another plus was that the finished roast, free of bones, was even easier to carve.

Thinking of our pork roast as prime rib also gave us a potential solution to the problem of an overcooked exterior: We could use a low-and-slow approach (our prime rib cooks at 250 degrees). In general, the lower the oven temperature and the longer the cooking time the more evenly cooked the meat will be. Here's why: With traditional high-heat cooking, the final temperature of the center of the roast (145 degrees for pork) will be a few hundred degrees lower than the oven temperature. This means that by the time the core of the roast is properly cooked, the outermost layers are well past the ideal temperature. Bring the oven temperature closer to the desired internal temperature and this differential mostly goes away.

To put the theory into practice, we cooked a series of roasts at temperatures from 200 to 375 degrees. Sure enough, the roasts cooked at the low end of the range were the most evenly cooked. But because pork is cooked to a higher final temperature than beef (145 versus 125), the pork cooked in a 200-degree oven required a whopping 6 hours. We knew that no one would want to wait that long. Thankfully, the 250-degree-oven roast clocked in at a more reasonable 3½ hours and was nearly as evenly cooked. As a final measure, we crisped up the fat by blasting the roast under the broiler for a couple of minutes just prior to serving.

With juicy, well-seasoned meat ready for the table, all that remained was to create an elegant sauce. Nothing is more luxurious than a classic French beurre rouge, a reduction of red wine and wine vinegar emulsified with butter. Pork loin is relatively lean, so we knew that it would benefit from this rich, concentrated sauce. To give the mixture real character, we traded the red wine for tawny port and the wine vinegar for balsamic. We also incorporated cream, minced shallots, fresh thyme, and a couple of handfuls of plump dried cherries.

This combination was a terrific match with the pork: The complex flavor with echoes of fruit and herbs balanced beautifully with the meaty roast. This was a dish that anyone could be proud to serve at any special occasion. And only the cook would need to know how dead simple it was to prepare.

Slow-Roasted Bone-In Pork Rib Roast

SERVES 6 TO 8

This recipe requires refrigerating the salted meat for at least 6 hours before cooking. For easier carving, ask the butcher to remove the chine bone. Monitoring the roast with an oven probe thermometer is best. If you use an instant-read thermometer, open the oven door as infrequently as possible and remove the roast from the oven while taking its temperature. The sauce may be prepared in advance or while the roast rests in step 3.

- 1 (4- to 5-pound) center-cut bone-in pork rib roast, chine bone removed
- 2 tablespoons packed dark brown sugar
- 1 tablespoon kosher salt
- 1½ teaspoons pepper
- 1 recipe sauce (recipes follow)

BUTCHERING PORK "PRIME RIB"
Removing the bones encourages even seasoning, and tying them back onto the roast guards against overcooking.

1. Using sharp knife, remove roast from bones, running knife down length of bones and closely following contours.

2. Trim surface fat to ¼ inch and score with crosshatch slits; rub roast with sugar mixture and refrigerate.

3. Sprinkle roast with pepper, then place roast back on ribs; using kitchen twine, tie roast to bones between ribs.

SHOPPING: BONE-IN PORK RIB ROAST
When making our Slow-Roasted Bone-In Pork Rib Roast, you'll want a 4- to 5-pound center-cut roast with a fat cap that's ¼ to ½ inch thick. But some roasts also come with the chine bone attached. Ask the butcher to remove as much of this bone as possible to facilitate carving.

WITH CHINE BONE   WITHOUT CHINE BONE

WHY ADD CREAM TO A BUTTER SAUCE?

To dress up our pork, we turned to a classic French preparation: beurre rouge. The beauty of this sauce, which translates as "red butter," is that at its most basic it requires just two components: butter and an acidic liquid. (Red wine and red wine vinegar are traditional.) The preparation is equally simple: Just whisk cold butter into the reduced acidic liquid.

The problem is that butter sauces, like any mixture of fat and water, don't always stay emulsified. That's because the butter is highly temperature-sensitive: If the sauce gets too hot (above 135 degrees), the butter—itself an emulsion of fat and water—will "break" and the butterfat will leak out. If it gets too cold (below 85 degrees), the butterfat solidifies and forms crystals that clump together and separate when the sauce is reheated.

The key to foolproofing a butter sauce is thus stabilizing the butterfat so that it doesn't separate. We do this by whisking in the butter a little bit at a time, which keeps the temperature of the sauce relatively stable. Even more important, we also add cream. Cream contains a relatively high proportion of casein proteins that surround and stabilize the butterfat droplets so that they don't separate from the emulsion. Cream is such an effective stabilizer that our sauce can be made ahead, chilled, and gently reheated before serving.

1. Using sharp knife, remove roast from bones, running knife down length of bones and following contours as closely as possible. Reserve bones. Combine sugar and salt in small bowl. Pat roast dry with paper towels. If necessary, trim thick spots of surface fat layer to about ¼-inch thickness. Using sharp knife, cut slits, spaced 1 inch apart and in crosshatch pattern, in surface fat layer, being careful not to cut into meat. Rub roast evenly with sugar mixture. Wrap roast and ribs in plastic wrap and refrigerate for at least 6 hours or up to 24 hours.

2. Adjust oven rack to lower-middle position and heat oven to 250 degrees. Sprinkle roast evenly with pepper. Place roast back on ribs so bones fit where they were cut; tie roast to bones with lengths of kitchen twine between ribs. Transfer roast, fat side up, to wire rack set in rimmed baking sheet. Roast until meat registers 145 degrees, 3 to 4 hours.

3. Remove roast from oven (leave roast on sheet), tent loosely with aluminum foil, and let rest for 30 minutes.

4. Adjust oven rack 8 inches from broiler element and heat broiler. Return roast to oven and broil until top of roast is well browned and crispy, 2 to 6 minutes.

5. Transfer roast to carving board; cut twine and remove meat from ribs. Slice meat into ¾-inch-thick slices and serve, passing sauce separately.

Port Wine–Cherry Sauce

MAKES ABOUT 1¾ CUPS

- 2 cups tawny port
- 1 cup dried cherries
- ½ cup balsamic vinegar
- 4 sprigs fresh thyme, plus 2 teaspoons minced
- 2 shallots, minced
- ¼ cup heavy cream

16 tablespoons unsalted butter,
    cut into ½-inch pieces and chilled

1   teaspoon salt

½   teaspoon pepper

1. Combine port and cherries in bowl and microwave until steaming, 1 to 2 minutes. Cover and let stand until cherries are plump, about 10 minutes. Strain port through fine-mesh strainer into medium saucepan, reserving cherries.

2. Add vinegar, thyme sprigs, and shallots to port and bring to boil over high heat. Reduce heat to medium-high and reduce mixture until it measures ¾ cup, 14 to 16 minutes. Add cream and reduce again to ¾ cup, about 5 minutes. Discard thyme sprigs. Off heat, whisk in butter, a few pieces at a time, until fully incorporated. Stir in cherries, minced thyme, salt, and pepper. Cover pan and hold, off heat, until serving. Alternatively, let sauce cool completely and refrigerate for up to 2 days. Reheat in small saucepan over medium-low heat, stirring frequently, until warm.

VARIATIONS

Cider–Golden Raisin Sauce

Substitute 2 cups apple cider for port and 1 cup golden raisins for cherries. In step 2, substitute ½ cup cider vinegar for balsamic. Stir in 2 teaspoons cider vinegar and 1 tablespoon Calvados with raisins and minced thyme.

Orange-Cranberry Sauce

Substitute 2 cups white wine for port and 1 cup dried cranberries for cherries. In step 2, substitute ½ cup orange juice for balsamic and 4 fresh sage leaves for thyme sprigs. Omit minced thyme and stir in 1 tablespoon orange zest, 1 tablespoon Grand Marnier, and 2 teaspoons minced fresh sage with the cranberries.

ROASTED BUTTERNUT SQUASH

✔ WHY THIS RECIPE WORKS: Taking a cue from famed chef Yotam Ottolenghi, we sought to create a savory recipe for roasted butternut squash that was simple and presentation-worthy. We chose to peel the squash thoroughly to remove not only the tough outer skin but also the rugged fibrous layer of white flesh just beneath, ensuring supremely tender squash. To encourage the squash slices to caramelize, we used a hot 425-degree oven, placed the squash on the lowest oven rack, and increased the baking time to evaporate the water. We also swapped in melted butter for olive oil to promote the flavorful Maillard reaction. Finally, we selected a mix of toppings that added crunch, creaminess, brightness, and visual appeal.

WHEN IT COMES TO PREPARING WINTER SQUASH, WE often find ourselves taking an all-too-familiar route: sprinkling the halves with some brown sugar, dotting them with butter, and sliding them into a hot oven. Or we cube the squash and toss it with oil before roasting to help it develop a bit more color and flavorful caramelization. Comforting, yes, but not all that inspiring.

A recipe in London-based chef Yotam Ottolenghi's book *Plenty* introduced us to an alternative squash universe. He slices the squash (skin and all) into thin half-moons to create more surface area for browning. And rather than add more sweetness, he tosses the roasted squash with savory ingredients, from chiles and lime to toasted nuts and spiced yogurt, which serve as a surprisingly successful foil to the squash's natural sweetness. We decided to put our own spin on this approach.

Tasters were smitten with Ottolenghi's approach, but they also had a few comments. While they liked the toppings, most found the texture of the roasted squash skin unappealing, and they noted that the squash wasn't especially caramelized.

ROASTED BUTTERNUT SQUASH WITH BROWNED BUTTER AND HAZELNUTS

Our first move was to lose the skin. We opted to forgo prepeeled squash, since we've found that the flavor of whole squash that you peel yourself is superior. As for the roasting method, Ottolenghi uses a relatively hot oven but a short cooking time of 15 minutes—sufficient to tenderize but not long enough for caramelization. We found that when the squash slices were roasted on the middle oven rack, they turned a light golden brown in about 40 minutes—but only on the side in contact with the baking sheet. For deeper caramelization on both sides, the solution was simple. We moved the sheet to the lowest oven rack, where it would absorb even more heat from the main heating element on the oven's floor. We then flipped the squash (and rotated the baking sheet) partway through roasting so that both sides could caramelize.

So far so good, but we had another idea. We had been tossing the squash with olive oil before roasting, but melted butter produced better browning, thanks to its milk proteins that undergo the Maillard reaction, leading to more complex flavors and aromas. These slices emerged perfectly caramelized, wonderfully sweet, and tender—until we got to the edge of each slice. Despite our having removed the skin, the outer edge of each slice was tough.

The reason is this: Below the skin sits a white layer of flesh laced with greenish fibers, and we discovered that this rugged matrix resists turning tender, even with prolonged cooking. The fix? A few more swipes with a vegetable peeler revealed a pumpkin-orange interior that baked up tender from the center to the outer edge of each slice.

The last step was to come up with toppings that provided a mix of contrasting textures and bold flavors—including one with browned butter, hazelnuts, lemon juice, and chives. With this new approach we felt emboldened to come up with several more sweet-savory topping combinations. You may not immediately recognize these dishes as the familiar roasted butternut squash, but actually, that's the point.

Roasted Butternut Squash with Browned Butter and Hazelnuts

SERVES 4 TO 6

For plain roasted squash omit the topping. This dish can be served warm or at room temperature. For the best texture it's important to remove the fibrous flesh just below the squash's skin.

SQUASH

- 1 large (2½- to 3-pound) butternut squash
- 3 tablespoons unsalted butter, melted
- ½ teaspoon salt
- ½ teaspoon pepper

TOPPING

- 3 tablespoons unsalted butter, cut into 3 pieces
- ⅓ cup hazelnuts, toasted, skinned, and chopped coarse
- 1 tablespoon water
- 1 tablespoon lemon juice
  Pinch salt
- 1 tablespoon minced fresh chives

1. **FOR THE SQUASH:** Adjust oven rack to lowest position and heat oven to 425 degrees. Using sharp vegetable peeler or chef's knife, remove skin and fibrous threads from squash just below skin (peel until squash is completely orange with no white flesh remaining, roughly ⅛ inch deep). Halve squash lengthwise and scrape out seeds. Place squash, cut side down, on cutting board and slice crosswise ½ inch thick.

2. Toss squash with melted butter, salt, and pepper until evenly coated. Arrange squash on rimmed baking sheet in single layer. Roast squash until side touching sheet toward back of oven is well browned, 25 to 30 minutes. Rotate sheet and continue to bake until side touching sheet toward back of oven is well browned, 6 to 10 minutes. Remove squash from oven and use metal spatula to flip each piece. Continue to roast until squash

is very tender and side touching sheet is browned, 10 to 15 minutes longer.

3. **FOR THE TOPPING:** While squash roasts, melt butter with hazelnuts in 8-inch skillet over medium-low heat. Cook, stirring frequently, until butter and hazelnuts are brown and fragrant, about 2 minutes. Immediately remove skillet from heat and stir in water (butter will foam and sizzle). Let cool for 1 minute; stir in lemon juice and salt.

4. Transfer squash to large serving platter. Drizzle butter mixture evenly over squash. Sprinkle with chives and serve.

VARIATIONS

Roasted Butternut Squash with Radicchio and Parmesan

Omit topping. Whisk 1 tablespoon sherry vinegar, ½ teaspoon mayonnaise, and pinch salt together in small bowl; gradually whisk in 2 tablespoons extra-virgin olive oil until smooth. Before serving, drizzle vinaigrette over squash and sprinkle with ½ cup coarsely shredded radicchio; ½ ounce Parmesan cheese, shaved into thin strips; and 3 tablespoons toasted pine nuts.

Roasted Butternut Squash with Goat Cheese, Pecans, and Maple

Omit topping. Stir 2 tablespoons maple syrup and pinch cayenne pepper together in small bowl. Before serving, drizzle maple mixture over squash and sprinkle with ⅓ cup crumbled goat cheese; ⅓ cup pecans, toasted and chopped coarse; and 2 teaspoons fresh thyme leaves.

Roasted Butternut Squash with Tahini and Feta

Omit topping. Whisk 1 tablespoon tahini, 1 tablespoon extra-virgin olive oil, 1½ teaspoons lemon juice, 1 teaspoon honey, and pinch salt together in small bowl. Before serving, drizzle tahini mixture over squash and sprinkle with ¼ cup finely crumbled feta cheese; ¼ cup shelled pistachios, toasted and chopped fine; and 2 tablespoons chopped fresh mint.

RATING FREEZER STORAGE BAGS

Too often, plastic food storage bags are flimsy, their closures don't work without a fight, and when you finally get them closed, they leak. In our tests, we found that while thick plastic helps, strong seals are more important. We also wanted to find a bag that could be propped open for filling. We put our samples through the wringer—dropping them, freezing them, filling them to capacity—and only one bag stood up to every challenge. Our winner, Ziploc Brand Double Zipper Gallon Freezer Bags with the Smart Zip Seal, kept frozen food free of freezer burn after two months, and its band of thicker plastic extending below the zipper made for easier filling and offered an extra barrier of protection. Products are listed in order of preference. See AmericasTestKitchen.com for updates and complete testing results.

HIGHLY RECOMMENDED

ZIPLOC BRAND Double Zipper Gallon Freezer Bags with the Smart Zip Seal
MODEL: UPC #0-25700-00382-3
PRICE: $3.99 for 30 bags ($0.13 per bag)
STYLE: Zipper-lock THICKNESS: 2.4 mil
FREEZER PROTECTION: ★★★ DURABILITY: ★★★
LEAKPROOF: ★★★ EASE OF USE: ★★★
COMMENTS: Frozen food stayed fresh in this bag even after two months. Its band of thicker plastic extending 2 inches below the zipper provided structure that made for easier filling and offered an extra barrier of protection. Its double zipper helped it remain leakproof and stand up to abuse.

ELKAY PLASTICS Ziplock Heavy Weight Freezer Bag
MODEL: UPC #6-54866-01303-4
PRICE: $9.69 for 100 bags ($0.10 per bag), plus shipping
STYLE: Zipper-lock THICKNESS: 3.7 mil
FREEZER PROTECTION: ★★★ DURABILITY: ★★
LEAKPROOF: ★★½ EASE OF USE: ★★★
COMMENTS: With the thickest plastic in the lineup and a tight seal, this bag provided excellent protection. Frozen cookie dough and pork chops had virtually no ice crystals and were fresh-looking after two months. A side seam split when we dropped this bag (full of tomato sauce), and the bag let in a little moisture when we submerged it.

RECOMMENDED

GREEN'N'PACK Food Storage Freezer Gallon Bags
MODEL: UPC #8-54347-00303-9
PRICE: $11.90 for 30 bags ($0.40 per bag)
STYLE: Zipper-lock THICKNESS: 2.7 mil
FREEZER PROTECTION: ★★½ DURABILITY: ★★
LEAKPROOF: ★★½ EASE OF USE: ★★½
COMMENTS: This eco-friendly bag, designed to biodegrade, performed well, though it didn't quite match our top bags. Frozen food stayed in excellent shape for a month but began to show a few signs of ice crystals after two months. Its seal could be a little bigger and stronger.

RECOMMENDED (*cont.*)

HEFTY Slider Bag, Gallon Freezer
MODEL: UPC #0-13700-82413-5
PRICE: $3.29 for 13 bags ($0.25 per bag)
STYLE: Slider THICKNESS: 2.5 mil
FREEZER PROTECTION: ★★ DURABILITY: ★★★
LEAKPROOF: ★★½ EASE OF USE: ★★
COMMENTS: Frozen food quickly acquired a moderate amount of "snow" around the edges. This bag claims to have "a stronger seal than Ziploc bags when shaken, dropped, or stacked," and it tied our top-ranked Ziploc when dropped and shaken, but its zipper leaked. It was also a bit too floppy.

RECOMMENDED WITH RESERVATIONS

ZIPLOC BRAND Gallon Freezer Slider Bags
MODEL: UPC #0-25700-02313-5
PRICE: $2.49 for 10 bags ($0.25 per bag)
STYLE: Slider THICKNESS: 2.8 mil
FREEZER PROTECTION: ★★★ DURABILITY: ★
LEAKPROOF: ★★ EASE OF USE: ★★★
COMMENTS: We really liked this bag's gusseted, expandable bottom, and foods stayed in good condition in the freezer. We only wish its sliding seal were stronger: It failed during abuse testing, dripped when full, and let in some moisture when submerged.

NOT RECOMMENDED

ZIPLOC BRAND Double Guard Double Layer Gallon Freezer Bags
MODEL: UPC #0-25700-01261-0
PRICE: $6.37 for 13 bags ($0.49 per bag)
STYLE: Zipper-lock
THICKNESS: 2.0 mil outer layer, 1.0 mil inner layer
FREEZER PROTECTION: ★★ DURABILITY: ★
LEAKPROOF: ★ EASE OF USE: ★
COMMENTS: This pricey double-layer bag claims to provide a better barrier against freezer burn; we found it only middling. Floppy and flimsy, this bag was also hard to fill and its weak seal burst during abuse tests. The side seams above the zipper ripped as we filled bags and leaked steadily when filled with liquids.

Favorite Ways with the Catch of the Day

Tahini, a thick paste made from ground sesame seeds, works to enhance the coating's nutty flavor and help the seeds stick to the salmon.

WE LIKE TO HAVE FUN WITH OUR FISH. WHAT DOES THAT MEAN? WHILE fresh fish cooked simply with a squeeze of fresh lemon is great, we sometimes get a bit bored. Enter two catch-of-the-day favorites: fish tacos and sesame-crusted salmon.

When it comes to fish tacos, most of us think of Baja-style tacos, with chunks of batter-fried white fish and a smooth, creamy sauce. But we were intrigued by another fish taco tradition, which hails from the Yucatán Peninsula. These lighter tacos dispense with frying and take a lighter approach using the grill. Typically a whole fish is split, seasoned, and grilled and then the whole thing is brought to the table with warm corn tortillas and garnishes. We wanted to keep things simple (i.e., not have to wrestle with a whole fish), so we set out to streamline.

Sesame and salmon are a natural pair, but getting a good sesame crust while not overcooking the fish can be a challenge. Furthermore, the somewhat monotonous richness of both the sesame seeds and the salmon can make the dish taste flat. Our goals here were multiple: perfectly cooked fish, a crunchy sesame crust, and a flavor boost to yield a new twist on this classic.

GRILLED FISH TACOS

GRILLED FISH TACOS

✔ **WHY THIS RECIPE WORKS:** For a fish taco with fresh, bold flavors, we fired up the grill. For simplicity we opted for skinless fillets instead of the traditional whole butterflied fish. Meaty swordfish held up on the grill better than flaky options like snapper and cod. A thick paste featuring ancho and chipotle chile powders, oregano, and just a touch of citrus juice developed deep, flavorful charring on the grill without promoting sticking. Refreshing grilled pineapple salsa, avocado, and crunchy iceberg lettuce completed our tacos with flavor and texture contrasts.

BATTER-FRIED BAJA-STYLE FISH TACOS HAVE THEIR place, but when we don't want to deal with a pot of hot oil—or be left with that heavy feeling that inevitably sets in after eating fried food—we go for the grilled kind. Nicely charred but moist fillets wrapped in tortillas with a few cool, crunchy garnishes and a squeeze of lime have the potential to be lighter on both the fuss and the stomach.

The problem is this leaner preparation can also be light on flavor and complexity. For grilled fish tacos with more punch, we looked for inspiration in preparations popular in the Yucatán Peninsula and along the Pacific coast of Mexico. Here they split a whole fish in half lengthwise, bathe it in a deep red chile–citrus mixture, then grill it wrapped in banana leaves or in a grill basket. This flavor-packed fish is served on a platter whole, to be flaked off and eaten with tortillas and some simple sides. We wanted grilled fish tacos featuring a similarly bold flavor profile, but a simpler approach—no dealing with whole, skin-on fish—plus, we wanted a few complementary toppings to complete the package.

Our first task was finding the best substitute for the whole fish. Traditional recipes usually start with a whole butterflied snapper or grouper. We knew we wanted to grill smaller portions, but a quick test in which we grilled both snapper and grouper fillets confirmed they weren't going to work out. Keeping the skin on was key with these flakier fish to prevent sticking, and that meant at serving time almost all of their charred flavor went into the trash with the skin. Relying on banana leaves or a grilling basket, like the traditional recipes, would circumvent sticking, but tracking down such an obscure item or requiring special equipment were both out of the question. We needed a different variety of fish.

All flaky fish, like cod and hake, were out for the same reason. Fish with a denser, meatier texture were more promising, so we gave mahi-mahi, tuna, swordfish, and halibut a chance. In the end, swordfish was the favorite. It's easy to find, it stands up well to flipping on the grill, and steaks that were 1 inch thick had enough time to pick up plenty of flavorful char before the interior cooked through. Cutting the fish into 1-inch-wide strips made it even easier to handle and also meant that the fish could go from grill to taco without any further prep.

Some of the more modern recipes we found called for marinating the fish in lots of citrus juice with a hit of warm chile spice and other seasonings. Such a brightly flavored approach offered lots of appeal, but we quickly discovered this sort of pretreatment created more problems than benefits. First, the flavor was lackluster since the fish spent only about 30 minutes in the marinade, and letting it sit long enough to make a noticeable difference led to fish that cooked in its high-acid bath (think ceviche). Worse, the significant amount of sugar in the fruit juice meant that, even with oil in the marinade, the fish had to be chiseled off the cooking grate. In the past, we've combatted sticking and lack of flavor by using a postgrilling marinade, but in this case it left the spices tasting raw. We briefly considered putting a piece of foil between the fish and the grate, but, aside from the fact this isn't recommended by some grill manufacturers, it prevented the fish from picking up flavorful char. We moved on to option two.

Many of the traditional recipes we'd found called for coating the fish in a thick paste featuring ground annatto seeds (the same spice used to color yellow cheese) or ground dried chiles, various warm spices, and just enough citrus juice to make it spreadable. But we knew we'd have to vary from tradition at least a little. Annatto seeds, which come from the tropical achiote tree, might be easy to find in Mexico, but they can be tough to ferret out stateside. We hoped that landing on the right mix of chiles and spices could make up for the loss of the annatto's earthy, peppery flavor.

Starting with whole dried chiles is the authentic approach, but the fuss of toasting them in a dry skillet or softening them in oil, then grinding them to a powder was more work (not to mention shopping effort)

than we cared to deal with. At the other end of the spectrum—and also not an option in our minds—was chili powder. With its blend of ground chiles and other spices and herbs, it made a paste that was passable but not distinctive.

Instead, we created a blend of chile powders and ground herbs, singling out ancho chile powder for its fruitiness and chipotle chile powder for smoky heat and earthiness, while some oregano and ground coriander boosted complexity. Blooming this mixture in oil, along with some minced garlic and salt, rounded out the flavors. But it still needed a bigger punch of savory sweetness. Adding a few tablespoons of tomato paste took care of that.

The last component: the citrus juice. Looking back at the recipes we'd compiled, sour or Seville oranges appeared most frequently. Instead, we employed a commonly suggested substitute: orange juice with a little lime juice added to give it the right tart, bright acidity.

After coating the fish in the paste, we let it sit in the refrigerator while the grill heated up to give the salt time to penetrate and season the fish. Despite fish's reputation for delicacy, we found there was no need to hold back on heat. A heaping chimney of charcoal (about 7 quarts) gave the coating great char that further deepened the swordfish's flavor and just cooked it through. We were also happy to find that as long as we thoroughly oiled the grate, the paste (helped no doubt by the grittiness of the chile powders and herbs) didn't exacerbate any sticking issues.

All that was left was coming up with the right combination of garnishes. Fresh, crunchy iceberg lettuce and rich, silky avocado were both in. A fresh fruit salsa also sounded promising. Mango and papaya both had potential, but pineapple won out for its acidity and sweetness, which balanced the spicy earthiness of the fish. A little jalapeño for some fresh heat and bell pepper and cilantro for color and freshness rounded out the salsa.

Since there was plenty of room on the grill, we threw the pineapple and jalapeño on the cooking grate opposite the fish, an easy step that caramelized the fruit and deepened the chile's flavors and brought more of the flavor of the grill to our tacos. Once the fish and salsa ingredients came off the grate, we quickly warmed the tortillas over the fire.

Loaded up with the smoky, boldly flavored fish, salsa, and garnishes, these tacos were satisfying yet still refreshingly light. They didn't need anything else but a cold beer to drink alongside.

Grilled Fish Tacos

SERVES 6

Mahi-mahi, tuna, and halibut fillets are all suitable substitutes for the swordfish, but to ensure the best results buy 1-inch-thick fillets and cut them in a similar fashion as the swordfish.

  3 tablespoons vegetable oil
  1 tablespoon ancho chile powder
  2 teaspoons chipotle chile powder
  1 teaspoon dried oregano
  1 teaspoon ground coriander
  2 garlic cloves, minced
     Salt
  2 tablespoons tomato paste
  ½ cup orange juice
  6 tablespoons lime juice (3 limes)
  2 pounds skinless swordfish steaks, 1 inch thick,
     cut lengthwise into 1-inch-wide strips
  1 pineapple, peeled, quartered lengthwise, cored,
     and each quarter sliced in half lengthwise
  1 jalapeño chile
 18 (6-inch) corn tortillas
  1 red bell pepper, stemmed, seeded, and cut into
     ¼-inch pieces
  2 tablespoons minced fresh cilantro, plus extra for serving
  ½ head iceberg lettuce, cored and sliced thin
  1 avocado, halved, pitted, and sliced thin
     Lime wedges

GRILLED FISH TACOS THAT ARE LIGHT BUT NOT LEAN
For grilled fish that's infused with flavor from start to finish, we made a bold spice paste and a grilled-fruit salsa.

1. MAKE PASTE: A thick spice paste, brightened by lime and orange juices, adds a layer of complexity to the fish.

2. CHILL FILLETS: Refrigerating the paste-covered fish for at least 30 minutes gives salt in the paste time to penetrate and season the fish.

3. GRILL FISH, FRUIT, AND JALAPEÑO: The grill gives the pineapple and pepper destined for the salsa deeper flavor.

4. WARM TORTILLAS: Grill the tortillas for about 30 seconds per side and then wrap them in a dish towel or foil to stay warm.

5. FINISH SALSA: Finely chop the pineapple and jalapeño and then combine them with red bell pepper, cilantro, and the remaining lime juice.

1. Heat 2 tablespoons oil, ancho chile powder, and chipotle chile powder in 8-inch skillet over medium heat, stirring constantly, until fragrant and some bubbles form, 2 to 3 minutes. Add oregano, coriander, garlic, and 1 teaspoon salt and continue to cook until fragrant, about 30 seconds longer. Add tomato paste and, using spatula, mash tomato paste with spice mixture until combined, about 20 seconds. Stir in orange juice and 2 tablespoons lime juice. Cook, stirring constantly, until thoroughly mixed and reduced slightly, about 2 minutes. Transfer chile mixture to large bowl and let cool for 15 minutes.

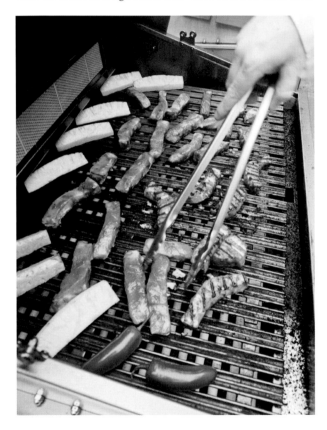

2. Add swordfish to bowl with chile mixture and stir gently with rubber spatula to coat fish. Cover and refrigerate for at least 30 minutes or up to 2 hours.

3A. FOR A CHARCOAL GRILL: Open bottom vent completely. Light large chimney starter mounded with charcoal (7 quarts). When top coals are partially covered with ash, pour coals evenly across bottom of grill. Set cooking grate in place. Cover and open lid vent completely. Heat grill until hot, about 5 minutes.

3B. FOR A GAS GRILL: Turn all burners to high, cover, and heat grill until hot, about 15 minutes. Turn all burners to medium-high.

4. Clean and thoroughly oil cooking grate. Brush both sides of pineapple with remaining 1 tablespoon oil. Place fish on half of grill. Place pineapple and whole jalapeño on other half. Cover and cook until fish, pineapple, and jalapeño have begun to brown, 3 to 5 minutes. Using thin spatula, turn fish, pineapple, and jalapeño. Cover and continue to cook until the second half of pineapple and jalapeño have browned and swordfish registers 140 degrees, 3 to 5 minutes. Transfer fish to large platter, flake into pieces, and tent with foil. Transfer pineapple and jalapeño to cutting board.

5. Clean cooking grate. Place half of tortillas on grill. Cook on each side until softened and speckled with brown spots, 30 to 45 seconds per side. Wrap tortillas in dish towel or foil to keep warm. Repeat with remaining tortillas.

6. When cool enough to handle, finely chop pineapple and jalapeño. Transfer to medium bowl and stir in bell pepper, cilantro, and remaining ¼ cup lime juice. Season with salt to taste. Top tortillas with flaked fish, salsa, lettuce, and avocado. Serve with lime wedges and extra cilantro.

SESAME-CRUSTED SALMON

✓ WHY THIS RECIPE WORKS: Often, sesame-crusted salmon is a one-note affair in which rich salmon is coated with sesame seeds that provide little more than crunch. We wanted to highlight both the fish and the natural contrasts of these two elements and give them some bolder, brighter flavor. We brined the salmon fillets to ensure that each piece was thoroughly seasoned and remained moist after cooking. Giving the sesame seeds a dunk in the salmon brine and then toasting them brought out their deep, nutty flavor. To liven up the dish, we added minced scallion whites, lemon zest, grated fresh ginger, and a pinch of cayenne pepper for zing. To make the flavorings and the sesame seeds adhere to the fish, we used rich tahini paste thickened with lemon juice.

THE FISH-AND-SESAME DUO GETS AROUND, SHOWING up in cuisines from Asia to California to the Middle East. The simplest approach is to coat fillets with the seeds (they stick easily) and then pan-sear the fish. Tuna is often used, but so is less-expensive salmon—perfect for a weeknight meal. We thought that only minor tweaks would be necessary to correct the ho-hum sesame flavor and slightly dry, unevenly cooked fish that most recipes turned out. But halfway through our tasting, we realized that the problems ran deeper. Both salmon and sesame have a monotonous richness, so finishing a whole serving was a chore. We wanted a lively dish in which the salmon and sesame would be offset with bolder, brighter flavors.

Brining the fish for just 15 minutes took care of any dryness. It may seem odd to brine something that basically lived in a brine, but the saltwater soak seasoned the flesh and subtly changed its protein structure, helping it retain moisture. We blotted the brined fillets with paper towels, applied the seeds to both sides, and eased the fillets into an oil-slicked nonstick skillet. When the seeds turned golden, we transferred the skillet to the oven for gentle, even cooking. Flawlessly cooked, moist fish? Check.

On to the dull sesame flavor. While discussing possible solutions, one cook mentioned Japanese *gomashio*. The term translates as "sesame salt" and at its most basic is just those two ingredients. To make the savory blend, you toast the seeds and then mix or grind them with salt.

Maybe salt and a little toasting were just what the seeds needed. But instead of grinding the seeds with salt after toasting them, we submerged them in some of the brine that we had mixed up for the fish, drained them, and then toasted them whole in a skillet. The brine woke up the nutty flavor of the seeds by infusing each one with salt. What's more, because the starch in the seeds absorbed water from the brine and then gelatinized during toasting, the seeds were now crispier than ever.

But we wanted an even more potent sesame punch. We experimented with cooking the fillets in sesame oil, but most of the oil's flavorful compounds vaporized in the hot skillet. We scanned the test kitchen pantry and came away with a Middle Eastern staple: tahini, which is basically ground sesame seeds. The only problem was its runny consistency—it would slide right off the slippery fillets. Before experimenting with thickeners, we decided to enliven the tahini with some lemon juice. We drizzled in the juice a little at a time, tasting after each addition. Oddly, the more juice we added the more viscous the tahini became. It turns out that because much of tahini's makeup is carbohydrates, when a small amount of lemon juice (or any water-containing liquid) is added to tahini, a portion of each carbohydrate molecule is drawn to the water. As a result, clumps of carbohydrates appear and the tahini is actually thickened. Two teaspoons of juice produced great tang and a miso-like texture. Happily, the thick paste was ideal for adhering other flavorful elements to the salmon, so we added minced scallion whites, lemon zest, grated fresh ginger, and a dash

of cayenne. We smeared the flavor-packed mixture onto the fillets, pressed on the sesame seeds, seared the fish, and popped the pan into the oven. Now we had a real winner. The contrasting flavors shone through—and the last bite was as interesting as the first.

Sesame-Crusted Salmon with Lemon and Ginger

SERVES 4

For even cooking, purchase fillets that are about the same size and shape. If any of your fillets have a thin belly flap, fold it over to create a more even thickness.

> Salt
> ¾ cup sesame seeds
> 4 (6- to 8-ounce) skinless salmon fillets
> 2 scallions, white parts minced, green parts sliced thin
> 1 tablespoon grated lemon zest plus
>   2 teaspoons juice
> 4 teaspoons tahini
> 2 teaspoons grated fresh ginger
> ⅛ teaspoon cayenne pepper
> 1 teaspoon vegetable oil

1. Adjust oven rack to middle position and heat oven to 325 degrees. Dissolve 5 tablespoons salt in 2 quarts water. Transfer 1 cup brine to bowl, stir in sesame seeds, and let stand at room temperature for 5 minutes. Submerge fillets in remaining brine and let stand at room temperature for 15 minutes.

2. Drain seeds and place in 12-inch nonstick skillet. Cook seeds over medium heat, stirring constantly, until golden brown, 2 to 4 minutes. Transfer seeds to pie plate and wipe out skillet with paper towels. Remove fillets from brine and pat dry.

3. Place scallion whites and lemon zest on cutting board and chop until whites and zest are finely minced

SCIENCE DESK

A SURPRISING TAHINI THICKENER

For our sesame-crusted salmon recipes, a smear of tahini on each fillet helps boost the sesame flavor. But tahini has a thin consistency, which means that it won't stay put on the moist, slick surface of a fish fillet. To thicken the tahini and give it some holding power, our solution was a bit surprising: We stirred in 2 teaspoons of lemon juice.

You'd think that adding a liquid would thin tahini rather than thicken it. Why the opposite? Tahini is sesame-seed butter, made by grinding hulled sesame seeds into a paste. Much of its makeup is carbohydrates, and when a small amount of lemon juice (or any water-containing liquid) is added to it, a portion of each carbohydrate molecule is drawn to the water. As a result, clumps of carbohydrates appear. As the amount of water is increased, more clumps develop, causing the tahini to thicken overall. If you keep adding water, eventually you'll cross over the threshold of thickening it; enough water in the system will cause the tahini to loosen and thin out. This is similar to what happens when chocolate seizes. A small amount of added water acts like a glue, wetting particles just enough to get them to stick together, but eventually if you add too much water, the mixture turns into an evenly thinned-out liquid.

SESAME-CRUSTED SALMON WITH LEMON AND GINGER

NOTES FROM THE TEST KITCHEN

HOW TO REHEAT FISH

Fish is notoriously susceptible to overcooking, so reheating previously cooked fillets is something that makes nearly all cooks balk. But since almost everyone has leftover fish from time to time, we decided to figure out the best approach to warming it up.

As we suspected, we had far more success reheating thick fillets and steaks than thin ones. Both swordfish and halibut steaks reheated nicely, retaining their moisture well and with no detectable change in flavor. Likewise, salmon reheated well, but, thanks to the oxidation of its abundant fatty acids into strong-smelling aldehydes, doing so brought out a bit more of the fish's pungent aroma. There was little we could do to prevent trout from drying out and overcooking when heated a second time.

To reheat thicker fish fillets, use this gentle approach: Place the fillets on a wire rack set in a rimmed baking sheet, cover them with foil (to prevent the exteriors of the fish from drying out), and heat them in a 275-degree oven until they register 125 to 130 degrees, about 15 minutes for 1-inch-thick fillets (timing varies according to fillet size). We recommend serving leftover cooked thin fish in cold applications like salads.

and well combined. Transfer scallion-zest mixture to bowl and stir in lemon juice, tahini, ginger, cayenne, and ⅛ teaspoon salt.

4. Evenly distribute half of paste over bottoms (skinned sides) of fillets. Press coated sides of fillets in seeds and transfer, seed side down, to plate. Evenly distribute remaining paste over tops of fillets and coat with remaining seeds.

5. Heat oil in now-empty skillet over medium heat until shimmering. Place fillets in skillet, skinned side up, and reduce heat to medium-low. Cook until seeds begin to brown, 1 to 2 minutes. Remove skillet from heat and, using 2 spatulas, carefully flip fillets over. Transfer skillet to oven. Bake until center of fish is translucent when checked with tip of paring knife and registers 125 degrees, 10 to 15 minutes. Transfer to serving platter and let rest for 5 minutes. Sprinkle with scallion greens and serve.

VARIATIONS

Sesame-Crusted Salmon with Lime and Coriander
Substitute 4 teaspoons lime zest for lemon zest, lime juice for lemon juice, and ¼ teaspoon ground coriander for cayenne.

Sesame-Crusted Salmon with Orange and Chili Powder
Substitute orange zest for lemon zest, orange juice for lemon juice, and ¼ teaspoon chili powder for cayenne.

RATING BENCH SCRAPERS

Also known as a bench knife, board scraper, or dough cutter, a bench scraper has as many and varied uses as its many names suggest. We rounded up bench scrapers in a range of styles to square off against each other. For scraping, trimming, or cutting dough into smaller pieces, testers strongly preferred thin, deeply beveled edges, which made it easier to dislodge sticky pie dough from the counter and neatly portion bread and pizza doughs. One model's extra-long plastic blade was an advantage for speedy cleanup, but its ultrathin, slippery plastic handle made it unwieldy for much else. Our winner, the Dexter-Russell 6" Dough Cutter/Scraper—Sani-Safe Series, has a deeply beveled edge that quickly slid under pie dough and effortlessly sliced bread and pizza dough. Its textured polypropylene handle was just slender enough, making it easy to grasp and keep flat to the work surface for fast and efficient cleanup. Products are listed in order of preference. See AmericasTestKitchen.com for updates and complete testing results.

RECOMMENDED

DEXTER-RUSSELL 6" Dough Cutter/Scraper—Sani-Safe Series
PRICE: $7.01
EASE OF USE: ★★★   PERFORMANCE: ★★★
COMMENTS: The deeply beveled edge of this scraper cut through pizza and bread dough quickly and scraped the work surface effectively. The textured polypropylene handle was easy to hold on to, even with greasy or floury hands, and was thinner than other scrapers' handles, helping us hold it flat to the work surface for easier, more effective scooping and scraping.

NORPRO Grip EZ Chopper Scraper
PRICE: $6.06
EASE OF USE: ★★½   PERFORMANCE: ★★★
COMMENTS: The slightly bulkier rubber handle on this scraper meant that testers couldn't hold it flat to get under pie dough to lift it from the counter. But its beveled edge neatly scooped up vegetables and portioned dough, and it features accurate inch-measurement marks.

RECOMMENDED WITH RESERVATIONS

OXO Good Grips Stainless Steel Multi-Purpose Scraper & Chopper
PRICE: $9.99
EASE OF USE: ★★   PERFORMANCE: ★★
COMMENTS: This scraper, our former favorite, had a duller edge than the previous copy we tested, making cutting through pizza and bread dough and dislodging pie dough a struggle. (This was a problem with multiple copies.) Although great for scooping up vegetables and herbs, this model was not our first choice for cutting doughs.

RECOMMENDED WITH RESERVATIONS (cont.)

KEREKES Dough Scraper, Poly
PRICE: $4.00
EASE OF USE: ★½   PERFORMANCE: ★★
COMMENTS: This flat, all-plastic scraper has an extra-long, deeply beveled edge that made it ideal for scraping up stuck-on pie dough and cleaning work surfaces. But the raised tab that serves as a handle was awkward, and both blade and handle were very flexible and uncomfortable when it came to cutting pizza and bread dough.

NOT RECOMMENDED

RACHAEL RAY Bench Scrape Shovel
PRICE: $7.99
EASE OF USE: ★   PERFORMANCE: ★½
COMMENTS: Since it had neither a sharp edge nor a comfortable, symmetrical handle, this model was not a favorite for dough cutting or scraping. One unique feature did work well for scooping up and transferring vegetables and herbs: raised sides like those on a dustpan, which kept scooped-up veggies on board.

CRESTWARE Dough Scraper, Steel/Plastic, 6½ Inch
PRICE: $3.70
EASE OF USE: ★   PERFORMANCE: ★
COMMENTS: This scraper, which has a thick, dull edge, required testers to use brute force to cut all types of dough, and the cuts were never clean; instead, the dough was squashed into odd shapes. This model's thin, slick plastic handle also proved impossible to grasp with greasy hands.

Seafood Specials

Browning the usually discarded shrimp shells helps create a quick seafood stock. Using this stock as a base for our tomato sauce maximizes seafood flavor while minimizing waste.

WHEN SEAFOOD IS PART OF THE DISH, RATHER THAN THE MAIN EVENT, balancing flavors can be a challenge. Take shrimp fra diavolo and cioppino. There are a lot of bright, spicy flavors in both of these dishes. But what's the secret to versions where the seafood and supporting players work in harmony?

Cioppino, a gently spiced seafood stew made with a variety of shellfish and white fish in a rich tomato-based broth, is a seafood lover's perfect meal—if it's done well. We wanted to scale back the ocean's worth of seafood found in many restaurant versions and come up with a manageable recipe for the home cook, without sacrificing any flavor. We think we succeeded—but we'll let your guests' empty bowls prove it.

In most versions of shrimp fra diavolo, the shrimp end up hopelessly overcooked and their flavor (if there had been any) is cancelled out by the spicy tomato sauce. Sure, a plain old spicy red sauce has its place, but it's not in shrimp fra diavolo. We wanted perfectly tender shrimp napped with a tomatoey, piquant sauce bursting with briny shrimp flavor. We'll show you how to make the most of your shrimp, while still producing a sauce that's spicy but not overpowering. In short, we'll show you how to make the best shrimp fra diavolo ever.

CIOPPINO

✔ **WHY THIS RECIPE WORKS:** Cioppino, a seafood stew popularized by Italian immigrants to San Francisco, offers up an appealing assortment of fish and shellfish in a tomato-based broth. But modern restaurant versions can be intimidating to home cooks, with half a dozen types of seafood and a long-simmered base. We streamlined our stew in several ways. First, we settled on using only halibut, clams, and mussels, which offered plenty of flavor and were easy to find and prepare. For the stew base, we lightly browned onions, which we then simmered with canned tomatoes, garlic, oregano, and clam juice. To ensure that the clams and mussels didn't break up the flaky halibut fillets, we poached the halibut in the tomato broth and then transferred it to a platter to keep it warm. Then we steamed the mollusks in white wine and butter. For a briny flavor boost, we added the flavorful steaming liquid to the broth. A handful of chopped parsley and a drizzle of olive oil completed the dish.

WHEN IT COMES TO STEW, WORDS LIKE "HUMBLE" AND "simple" usually spring to mind. The seafood stew known as cioppino, however, is a different matter. True, it has modest origins. Brought to San Francisco by Italian immigrants, the earliest versions were uncomplicated affairs made by fishermen, featuring the catch of the day in a simple broth created from little more than water, tomato paste, and garlic. Today's restaurant versions have taken it to another level. Showcasing an assembly of fish and shellfish piled high in a bright, complex broth and anointed with fruity olive oil, cioppino is an indulgence for a seafood lover. From the first whiff of briny clams and mussels to the last drops of the flavorful broth, mopped up with a crust of bread, this stew is a serious treat—but it's also a production that can intimidate the home cook. Many recipes call for up to a half-dozen different types of seafood and a tomatoey fish stock that is simmered for hours. We did find shortcut versions,

but these proved disappointing: The broth tasted thin and there wasn't enough variety to make a dish that felt special. Our goal: a restaurant-worthy cioppino in which every component was perfectly cooked and the broth was rich-tasting but which could be on the table quickly and with minimal fuss.

We began by selecting the seafood. We needed to scale down the list to a choice few that presented a good mix of textures and flavors. For the fish, a white variety is most traditional and the best choice, since oily varieties like salmon muddy the stew's light flavors. Swordfish seemed promising, but tasters found its texture too meaty. Sea bass was acceptable, although it fell apart slightly. Halibut fillets worked perfectly—they were tender and had just enough heft. As for the shellfish, even though just about all the cioppino recipes from San Francisco feature Dungeness crab, we decided to omit it. Other seafood options offer enough briny-sweet flavor—plus, having to source, cook, crack, and shell the crab just complicated things. We also agreed that the sweetness of shrimp seemed out of place. But a combination of briny littleneck clams and savory-sweet mussels had just the flavors we were looking for.

With the seafood lineup ready to go, we moved on to the cooking method. Recipes that we found typically followed one of two approaches. The first method called for putting everything in the broth at the same time—submerging the fish in the broth so that it could poach while also serving as a raft for the shellfish, which rested on top to steam. We quickly discovered the flaw here: To generate enough steam to cook the shellfish, we had to bring the broth (a placeholder mixture for now) to a boil. That left us with overcooked, wrung-out halibut, not to mention chewy mussels, since they take less time to cook than clams do. The second approach, staggered additions, seemed much more promising. We put the halibut in the Dutch oven first, let it simmer until about halfway done, and then added the clams, followed by the mussels a few minutes later. The big problem here was that there's little leeway if one component happens to cook more quickly or more slowly than expected. A minute or two on either end makes a huge difference

CIOPPINO

for seafood, and if one component strayed from the projected cooking time, the others suffered. This one-pot approach was clearly not going to work. The only way to perfectly cook three varieties of seafood was to cook each one separately and bring them all together in the hot broth to serve.

With this in mind, we poached the halibut in the broth and then turned off the heat and let it sit while we steamed the clams and then the mussels in water and butter in a shallow skillet. As the shellfish opened we transferred them to the pot with the halibut. This ensured ideal doneness for each one, and the cooked shellfish stayed warm in the pot of broth until they were all done.

This was a huge improvement: Finally each seafood component was perfectly cooked. But there was still a small problem that had plagued every version we'd made. When we went to serve the cioppino, no matter how careful we were when ladling the stew into bowls, it was impossible to avoid knocking the clams and mussels around, and their hard shells broke the halibut into unappealing shreds. The solution? We transferred the halibut to a plate as soon as it was done and kept it covered with foil while we steamed the shellfish. (Keeping the halibut in large pieces ensured that it was easy to remove from the pot.) Then we divided the still-warm halibut among serving bowls and ladled the broth and shellfish on top. This worked seamlessly, so we focused on fine-tuning the broth. It was taking too long, and it seemed more like pasta sauce than like the base for a seafood stew.

Up to this point, we had been sautéing onions in oil until golden and then stirring in garlic and a few spices (bay leaves, dried oregano, and red pepper flakes) and, finally, canned tomatoes and water. Following precedent set by the recipes we'd found, we simmered this mixture for about an hour before adding the halibut.

We decided to start our revision of the broth with the flavor. As the clams and mussels opened, they released their briny juices into the steaming water. Why not put

that to use? For the next test we cut back on the water in the broth and poured the clams' and mussels' cooking liquid into the pot once they were done. As long as we poured slowly, it was easy to leave any sand and grit from the clam shells behind in the skillet. This was a definite improvement, but the stew really hit the mark when we replaced the rest of the water in the broth with bottled clam juice.

Now the stew had a clean, briny flavor appropriate to a seafood stew, but tasters wanted a bit more acidity and complexity. The answer was using white wine to steam the shellfish.

Flavor squared away, we moved on to seeing what we could do about the broth's lengthy simmer. The idea was to concentrate and meld the broth's components, but we wondered how essential that really was. After all, we weren't making a stock or a tomato-based pasta sauce. As it turned out, a long simmer was entirely unnecessary. In fact, once we poured the clam juice and tomatoes into the sautéed onions and aromatics, the broth tasted just right after a mere 5 minutes of cooking. We added the halibut and let it poach in the broth for 15 minutes.

A little parsley stirred into the pot and a generous drizzle of olive oil were the finishing touches. In an hour, we had created a restaurant-worthy cioppino.

Cioppino

SERVES 4 TO 6

Any firm-fleshed, ¾- to 1-inch-thick white fish (such as cod or sea bass) can be substituted for halibut. Our favorite bottled clam juices are Bar Harbor Clam Juice and Look's Atlantic Clam Juice. Discard clams or mussels with unpleasant odors, cracked shells, or shells that won't close. If littlenecks are not available, substitute Manila or mahogany clams, or use 2 pounds of mussels. If using only mussels, skip step 3 and cook them all at once with the butter and wine for 3 to 5 minutes. Adjust the amount of pepper flakes depending on how spicy you want the dish. Serve with sourdough or rustic bread.

- ¼ **cup vegetable oil**
- 2 **large onions, chopped fine**
-    **Salt and pepper**
- ¼ **cup water**
- 4 **garlic cloves, minced**
- 2 **bay leaves**
- 1 **teaspoon dried oregano**
- ⅛–¼ **teaspoon red pepper flakes**
- 1 **(28-ounce) can whole peeled tomatoes, drained with juice reserved, chopped coarse**
- 1 **(8-ounce) bottle clam juice**
- 1 **(1½-pound) skinless halibut fillet, ¾ to 1 inch thick, cut into 6 pieces**
- 1 **pound littleneck clams, scrubbed**
- 1¼ **cups dry white wine**
- 4 **tablespoons unsalted butter**

COOK IN STAGES
Cooking the halibut, then the clams, and finally the mussels ensures that each component is perfectly done.

1. SIMMER HALIBUT IN POT: The halibut needs just 15 minutes in the pot; set the cooked fish aside before adding the cooked shellfish.

2. STEAM CLAMS AND THEN MUSSELS IN SKILLET: Transfer the clams and mussels to the pot as they open; using a skillet makes it easy to leave grit behind when pouring the cooking liquid into the pot.

CLEANING CLAMS
Most clams these days are cultured. After being dug, they are usually held on flats submerged in salt water for several days. During this time they expel grit they have ingested; scrubbing is only necessary to remove exterior sand and grit before cooking.

- 1 **pound mussels, scrubbed and debearded**
- ¼ **cup chopped fresh parsley**
-    **Extra-virgin olive oil**

1. Heat vegetable oil in Dutch oven over medium-high heat until shimmering. Add onions, ½ teaspoon salt, and ½ teaspoon pepper; cook, stirring frequently, until onions begin to brown, 7 to 9 minutes. Add water and cook, stirring frequently, until onions are soft, 2 to 4 minutes. Stir in garlic, bay leaves, oregano, and pepper flakes and cook for 1 minute. Stir in tomatoes and reserved juice and clam juice and bring to simmer. Reduce heat to low, cover, and simmer for 5 minutes.

2. Submerge halibut in broth, cover, and gently simmer until fish is cooked through, 12 to 15 minutes. Remove pot from heat and, using slotted spoon, transfer halibut to plate; cover with aluminum foil and set aside.

3. Bring clams, wine, and butter to boil in covered 12-inch skillet over high heat. Steam until clams just open, 5 to 8 minutes, transferring them to pot with tomato broth as they open.

4. Once all clams have been transferred to pot, add mussels to skillet, cover, and cook over high heat until mussels have opened, 2 to 4 minutes, transferring them to pot with tomato broth as they open. Pour cooking liquid from skillet into pot, being careful not to pour any grit from skillet into pot. Return broth to simmer.

5. Stir parsley into broth and season with salt and pepper to taste. Divide halibut among serving bowls. Ladle broth over halibut, making sure each portion contains both clams and mussels. Drizzle with olive oil and serve immediately.

RATING FIRE-ROASTED TOMATOES

Fresh tomatoes charred over an open fire possess a sweet, smoky depth that plain tomatoes can't match. We wondered if canned versions could meet that ideal, so we gathered three nationally available diced fire-roasted tomato products to find out. Although they all looked the part, with char-flecked tomatoes in every can, flavor told another story. Two of the brands had wimpy or artificial smoke flavor. DeLallo Fire-Roasted Diced Tomatoes tasted aggressively smoky when sampled plain, but in salsa and chili that intensity mellowed, providing a smoky background flavor that tasters appreciated. Tasters also liked the sweeter, fruitier notes of the winning tomatoes, as well as the added flavorings and spices, which bolstered savory flavor. Products are listed in order of preference. See AmericasTestKitchen.com for updates and complete tasting results.

RECOMMENDED

DELALLO Fire-Roasted Diced Tomatoes in Juice with Seasonings
PRICE: $2.50 for 14.5-oz can ($0.17 per oz)
SODIUM: 280 mg per ½-cup serving   SUGARS: 5 g
INGREDIENTS: Fire-roasted diced tomatoes, tomato juice, salt, garlic powder, natural flavoring, onion powder, onion juice, yeast extract, calcium chloride, citric acid
COMMENTS: Tasters liked the "rich red" color of these tomatoes. Sampled plain, many tasters liked the "sweet," roasted flavor, though some took off points for a taste "like fake smoke." However, when used in salsa, the tomatoes' smoky flavor mellowed and gained depth.

RECOMMENDED WITH RESERVATIONS

MUIR GLEN Organic Diced Tomatoes, Fire Roasted
PRICE: $2.19 for 14.5-oz can ($0.15 per oz)
SODIUM: 200 mg per ½-cup serving   SUGARS: 3 g
INGREDIENTS: Fire-roasted tomatoes, tomato juice, sea salt, naturally derived citric acid and calcium chloride
COMMENTS: These tomatoes looked the part but their flavor didn't play it: "They just taste like regular old tomatoes." Despite this complaint, tasters found the tomatoes' basic flavor "fresh" and "nicely sweet."

HUNT'S Fire Roasted Diced Tomatoes
PRICE: $1.25 for 14.5-oz can ($0.09 per oz)
SODIUM: 280 mg per ½-cup serving   SUGARS: 3 g
INGREDIENTS: Unpeeled diced tomatoes, tomato juice, less than 2 percent of: salt, citric acid, yeast extract, calcium chloride, natural flavor, onion juice, garlic powder, onion powder
COMMENTS: Tasted plain, these tomatoes exhibited a smoke flavor that was "strong" but "artificial." These "fake" notes still surfaced in salsa. And while tasters praised the tomatoes for being "juicy" and "bright," some found their "chewy" skins "a drawback."

SHRIMP FRA DIAVOLO

✔ **WHY THIS RECIPE WORKS:** Ideally, shrimp fra diavolo is a lively, piquant dish full of briny, plump shrimp and juicy chunks of tomato, with red pepper flakes and garlic providing an aromatic backbone. But too often, the shrimp are overcooked and the spice obliterates the other flavors, leaving the dish hot but one-dimensional. To highlight the sweet shrimp flavor in our spicy sauce, we browned the shrimp shells to make a stock. We also amped up the savory seafood flavor with minced anchovies. Poaching the shrimp directly in the sauce cooked them to succulent perfection. In addition, we intensified the heat and depth of the red pepper flakes by adding minced pepperoncini. A generous handful of chopped herbs, stirred in at the end, contributed freshness, while extra-virgin olive oil gave the dish a bright, peppery finish.

SHRIMP *FRA DIAVOLO* (OR "BROTHER DEVIL") IS A 20th-century Italian American combo of shrimp, tomatoes, garlic, and hot pepper, often served over spaghetti or with crusty bread. At its best, it's lively and piquant, the tangy tomatoes countering the sweet and briny shrimp, and the pepper and garlic providing a spirited kick. Unfortunately, this "devilish" dish is often so in-your-face spicy and pungent that it's about as suavely enticing as a cartoon Beelzebub. The heavy-handed spice completely overwhelms the other flavors.

What's more, the fragile shrimp are often flambéed (for flavor or fiery effect, we've never been sure which) or pan-seared before being cooked further in the sauce, transforming them into chunks of overcooked, flavorless protein, identifiable only by their shape.

Simply taming the heat of shrimp fra diavolo would be as easy as cutting back on the spice (usually red pepper flakes), but that would make it another dish entirely: more like shrimp marinara. No, we intended to not only preserve the fiery character of fra diavolo but also heighten the other flavors—particularly the brininess of the shrimp—so that they could stand up to the heat. And we'd make sure that those shrimp remained succulent.

We started with the simplest sauce recipe we could find: a goodly amount of both garlic and red pepper flakes and a bit of dried oregano—all sautéed in a few tablespoons of vegetable oil until fragrant—plus chopped canned whole tomatoes and their juice, cooked down for a few minutes until thickened. The first question was how to cook the shrimp. Recipes that we found called for one of three techniques: sautéing the peeled shrimp (1½ pounds would yield four servings) along with the aromatics in oil before adding the sauce components; flambéing the sautéed shrimp by adding a few glugs of cognac to the pan and waving a lit match over the surface; and, the simplest method, slipping raw shrimp into the simmering tomato sauce, where they poached until just opaque and cooked through.

Flambéing turned out to be more impressive for its pyrotechnic display than for its flavor contribution. Besides, the technique produced rubbery shrimp. We hoped that by simply sautéing the shrimp we could coax out good briny flavor without overcooking them. Even

SHRIMP FRA DIAVOLO

more important, we hoped that the method would yield a valuable by-product: the flavorful browned bits known as fond, which would serve as a rich shrimp base for the sauce. But alas, even browning the shrimp enough to develop fond had them teetering on the edge of overcooked, and stirring them back into the sauce before serving to meld their flavors sealed the deal.

Poaching, meanwhile, produced the tender shrimp that we were after, but with little briny seafood flavor to speak of. The finished product tasted like what we were trying to avoid: spicy shrimp marinara. If only we could use this poaching method but along the way boost the flavor presence of the shrimp.

We considered sacrificing a small portion of the shrimp by searing them to build fond and then throwing them away. That way, we'd develop a rich seafood backbone for the sauce before gently poaching the remaining raw shrimp in the sauce. But then it occurred to us that we already had a flavor-building ingredient at our disposal.

Crustacean shells contain loads of proteins, sugars, and flavor-boosting compounds called glutamates and nucleotides that are ideal for building the flavorful browning known as the Maillard reaction—a discovery we capitalized on in a past recipe for roasted shrimp, in which roasting the shrimp shell-on considerably amped up their savory seafood flavor. Searing these smaller shell-on shrimp would only overcook them, but browning the to-be-discarded shells as a foundation for the sauce was a possibility. The concept is a classic first step when making shrimp bisque—but oddly not a technique that we found during our fra diavolo research.

We started a new batch, this time sautéing the shrimp shells in a little oil until they and the surface of the pan were spotty brown. Then we deglazed the pan with wine—another pickup technique from seafood bisques. The puff of heady, seafood-rich steam that rose up from the pan indicated that we were on the right track. From there, we added the juice from a can of whole tomatoes (we'd add the solids later) and let the shells simmer,

essentially creating a tomatoey shrimp "stock," which we strained from the shells about 5 minutes later. When we took a whiff of the cooking liquid, the intensity of its seafood aroma impressed us—but not as much as the flavor did. A spoonful was remarkably rich and savory, like shrimp pot liquor.

The rest of the sauce was quick to pull together. We wiped out the skillet and sautéed the garlic, pepper flakes, and oregano in a couple of tablespoons of oil until fragrant and then added the reserved tomato solids. To break up the large chunks, we pummeled the pieces with a potato masher until we had a pulpy puree. In went the

tomato stock, which needed more body, so we cranked up the heat a bit and let the mixture simmer for about 5 minutes, by which time it had thickened. Finally, we added the shrimp, turning them a few times to ensure that they cooked evenly, and finished the dish with handfuls of chopped basil and parsley and a drizzle of fruity extra-virgin olive oil.

We were almost satisfied: The shrimp were plump and juicy, and the sauce boasted true (but not overwhelming) heat. Searing the shells had paid off; there was more than a hint of rich shrimp flavor and brininess. And yet we hadn't nailed the intensity of either one of those flavors, so we looked to the test kitchen pantry for something that might help.

Minutes later, we had our answers. The first: a jar of anchovies. Don't underestimate the potential of these little fish. Mincing a pair of fillets (rinsed first to reduce their saltiness) and browning them with the aromatics added remarkably savory, not fishy, depth. The second, more unexpected find was a jar of pepperoncini. When we stirred in two of these minced pickled peppers at the end with the herbs, the acidity—and heat—of the sauce perked up just a bit more. On a whim, we stirred in a teaspoon of the brine from the jar, too, which amplified the effect.

This version of shrimp fra diavolo had enough fire from the garlic and pepper to please the most daring of diners and—thanks to the browned shells and anchovies—a round, rich seafood flavor, too. Served with warm, crusty bread, it made a meal that would tempt the devil himself.

Shrimp Fra Diavolo

SERVES 4

If the shrimp you are using have been treated with salt (check the bag's ingredient list), skip the salting in step 1 and add ¼ teaspoon of salt to the sauce in step 3. Adjust the amount of red pepper flakes depending on how spicy you want the dish. Serve the shrimp with a salad and crusty bread or over spaghetti. If serving with spaghetti, adjust the consistency of the sauce with some reserved pasta cooking water.

- 1½   pounds large shrimp (26 to 30 per pound), peeled and deveined, shells reserved
-      Salt
- 1   (28-ounce) can whole peeled tomatoes
- 3   tablespoons vegetable oil
- 1   cup dry white wine
- 4   garlic cloves, minced
- ½–1   teaspoon red pepper flakes
- ½   teaspoon dried oregano
- 2   anchovy fillets, rinsed, patted dry, and minced
- ¼   cup chopped fresh basil
- ¼   cup chopped fresh parsley
- 1½   teaspoons minced pepperoncini, plus 1 teaspoon brine
- 2   tablespoons extra-virgin olive oil

1. Toss shrimp with ½ teaspoon salt and set aside. Pour tomatoes into colander set over large bowl. Pierce tomatoes with edge of rubber spatula and stir briefly to release juice. Transfer drained tomatoes to small bowl and reserve juice. Do not wash colander.

2. Heat 1 tablespoon vegetable oil in 12-inch skillet over high heat until shimmering. Add shrimp shells and cook, stirring frequently, until they begin to turn

NOTES FROM THE TEST KITCHEN

THE SECRET'S IN THE STOCK
The sauce in most versions of shrimp fra diavolo tastes largely of cooked tomato and chile, but not really of seafood. To amp up savory shrimp flavor and brightness, we took a cue from classic seafood bisques and created a shrimp stock by browning the shells—an ingredient we would have otherwise discarded—deglazing the pan with white wine, and simmering the mixture with the juice from canned tomatoes. In just minutes, the shells give up remarkably rich flavor, which the wine and tomato juice balance with acidity.

spotty brown and skillet starts to brown, 2 to 4 minutes. Remove skillet from heat and carefully add wine. When bubbling subsides, return skillet to heat and simmer until wine is reduced to about 2 tablespoons, 2 to 4 minutes. Add reserved tomato juice and simmer to meld flavors, 5 minutes. Pour contents of skillet into colander set over bowl. Discard shells and reserve liquid. Wipe out skillet with paper towels.

3. Heat remaining 2 tablespoons vegetable oil, garlic, pepper flakes, and oregano in now-empty skillet over medium heat, stirring occasionally, until garlic is straw-colored and fragrant, 1 to 2 minutes. Add anchovies and stir until fragrant, about 30 seconds. Remove from heat. Add drained tomatoes and mash with potato masher until coarsely pureed. Return to heat and stir in reserved tomato juice mixture. Increase heat to medium-high and simmer until mixture has thickened, about 5 minutes.

4. Add shrimp to skillet and simmer gently, stirring and turning shrimp frequently, until they are just cooked through, 4 to 5 minutes. Remove pan from heat. Stir in basil, parsley, and pepperoncini and brine and season with salt to taste. Drizzle with olive oil and serve.

Introducing Caldo Verde and White Gazpacho

Instead of relying on dairy-rich cream, we turned to pureed soaked bread to thicken our chilled Spanish soup, which allows its refined character to shine.

SOUP HAS MANY PERSONALITIES: IT CAN BE WARM AND COMFORTING or cool and refreshing. It can be meaty or vegetarian, creamy or brothy, sweet or savory. Here in the test kitchen, we are always on the lookout for new ways to enjoy soup, and sometimes our searches lead us to surprising places. Join us as we cross the Atlantic and delve into two dramatically different soups from Portugal and Spain.

Caldo verde, or "green soup," is a simple Portuguese soup made with linguiça sausage, potatoes, and, of course, hearty greens called *couve tronchuda*. Although it's often served as a starter, we wanted it to function as a satisfying main course, and we wanted to use commonly available ingredients in place of the hard-to-find linguiça and couve.

When most of us think of gazpacho, we think of tomatoes, cucumbers, and bell peppers. But Spanish *ajo blanco* doesn't rely on fresh summer veggies for flavor. This elegant white gazpacho is made with ground almonds, bread, garlic, and sherry vinegar, and garnished with crunchy toasted almonds, sweet green grapes, and peppery olive oil. The flavors are complex, but our recipe is amazingly simple. Two ways with soup, coming up.

CALDO VERDE

CALDO VERDE

✔ WHY THIS RECIPE WORKS: Caldo verde is a traditional Portuguese soup of shredded greens, potatoes, and sausage. In our version, we pureed some of the potatoes with olive oil to make a thick, cohesive, silky-smooth base. Replacing some of the water with chicken broth added depth of flavor and a splash of white wine vinegar at the end of cooking provided brightness. Increasing the amount of potato and sausage turned this simple first course into a hearty and filling meal.

IN PORTUGUESE COMMUNITIES IN MASSACHUSETTS, caldo verde, a soup of sausage, potato, and hearty greens, is a staple in many households. Although recipes vary, they generally follow similar outlines: Sauté onion and garlic in extra-virgin olive oil, add cubed russet potatoes and a couple of quarts of water, bring the pot to a boil, and let the soup simmer until the potatoes are tender. As that is cooking, pieces of smoky, garlicky linguiça sausage are browned in a skillet and hearty greens are finely shredded (kale or collards often stand in for *couve tronchuda*, the traditional greens used for the dish). After about 10 minutes, the pot is stirred to break down the potatoes and introduce body to the broth; then the sautéed sausage and greens are added. The greens soften during the last few minutes of cooking and give the soup its generally verdant appearance—and its name.

What we like best about this dish is that, while the flavors are rich, it's not a heavy soup. In fact, some families serve it as a starter. Without changing the soup's essentially light character, we wanted to create a slightly heartier result—something that could function as a main course.

To start, we decided to increase the amount of sausage, greens, and potatoes to give the soup more heft. We replaced the hard-to-find Portuguese linguiça sausage with widely available Spanish-style chorizo, which boasts a similar garlicky profile. We also sautéed the sausage right in the Dutch oven—no need to dirty a skillet. The ¼ cup of extra-virgin olive oil that many recipes suggest for cooking the sausage seemed excessive, so we reduced it to just 1 tablespoon. One more tweak: We split the water with an equal amount of chicken broth for deeper flavor.

While the soup simmered, we dealt with the greens. In a side-by-side test of kale and collard greens, tasters preferred the collards, which offered a delicate sweetness and a meatier bite. One last problem to solve: The wilted strips of shredded greens dangled from the spoon, making the soup messy to eat. Chopping the leaves into bite-size pieces made them more spoon-friendly.

So far, our caldo verde was shaping up nicely, save for the broth itself, which was too thin. We also didn't love how three separate layers developed as the soup sat: a thin film of flavorful chorizo oil on top, broth beneath it, and a bed of grainy potato bits on the bottom of the pot. We wanted something with creamier, more even body.

Until now we'd been vigorously stirring the broth once the potatoes had softened so that they broke down. But it was becoming clear that using this mixing method would never produce the smooth body we wanted: We realized that we should just puree some of the softened potatoes into the liquid. This way, the broth would thicken up and become uniformly silky. We blitzed ¾ cup of the russets with an equal amount of broth in a blender. The resulting puree was definitely smooth-textured. The problem was that by the time the soup was simmering with the greens and the sausage, the unpureed potato pieces (which we wanted to remain intact) were completely blown out. Switching to lower-starch Yukon Golds, which hold their shape even during long cooking, was the easy solution.

And yet the broth was not quite as silky as we wanted it to be, which made us think of those 3 extra tablespoons of oil that we'd vetoed early on in testing. Maybe emulsifying that fat in the broth would be just what the soup needed. We drizzled the oil into the blender with the softened potatoes and broth, and as we'd hoped, a brief whirl left us with a uniform, velvety puree. We added the greens to the broth and then stirred in the chorizo a few minutes later. When the greens were tender, we poured the potato-oil emulsion into the soup along with a bit of white wine vinegar to brighten the pot.

Here were all the flavors we loved in the classic soup, but in a heartier and more satisfying form.

Caldo Verde

SERVES 6 TO 8

We prefer collard greens, but kale can be substituted. Serve this soup with hearty bread and, for added richness, a final drizzle of extra-virgin olive oil.

¼ cup extra-virgin olive oil
12 ounces Spanish-style chorizo sausage,
     cut into ½-inch pieces
1 onion, chopped fine
4 garlic cloves, minced
   Salt and pepper
¼ teaspoon red pepper flakes
2 pounds Yukon Gold potatoes, peeled and
     cut into ¾-inch pieces
4 cups chicken broth
4 cups water
1 pound collard greens, stemmed and cut into
     1-inch pieces
2 teaspoons white wine vinegar

1. Heat 1 tablespoon oil in Dutch oven over medium-high heat until shimmering. Add chorizo and cook, stirring occasionally, until lightly browned, 4 to 5 minutes. Transfer chorizo to bowl and set aside. Reduce heat to medium and add onion, garlic, 1¼ teaspoons salt, and pepper flakes and season with pepper to taste. Cook, stirring frequently, until onion is translucent, 2 to 3 minutes. Add potatoes, broth, and water; increase heat to high and bring to boil. Reduce heat to medium-low and simmer, uncovered, until potatoes are just tender, 8 to 10 minutes.

2. Transfer ¾ cup solids and ¾ cup broth to blender. Add collard greens to pot and simmer for 10 minutes. Stir in chorizo and continue to simmer until greens are tender, 8 to 10 minutes longer.

3. Add remaining 3 tablespoons oil to soup in blender and process until very smooth and homogeneous, about 1 minute. Remove pot from heat and stir pureed soup mixture and vinegar into soup. Season with salt and pepper to taste, and serve. (Soup can be refrigerated for up to 2 days.)

SPANISH GARLIC AND ALMOND SOUP

✓ **WHY THIS RECIPE WORKS:** Spanish white gazpacho, or *ajo blanco,* is a silky cold soup that relies on just a few ingredients for intense flavor. At its best, it is a study in contrasts: Some bites offer a nutty crunch, while others are sharply fruity and floral. But the versions we tried were watery and bland or even grainy. We wanted to nail down a foolproof way to make this chilled soup. We found that the order in which we added ingredients to the blender made all the difference. First, we buzzed almonds until they were powdery, then added bread (which had been soaked in water), a clove of garlic, a splash of sherry vinegar, and salt and pepper. Then we drizzled olive oil into the puree and thinned the soup with more water. For just a hint of bitter almond flavor, we mixed a tablespoon of the pureed soup with ⅛ teaspoon of almond extract, then stirred a teaspoon of the mixture back into the soup. For garnishes, we thinly sliced green grapes and toasted a few almonds in oil to add crunch. An extra drizzle of olive oil made for a rich finish and a beautiful presentation.

SPANISH WHITE GAZPACHO, OR *AJO BLANCO*, BEARS little resemblance to its red cousin. The silky soup is served ice-cold, decorated with a delicate mosaic of almonds, sliced grapes, and vibrantly green olive oil. Its flavors are as intricate as its appearance: Some bites offer a nutty crunch, while others are sharply fruity and floral; in still others, peppery extra-virgin olive oil is at the fore. And all of this complexity is coaxed from just a handful of ingredients. We were intrigued.

A little research taught us that white gazpacho pre-dates the familiar red version since tomatoes didn't reach Spain until after Columbus. The rock-bottom-cheap ajo blanco was prepared by peasants with five ingredients at their disposal: stale bread, garlic, vinegar, oil, and salt. They pounded the bread and garlic with a mortar and pestle, added slugs of vinegar and oil with salt to taste, and either ate the gazpacho in that form or stirred in water to make it drinkable. When the dish migrated from the tables of laborers to those of aristocrats, upscale ingredients like almonds and grapes (or even fish or pickled vegetables) went into the mix, transforming a humble mush into a dish meant to impress.

And yet, the first couple of batches we whipped up from modern recipes were far from impressive. Some were watery and bland; others were grainy and salad dressing–esque. We decided to nail down the technique before figuring out the flavor.

Although traditionalists rely on a mortar and pestle (and elbow grease), we planned on putting a kitchen appliance to work. We pulled out a blender and a food processor and loaded each with placeholder amounts of bread, almonds, garlic, vinegar, and water. We pureed the ingredients and then streamed oil into each machine. When we strained the soups, we could plainly see that the blender had done the better job of breaking down the solids, but the soup was still marred by tiny almond bits.

We recalled that the recipes employing a mortar and pestle proceeded in a specific manner. First, the almonds were finely crushed. Meanwhile, the bread was soaked in water to facilitate grinding. The almonds and bread were then mixed into a paste and only then was liquid incorporated. We mimicked the process in a blender: We buzzed the almonds until they were powdery and then added the soaked bread, garlic, a splash of vinegar, and salt and pepper. Once these ingredients were pureed, we drizzled in the olive oil and finally thinned the soup with more water. This soup was thicker, creamier, and smoother than ever.

Now that we had a foolproof procedure, we examined the ingredients. Stale bread never produced a soup that was significantly different from fresh, and plain old sandwich bread worked as well as (if not better than) fancy artisanal types. Blanched sliced almonds were best since they didn't create brown flecks in the ivory soup. Brightened with sherry vinegar and a pinch of cayenne pepper, the gazpacho was tasty, but we had yet to capture the fruity, floral flavors that had drawn us to this unique recipe in the first place.

SPANISH CHILLED ALMOND AND GARLIC SOUP

Switching from everyday extra-virgin olive oil to a premium brand added a fruity, peppery pop. We tried toasting the almonds but this darkened the soup and gave it a toasted flavor that was less than refreshing. Finally, we realized that the sharper, almost flowery profile of bitter almonds (found in almond extract) would be a better fit. We made another batch with just a drop of extract, and this hit the mark. However, even an extra drop of extract ruined the gazpacho. For foolproof measuring, we mixed ⅛ teaspoon of the extract into a tablespoon of soup and then stirred 1 teaspoon of the extract mixture back into the soup.

As for garnishes, thinly sliced green grapes were a given. For crunch, we toasted a few almonds in oil and sprinkled them lightly with salt. After ladling the soup into bowls, we mounded the garnishes in the center and then drizzled more oil on top. This gazpacho had the taste to back up its looks.

Spanish Chilled Almond and Garlic Soup
SERVES 6 TO 8

This rich soup is best when served in small portions (about 6 ounces). Use a good-quality extra-virgin olive oil. Our favorite is Columela Extra Virgin Olive Oil. Too much almond extract can ruin the soup. Hence, the unusual mixing technique in step 4.

    6 slices hearty white sandwich bread, crusts removed
    4 cups water
2½ cups (8¾ ounces) plus ⅓ cup sliced blanched almonds
    3 tablespoons sherry vinegar
    1 garlic clove, peeled
       Kosher salt and pepper
       Pinch cayenne pepper
    ½ cup extra-virgin olive oil, plus extra for drizzling
    ⅛ teaspoon almond extract
    2 teaspoons vegetable oil
    6 ounces seedless green grapes, sliced thin (1 cup)

1. Combine bread and water in bowl and let soak for 5 minutes. Process 2½ cups almonds in blender until finely ground, about 30 seconds, scraping down sides of blender jar as needed.

2. Using your hands, remove bread from water, squeeze it lightly, and transfer to blender with almonds. Measure 3 cups soaking water and set aside; transfer remaining soaking water to blender.

3. Add vinegar, garlic, 1¼ teaspoons salt, and cayenne to blender and process until mixture has consistency of cake batter, 30 to 45 seconds. With blender running, add olive oil in thin, steady stream, about 30 seconds. Add reserved soaking water and process for 1 minute. Season with salt and pepper to taste. Strain soup through fine-mesh strainer set in bowl, pressing on solids to extract liquid. Discard solids.

4. Measure 1 tablespoon of soup into second bowl and stir in almond extract. Return 1 teaspoon of extract mixture to soup; discard remainder. Chill for at least 3 hours or up to 24 hours.

5. Heat vegetable oil in 8-inch skillet over medium-high heat until oil begins to shimmer. Add remaining ⅓ cup almonds and cook, stirring constantly, until golden brown, 3 to 4 minutes. Immediately transfer to bowl and stir in ¼ teaspoon salt.

6. Ladle soup into shallow bowls. Mound equal amount of grapes in center of each bowl. Sprinkle cooled almonds over soup and drizzle with extra olive oil. Serve immediately.

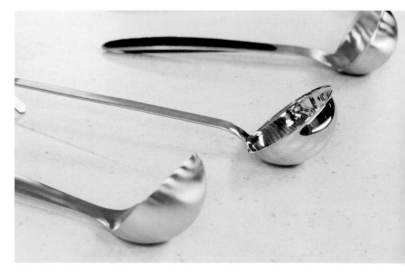

The Italian Vegetarian

Using just a portion of ricotta thinned with cream creates a sauce that stays silky when tossed with the hot pasta and spinach. Any lost richness is replaced by spoonfuls of ricotta dolloped over the pasta just before serving.

PERENNIAL ITALIAN RESTAURANT FAVORITES LIKE EGGPLANT *INVOLTINI* and stuffed shells make use of classic ingredient combinations—eggplant, red sauce, and cheese; or pasta, spinach, and ricotta—to create rich, stick-to-your-ribs vegetarian dishes. These dishes are classics for a reason: They taste great. But making eggplant involtini or stuffed shells at home can be a daunting process. We wanted an easier way to take these flavors into the busy home kitchen.

Eggplant involtini, though similar to its Parmesan cousin, requires rolling planks of fried eggplant around a rich ricotta filling and then baking the rolls with tomato sauce and cheese. But this time-consuming dish is plagued by greasy eggplant and a mountain of dishes to clean afterward. To solve these problems, we started with the eggplant, which we typically salt to remove its excess moisture before cooking. But that process can take almost an hour. Finding a way to slash the salting time would be the first of several hurdles to perfect our dish.

Deconstructed versions of stuffed shells have been making the rounds for years. It was time for us to give one a try. The appeal is apparent: traditional stuffed pasta ingredients, like creamy ricotta and fresh baby spinach, are tossed with warm pasta. It should make for an easy weeknight dish, but often that simplicity translates into dullness—or worse, a wan, gritty-textured entree. We made some adjustments to bring out the best flavor and texture, but kept the streamlined nature of the dish intact.

EGGPLANT INVOLTINI

✔ **WHY THIS RECIPE WORKS:** Eggplant *involtini* recipes are often complicated and messy and produce heavy, oily results. We wanted a lighter, less fussy take on these bundles that would make the most of the classic combination of eggplant, tomato sauce, and cheese. To streamline the eggplant prep, we skipped salting and frying in batches in favor of baking the planks, which eliminated excess water and produced tender and lightly browned eggplant. We lightened up the cheesy filling by using half the usual amount of ricotta and supplementing with bold Pecorino Romano. To ensure that the filling stayed creamy, we added bread crumbs, which prevented the cheese from forming a dense protein network. Finally, we put together a simple skillet tomato sauce where the involtini could warm through. A final sprinkle of basil and Pecorino finished off our streamlined involtini.

OFTEN, RECIPES FOR EGGPLANT *INVOLTINI* ("LITTLE bundles" in Italian) are so complicated and messy that they can make you wonder if they were the malicious invention of someone who wanted cooks to suffer.

One of the first recipes we tried started innocently enough with a homemade tomato sauce. While that simmered, we cut two eggplants lengthwise into ½-inch-thick planks and fried them. Frying sounds like one step, but in this case it was actually several: Before frying, we had to salt the planks for 45 minutes to remove excess moisture, pat them dry, and coat them in flour, eggs, and bread crumbs. After doing that with four batches, we were still only halfway done.

We mixed up a ricotta filling, spread a dollop of it on each slice, rolled up the slices, and arranged them in a baking dish. We poured the sauce over the bundles, topped the assembly with mozzarella and Parmesan, and baked it for 30 minutes—barely enough time to clear up the devastation the project had left in its wake.

The resulting dish was rich and hefty, similar to classic eggplant Parmesan, though the process had been slightly more arduous, thanks to that rolling-rather-than-layering step. While eggplant Parmesan is justifiably popular, both the making and the eating can be a bit heavy going.

But we were charmed by those tidy little involtini, and the combination of eggplant, tomato sauce, and cheese has timeless appeal. Our goal: Come up with a version of involtini that would emphasize the eggplant and minimize the fuss.

Many eggplant recipes begin by treating the cut vegetable with a heavy dose of salt to draw out excess moisture. It supposedly pulls out bitterness, too.

Let's start with the second claim: It's true that unsalted eggplant can taste a tad bitter from compounds called alkaloids that are found under the skin and in the seeds, but salt doesn't really draw many of those compounds out. As we've found with other bitter-tasting foods, like coffee and grapefruit, salt merely masks bitter flavors; it doesn't eliminate them. And though eggplants were once very bitter indeed, as food scientist Harold McGee points out in *On Food and Cooking*, this trait has been significantly reduced through selective breeding methods. In short, bitterness is less of an issue than it once was. But the excess water problem? That's real.

The flesh of an eggplant is made up of millions of tiny air-filled compartments enclosed by water-fortified walls. If you fry eggplant without removing some of that water beforehand, two things happen: First, those air sacs flood with oil, turning the eggplant greasy. Second, when heat turns the water to steam, some of it will become trapped in the eggplant's flesh. And as the steam forcibly tries to escape, it will damage the cell structure of the fruit. The result? Mushy, oily, and entirely unappetizing eggplant.

When you salt eggplant, some of that potentially destructive water is removed, so the walls of the air sacs weaken and collapse. That sounds bad, but it's actually good: The end result is eggplant with a more compact, meatier consistency. And a denser texture means that there are fewer places for oil to get trapped.

EGGPLANT INVOLTINI

But we didn't want to devote 45 minutes to drying out the eggplant if we didn't have to. Instead, we tried a test kitchen shortcut: microwaving the planks in a single layer for about 6 minutes. Unfortunately, the microwave's limited capacity meant that we could work with only one-quarter of the eggplant at a time, so 12 slices of eggplant required almost half an hour of intermittent engagement. It wasn't ideal.

But maybe there was another, unorthodox solution. Maybe we wouldn't fry the eggplant. True, most recipes we found required frying the planks, either breaded or plain, but we were after a simpler, lighter, cleaner-tasting dish. And if we didn't fry, maybe we wouldn't have to salt.

Recipes for grilled eggplant rarely call for preliminary salting. That's because there's little oil on the grill for the flesh to soak up, and the eggplant's excess water quickly evaporates. We weren't about to fire up the grill, but we wondered if other dry-heat cooking methods might offer the same benefits.

We peeled two eggplants and cut them into ½-inch-thick planks. Broiling the plain slices (we skipped the breading to lighten the dish and its workload) on a wire rack set in a rimmed baking sheet worked pretty well but demanded near-constant vigilance and flipping halfway through to prevent burning. It also required working in two batches. Hoping for a hands-off method, we tried baking instead.

We brushed the planks with oil, seasoned them with salt and pepper, and then baked them on two greased parchment-lined baking sheets in a 375-degree oven for about 30 minutes. Happily, they emerged light brown and tender, with a compact texture that was neither mushy nor sodden. Though the tops and sides of the slices had dried out nicely, there was still a bit of residual moisture on the undersides, so we let the planks cool and firm up on the baking sheet for 5 minutes and then flipped them to allow the remaining steam to escape. These slices were meaty and tender, but not at all squishy, and we didn't miss frying. It was time to move on to the filling.

Ricotta, which forms the base for most involtini fillings, is subtle, so you have to use a lot of it if you want it to stand up to the tomato sauce. But for these lighter involtini, we wanted to decrease the overall amount of cheese. Swapping some of the ricotta for a lesser amount of a more assertive cheese seemed like the way to go.

We limited ourselves to 1 cup of ricotta, which was half the amount required by that initial recipe. Adding ½ cup of grated Parmesan and a handful of chopped basil to bump up its flavor didn't cut it, though, and the texture of the filling was unexpectedly tight and bouncy. In the next batch, we used bolder Pecorino Romano instead of the Parmesan, and we stirred in a tablespoon of lemon juice. Things started looking (and tasting) brighter—but that resilient texture remained.

It was clear that the dry, aged cheese—whether Parmesan or Pecorino—was the source of that tight, granular texture. Just a small handful was fine, but when we added a full ½ cup to 1 cup of ricotta, the texture of the filling deteriorated from creamy to firm. In fact, it was reminiscent of ground meat that had been overcooked, and we wondered if it was indeed the same problem: an excessive linking of proteins. And that thought led us to the solution: bread crumbs.

When you add a paste of bread crumbs and milk (called a panade) to ground meat, it interferes with the linking of the meat proteins so that the cooked meat stays loose and soft. Bingo. When we incorporated just one slice of bread, whizzed to crumbs in the food processor, into the ricotta-Pecorino combo (no milk required), the filling remained creamy.

It was time to circle back to the beginning: the tomato sauce. The placeholder recipe we had been working with called for sautéing onions and garlic, adding canned diced tomatoes and seasonings, and simmering the sauce for at least an hour. It wasn't all that onerous, but our success with the eggplant and the filling had raised the bar, and now we wanted a sauce that could be made from start to finish while the eggplant had its 30-minute stint in the oven.

Diced tomatoes don't break down easily because they're treated with calcium chloride during processing to help them keep their chunky shape, hence the lengthy cooking time. We briefly flirted with the idea of going with fresh summer tomatoes, but blanching, peeling, and cooking them down wasn't consistent with our goals of speed and simplicity. Instead we swapped the diced tomatoes for more-tender canned whole tomatoes (where the calcium chloride works only on the exterior of the tomato) that we chopped roughly, and the sauce came together in about half the time. To trim a few more minutes, we stripped the sauce down to the bare bones: just garlic, oregano, tomatoes, and a pinch of red pepper flakes. This simpler sauce fit perfectly into the more streamlined dish.

Between ditching the salting, trading frying for baking, and making a quick rather than long-simmered sauce, we had saved loads of time on prep, but it occurred

to us that we could save a bit more time on cleanup, too. We made the sauce in a 12-inch skillet instead of a saucepan, and we nestled the filled eggplant rolls directly in the simmering sauce. When the rolls had begun to warm through, we moved the whole skillet to the broiler instead of the oven.

After about 5 minutes, the eggplant was nicely browned and the sauce was bubbly and hot. We let our creation cool slightly and then crowned it with an additional dusting of Pecorino and a sprinkling of basil before serving directly from the skillet.

No one would mistake this light, fresh skillet supper for rich and heavy eggplant Parmesan. The eggplant truly shines, and the cheese and sauce complement it rather than weigh it down. And the best part might just be how easy it is to make—no one will ever blame us for taking advantage of a cook's precious time.

Eggplant Involtini
SERVES 4 TO 6

Select shorter, wider eggplants for this recipe. Part-skim ricotta may be used, but do not use fat-free ricotta. Serve the eggplant with crusty bread and a salad.

2 large eggplants (1½ pounds each), peeled

6 tablespoons vegetable oil

Kosher salt and pepper

2 garlic cloves, minced

¼ teaspoon dried oregano

Pinch red pepper flakes

1 (28-ounce) can whole peeled tomatoes, drained with juice reserved, chopped coarse

1 slice hearty white sandwich bread, torn into 1-inch pieces

8 ounces (1 cup) whole-milk ricotta cheese

1½ ounces grated Pecorino Romano cheese (¾ cup)

5 tablespoons chopped fresh basil

1 tablespoon lemon juice

1. Slice each eggplant lengthwise into ½-inch-thick planks (you should have 12 planks). Trim rounded surface from each end piece so it lies flat.

2. Adjust 1 oven rack to lower-middle position and second rack 8 inches from broiler element. Heat oven to 375 degrees. Line 2 rimmed baking sheets with parchment paper and spray generously with vegetable oil spray. Arrange eggplant slices in single layer on prepared sheets. Brush 1 side of eggplant slices with 2½ tablespoons oil and sprinkle with ½ teaspoon salt and ¼ teaspoon pepper. Flip eggplant slices and brush with 2½ tablespoons oil and sprinkle with ½ teaspoon salt and ¼ teaspoon pepper. Bake until tender and lightly browned, 30 to 35 minutes, switching and rotating sheets halfway through baking. Let cool for 5 minutes. Using thin spatula, flip each slice over. Heat broiler.

3. While eggplant cooks, heat remaining 1 tablespoon oil in 12-inch broiler-safe skillet over medium-low heat until just shimmering. Add garlic, oregano, pepper flakes, and ½ teaspoon salt and cook, stirring occasionally, until fragrant, about 30 seconds. Stir in tomatoes and their juice. Increase heat to high and bring to simmer. Reduce heat to medium-low and simmer until thickened, about 15 minutes. Cover and set aside.

4. Pulse bread in food processor until finely ground, 10 to 15 pulses. Combine bread crumbs, ricotta, ½ cup Pecorino, ¼ cup basil, lemon juice, and ½ teaspoon salt in medium bowl.

5. With widest ends of eggplant slices facing you, evenly distribute ricotta mixture on bottom third of each slice. Gently roll up each eggplant slice and place seam side down in tomato sauce.

6. Bring sauce to simmer over medium heat. Simmer for 5 minutes. Transfer skillet to oven and broil until eggplant is well browned and cheese is heated through, 5 to 10 minutes. Sprinkle with remaining ¼ cup Pecorino and let stand for 5 minutes. Sprinkle with remaining 1 tablespoon basil and serve.

BAKE, DON'T FRY

We trade the salting, breading, and frying steps that classic recipes employ for a lighter, no-fuss approach.

1. SLICE: Lay each peeled eggplant on its side and slice it lengthwise into ½-inch-thick planks (you should have 12 planks).

2. BAKE: Brush both sides of slices with oil, season with salt and pepper, and bake until tender and lightly browned, about 30 minutes.

3. STUFF AND ROLL: With widest end facing you, place portion of ricotta mixture on bottom third of slice. Roll into cylinder.

BREAD CRUMBS: OUTSIDE TO INSIDE

In most *involtini* recipes bread crumbs are used to coat the eggplant, but in our version we put them in the cheese. The bread crumbs keep the filling creamy by preventing the Pecorino Romano proteins from linking tightly.

FUSILLI WITH RICOTTA AND SPINACH

✔ **WHY THIS RECIPE WORKS:** Pasta like manicotti and tortellini are often stuffed with a creamy mixture of ricotta and fresh spinach. The combination is irresistible, but making fresh stuffed pasta is a work-intensive project. We decided to turn this dish inside out for a weeknight meal that would make the most of these classic flavors. To keep the ricotta texture and flavor distinct (and to prevent the graininess that comes from heating ricotta), we opted to add most of it in dollops over the finished dish rather than fold it into the sauce. To keep the spinach bright and green (and eliminate the tedious task of blanching and squeezing it dry), we cooked it very briefly in the pot along with the pasta. For complexity and balance, we added lots of minced garlic, cayenne pepper, nutmeg, lemon juice and zest, and Parmesan cheese to our sauce.

EVERY SO OFTEN WE COME ACROSS A RECIPE THAT teams simple boiled pasta with spinach and ricotta as a sort of quick "deconstructed" version of stuffed shells, manicotti, or ravioli. Since the labor involved in cooking a stuffed pasta dish makes it the sort of project that most of us reserve for special occasions, a no-fuss dish created by simply tossing the same ingredients together has a lot of appeal.

But when we gave a few recipes of this sort a try, our enthusiasm faded. The authors all seemed to forget that the stuffed pasta is only one component of the dish: Ravioli and the like are typically served with a bright marinara, a meaty ragu, or even a nutty browned butter. When you take these contrasting flavors away, the dish loses complexity, and the richness of the ricotta hijacks the mild spinach and pasta. Our goal was to punch up the flavor to make up for what a sauce contributes to a stuffed pasta.

FUSILLI WITH RICOTTA AND SPINACH

Most of the recipes we found employ one of two basic methods: The first calls for buzzing raw spinach and ricotta in a food processor along with bold ingredients like garlic, Parmesan, and toasted nuts to create a "pesto." The uncooked puree is then tossed with hot pasta just prior to serving. The second approach requires sautéing chopped, blanched spinach with aromatics; stirring in the ricotta; and cooking it just long enough to create a uniform sauce. Unfortunately, the pesto tasted neither of mineral-y spinach nor of milky ricotta. Pureed together, the two components seemed to cancel each other out. The result of the latter method also tasted somewhat wan, but we could at least discern the ingredients, so that's where we began our testing.

First we set out to tackle the sauce's gritty, chalky texture. Heat causes the ricotta curds to release water and coagulate, rendering the sauce grainy. We tried cooking the cheese as briefly as possible to prevent this from happening, but it doesn't take much heat to induce the effect, and we had to at least bring the sauce to a simmer before dressing the pasta.

Adding cream would minimize grittiness (the fat in the cream coats the milk proteins in the cheese to slow down coagulation), but to prevent curdling entirely, we had to either add an excessive amount of cream or dial down the ricotta to the point that its presence was lost completely. Then we had a better idea: Simply withhold most of the cheese and dollop it onto the finished dish. This would prevent graininess while keeping the ricotta presence distinct.

To bring out the best from the cheese, we seasoned it with extra-virgin olive oil, salt, and pepper. And to make sure it didn't go onto the pasta cold, we let it sit out on the counter to warm up to room temperature while the pasta cooked. After combining a small amount of ricotta with cream and using it to dress the pasta, we spooned the remaining seasoned ricotta on top of the dish. This worked perfectly: Instead of a dilute amount of cheese in each bite, tasters got concentrated hits here and there, much as they would when eating filled pasta.

With the ricotta sorted out, we turned our attention to the spinach. We wanted to use baby spinach since

RICOTTA

Originally crafted from the whey by-product that forms during the making of Pecorino Romano cheese, ricotta cheese has garnered fame on its own as a white, cushiony filling for baked pasta dishes. As ricotta has gained global popularity, however, preservation methods used by many large-scale manufacturers have turned these once fluffy, buttery, sweet curds into chalky, sour spreads. We are not big fans of most supermarket ricottas, as they are packed with gums and other stabilizers to guarantee a shelf life of weeks. Our favorite brand is **Calabro**, whose curds are fresh drawn from nothing other than Vermont farm whole milk, skim milk, a starter, and a sprinkle of salt. Granted, its shelf life spans only a matter of days, but one spoonful should be enough to guarantee its quick disappearance from your fridge. If you can't find this particular brand, check labels and look for another fresh ricotta without gums or preservatives. We prefer whole-milk ricotta but part-skim ricotta is fine. Do not try to use nonfat ricotta, as it is very dry and flavorless.

Fusilli with Ricotta and Spinach

SERVES 4 TO 6

We like fusilli for this recipe since its corkscrew shape does a nice job of trapping the sauce, but penne and campanelle also work well.

11 ounces (1⅓ cups) whole-milk ricotta cheese
3 tablespoons extra-virgin olive oil
   Salt and pepper
1 pound fusilli
1 pound (16 cups) baby spinach, chopped coarse
4 garlic cloves, minced
¼ teaspoon ground nutmeg
⅛ teaspoon cayenne pepper
¼ cup heavy cream
1 teaspoon grated lemon zest plus 2 teaspoons juice
1 ounce Parmesan cheese, grated (½ cup), plus extra for serving

it requires very little prep. Figuring that it was worth trying the most straightforward approach to cooking it, too, we simply threw the coarsely chopped leaves into the pot with the pasta (curly fusilli nicely trapped the sauce) once it was al dente. This worked like a charm: In just 30 seconds, the spinach was wilted yet still brilliant green.

To make the flavors pop, we opted for a healthy dose of sautéed garlic mixed into the ricotta and cream mixture, along with sprinklings of nutmeg and cayenne pepper for an underlying warmth. A generous dusting of grated Parmesan cheese provided additional depth, and lemon zest and lemon juice introduced welcome brightness. Finally, to produce a nice, velvety texture, we employed a dead-simple trick we've used in the past: Let the dressed pasta sit for a few minutes, stirring it occasionally, to draw out some of the pasta's starches. Together, these elements combined to give us a dish that was as easy to make as it was delicious.

1. Whisk 1 cup ricotta, 1 tablespoon oil, ¼ teaspoon pepper, and ⅛ teaspoon salt in medium bowl until smooth; set aside.

2. Bring 4 quarts water to boil in large pot. Add pasta and 1 tablespoon salt and cook, stirring often, until al dente. Reserve 1 cup cooking water. Stir spinach into pot with pasta and cook until wilted, about 30 seconds. Drain pasta and spinach and return them to pot.

3. While pasta cooks, heat remaining 2 tablespoons oil, garlic, nutmeg, and cayenne in small saucepan over medium heat until fragrant, about 1 minute. Remove pan from heat and whisk in remaining ⅓ cup ricotta, cream, lemon zest and juice, and ¾ teaspoon salt until smooth.

4. Add ricotta-cream mixture and Parmesan to pasta and toss to combine. Let pasta rest, tossing frequently, until sauce has thickened slightly and coats pasta, 2 to 4 minutes, adjusting consistency with reserved cooking water as needed. Transfer pasta to serving platter, dot evenly with reserved ricotta mixture, and serve, passing extra Parmesan separately.

RATING PROSCIUTTO

Let's face it: Italian food has more to offer than just great vegetarian entrées. Lately, pre-sliced prosciutto has made an appearance in many supermarket deli cases. We wondered if these packaged products (all made outside Italy) could match the depth of flavor and soft texture that we expect from Italian prosciutto that's sliced to order. We rounded up nine products, with per-pound prices ranging from just over $19 to a whopping $58-and-change. We tried each one plain and also seared in chicken saltimbocca. A few boasted some of the complexity and silky texture that we expect from the Italian imports. We found that longer aging produced the most complex flavor, and tasters preferred those products with no added flavorings or nitrates. Sodium was another key factor in our likes and dislikes. Most of our favorite prosciutti (including our winner) were salty. Finally, low-moisture hams that were sliced thinner delivered that ideal combination of complex flavor and supple texture. Our winner from Volpi was worthy of any salumi plate and can be quickly picked up at any supermarket. Sodium amounts are per 1-ounce serving. Products are listed in order of preference. See AmericasTestKitchen.com for updates and complete tasting results.

RECOMMENDED

VOLPI Traditional Prosciutto
PRICE: 3 oz for $5.75
($1.92 per oz/$30.67 per pound)
MADE IN: Missouri **AGED:** 9 months
INGREDIENTS: Pork, sea salt
SODIUM: 771 mg **FAT:** 15.64%
MOISTURE: 45.91% **SLICE THICKNESS:** 0.5 mm
COMMENTS: "Tender" with a "nice porky complexity" and a "salty punch" that came from its high sodium level, our top choice has an "ultra-supple" texture that was highlighted by the meat being sliced very thinly.

DEL DUCA Prosciutto
PRICE: 3 oz for $3.59
($1.20 per oz/$19.15 per pound) **BEST BUY**
MADE IN: Rhode Island **AGED:** Just over 1 year
INGREDIENTS: Pork, salt
SODIUM: 522 mg **FAT:** 12.58%
MOISTURE: 51.61% **SLICE THICKNESS:** 0.9 mm
COMMENTS: With a "nice porky sweetness" and "clean" but "intense" flavor, this prosciutto was one of the most thickly sliced in the lineup, but its ample moisture also gave it a "supple," "silky" texture.

CITTERIO All Natural Prosciutto
PRICE: 4 oz for $6.99
($1.75 per oz/$27.96 per pound)
MADE IN: Pennsylvania **AGED:** 9 to 11 months
INGREDIENTS: Pork, sea salt
SODIUM: 857 mg **FAT:** 9.90%
MOISTURE: 53.92%
SLICE THICKNESS: 0.58 mm
COMMENTS: This product's "salty, sweet, oaky" flavor was deemed "classic" and "very pleasant." Citterio's thin, tender slices became extra-crispy when fried in chicken saltimbocca, although its flavor contribution in that dish was considered "mild."

RECOMMENDED WITH RESERVATIONS

LA QUERCIA Prosciutto Americano
PRICE: 3 oz for $10.99 plus shipping
($3.66 per ounce/$58.61 per pound)
MADE IN: Iowa **AGED:** 9 to 12 months
INGREDIENTS: Pork, sea salt
SODIUM: 384 mg **FAT:** 17.36%
MOISTURE: 44.12% **SLICE THICKNESS:** 0.75 mm
COMMENTS: There were near-unanimous raves for the complex flavor of this prosciutto: "rich, with notes of toasty nuts, wine, and a lovely sweet finish." But tasters found it "dry", "tough" and "leathery"—whether plain or in saltimbocca.

NOT RECOMMENDED

APPLEGATE NATURALS Prosciutto
PRICE: 4 oz for $6.99
($1.75 per oz/$27.96 per pound)
MADE IN: Canada **AGED:** 6 to 9 months
INGREDIENTS: Pork, salt, spice
SODIUM: 729 mg **FAT:** 15.62%
MOISTURE: 49.09% **SLICE THICKNESS:** 1 mm
COMMENTS: "Chewy" was the oft-repeated description of this ham. While some tasters liked its "sweet porkiness," others found that it tasted "supermild," not to mention "a bit gummy." In saltimbocca, its inclusion of unspecified spice flavoring may have helped remind one taster of "Domino's pepperoni."

DIETZ & WATSON Prosciutto
PRICE: 3 oz for $5.49
($1.83 per oz/$29.28 per pound)
MADE IN: Pennsylvania **AGED:** Up to 1 year
INGREDIENTS: Pork ham, salt, contains less than 2% of sugar, sodium nitrate, natural flavorings, sodium ascorbate, sodium nitrite, lactic acid starter culture
SODIUM: 397 mg **FAT:** 5.78%
MOISTURE: 58.49% **SLICE THICKNESS:** 0.46 mm
COMMENTS: The lactic acid starter culture, along with the inclusion of nitrates, doomed this prosciutto. One taster summed it up: "Too lean, and tastes funky and tangy like salami." High moisture and paper-thin slicing made its texture "wet," though it still crisped up well in saltimbocca.

Dinner in the Mediterranean

Reserving some of the olive oil–lemon marinade to mix with the chicken after grilling makes for a brighter, more pronounced flavor in our souvlaki.

MEDITERRANEAN FOOD IS FAMOUSLY FRESH AND FLAVORFUL, REDOLENT with bright lemon, rich olive oil, and fresh herbs. So why is it that here in the United States, many "Mediterranean" recipes turn out dull, heavy, and bland? Here, we'll explain how we revitalized two recipes to put together a summery dinner that reflects all the best qualities of this popular cuisine.

Chicken souvlaki works great on a home grill—the small pieces of chicken cook quickly, and a few simple add-ons, like soft pita bread and cool *tzatziki* sauce, make it a meal. But the traditional method of cooking chunks of chicken on skewers is hardly foolproof. To get our chicken to cook evenly and boast bold, lemony flavor, we had to rethink our ingredient list and our marinade.

Supermarket versions of tabbouleh usually aren't worth buying, but we think this herb-heavy salad deserves a place on the table. We wanted tabbouleh bursting with peppery parsley and crisp mint, balanced with a smattering of flavorful bulgur. To cram as much flavor as possible into so few ingredients, we had to stop pouring a key element down the drain. With dishes this good, you won't need to leave home to experience the best the Mediterranean has to offer.

GRILLED CHICKEN SOUVLAKI

GRILLED CHICKEN SOUVLAKI

✔ **WHY THIS RECIPE WORKS:** Nicely charred, lemony chicken drizzled with creamy *tzatziki* sauce and wrapped in a soft pita makes a perfect summer weeknight meal, but achieving evenly cooked, moist chicken on skewers can be a challenge. We started by brining the chicken to help it retain moisture and to season it throughout. To keep the pieces on the ends of the skewers from cooking faster than the pieces in the middle, we used chunks of red onion and bell pepper as "shields." We reserved a bit of our lemony marinade mixture to toss with the chicken after grilling for a bright, fresh hit of flavor. We warmed and softened the pitas by moistening them and steaming them in a foil packet on the grill. Our cool tzatziki made a perfect counterpoint to our charred chicken.

"SOUVLAKI" IS BASICALLY A GREEK TERM FOR MEAT grilled on a stick. Just about every meat-eating culture has a version, but when it comes to being documented masters (if not the originators) of the technique, Greek credentials are hard to beat. Homer's *Iliad* and *Odyssey* are rich with detailed accounts of the heroes skewering meat and cooking it over fire, souvlaki-style.

In modern Greece, souvlaki is usually made with pork, but at Greek restaurants here in the United States, boneless, skinless chicken breast is common. The chunks of white meat are marinated (often overnight) in a tangy mixture of lemon juice, olive oil, oregano, parsley, and sometimes garlic before being skewered and grilled until nicely charred. Souvlaki may be served with rice and cooked vegetables or a salad, but just as often the chicken is placed on a lightly grilled pita, slathered with a yogurt-based *tzatziki* sauce, wrapped snugly, and eaten out of hand. This sandwich is a perfect way to eat souvlaki: The creamy sauce, freshened with herbs and cucumber, complements the char of the chicken, and the soft pita pulls it all together.

At least as appealing as the dish itself is how easily it translates to a home grill. The ingredients are readily available, and small chunks of boneless chicken cook quickly, making souvlaki a prime candidate for weeknight backyard fare. We just needed to come up with a good recipe.

Because boneless, skinless chicken breasts easily turn dry and leathery on the grill, we wondered if we could buck tradition and substitute fattier and more forgiving boneless thighs instead. But when we experimented with grilling cubes of both thighs and breasts (marinated overnight first), wrapping them in warm pitas with a placeholder yogurt sauce, we had to admit that the richer flavor of the thighs actually seemed ill-suited for souvlaki. In the end, we decided to stick with white meat, which had a cleaner flavor that melded much more companionably with the other components.

Still, the breast meat was bland. It was also mushy on the outside and dry within, and we recognized that the long soak in the acidic marinade was to blame. Tests have shown us that, over time, acid weakens the protein bonds on the surface of meat, which causes that mushy texture. What's more, the marinade never penetrates much below the meat's surface, so its flavor is superficial at best. Bottom line: The long marinating step had to go.

In the next test, we went to the other extreme: We tossed the 1-inch cubes of chicken with lemon juice and olive oil and then immediately skewered and grilled them over very hot coals. It was only a modest success. The pasty exterior was gone, but the meat was still bland and dry, especially those more exposed chunks that had been on either end of each skewer.

So we mixed up a brine. We've long known that soaking meat in a saltwater solution before cooking encourages it to take up extra moisture, and the salt, some of which is also absorbed, not only seasons the meat but also changes its physical structure in such a way that it retains more moisture when cooked. Brining the chicken after cutting it into chunks would be particularly effective, as there would be more exposed surface area in contact with the solution.

We soaked the chicken for 30 minutes while the grill heated and then drained it, patted it dry, and tossed it with olive oil, lemon juice, dried oregano, parsley, and black pepper. We also added a bit of honey, which we had seen in a few souvlaki recipes; we suspected that a sweetener would add complexity and help with browning. The one thing we left out was garlic. In previous tests most of it had fallen off, and what had remained on the meat burned. We'd try to make up for it in the tzatziki. In the meantime, we threaded the dressed chunks onto skewers and grilled them over very hot coals for about 15 minutes, at which point they were cooked through and well charred.

The brine had helped, as most of the chicken was now moist, but those end pieces were still parched. That brought up a fundamental problem with the meat-on-a-stick method: Meat that's packed tightly on a skewer doesn't cook evenly. The middle pieces are insulated from the fierce heat, while the exposed end pieces cook faster. Poking around with a thermometer, we found that the end pieces reached the target 160 degrees at least 4 minutes before the middle ones did.

Spacing the pieces at intervals instead of packing them snugly helped even out the cooking, but it required more skewers (which meant more to watch and turn). Also, since the chunks weren't packed tightly, they spun around when we tried turning the skewers.

We came up with a better idea. Instead of packing only meat onto the skewers, we started each one with a stack of bell pepper chunks, then threaded on the chicken pieces, and finished each skewer with two chunks of red onion. The vegetables functioned as shields, protecting the end pieces of chicken from the heat so they cooked at the same rate as the middle pieces. A bonus: They added more char flavor to the wrap and broke up the all-meat filling with some crunch.

What was missing from the chicken was the lemon punch that we associate with souvlaki, so we made a quick adjustment. Instead of using all the lemon–olive oil mixture to coat the raw chicken, we reserved ¼ cup of it to use after cooking. When the skewers came off the grill, we unloaded the chicken and vegetables into a bowl with the reserved sauce. Covering the bowl and letting the contents steam for a bit to absorb the sauce resulted in bright-tasting chicken and vegetables.

Next up: the sauce. Tzatziki is plain yogurt flavored with garlic, cucumber, herbs, salt, and maybe a bit of acid like lemon juice or vinegar. Since raw garlic can be too assertive, we used a trick we discovered when making Caesar salad dressing: grating the garlic to a paste and briefly steeping it in lemon juice before adding both to the sauce. The acid converts the harsh-tasting garlic compound, allicin, into mellower compounds in the same way that cooking does.

Thick Greek yogurt is typically used and the cucumbers, either grated or minced, are usually pretreated with salt to remove excess moisture. But the mixture of yogurt and salted cucumbers was so heavy and thick that it dominated the wrap. To thin out the sauce, we skipped salting the cucumbers and relied on the salt in the tzatziki to pull water from the cucumbers into the yogurt as it sat (from that point on, we prepared the sauce before the chicken). When it came time to assemble the wraps, the tzatziki had a thinner consistency.

Finally, we made a subtle, but important, change to how we handled the pita bread. Traditionally, souvlaki is wrapped in soft pocketless pitas, which are hard to find at regular supermarkets. The trouble with conventional pocketed pitas was that when we warmed them on the grill the way some Greek cooks do, they turned dry and brittle and were nearly impossible to fold around the cooked chicken. Brushing them with oil and water before grilling didn't help.

We were happy to trade char on the pita (the chicken had plenty) for a pillowy texture, so we wrapped a stack of four pitas tightly in foil after moistening the top and bottom surfaces of the stack with water. We placed the packet on a cooler side of the grill, so the bread could steam while the chicken cooked. By the time the chicken had rested, the pitas were soft, warm, and floppy—perfect for wrapping.

With our goals of charred, lemony chicken, creamy tzatziki, and soft bread met, we wrapped up our sandwiches, and our testing.

NOTES FROM THE TEST KITCHEN

A VEGETABLE SHIELD

The age-old problem with grilling meat on a stick: The end pieces overcook. We protect the chicken by threading pepper and onion pieces on the ends. The charred vegetables taste great in the sandwich, too.

SOFTENING SUPERMARKET PITA

To soften up dry, tough supermarket pita, we moisten two of the breads with a little water and then stack them on either side of two unmoistened pieces. Then we steam the breads in a foil-wrapped stack on the cooler side of the grill while the cooked chicken rests.

MARINATE TWICE

Briefly soaking the grilled chicken and vegetables in some reserved marinade before wrapping them in a pita rehydrates their dry exteriors and delivers a bright citrus punch.

Grilled Chicken Souvlaki

SERVES 4

This tzatziki is fairly mild; if you like a more assertive flavor, double the garlic. A rasp-style grater makes quick work of turning the garlic into a paste. We like the chicken as a wrap, but you may skip the pita and serve the chicken, vegetables, and tzatziki with rice. You will need four 12-inch metal skewers.

TZATZIKI SAUCE

- 1 tablespoon lemon juice
- 1 small garlic clove, minced to paste
- ¾ cup plain Greek yogurt
- ½ cucumber, peeled, halved lengthwise, seeded, and diced fine (½ cup)
- 3 tablespoons minced fresh mint
- 1 tablespoon minced fresh parsley
- ⅜ teaspoon salt

CHICKEN

- Salt and pepper
- 1½ pounds boneless, skinless chicken breasts, trimmed and cut into 1-inch pieces
- ⅓ cup extra-virgin olive oil
- 2 tablespoons minced fresh parsley
- 1 teaspoon finely grated lemon zest plus ¼ cup juice (2 lemons)
- 1 teaspoon honey
- 1 teaspoon dried oregano
- 1 green bell pepper, quartered, stemmed, seeded, and each quarter cut into 4 chunks
- 1 small red onion, ends trimmed, peeled, halved lengthwise, and each half cut into 4 chunks
- 4 (8-inch) pita breads

1. FOR THE TZATZIKI SAUCE: Whisk lemon juice and garlic together in small bowl. Let stand for 10 minutes. Stir in yogurt, cucumber, mint, parsley, and salt. Cover and set aside.

2. FOR THE CHICKEN: Dissolve 2 tablespoons salt in 1 quart cold water. Submerge chicken in brine, cover, and refrigerate for 30 minutes. While chicken is brining, combine oil, parsley, lemon zest and juice, honey, oregano, and ½ teaspoon pepper in medium bowl. Transfer ¼ cup oil mixture to large bowl and set aside to toss with cooked chicken.

3. Remove chicken from brine and pat dry with paper towels. Toss chicken with remaining oil mixture. Thread 4 pieces of bell pepper, concave side up, onto one 12-inch metal skewer. Thread one-quarter of chicken onto skewer. Thread 2 chunks of onion onto skewer, and place skewer on plate. Repeat skewering remaining chicken and vegetables on 3 more skewers. Lightly moisten 2 pita breads with water. Sandwich 2 unmoistened pita breads between moistened pita breads and wrap stack tightly in lightly greased heavy-duty aluminum foil.

4A. FOR A CHARCOAL GRILL: Open bottom vent completely. Light large chimney starter mounded with charcoal briquettes (7 quarts). When top coals are partially covered with ash, pour evenly over half of grill. Set cooking grate in place, cover, and open lid vent completely. Heat grill until hot, about 5 minutes.

4B. FOR A GAS GRILL: Turn all burners to high, cover, and heat grill until hot, about 15 minutes. Leave primary burner on high and turn off other burner(s).

5. Clean and oil cooking grate. Place skewers on hotter side of grill and cook, turning occasionally, until chicken and vegetables are well browned on all sides and chicken registers 160 degrees, 15 to 20 minutes. Using fork, push chicken and vegetables off skewers into bowl of reserved oil mixture. Stir gently, breaking up onion chunks; cover with foil and let sit for 5 minutes.

6. Meanwhile, place packet of pitas on cooler side of grill. Flip occasionally to heat, about 5 minutes.

7. Lay each warm pita on 12-inch square of foil. Spread each pita with 2 tablespoons tzatziki. Place one-quarter of chicken and vegetables in middle of each pita. Roll into cylindrical shape and serve.

TABBOULEH

☑ **WHY THIS RECIPE WORKS:** At its best, tabbouleh is a light, fresh salad full of the bright flavors of parsley, lemon, and tomato, with textural interest from bulgur. But supermarket versions are usually bland and flavorless. We wanted to find a way to make this meze staple the best it could be. To avoid a soggy salad, we salted the tomatoes, and then used the flavorful liquid (along with a generous squeeze of lemon juice) to soak the bulgur and imbue it with flavor. We used plenty of chopped fresh parsley and mint for a salad with balance and contrast.

TABBOULEH HAS LONG BEEN A MEZE STAPLE IN THE Middle East, but these days it can be found in the refrigerator case of virtually every American supermarket. Its brief (and healthful) ingredient list explains its popularity: Chopped fresh parsley and mint, tomatoes, onion, and bits of nutty bulgur are tossed with lemon and olive oil for a refreshing appetizer or side dish. It all sounds easy enough, but following a recipe or picking up a pint at the market reveals that most versions are hopelessly soggy, with flavor that is either too bold or too bland.

Another problem is that there's no agreement on the correct proportions for tabbouleh. Middle Eastern cooks favor loads of parsley (75 to 90 percent of the salad), only employing a sprinkle of bulgur as a texturally interesting garnish. Most American recipes, on the other hand, invert the proportions, transforming the green salad into an insipid pilaf smattered with herbs. We decided to take a middle-of-the-road approach for a dish that would feature a hefty amount of parsley as well as a decent amount of bulgur.

Bulgur is made by boiling, drying, and grinding wheat kernels, so it only needs to be reconstituted in cool water. But specific advice on how to prepare the grains is all over the map. Rehydration times range from a cursory

TABBOULEH

5 minutes all the way up to several hours. And then there's the amount of liquid: Some recipes call for just enough to plump the grains; others employ the "pasta method," soaking the bulgur in lots of water and then squeezing out the excess.

Working with ½ cup of medium-grind bulgur (the easiest size to find) and first rinsing the grains to remove any detritus, we experimented with innumerable combinations of time and amount of water. Our initial finding: The grains required at least 90 minutes to tenderize fully. Second: The less liquid we used the better the texture. Soaking the bulgur in excess water only made it heavy, damp, and bland. In the end, a mere ¼ cup of liquid was enough for ½ cup of dried bulgur. The grains absorbed the liquid almost instantly and then slowly swelled into 1 cup of tender, fluffy grains as they rested.

With the method settled, we switched to soaking the bulgur in lemon juice instead of water, as some cookbooks recommend. This was a no-brainer—eliminating water from the recipe only made sense for a salad that can taste washed out.

Next up: parsley. To our 1 cup of reconstituted bulgur, we added 1½ cups of chopped parsley and ½ cup of chopped mint. These quantities still put the emphasis on the bright, peppery parsley but didn't discount the lemony bulgur and refreshing mint.

As for the rest of the salad, 6 tablespoons of extra-virgin olive oil tempered the tart lemon juice, and three chopped ripe tomatoes and two sliced scallions (preferred over red or white onion) rounded out the mix. A smidge of cayenne pepper along with the usual salt and pepper added zing. Finally, we considered garlic and cucumbers. Tasters soundly rejected these additions, complaining that they detracted from the salad's clean flavor (in the case of the former) and overall texture (in the case of the latter).

We set out pita bread wedges and romaine lettuce leaves (traditional accompaniments) and summoned tasters for feedback. They were happy enough with the texture, but the flavors of the salad, they lamented, weren't cohesive—tabbouleh features bold ingredients

and this method wasn't giving them time to blend. This was easy to resolve: We simply reworked our method to give the bulgur a chance to absorb more of the liquids—namely, olive oil and juices from the tomatoes—in the salad. Soaking the bulgur for 30 to 40 minutes, until it began to soften, and then combining it with the remaining ingredients and letting it sit for an hour until fully tender gave everything time to mingle, resulting in a perfectly well-balanced dish.

We had just one final issue to deal with. Over the course of testing, we had noticed that depending on variety, the tomatoes contributed different amounts of liquid to the tabbouleh, sometimes diluting its flavor and making it soupy. The solution? Salting. Tossing the tomatoes in salt and letting them drain in a colander drew out their moisture, precluding sogginess. We were about to pat ourselves on the back when a light bulb went on: By discarding the tomato juice, we were literally pouring flavor down the drain. What if we reserved this savory liquid and used it to soak the bulgur? For our next try, we put a bowl under the colander to catch the juices

and prepared a salad using 2 tablespoons of the tomato liquid (along with an equal amount of lemon juice) to soak the bulgur, whisking the remaining 2 tablespoons of lemon juice with oil for the dressing. At last, here was tabbouleh with fresh, penetrating flavor and a light texture that would make cooks—from anywhere around the globe—proud.

Tabbouleh

SERVES 4

Serve the salad with the crisp inner leaves of romaine lettuce and wedges of pita bread.

- 3 tomatoes, cored and cut into ½-inch pieces
  Salt and pepper
- ½ cup medium-grind bulgur
- ¼ cup lemon juice (2 lemons)
- 6 tablespoons extra-virgin olive oil
- ⅛ teaspoon cayenne pepper
- 1½ cups chopped fresh parsley
- ½ cup chopped fresh mint
- 2 scallions, sliced thin

1. Toss tomatoes and ¼ teaspoon salt in large bowl. Transfer to fine-mesh strainer, set strainer in bowl, and let stand for 30 minutes, tossing occasionally.

2. Rinse bulgur in fine-mesh strainer under cold running water. Drain well and transfer to second bowl. Stir in 2 tablespoons lemon juice and 2 tablespoons juice from draining tomatoes. Let stand until grains are beginning to soften, 30 to 40 minutes.

3. Whisk oil, cayenne, ¼ teaspoon salt and remaining 2 tablespoons lemon juice together in large bowl. Add parsley, mint, scallions, drained tomatoes, and soaked bulgur; toss gently to combine. Cover and let stand at room temperature until flavors have blended and bulgur is tender, about 1 hour. Toss to recombine, season with salt and pepper to taste, and serve immediately.

RATING MIXING BOWLS

A good bowl should be steady, durable, and comfortable to use. To find the perfect small, medium, and large bowls, we scooped up three stainless-steel sets and four sets made of tempered glass (glass that has undergone a mechanical strengthening process to increase its impact and thermal resistance), all priced from $13.19 to $59.99. We subjected the bowls to a variety of core tasks. In the small bowls, we whisked oil into vinegar to make dressing. In the medium and large bowls we mixed up muffin and pancake batters. We also used the large bowls to mix bread dough and the medium bowls to melt chocolate in a double boiler, with the bowl set over a saucepan of simmering water. Testers disliked bowls with walls that were too tall or steep, or materials that were too heavy for comfortable use. Models with wide, grippable rims, gently curved bowls, and steady bases that didn't shift during vigorous mixing won top marks. In the end we chose one stainless-steel winner and one glass winner. The metal Vollrath set is lightweight and great at conducting heat while the durable Pyrex set is transparent, which lets you check for pockets of unmixed ingredients, and it can be used in the microwave. Products are listed in order of preference. See AmericasTestKitchen.com for updates and complete testing results.

STAINLESS-STEEL BOWLS

HIGHLY RECOMMENDED

VOLLRATH Economy Stainless Steel Mixing Bowls
MATERIAL: Stainless steel
SOLD AS: Open stock
SIZES TESTED: 1½ qt ($2.90, model 47932); 3 qt ($4.50, model 47933); 5 qt ($6.90, model 47935)
WEIGHTS: 4⅝ oz (1½ qt); 6⅛ oz (3 qt); 8⅞ oz (5 qt)
PERFORMANCE: ★★★ **EASE OF USE:** ★★★ **DURABILITY:** ★★★
COMMENTS: The broad, shallow shape of these lightweight, inexpensive bowls put food within easy reach.

RECOMMENDED

CUISINART Set of 3 Stainless Steel Mixing Bowls with Lids
MATERIAL: Stainless steel with plastic lids
SOLD AS: Three-bowl set ($29.99, model CTG-00-SMB)
SIZES TESTED: 1½ qt; 3 qt; 5 qt
WEIGHTS: 9¾ oz (1½ qt); 13¾ oz (3 qt); 1 lb, 3⅝ oz (5 qt)
PERFORMANCE: ★★★ **EASE OF USE:** ★★ **DURABILITY:** ★★★
COMMENTS: Though their relatively tall and narrow build made it a little challenging to access their contents, these bowls were lightweight and sported a generous rim which made them easy to grasp.

NOT RECOMMENDED

OXO Good Grips Stainless Steel Mixing Bowl Set
MATERIAL: Stainless-steel interior, white plastic exterior with non-skid Santoprene base
SOLD AS: Three-bowl set ($59.99, model 1107600V1)
SIZES TESTED: 1½ qt; 3 qt; 5 qt
WEIGHTS: 11½ oz (1½ qt); 1 lb, 3 oz (3 qt); 1 lb, 10¾ oz (5 qt)
PERFORMANCE: ★ **EASE OF USE:** ★½ **DURABILITY:** ★★★
COMMENTS: These bowls were not user-friendly—and not worth the high price. Their small bases spun as we mixed and we could not use them in a double boiler.

GLASS BOWLS

HIGHLY RECOMMENDED

PYREX Smart Essentials Mixing Bowl Set with Colored Lids
MATERIAL: Tempered glass with plastic lids
SOLD AS: Four-bowl set ($13.19, model 1086053); or open stock
SIZES TESTED: 1 qt; 2½ qt; 4 qt
WEIGHTS: 1 lb, 3½ oz (1 qt); 2 lb, 4¼ oz (2½ qt); 3 lb, 7⅜ oz (4 qt)
PERFORMANCE: ★★★ **EASE OF USE:** ★★★ **DURABILITY:** ★★★
COMMENTS: Even though these bowls were heavy, they never felt cumbersome, thanks to their gently curved walls and easy-to-grip rims. Tight-fitting lids kept food well protected.

RECOMMENDED

ARC INTERNATIONAL LUMINARC 10 Piece Stackable Bowl Set
MATERIAL: Tempered glass
SOLD AS: Ten-bowl set ($29.75, model E4371)
SIZES TESTED: 1 qt (5½ in); 3 qt (9 in); 4½ qt (10¼ in)
WEIGHTS: 15⅛ oz (1 qt); 2 lb, 1⅛ oz (3 qt); 3 lb, ⅜ oz (4½ qt)
PERFORMANCE: ★★½ **EASE OF USE:** ★★ **DURABILITY:** ★★★
COMMENTS: These shallow, wide bowls were easy to navigate with a whisk or a spatula. They were also one of the lighter glass sets, although they would have been easier to grip if they'd had rims instead of food-trapping collars.

NOT RECOMMENDED

ANCHOR Hocking Mixing Bowls with Red Plastic Lids
MATERIAL: Tempered glass with plastic lids
SOLD AS: Four-bowl set ($21.99, model 918508K) or open stock
SIZES TESTED: 1 qt; 2½ qt; 4 qt
WEIGHTS: 1 lb, 6⅜ oz (1 qt); 2 lb, 7⅝ oz (2½ qt); 3 lb, 9⅝ oz (4 qt)
PERFORMANCE: ★ **EASE OF USE:** ½ **DURABILITY:** ★½
COMMENTS: The weight of these hefty bowls made them challenging to handle. Reaching over their high sides was a struggle.

Beefing Up Mexican Favorites

*A braising liquid enriched
with beer, vinegar, garlic,
and ancho chiles infuses
our* carne deshebrada *with
complex flavor and makes
a perfect base for a silky,
meaty sauce.*

AUTHENTIC MEXICAN FOOD IS A FAR CRY FROM THE OVERSTUFFED AND over-cheesed burritos and enchiladas found in many restaurants. Here, we'll introduce you to two Mexican classics that will change the way you think about Mexican food: *carne asada,* a well-charred, thin steak eaten with a variety of sides; and *carne deshebrada,* a traditional shredded beef taco filling.

Carne asada was invented in the 1940s at the Tampico Club in Mexico City. Platters consisted of strips of beef jerky, folded enchiladas, beans, and *queso fresco*; later, the jerky was traded out for fresh grilled beef. We wanted to capture the original essence of the dish, but pare it down to make it more approachable. We started by choosing the best cut of meat for the job—but that was only half the battle.

Saucy, spicy carne deshebrada is the perfect Mexican comfort food. The beef is gently braised, then shredded and added to a sauce before being served with soft corn tortillas. But traditional methods produced uninspiring results. Our goal was to develop shredded beef tacos full of big, bold flavors that could compete with even the best taqueria versions.

MEXICAN-STYLE GRILLED STEAK

✔ WHY THIS RECIPE WORKS: Traditionally, well-charred Mexican carne asada is served on a platter with a bevy of sides. To create a recipe for a satisfying, well-balanced carne asada platter, we started with skirt steak. Since skirt steak is tender and juicy when cooked to medium, we had plenty of time to create a nice char on the exterior without overcooking the interior. We eschewed the standard lime juice marinade in favor of a dry salting to promote faster browning on the grill. To speed up charring even more and create a large enough area of concentrated heat to cook all four steaks at once, we cut the bottom from a disposable aluminum roasting pan and used it to corral the coals. For heady garlic flavor, we treated the cooked steaks like bruschetta, rubbing their rough crusts with a smashed garlic clove. To round out the platter, we whipped up a quick red chile salsa and a speedy batch of smooth, creamy refried beans by starting with canned pintos and rendering bacon fat.

THESE DAYS CARNE ASADA USUALLY REFERS TO A supercharred, thin steak, but traditionally the dish involves a platter of food. Created around 1940 at the Tampico Club in Mexico City, carne asada began as a plate of fried strips of lime-and-salt-seasoned beef jerky, folded enchiladas, beans, and queso fresco. At some point a fresh grilled or seared steak was swapped in and the number of sides was upped. Thus carne asada *de Tampico* was born.

For our version, we wanted to stick close to the original while keeping it approachable for the home cook. A juicy, thin, well-charred steak was a must, and we settled on two extras: a salsa that would complement the meat and quick refried beans.

Mexican cookbooks are divided on the best cut for the job. Some take the thriftier route, calling for shell steak or chuck roast, but pricier tenderloin and strip steak appear, too. We tested them all, sliced or pounded to ¼ inch thick, marinated in salt and lime juice, and grilled until charred. Inexpensive cuts may have been ideal for the jerky version, but their tough connective tissue and pockets of sinew and fat made them a flop for the update. Supertender steaks didn't fare much better. While we weren't cooking any of the steaks to well-done as a number of traditional recipes suggest, to get good charring on a thin steak, medium was the most realistic goal. Cooked to this degree, both tenderloin and strip were inevitably dry and mealy. Flank steak was better, but it was hard to pound thin enough, so it also fell out of the running.

At the top of the heap were skirt steak and sirloin steak tips. Not only do these cuts have a beefier flavor, but because of their muscle structure, they were tender when grilled to medium. In the end, skirt steak won out for both flavor and texture, and since it's inherently thin, all we needed to do was give it a few good whacks with a meat pounder.

Next we focused on the marinade. Purist recipes call for lime juice and maybe salt. Outside this circle, recipes go to the other extreme, calling for everything from wine, herbs, and garlic to cumin, chiles, and even soy sauce. We tried every combination that we found in print. The verdict? Steaks bathed in unexpected ingredients like red wine and soy sauce garnered few fans. Our tasters liked simple—though not dead simple. While salt and lime alone were OK, a little warmth from cumin and sharpness from garlic were welcome. A 45-minute soak allowed the salt to penetrate the meat, helping make it more tender and juicy, but any longer and the acidic mixture broke down the structure and made the meat mushy. When time was up, we removed the steaks from the marinade, patted them dry, and fired up the grill.

For the grill setup, we needed a ripping-hot fire to ensure that the meat charred well before the interior overcooked. Starting with a full chimney starter (about 6 quarts of charcoal briquettes) was essential. First we tried steeply banking the coals on one side to put

MEXICAN-STYLE GRILLED STEAK

concentrated heat close to the cooking grate, but with the coals packed into such a small footprint, we couldn't cook more than one steak at a time. We needed coals mounded into a relatively thick layer for intense heat but spread out just enough to cook all the steaks at once. Arranging them just so was too fussy; we needed something to corral the coals.

A disposable aluminum roasting pan seemed like just the answer, but even when we punched numerous holes in the bottom to allow for airflow, the heat was tempered too much. We eventually grabbed kitchen shears and cut the bottom out, leaving just the pan collar to contain the coals. This setup delivered the fastest browning yet—about 4 minutes per side—but we still ended up with overcooked meat. We had a hunch that our marinade might be part of the problem.

For browning to kick into high gear, the surface of a steak must dry out. The soaking step was introducing unwanted moisture, so we ditched the marinade and instead treated the steaks to a dry rub of salt, cumin, and minced garlic. To further encourage a dry exterior, we also refrigerated them uncovered on a wire rack for 45 minutes before grilling. These steaks browned and crisped in record time—just longer than 2 minutes per side—leaving the interior moist and tender. To work in the lime flavor, we simply gave the grilled steaks a squeeze of citrus before serving. This all worked great, except that without the moisture the garlic in the rub burned. So we stole a technique often used for bruschetta: We took a smashed garlic clove and rubbed it over the steak's charred crusts after they came off the grill. This simple step brought a burst of fresh garlic flavor and aroma to the meat.

Many carne asada recipes call for a tomatillo salsa, but it was the versions that had a red chile salsa that really stuck with us. The chiles' fruity, slightly smoky flavor added incredible depth to the steak. We started by toasting dried guajillo chiles, which have the right bright, slightly tangy flavor with a hint of heat, in a hot skillet before grinding them in a blender. From there we added a can of fire-roasted diced tomatoes, water, garlic, vinegar, oregano, pepper, cloves, cumin, and salt. Punchy and intense, this salsa complemented the charred steaks perfectly.

Finally, no carne asada platter would be complete without beans. We opted for creamy refried beans over the brothy boiled kind. A quick homemade version with canned pinto beans, onion, garlic, and rich meaty depth from bacon was easy to prepare and tasted far superior to the canned stuff. Our recipe was streamlined and simple, since we could prepare the salsa and beans in the time the meat sat in the refrigerator. Combined with the juicy, perfectly charred steak, this was carne asada that lived up to the Mexico City favorite.

Mexican-Style Grilled Steak (Carne Asada)
SERVES 4 TO 6

We like skirt steak for this recipe, but 2 pounds of sirloin steak tips, also sold as flap meat, may be substituted. The steak can also be used in tacos or burritos.

- **2 teaspoons kosher salt**
- **¾ teaspoon ground cumin**
- **1 (2-pound) skirt steak, trimmed, cut with grain into 4 equal steaks, and pounded ¼ inch thick**
- **1 (13 by 9-inch) disposable aluminum roasting pan (if using charcoal)**
- **1 garlic clove, peeled and smashed**
- **Lime wedges**

1. Combine salt and cumin in small bowl. Sprinkle salt mixture evenly over both sides of steaks. Transfer steaks to large plate, and refrigerate, uncovered, for at least 45 minutes or up to 24 hours. Meanwhile, if using charcoal, use kitchen shears to remove bottom of disposable pan and discard, reserving pan collar.

2A. FOR A CHARCOAL GRILL: Open bottom vent completely. Light large chimney starter filled with charcoal briquettes (6 quarts). When top coals are partially covered with ash, place disposable pan collar in center of grill over bottom vent and pour coals into even layer in collar. Set cooking grate in place, cover, and open lid vent completely. Heat grill until hot, about 5 minutes.

2B. FOR A GAS GRILL: Turn all burners to high, cover, and heat grill until hot, about 15 minutes. Leave all burners on high.

3. Clean and oil cooking grate. Place steaks on grill (if using charcoal, arrange steaks over coals in collar) and cook, uncovered, until well browned on first side, 2 to 4 minutes. Flip steaks and continue to cook until well browned on second side and meat registers 130 degrees, 2 to 4 minutes longer. Transfer steaks to cutting board, tent loosely with aluminum foil, and let rest for 5 minutes.

4. Rub garlic thoroughly over 1 side of steaks. Slice steaks across grain into ¼-inch-thick slices and serve with lime wedges.

Red Chile Salsa
MAKES 2 CUPS

Regular diced tomatoes can be used in place of the fire-roasted tomatoes; you will sacrifice some flavor.

- **1¼ ounces dried guajillo chiles, wiped clean**
- **1 (14.5-ounce) can fire-roasted diced tomatoes**
- **¾ cup water**
- **¾ teaspoon salt**
- **1 garlic clove, peeled and smashed**
- **½ teaspoon distilled white vinegar**
- **¼ teaspoon dried oregano**
- **⅛ teaspoon pepper**
- **Pinch ground cloves**
- **Pinch ground cumin**

Toast guajillos in 10-inch nonstick skillet over medium-high heat until softened and fragrant, 1 to 2 minutes per side. Transfer to large plate and, when cool enough

to handle, remove stems and seeds. Place guajillos in blender and process until finely ground, 60 to 90 seconds, scraping down sides of blender jar as needed. Add tomatoes and their juice, water, salt, garlic, vinegar, oregano, pepper, cloves, and cumin to blender and process until very smooth, 60 to 90 seconds, scraping down sides of blender jar as needed. (Salsa can be stored in refrigerator for up to 5 days or frozen for up to 1 month.)

FOR TENDER SKIRT STEAK, COOK IT A LITTLE LONGER
Cooking most steaks to 125 degrees, or medium-rare, delivers the juiciest, most tender results. But skirt steak is one exception. When a piece of beef is heated, its muscle fibers shrink in width, separating them from one another and making them easier to chew. For cuts like strip steak, which have comparatively thin fibers, the amount of shrinking, and thus tenderizing, that occurs when the meat is cooked to 125 degrees is sufficient. But skirt steak has wider muscle fibers that need to shrink further, and thus require cooking to 130 degrees before they are acceptably tender.

However, this tenderizing effect doesn't continue the more you cook the steak. Once any cut of meat hits 140 degrees, muscle fibers begin to shrink not just in width but also in length, and that causes the meat to toughen again. This lengthwise shrinking also squeezes out juices, which means your steak will end up not just tough but also dry.

Simple Refried Beans

MAKES ABOUT 1½ CUPS

If desired, the bacon can be crumbled and served over the beans.

- 2 slices bacon
- 1 small onion, chopped fine
- 2 garlic cloves, minced
- 1 (15-ounce) can pinto beans
- ¼ cup water
- Kosher salt

Heat bacon in 10-inch nonstick skillet over medium-low heat until fat renders and bacon crisps, 7 to 10 minutes, flipping bacon halfway through cooking. Remove bacon and reserve for another use. Increase heat to medium, add onion to fat in skillet and cook until lightly browned, 5 to 7 minutes. Add garlic and cook until fragrant, about 30 seconds. Add beans and their canning liquid and water and bring to simmer. Cook, mashing beans with potato masher, until mixture is mostly smooth, 5 to 7 minutes. Season with salt to taste, and serve.

SHREDDED BEEF TACOS

✔ **WHY THIS RECIPE WORKS:** Many recipes for *carne deshebrada*, a Mexican beef taco filling, are sorely lacking in meaty flavor. To achieve moist, tender, and richly flavored beef, we cooked boneless short ribs slowly and gently in a covered Dutch oven. Our braising liquid, made from beer, vinegar, and dried ancho chiles, doubled as a flavorful sauce base. To maximize browning during the braise (and skip searing beforehand), we set the meat over thick onion slices to expose more of its exterior to the oven's heat. A bright cabbage-carrot slaw provided a nice counterbalance to the rich meat.

WHEN AMERICANS THINK OF SHREDDED MEAT TACOS, we tend to think of those filled with pork carnitas. But in Mexico, the saucy beef filling called *carne deshebrada* (which translates as "shredded meat") is also hugely popular. A taqueria standard as well as a home-cooked favorite, it's made by braising a large cut of beef (usually brisket, chuck roast, or even flank or skirt steak) until ultratender and then shredding the meat and tossing it with either a *rojo* sauce made with tomatoes and/or dried chiles or a *verde* sauce made with tomatillos. Our preference is for the robust rojo style, particularly those versions that feature warm, earthy spices. Instead of having to seek out a good local taqueria every time we get a craving for this Mexican comfort food, we wondered how hard it would be to make a great version at home.

The handful of carne deshebrada recipes that we found didn't look complicated. They started with the same basic procedure: Cover the cut of choice with water in a large pot, add some flavorings (onion, garlic, cilantro, and sometimes various others), and braise the meat for several hours until tender. Then remove the meat, shred it, and combine it with a sauce that has been prepared separately. The sauce recipes showed more variation. Some were as simple as canned whole or diced tomatoes simmered quickly with onion and garlic, while others went on to add a mix of spices as well as dried and sometimes fresh chiles. Some sauces were pureed, while others were left a bit chunky.

No matter the sauce used, one flaw was clear: For a dish known for its meatiness, the beef flavor was noticeably wan. One contributing factor seemed obvious: Once the roast or steak was cooked and removed from the pot, the cooking liquid, along with all the flavor released by the beef, was poured down the drain. Our goal was clear: we wanted a recipe for this shredded meat filling that really emphasized beef flavor. For the rojo sauce, we weren't sold on any particular style, but we wanted it to boast meaty depth and complexity.

Since discarding the cooking liquid was clearly detracting from our goal of meaty flavor, our first move was to put the braising liquid to use in the sauce. Having it pull double duty would not only ensure more flavor but also streamline things by allowing us to skip preparing a sauce separately.

It made sense to swap out the water for beef broth. We wanted to add only as much broth as we'd need to adequately sauce the beef; our guess was that 2 cups would be about right. We added it to the pot with the meat (we went with a chuck roast for the moment), along with diced canned tomatoes, chopped onion, a little minced jalapeño, and garlic. At this point, we opted not to use dried chiles, which allowed us to skip pureeing the sauce. We cooked the meat until tender before shredding it and returning it to the pot to toss with the sauce. The filling was definitely meatier but still not nearly meaty enough.

We took a step back. What about the cut of meat? Chuck roast is reasonably flavorful, but there are definitely cuts that are beefier, plus it took a full 5 hours of cooking to turn tender. Other popular choices, flank and skirt steak, held promise in terms of flavor and are fairly quick-cooking, but because they don't have much marbling, they tended to dry out. Ditto for brisket. So we turned to a test kitchen favorite for braising: boneless beef short ribs. While they were not traditional to the

SHREDDED BEEF TACOS

dish, tasters agreed that short ribs delivered the meatiest, richest taco filling yet. And cutting them into 2-inch cubes reduced the cooking time by half, to a comparatively quick 2½ hours. Because short ribs are fairly fatty, the filling was a little greasy, but trimming the meat well before cooking and skimming the cooking liquid before saucing the meat were easy fixes.

Our recipe was shaping up nicely: The flavor was much improved, it used easy-to-find ingredients, and its preparation was fairly simple. The meat required trimming before cooking and shredding afterward, but it was hands-off for most of the cooking time. We wanted to keep it that way, but we had to wonder if we couldn't develop even more meaty flavor.

We didn't want to tack on the extra step of browning the meat at the start, but we'd developed enough braising recipes to know that meat that isn't submerged in liquid will brown during cooking. Our short ribs were just peeking above the liquid and thus barely browning. What if we gave the meat a lift so that more of it was exposed? We sliced an onion into thick rounds, arranged them in the pot with the cooking liquid, and placed the chunks of short ribs on top. When we pulled the pot from the oven about 2½ hours later and removed the lid, at first glance we weren't hopeful about the results. The onion rounds had softened and sunk, taking the meat down with them. But when we removed the meat from the sauce to shred it, we realized that it had stayed afloat long enough to develop really good browning, and the beef had tons of meaty flavor. What about the sauce? We fished the onion slices out of the pot and gave it a taste. It was certainly good and meaty—but it wasn't much else.

We wondered if broth really made the best choice for the cooking liquid, which was now incredibly meaty but lacking in depth and brightness. Our recipe was really nothing more than a braise, and many braises use some form of alcohol to provide both traits that our sauce was missing. Wine didn't seem appropriate for this Mexican braise, but beer did, and when we swapped in a bottle of good ale for most of the broth, tasters found the sauce

much improved. It still lacked acidity, so we ditched the remaining broth in favor of cider vinegar. We also decided to swap out the canned tomatoes for the concentrated umami-rich flavors of tomato paste.

The switch to tomato paste whetted our appetites for a smoother sauce; without the chunks of tomatoes, the sauce was incorporating much more thoroughly with the shreds of meat. For the next batch, we gave the cooking liquid a quick whiz in the blender before combining it with the shredded meat. This sauce was better still, with a silky, unctuous texture.

Now that we were pureeing the sauce, there was no reason not to use dried chiles. Recipes called for a wide variety, from fruity, moderately hot guajillos to mildly flavored, slightly spicy New Mexican reds to smoky-sweet anchos and earthy, raisiny pasillas. While each variety had its merits, anchos came out on top. By the end of the cooking time, they were plenty soft and easily pureed into the sauce, giving it the smoky, spicy kick it needed.

Up to this point, we hadn't been adding herbs or spices to the sauce. Traditional choices ranged from only a little dried oregano to up to 10 different seasonings. For increased complexity without going overboard, we settled on the warm notes of ground cumin, cinnamon, and cloves, along with dried oregano and bay leaves.

For taco toppings, we usually stick with reliable standbys like salsa, pico de gallo (chopped fresh tomatoes, onions, and chiles), guacamole, and cheese, but we felt that given the filling's richness, a topping that was bright and added crunch would provide perfect contrast.

To that end, we looked past Mexico to El Salvador and homed in on *curtido*, a crunchy, tart cabbage-carrot slaw with a spicy kick that's a specialty of that country. While the slaw is often fermented to develop flavor (a process that takes several days or even weeks), we found that a quick version tossed together while the meat was

braising and then refrigerated for 1 hour had all the punch that our tacos required. The key was marinating the shredded vegetables, onion, and jalapeño in a fruity cider vinegar–based pickling liquid before draining and serving them. In addition to the curtido, a sprinkling of crumbled *queso fresco* (or feta if you're in a pinch) introduced the right salty, creamy finish to the tacos.

With that, we had a carne deshebrada taco that could hold its own against the best of the rest.

Shredded Beef Tacos (Carne Deshebrada)
SERVES 6 TO 8

Use a full-bodied lager or ale such as Dos Equis or Sierra Nevada. If you can't find *queso fresco*, substitute feta. If your Dutch oven does not have a tight-fitting lid, cover the pot tightly with a sheet of heavy-duty aluminum foil and then replace the lid. To warm the tortillas, place them on a plate, cover them with a damp dish towel, and microwave them for 60 to 90 seconds. The shredded beef also makes a great filling for empanadas, tamales, and chiles rellenos.

BEEF

- 1½ cups beer
- ½ cup cider vinegar
- 2 ounces (4 to 6) dried ancho chiles, stemmed, seeded, and torn into 1-inch pieces
- 2 tablespoons tomato paste
- 6 garlic cloves, lightly crushed and peeled
- 3 bay leaves
- 2 teaspoons ground cumin
- 2 teaspoons dried oregano
  Salt and pepper
- ½ teaspoon ground cloves
- ½ teaspoon ground cinnamon
- 1 large onion, sliced into ½-inch-thick rounds
- 3 pounds boneless beef short ribs, trimmed and cut into 2-inch cubes

CABBAGE-CARROT SLAW

- 1 cup cider vinegar
- ½ cup water
- 1 tablespoon sugar
- 1½ teaspoons salt
- ½ head green cabbage, cored and sliced thin (6 cups)
- 1 onion, sliced thin
- 1 large carrot, peeled and shredded
- 1 jalapeño chile, stemmed, seeded, and minced
- 1 teaspoon dried oregano
- 1 cup chopped fresh cilantro

- 18 (6-inch) corn tortillas, warmed
- 4 ounces queso fresco, crumbled (1 cup)
  Lime wedges

GIVING BEEF(INESS) A BOOST

We found that many recipes for *carne deshebrada* produced results that weren't actually all that beefy. To improve meatiness, we used short ribs, one of the most flavorful braising cuts we know, and cut them into 2-inch cubes for faster cooking. We also propped up the cubes on onion rounds so that the exposed portions would brown during the 2-plus hours of cooking—thus avoiding the fuss of searing the meat before cooking.

Sliced onion lifts the short ribs above the braising liquid, which delivers more browning—and more meaty flavor.

WARMING TORTILLAS

To warm tortillas, stack on microwave-safe plate, cover with damp dish towel, and microwave for 60 to 90 seconds.

rounds in single layer. Cover and cook until meat is well browned and tender, 2½ to 3 hours.

2. FOR THE CABBAGE-CARROT SLAW: While beef cooks, whisk vinegar, water, sugar, and salt in large bowl until sugar is dissolved. Add cabbage, onion, carrot, jalapeño, and oregano and toss to combine. Cover and refrigerate for at least 1 hour or up to 24 hours. Drain slaw and stir in cilantro right before serving.

3. Using slotted spoon, transfer beef to large bowl, cover loosely with aluminum foil, and set aside. Strain liquid through fine-mesh strainer into 2-cup liquid measuring cup (do not wash pot). Discard onion rounds and bay leaves. Transfer remaining solids to blender. Let strained liquid settle for 5 minutes, then skim any fat off surface. Add water as needed to equal 1 cup. Pour liquid in blender with reserved solids and blend until smooth, about 2 minutes. Transfer sauce to now-empty pot.

4. Using 2 forks, shred beef into bite-size pieces. Bring sauce to simmer over medium heat. Add shredded beef and stir to coat. Season with salt to taste. (Beef can be refrigerated for up to 2 days; gently reheat before serving.)

5. Spoon small amount of beef into each warm tortilla and serve, passing slaw, queso fresco, and lime wedges separately.

1. FOR THE BEEF: Adjust oven rack to lower-middle position and heat oven to 325 degrees. Combine beer, vinegar, anchos, tomato paste, garlic, bay leaves, cumin, oregano, 2 teaspoons salt, ½ teaspoon pepper, cloves, and cinnamon in Dutch oven. Arrange onion rounds in single layer on bottom of pot. Place beef on top of onion

RATING DARK CHOCOLATE

To find an everyday chocolate that would work for both snacking and cooking, we gathered nine bars that contained at least 35 percent cacao (the FDA standard for the "bittersweet" or "semisweet" label). We tasted each bar plain, in brownies, and in pots de crème. Products with more than 50 percent sugar sank to the bottom of the ratings for their barely there chocolate flavor, while bars with high levels of cocoa solids earned accolades from tasters for their complexity. There was a tipping point though: Bars with the highest percentage of cocoa solids fared less well in creamy applications. Fat and sugar amounts are per 42-gram serving. Chocolates are listed in order of preference. See AmericasTestKitchen.com for updates and complete tasting results.

HIGHLY RECOMMENDED

GHIRARDELLI 60 Percent Cacao Bittersweet Chocolate Premium Baking Bar

PRICE: $2.99 for 4 oz ($0.75 per oz)
CACAO PERCENTAGE: about 60%   **COCOA SOLIDS:** about 22%
SUGAR: 16 g (38%)   **FAT:** 16 g (38%)
PLAIN: ★★★   **BROWNIES:** ★★½
POTS DE CRÈME: ★★★
COMMENTS: This bar rated the highest for eating plain, with a nice, complex flavor. Its high—but not too high—level of cocoa solids made this bar easy to work with in pots de crème.

CALLEBAUT Intense Dark Chocolate, L-60–40NV

PRICE: $8.39 for 1.05 lb ($0.50 per oz)
CACAO PERCENTAGE: about 60%   **COCOA SOLIDS:** about 30%
SUGAR: 15.12 g (36%)   **FAT:** 12.6 g (30%)
PLAIN: ★★★   **BROWNIES:** ★★★
POTS DE CRÈME: ★★½
COMMENTS: This bar was "intense," with "just the right amount of sweetness." Its high level of cocoa solids sometimes produced slightly grainy pots de crème.

RECOMMENDED

DOVE Silky Smooth Dark Chocolate

PRICE: $3.20 for 3.3 oz ($0.97 per oz)
CACAO PERCENTAGE: about 55%
COCOA SOLIDS: about 22%
SUGAR: 19 g (45%)   **FAT:** 14 g (33%)
PLAIN: ★★½   **BROWNIES:** ★★½
POTS DE CRÈME: ★★★
COMMENTS: This fudgy bar offered pleasing complexity with a "nutty, mocha flavor" and a notably smooth texture. A few tasters found it too sweet in desserts.

SCHARFFEN BERGER Semisweet Fine Artisan Dark Chocolate

PRICE: $4.29 for 3 oz ($1.43 per oz)
CACAO PERCENTAGE: about 62%
COCOA SOLIDS: about 25%
SUGAR: 15.6 g (37%)   Fat: 15.6 g (37%)
PLAIN: ★★½   **BROWNIES:** ★★½
POTS DE CRÈME: ★★½
COMMENTS: Many tasters praised the hints of berry and "background smokiness" in this chocolate. Others found it "pleasant but generic."

RECOMMENDED WITH RESERVATIONS

BAKER'S Bittersweet Baking Chocolate Squares

PRICE: $4.99 for 6 oz ($0.83 per oz)
CACAO PERCENTAGE: about 66%   **COCOA SOLIDS:** about 30%
SUGAR: 15 g (36%)   **FAT:** 15 g (36%)
PLAIN: ★★★   **BROWNIES:** ★★★
POTS DE CRÈME: ★★
COMMENTS: This basic supermarket product had a "rich" chocolate flavor that had notes of coconut and coffee. But with high levels of cocoa solids, it consistently made "gritty" pots de crème.

GHIRARDELLI Semi-Sweet Chocolate Premium Baking Bar

PRICE: $2.99 for 4 oz ($0.75 per oz)
CACAO PERCENTAGE: about 52%   **COCOA SOLIDS:** about 19%
SUGAR: 20 g (48%)   **FAT:** 14 g (33%)
PLAIN: ★★   **BROWNIES:** ★★½
POTS DE CRÈME: ★
COMMENTS: The pleasant complex flavors in this bar were muted by a milky sweetness. It was "enjoyable" in brownies, but it made runny pots de crème.

NOT RECOMMENDED

HERSHEY'S Semi-Sweet Chocolate Baking Bar

PRICE: $2.49 for 4 oz ($0.62 per oz)
CACAO PERCENTAGE: about 42%   **COCOA SOLIDS:** about 13%
SUGAR: 24 g (57%)   **FAT:** 12 g (29%)
PLAIN: ★½   **BROWNIES:** ★½
POTS DE CRÈME: ★★½
COMMENTS: This high-sugar, very low cocoa solids bar tasted far too sweet and milky. Its strong notes of hazelnut, caramel, and butterscotch overwhelmed its feeble chocolate flavor.

NESTLÉ Semi-Sweet Baking Chocolate Bar

PRICE: $3.31 for 4 oz ($0.83 per oz)
CACAO PERCENTAGE: about 43%   **COCOA SOLIDS:** about 14%
SUGAR: 24 g (57%)   **FAT:** 12 g (29%)
PLAIN: ★   **BROWNIES:** ★½
POTS DE CRÈME: ★
COMMENTS: Sampled plain, this bar was flat-out sweet. Brownies were its best application, though it was still overly sugary and weak on chocolate flavor. In pots de crème it was "runny."

Southeast Asian Specialties

CHAPTER 16

THE RECIPES
Vietnamese Beef Pho
Singapore Noodles

The beef for traditional pho bo *is sliced so thinly, it cooks right in the hot broth. We achieve paper-thin slices by briefly freezing the meat before cutting it.*

WHEN WE SAY "SPECIALTIES," WE AREN'T KIDDING AROUND: MANY Asian dishes contain ingredients or use methods that are difficult to reproduce in a typical American kitchen. But the intensity of flavors in dishes like *pho bo* and Singapore noodles gives these dishes such appeal, we couldn't resist trying our hand at making them accessible to home cooks.

Vietnamese pho bo owes its deeply complex, beefy broth to beef bones, which are simmered for hours along with aromatics like garlic and ginger, and warm spices like cloves and star anise. But therein lies the problem: beef bones? Hours? The very things that give pho its characteristic flavor are the same things we wanted to avoid. We set out to turn this project soup into a weeknight meal, without losing any of the fragrant, beefy flavor that made us love it in the first place.

Singapore noodles (which are actually from Hong Kong) are unique: The dish relies on typical Chinese aromatic ingredients like ginger, but also makes use of curry powder—an Indian spice blend influenced by British tastes. But the curry powder can give the sauceless dish a grainy texture, and we found its presence weak. Plus, the noodles often end up in an unappealing, tangled ball. Although the culture of this dish may be a bit ambiguous, we made sure the flavors (and the noodles) weren't.

VIETNAMESE BEEF PHO

VIETNAMESE BEEF PHO

✔ **WHY THIS RECIPE WORKS:** Traditional versions of this Vietnamese beef and noodle soup call for simmering beef bones for hours to make a deeply flavorful broth. We wanted to make this soup suitable for the home cook, which meant that beef bones were out of the question. Instead, we simmered ground beef in spiced store-bought broth, which gave us the complexity and depth we were after in a fraction of the time. To serve the soup, we poured our broth over thinly sliced strip steak and gathered a variety of essential garnishes, such as lime wedges, hoisin and chile sauces, and bean sprouts.

MANY ASIAN CUISINES LAY CLAIM TO A BROTHY NOODLE soup, but we can't think of one that's as universally popular as *pho bo*. This Vietnamese beef and noodle soup's biggest selling point is its killer broth—a beefy, fragrant, faintly sweet concoction produced by simmering beef bones and water for hours with aromatics like ginger and onions and warm spices like cinnamon and star anise. Notably, those bones are often the only form of meat added to the cooking liquid; actual pieces of beef aren't introduced until serving, when the broth is strained and ladled onto very thin slices of raw steak (typically sirloin) and thin rice noodles in large individual serving bowls. Fresh herbs and a few aromatic vegetables are presented as garnishes. Pouring hot broth over the contents cooks the meat just enough and softens the noodles and vegetables. Condiments such as salty-sweet hoisin sauce, chile sauce, and fish sauce and lime wedges are passed at the table for individual flavor tinkering.

While we love pho's exotic yet approachable flavors, we've never made this soup ourselves. Who has the time to spend a day boiling up a full-flavored beef stock, much less running around town trying to track down hard-to-find beef bones? Could we could devise an equally intense, complex-tasting broth in less time (and with easier-to-find ingredients)?

Ditching the bones was an obvious first move. The easiest shortcut, we figured, would be to doctor store-bought beef broth with typical pho flavors. We threw together a working recipe based on that: 14 cups of beef broth (since pho is a one-bowl meal, this amount of liquid feeds four to six people), a handful of quartered onions, peeled and thinly sliced ginger, a cinnamon stick, six each star anise pods and whole cloves, a couple of teaspoons of salt, and a teaspoon of black peppercorns, all simmered for about 1½ hours. To say the result was a failure would be an understatement. The soup tasted exactly like what it was: spiced-up commercial broth. We tried adding a little fish sauce and sugar to the cooking liquid, and both were keepers—they rounded out the salty-sweet profile we were after. But the broth needed more help.

At that point it dawned on us that doing without beef bones didn't mean we had to do without beef altogether. Our reference point was the test kitchen's trick for making an ultrameaty sauce for steak. In that recipe, we build rich, meaty flavor in a hurry by simmering some ground beef with the cooking liquid and then discarding the solids. We discovered that ground meat works well because its muscle fibers are broken up in the grinding process and, therefore, release meaty flavor very quickly.

Feeling hopeful, we pulled together another batch of broth, but this time we added 2 pounds of ground beef along with the commercial broth, aromatics, and spices. While that simmered, we used a sharp knife to peel ⅛-inch-thick slices off of a 1-pound piece of beef sirloin (a placeholder until we did further testing with other cuts). We also soaked strands of thin dried rice noodles in warm water and then briefly boiled them. Soaking helped them slough off excess starch and made them soften evenly and quickly in the boiling water. Then we loaded up individual bowls with the noodles and meat, as well as chopped cilantro and thin-sliced raw onion and scallions, before pouring hot broth over each serving.

The good news was that this broth was in a different league compared with our previous attempts: It was remarkably more savory and full-bodied, thanks to the ground beef. The downsides were that the ground beef had

BEEF SO THIN IT COOKS IN THE BOWL

Traditionally, the steak for *pho* is sliced very thin and placed raw in the serving bowl. (It cooks, but ideally remains slightly rare, in the hot broth.)

To cut thin slices against the grain, freeze the meat until it's very firm. Then stand the meat on its cut end and, using the sharpest, thinnest blade you have, point the tip downward and push the blade down and away from you in one stroke.

released "scum" into the liquid that turned it cloudy; the liquid retained a touch of that commercial broth tinniness and vegetal flavor; and, frankly, we weren't thrilled about throwing away 2 pounds of beef. But fortifying the broth with ground meat had improved its flavor so dramatically that we couldn't resist pursuing the technique further.

In the test kitchen, we've made our fair share of stocks, so we were familiar with that pesky layer of scum, which forms any time you boil meat or bones. Traditional stock recipes, pho included, call for blanching the bones before adding them to the cooking liquid, a step that washes away much of their surface proteins and fat, which form the scum. We gave it a try with the ground beef and were glad to see that the technique was effective: Covering the meat with water, bringing it up to a boil for 2 minutes, and then quickly draining and rinsing it (to remove clingy bits of protein and fat) before adding it to the beef broth made for a clearer, cleaner-tasting beef stock. Of course, it's not as easy to strain bits of ground meat as it is large beef bones, so we broke the 2-pound mass of meat into 1-inch chunks that weren't hard to fish out of the water. Swapping out a couple of cups of the broth for an equal amount of water took care of the tinny, vegetal notes without noticeably dampening the beefy flavor.

Making do with less beef broth also tempted our frugal side: Could we get away with less ground beef, too? Indeed, making our broth with 1 pound of ground beef

provided plenty of meaty flavor—and the flavor payoff for 1 pound of meat was worth the sacrifice.

We had to admit that this broth had a lot going for it: all the flavor and complexity of real-deal beef broth without the fuss. Our only hang-up was the 1½-hour simmer. For this pho to be part of our regular dinner rotation, not just a special-occasion dish, we'd need to hurry it along, so we tried skimping on the simmer time. To our delight, after testing various times, we discovered that the beef flavor peaked around the 45-minute mark—a change that put this soup on the table for a weeknight meal.

Some pho shops throw tough cuts like brisket and tripe into their long-simmered broths and offer them as garnishing options, but thin slices of raw, relatively tender steak are the most common and would do fine for our purposes. The question was which cut exactly, so we tried all the options we could think of: tenderloin, rib eye, strip steak, tri-tip, blade steak, flank, and eye of round. Tenderloin was favored for its supple texture, and its uniform cylindrical shape made thin-slicing it a breeze. But its prohibitive price meant that it was ill-matched for this humble soup. Plus, it offered nothing in the way of beefy flavor. Strip steak, tri-tip, and blade steak all offered good beefiness and reasonable tenderness at a fraction of the price. We chose to work with strip since it is usually the easiest to find. To make the steak less challenging to slice thin, we employed the test kitchen's favorite trick for prepping stir-fry meat: briefly freezing the whole steak, which firms it up enough for the blade to make clean cuts. As a bonus, freezing also ensured that the steak didn't overcook when it came in contact with the hot broth.

We also pared down the list of tableside garnishes and condiments to the essentials. The must-haves—bean sprouts for crunch, basil (preferably Thai basil, though Italian basil will work), lime wedges, hoisin and chile sauces, and additional fish sauce—balanced the straightforward meatiness and mellow sweetness of the broth with heat, acidity, and freshness.

As we ladled the fragrant broth into serving bowls, we remarked at how easily and quickly the complex flavors of pho had come together and how this seemingly exotic dish suddenly felt much closer to home.

Vietnamese Beef Pho

SERVES 4 TO 6

Use a Dutch oven that holds 6 quarts or more. An equal weight of tri-tip steak or blade steak can be substituted for the strip steak; make sure to trim all connective tissue and excess fat. Look for noodles that are about ⅛ inch wide; these are often labeled "small." Don't use Thai Kitchen Stir-Fry Rice Noodles since they are too thick and don't adequately soak up the broth.

1	pound 85 percent lean ground beef
2	onions, quartered through root end
12	cups beef broth
¼	cup fish sauce, plus extra for seasoning
1	(4-inch) piece ginger, sliced into thin rounds
1	cinnamon stick
2	tablespoons sugar, plus extra for seasoning
6	star anise pods
6	whole cloves
	Salt
1	teaspoon black peppercorns
1	(1-pound) boneless strip steak, trimmed and halved
14-16	ounces (⅛-inch-wide) rice noodles
⅓	cup chopped fresh cilantro
3	scallions, sliced thin (optional)
	Bean sprouts
	Sprigs fresh Thai or Italian basil
	Lime wedges
	Hoisin sauce
	Sriracha sauce

1. Break ground beef into rough 1-inch chunks and drop in Dutch oven. Add water to cover by 1 inch. Bring mixture to boil over high heat. Boil for 2 minutes, stirring once or twice. Drain ground beef in colander and rinse well under running water. Wash out pot and return ground beef to pot.

2. Place 6 onion quarters in pot with ground beef. Slice remaining 2 onion quarters as thin as possible and set aside for garnish. Add broth, 2 cups water, fish sauce, ginger, cinnamon, sugar, star anise, cloves, 2 teaspoons salt, and peppercorns to pot and bring to boil over high heat. Reduce heat to medium-low and simmer, partially covered, for 45 minutes.

3. Pour broth through colander set in large bowl. Discard solids. Strain broth through fine-mesh strainer lined with triple thickness of cheesecloth; add water as needed to equal 11 cups. Return broth to pot and season with extra sugar and salt (broth should taste overseasoned). Cover and keep warm over low heat.

4. While broth simmers, place steak on large plate and freeze until very firm, 35 to 45 minutes. Once firm, cut against grain into ⅛-inch-thick slices. Return steak to plate and refrigerate until needed.

5. Place noodles in large container and cover with hot tap water. Soak until noodles are pliable, 10 to 15 minutes; drain noodles. Meanwhile, bring 4 quarts water to boil in large pot. Add drained noodles and cook until almost tender, 30 to 60 seconds. Drain immediately and divide noodles among individual bowls.

6. Bring broth to rolling boil over high heat. Divide steak among individual bowls, shingling slices on top of noodles. Pile reserved onion slices on top of steak slices and sprinkle with cilantro and scallions, if using. Ladle hot broth into each bowl. Serve immediately, passing bean sprouts, basil sprigs, lime wedges, hoisin, Sriracha, and extra fish sauce separately.

SINGAPORE NOODLES

✓ **WHY THIS RECIPE WORKS:** Singapore noodles traditionally combine rice noodles, vegetables, and shrimp with aromatics like ginger, garlic, and curry powder, which gives the dish a distinct flavor profile—and a pervasive grittiness. Plus, the long noodles tend to bunch up into a ball. We set out to improve the noodles' flavor and texture, and, to make the dish work as a main course, we also wanted to revise the proportions of protein and veggies to noodles. To boost flavor and eliminate the sandy texture, we bloomed the curry powder in a few tablespoons of oil. To detangle the noodles, we cut them into shorter pieces. We gave the dish heft by adding a few scrambled eggs and some bean sprouts. We also cut the shrimp into smaller pieces that dispersed evenly. A squeeze of lime juice over the composed dish provided brightness.

NOMENCLATURE ASIDE, SINGAPORE NOODLES HAVE nothing to do with Singapore and are virtually unknown there. In fact, this light, almost fluffy stir-fry of thin, resilient rice noodles, vegetables, and shrimp is native to Hong Kong, and nobody seems to know for sure how it came to be named for a city that's more than 1,500 miles away.

The dish includes typical Chinese ingredients like garlic, ginger, and soy sauce, but also prominently features curry powder, a spice blend that probably trickled into Hong Kong's cuisine when it was under British rule. The heady spice blend lends the dish a pervasive aroma. It's a classic in Chinese restaurants outside Hong Kong, too, and one of our favorites.

But the curry powder can also be the most problematic element of Singapore noodles. Because this dish is not saucy, the dry powder doesn't distribute evenly, leading to patchy curry flavor (and color), not to mention gritty texture.

This was the core problem we set out to solve when we created our own version of Singapore noodles. And given that we wanted this dish to function as a light yet satisfying one-dish meal, we also vowed to revise the typical ratio of ingredients, which tends to be about 80 percent noodles, with the vegetables and protein acting almost as garnishes.

The ingredient list for Singapore noodles is simple—just dried rice noodles (usually thin vermicelli), ordinary vegetables, shrimp, a handful of seasonings, and maybe some eggs—and once the ingredients are prepped, the cooking takes all of 15 minutes.

The universal first step is to soak the rice noodles; you want them to be just pliable, but not fully softened since they'll continue to absorb liquid during cooking. Covering 6 ounces of noodles with boiling water, letting them soak for 2½ minutes, stirring them occasionally, and draining them produced exactly the texture we were hoping for.

From there, we broke out our large nonstick skillet (which we prefer to a wok) for stir-frying. Over a medium-high flame, we heated a couple of teaspoons of vegetable oil and sautéed 12 ounces of large shrimp in a single layer until they'd browned on the bottom. Then we slid the cooked shrimp onto a plate, lowered the heat, added another spoonful of oil, and stir-fried some grated ginger and minced garlic until fragrant. In went some thin-sliced red bell pepper and shallots, followed by the drained noodles, ⅔ cup of chicken broth, a couple of splashes of soy sauce, and 2 tablespoons of mild (or "sweet") curry powder—a generous amount that's about par for the course in this dish. Then we added back the shrimp, cranked the heat to high, and briefly tossed everything together until the mixture was relatively dry and the noodles were al dente.

At least, we tried to toss everything together. What actually happened was that the long noodles tangled, forming a tight ball that forced most of the vegetables and shrimp to the sides of the skillet. The dish was also still much too noodle-heavy. And the curry powder had given the whole ensemble a predictably gritty texture and a slightly bitter edge. While those qualities would normally signal spice overload to us, we actually found the curry flavor lacking.

Since increasing the amount of curry powder would only make the dish dustier, it occurred to us to try changing not the amount of curry powder, but how we were

SINGAPORE NOODLES

treating it. It's possible to increase the flavor of a given amount of spice by heating it in oil or butter—a technique called "blooming." That's because the flavor compounds in most spices are fat-soluble, so they infuse readily into oil, and like most chemical interactions, this happens more quickly in a warm environment. As the compounds are drawn from the spice granules into the warm oil, they produce stronger and more complex flavors. We also thought that making a curry-infused oil could provide the missing fat to the dish.

We heated 3 tablespoons of oil in the skillet and stirred in the 2 tablespoons of curry powder we had been using originally. Then we heated the spiced oil for 4 minutes over medium-low heat. By that point we could smell that we were on the right track from the rich curry aroma, and our tasters confirmed as much when they tasted the curry oil–dressed noodles, noting the richer, more complex flavor. Even better, blooming the curry powder had caused the spice granules to disperse evenly in the oil, so their grittiness was no longer noticeable. Tasters' only lingering flavor complaint was that the curry was

still a touch bitter, but it was nothing that a spoonful of sugar couldn't fix. On to tackling that ball of noodles.

In Chinese tradition long noodles symbolize a long life, but in wrestling with them we'd grown short-tempered, so we made a drastic move. After soaking and draining the vermicelli, we cut across them twice to make them shorter and less tangle-prone.

We also cut the shrimp into ½-inch pieces that dispersed nicely throughout the noodles, and we bulked up the protein and vegetables by adding four eggs (scrambled with a little salt), four scallions cut into ½-inch pieces, and a couple of cups of bean sprouts.

Tossing the cut noodles with the curry oil, soy sauce, and sugar in a large mixing bowl made it easier to distribute the dressing evenly throughout the noodles. Then, as each of the components finished cooking, we collected them in a second large bowl. To finish softening the dressed noodles, we simmered them in the skillet with chicken broth, tossing them for about 2 minutes until the broth had been absorbed. Finally, we slid the hot noodles into the bowl with the shrimp and vegetables and squeezed fresh lime juice over the bowl to brighten the flavor.

With bold, complex curry flavor and a more evenly balanced ratio of noodles, protein, and vegetables, our version of Singapore noodles was as satisfying as any we'd had in a Chinese restaurant, and would slip easily into our weeknight lineup.

Singapore Noodles
SERVES 4 TO 6

For spicier Singapore noodles, add the optional cayenne pepper. Look for dried rice vermicelli in the Asian section of your supermarket. A rasp-style grater makes quick work of turning the garlic into a paste.

- 4 **tablespoons plus 1 teaspoon vegetable oil**
- 2 **tablespoons curry powder**
- ⅛ **teaspoon cayenne pepper (optional)**
- 6 **ounces rice vermicelli**
- 2 **tablespoons soy sauce**

1 teaspoon sugar

12 ounces large shrimp (26 to 30 per pound), peeled,
   deveined, tails removed, and cut into ½-inch pieces

4 large eggs, lightly beaten

  Salt

3 garlic cloves, minced to paste

1 teaspoon grated fresh ginger

1 red bell pepper, stemmed, seeded, and cut into
   2-inch-long matchsticks

2 large shallots, sliced thin

⅔ cup chicken broth

4 ounces (2 cups) bean sprouts

4 scallions, cut into ½-inch pieces

2 teaspoons lime juice, plus lime wedges for serving

1. Heat 3 tablespoons oil, curry powder, and cayenne, if using, in 12-inch nonstick skillet over medium-low heat, stirring occasionally, until fragrant, about 4 minutes. Remove skillet from heat and set aside.

2. Bring 1½ quarts water to boil. Place noodles in large bowl. Pour boiling water over noodles and stir briefly. Soak noodles until flexible, but not soft, about 2½ minutes, stirring once halfway through soaking. Drain noodles briefly. Transfer noodles to cutting board. Using chef's knife, cut pile of noodles roughly into thirds. Return noodles to bowl, add curry mixture, soy sauce, and sugar; using tongs, toss until well combined. Set aside.

3. Wipe out skillet with paper towels. Heat 2 teaspoons oil in skillet over medium-high heat until shimmering. Add shrimp in even layer and cook without moving them until bottoms are browned, about 90 seconds. Stir and continue to cook until just cooked through, about 90 seconds longer. Push shrimp to 1 side of skillet. Add 1 teaspoon oil to cleared side of skillet. Add eggs to clearing and sprinkle with ¼ teaspoon salt. Using rubber spatula, stir eggs gently until set but still wet, about 1 minute. Stir eggs into shrimp and continue to cook, breaking up large pieces of egg, until eggs are fully cooked, about 30 seconds longer. Transfer shrimp-egg mixture to second large bowl.

4. Reduce heat to medium. Heat remaining 1 teaspoon oil in now-empty skillet until shimmering. Add garlic

CURRY POWDER: MILD VERSUS MADRAS

Most curry powders fall into one of two categories: mild or "sweet" (like we use in our Singapore Noodles; often identified by the lack of any description on the label) and hotter Madras style. Both types contain turmeric, which accounts for the yellow color, as well as warm spices like cumin, ginger, and cardamom. But Madras curry powder has a higher ratio of dried chile and black pepper, which makes it spicier. We control the spice in our dish by adding cayenne.

UNTANGLING SINGAPORE NOODLES

Two easy steps help avoid the usual ball of noodles that forms when you toss the rice vermicelli with the shrimp and vegetables.

1. SHORTEN THE STRANDS: Cutting the soaked and drained rice vermicelli into thirds makes the noodles less tangle-prone.

2. LUBRICATE WITH CURRY OIL: Coating the noodles with curry oil prevents them from sticking. "Blooming" the spice in oil also boosts its flavor, softens its gritty texture, and adds richness.

and ginger and cook, stirring constantly, until fragrant, about 15 seconds. Add bell pepper and shallots. Cook, stirring frequently, until vegetables are crisp-tender, about 2 minutes. Transfer to bowl with shrimp.

5. Return again-empty skillet to medium-high heat, add broth to skillet, and bring to simmer. Add noodles and cook, stirring frequently, until liquid is absorbed, about 2 minutes. Add noodles to bowl with shrimp and vegetable mixture and toss to combine. Add bean sprouts, scallions, and lime juice and toss to combine. Transfer to warmed platter and serve immediately, passing lime wedges separately.

Two Ways to Unlock Asian Flavor

*Browning our homemade
curry paste in oil helps
to deepen and enhance
the layers of flavor in the
finished dish.*

WHY IS IT THAT OUR FAVORITE ASIAN RESTAURANT DISHES SEEM SO unattainable at home? Is it the ingredients? The cooking methods? Or both? We set out to bring two of our favorites, Thai curry and Chinese braised beef, into the home kitchen. After you see how accessible our recipes are, we're pretty sure you'll think twice before reaching for a takeout menu.

The style of Thai curry known as *massaman* depends on a warmly spiced, lightly sweet, coconut milk–based sauce. Traditional massaman curry pastes call for exotic ingredients like galangal, tamarind, and fish paste, along with a host of whole toasted ground spices. We wanted to avoid a special trip to an Asian market, yet still come up with a curry that was deeply flavorful—and that wouldn't take all day.

When it comes to comfort foods, we're particularly fond of Chinese red-cooked beef: chunks of meltingly tender beef served in a thick, glaze-like sauce. The stew-like dish is full of potent flavors like soy sauce, ginger, cinnamon, and star anise, which come together in rich harmony. But traditional recipes use hard-to-find beef shank, which is braised for many hours, and the multistep preparation process can be arduous. To simplify, we started with beef short ribs—and it only got easier from there. These two Asian-inspired dishes are as good as any from your favorite restaurant—no tip required.

THAI CHICKEN CURRY

✔ WHY THIS RECIPE WORKS: Warm-spiced, savory-sweet *massaman* curry is a Thai specialty, but it presents problems for the home cook with difficult-to-find ingredients and work-intensive processes. We set out to streamline the traditional recipe. To make a deeply flavorful curry paste, we toasted chiles and broiled garlic and shallots per tradition, but we replaced hard-to-find galangal with readily available ginger and traded out toasted, ground whole spices for preground five-spice powder. Coconut milk and lime juice rounded out the flavor of our curry. We stuck with the traditional potatoes, onion, chicken, and peanuts, simmered in the sauce until they were tender. A final garnish of lime zest and cilantro added a splash of color and brightness.

THERE ARE AS MANY INTERPRETATIONS OF THAI CURRIES as there are cooks who prepare them, but the versions served in stateside restaurants tend to fit a similar profile: a coconut milk–based sauce that's flavored and thickened with a concentrated spice paste, filled out with meat or fish and vegetables, and served over plenty of steamed jasmine rice. Hot and tangy red and green curries, which get their respective colors from the type of chile in the paste, are most familiar to Americans, along with curries tinted golden yellow by spices like turmeric. And then there's an equally flavorful but somewhat less well-known variety called *massaman*.

Unlike many Thai dishes that feature hot, sour, salty, and sweet elements, massaman curry trades on a warm, faintly sweet, and not overly spicy profile, thanks to the mix of warm spices like cinnamon, cloves, cardamom, and cumin, as well as roasted dried chiles and aromatics like shallots, garlic, and fresh galangal (a sweet-spicy cousin of ginger) that make up its paste. A last-minute addition of either shrimp paste or fish sauce and a few

teaspoons of tangy tamarind balance the rich sauce, which is typically paired with chicken (or beef), potato chunks, and roasted peanuts.

Massaman is a dish that we've always wanted to tackle, but it presents challenges in an American kitchen. Ingredients like galangal and tamarind are hard to track down. Plus, precooking dried chiles and aromatic vegetables and toasting and grinding whole spices (another traditional step) make for one heck of a prep job—and that's just for the paste. We were determined to produce a massaman curry as fragrant and rich-tasting as any Thai restaurant would make, but with less work.

Pulling together the curry at the end would be easy, so we skipped right to streamlining the paste. To see what would happen if we cut the precooking step for both the dried chiles and the aromatics, we compared the dish made with two different batches of paste. The first we made the traditional way, using oven-toasted dried red chiles (we chose the New Mexican kind for their relatively moderate heat and wide availability) along with broiled skin-on shallots and garlic. In the second batch, the same ingredients (this time the alliums were peeled) went into the blender without precooking. Both pastes also got a knob of fresh ginger (the most obvious substitute for galangal), as well as a dash of fish sauce. As for the spices, some recipes we found called for up to a dozen different kinds—and just a little of each one—but to stick with our streamlining goal, we knocked down the list to whole cloves, cinnamon, cardamom, and cumin, all toasted and ground per tradition for now.

To finish both curries, we browned the pastes in a little oil to deepen their flavors, poured in chicken broth and coconut milk, and simmered the mixtures with Yukon Gold potatoes, onion, peanuts, and a little salt until the potatoes were tender. Finally we slipped in pieces of boneless, skinless chicken thighs. (Dark meat was a must for its rich flavor.)

The flavor difference between the two batches wasn't just noticeable. Tasters declared the paste made with

THAI CHICKEN CURRY WITH POTATOES AND PEANUTS

THAI CURRY BY COLOR AND SPICE

Several of the typical curries you'll see on a Thai menu are identifiable by their color—a reflection of the type and amount of chiles, aromatic vegetables, herbs, and spices in the curry paste. Massaman, a relative of yellow curry, is better known for its depth and fragrance from warm spices, which makes it stand out from other varieties.

RED

This curry, which has moderate salty sweetness, is fairly spicy and sour, thanks to lots of dried red chiles and a big hit of lime at the end.

GREEN

A high proportion of fresh green chiles plus raw aromatics and very little sugar typically makes this variation the hottest and most pungent type of Thai curry.

YELLOW

Stateside versions tend to be mild, though authentic yellow curries can be quite hot. All are heavy on turmeric—hence the color.

MASSAMAN

Though one of the mildest Thai curries, massaman is also one of the most complex. Traditionally, the paste combines cinnamon, star anise, cloves, cardamom, and cumin—all introduced to Thailand by Muslim merchants around the 12th century—as well as dried chiles and aromatics. To cut down on ingredients, our recipe swaps some of the individual spices for five-spice powder.

FOR COMPLEX CURRY, TURN ON THE OVEN

Massaman curry is richer-tasting and more complex than other varieties of Thai curry not just because of the mix of ingredients in its paste but also because of how they're prepared. By toasting the dried chiles and broiling the aromatic vegetables, we get a paste with a rounder and mellower flavor than we would if we added those components raw, as is done in sharper-tasting red and green curries.

precooked chiles and alliums in a different league altogether from its uncooked counterpart: richer-tasting, with rounder, more complex flavor, thanks to the caramelization of the sugars in these ingredients. We'd also discovered that there was a textural advantage to precooking: The heat had softened the vegetables, making them a bit easier to blend into a uniform paste, especially when we added a little water and several teaspoons of vegetable oil to the blender jar.

That meant that our only hope for a shortcut rested on the spices. Since they would end up blooming in oil, which also brings out their flavors, we wondered if toasting them beforehand was necessary—or if we could even sub in preground spices. We ran more tests, comparing whole spices that we'd toasted and ground against their preground equivalents. Fortunately, this timesaver worked: The depth and intensity of the preground spice paste was a little less potent, but the basic effect we were going for—warmth with faint sweetness—came across just fine.

In fact, we wondered if we could take this streamlining one step further and use a commercial spice blend instead of measuring out individual spices. After trying pumpkin pie spice (too much cinnamon) and curry powder (too much turmeric), we landed on five-spice powder. Though not an exact match with the traditional massaman lineup, the generally warm, fragrant profile of this blend (which typically includes fennel, cinnamon, star anise, cloves, and either pepper or ginger) made a nice stand-in, and its flavor was potent enough that just a teaspoon got the job done. Some cumin and a little extra black pepper went into the mix, and we were done.

From there, we had only a couple of technique and flavor issues to work through. Traditional Thai curry recipes call for frying the paste in coconut cream (either skimmed from the top of a can of coconut milk or bought separately) that's first heated until its oil separates out, or "cracks." We pitted a batch of curry in which we had fried the paste in the skimmed, cracked cream against our working recipe, which called for simply frying the paste in vegetable oil. Admittedly, a few tasters picked up on the more concentrated flavor of the cracked cream curry, but most agreed that vegetable oil worked fine.

Our colleagues were also clamoring for a bit of brightness, so we tried finishing the curry with a few teaspoons of lime juice—our best guess for a tamarind substitute. Alas, its effect was too sharp for massaman, and scaling back on the juice flattened its effect altogether.

What did work: changing the point at which we added the lime juice rather than the amount. When we replaced some of the water in the paste with a few teaspoons of juice, the lime's acid mellowed as it cooked in the curry but didn't disappear. Finishing the curry with lime zest and cilantro freshened it even more.

Served with a heap of fragrant jasmine rice, our version of massaman curry captured everything we love about this dish: richness and depth from the roasted chiles and aromatics, warmth from the spices, crunch from the peanuts, and a touch of freshness from the lime and cilantro, all brought together in a manageable amount of time.

Thai Chicken Curry with Potatoes and Peanuts
SERVES 4 TO 6

Serve the curry with jasmine rice. The ingredients for the curry paste can be doubled to make extra for future use. Refrigerate the paste for up to one week or freeze it for up to two months.

CURRY PASTE

- **6** dried New Mexican chiles
- **4** shallots, unpeeled
- **7** garlic cloves, unpeeled
- **½** cup chopped fresh ginger
- **¼** cup water
- **1½** tablespoons lime juice
- **1½** tablespoons vegetable oil
- **1** tablespoon fish sauce
- **1** teaspoon five-spice powder
- **½** teaspoon ground cumin
- **½** teaspoon pepper

CURRY

- **1** teaspoon vegetable oil
- **1¼** cups chicken broth
- **1** (13.5-ounce) can coconut milk
- **1** pound Yukon Gold potatoes, unpeeled, cut into ¾-inch pieces
- **1** onion, cut into ¾-inch pieces
- **⅓** cup dry-roasted peanuts
- **¾** teaspoon salt
- **1** pound boneless, skinless chicken thighs, trimmed and cut into 1-inch pieces
- **2** teaspoons grated lime zest
- **¼** cup chopped fresh cilantro

1. FOR THE CURRY PASTE: Adjust oven rack to middle position and heat oven to 350 degrees. Line rimmed baking sheet with aluminum foil. Arrange chiles on prepared sheet and toast until puffed and fragrant, 4 to 6 minutes. Transfer chiles to large plate. Heat broiler.

2. Place shallots and garlic on foil-lined sheet and broil until softened and skin is charred, 6 to 9 minutes.

3. When cool enough to handle, stem and seed chiles and tear into 1½-inch pieces. Process chiles in blender until finely ground, about 1 minute. Peel shallots and garlic.

CHINESE BRAISED BEEF

✓ **WHY THIS RECIPE WORKS:** Chinese braised beef (also called red-cooked beef) is a slow-braised dish in which a thick, ultraflavorful, stew-like sauce envelops tender pieces of beef. We wanted to maintain the deeply complex flavors of the original but simplify the recipe for the home kitchen. We decided to use readily available boneless beef short ribs in place of traditional shank of beef. To streamline the classic cooking method, we opted to skip blanching the meat, and we moved the pot from the stovetop to the even heat of the oven. A pair of thickeners—gelatin and cornstarch—added body to the sauce. Five-spice powder provided characteristic flavor without the bother of whole spices, and a combination of hoisin sauce and molasses contributed an underlying sweetness that completed the dish.

Add shallots, garlic, ginger, water, lime juice, oil, fish sauce, five-spice powder, cumin, and pepper to blender. Process to smooth paste, scraping down sides of blender jar as needed, 2 to 3 minutes. You should have 1 cup paste.

4. FOR THE CURRY: Heat oil in large saucepan over medium heat until shimmering. Add curry paste and cook, stirring constantly, until paste begins to brown, 2½ to 3 minutes. Stir in broth, coconut milk, potatoes, onion, peanuts, and salt, scraping up any browned bits. Bring to simmer and cook until potatoes are just tender, 12 to 14 minutes.

5. Stir in chicken and continue to simmer until chicken is cooked through, 10 to 12 minutes. Remove pan from heat and stir in lime zest. Serve, passing cilantro separately.

EVERY CULTURE HAS A VERSION OF SLOW-COOKED, satisfying, warm-you-from-the-inside-out comfort food, and Chinese red-cooked beef is a prime example of the genre. While the dish shares some of the same homey appeal of American beef stew, the Chinese take is arguably more appealing. What you get: chunks of ultratender meat moistened in a modest amount of sauce that makes up for what it lacks in volume with its potent flavor. Red-cooked beef also differs from American stews in that it doesn't have add-ins like carrots or potatoes. Instead, the focus is exclusively on the beef and the sauce, which is redolent with flavorings like ginger, cinnamon, star anise, Sichuan peppercorns, and cardamom. The meal is typically rounded out with plenty of steamed vegetables and rice, which provide a neutral background for the intensity of the sauce.

We learned quickly not to get hung up on the name. "Red-cooked" (or *hong shao*) comes from the notion that a protein (beef, pork, poultry, or fish) simmered in a lightly sweetened broth of soy sauce and spices takes on a ruddy hue, but every version that we've seen has a deep, rich brown color.

CHINESE BRAISED BEEF

BEEF SHANK—EVEN BETTER THAN SHORT RIBS

Shank is a cut from the lower leg of the steer. Though it is very sinewy, it is actually quite lean. In the United States, it's often used to make low-fat ground beef. This is a shame because with braising, it becomes meltingly tender, and its liquefied connective tissue imparts a silky richness to a sauce that requires little, if any, defatting. If you can find shank and have an extra hour or two, it's the best and most economical choice for red-cooked beef. You'll find shank sold as both long cut and cross cut (with or without the bone). If using cross cut, decrease the gelatin to 2¼ teaspoons and increase the cooking time in step 2 to 4 hours. If using long cut, cut it crossways into 1-inch-thick slabs, omit the gelatin, and increase the cooking time in step 2 to 5 hours.

LONG-CUT SHANK
Lots of connective tissue; cooks in 5 hours.

CROSS-CUT SHANK
Less connective tissue; cooks in 4 hours.

There are two approaches to red cooking. The first calls for braising the food in plenty of liquid and saving that liquid to be used repeatedly for the same purpose, imparting deeper flavor with each use. As appealing as that sounded, it wasn't really practical. We centered our attention on the second approach, in which the meat is braised in liquid and then removed from the pot, after which the braising liquid is reduced to an intensely flavored, demi-glace-like consistency.

All the recipes in this style that we'd rounded up started out the same way: Cube a large cut of beef (shank is the most traditional), blanch the cubes in water (a step that's said to remove impurities), and then set them aside while you make the braising liquid. The most basic of these stocks called for simply combining water with soy sauce, a bit of sugar, rice wine (or sherry), ginger, scallions, garlic, and one or two spices. But even when such stocks were reduced, we found that they didn't have the layers of flavor that are key to the dish. On the other hand, more elaborate recipes that incorporated caramelized sugar, pungent fermented condiments such as chili bean paste, and lengthy lists of whole spices were beautifully nuanced. Our challenge, then, would be maintaining the complex, aromatic flavor profile of this comfort food while making it as fuss-free as possible—no trips to an Asian market required.

To determine which cut of beef would be best, we blanched several braising cuts in boiling water (we'd revisit whether this step was really necessary later) and then simmered them in separate pots of water flavored with soy sauce, sugar, scallions, garlic, sherry, fresh ginger, and cinnamon sticks (likewise, we'd figure out the full spectrum of spices that we'd want to use when we were further along). The shank worked beautifully. It was amazingly tender and moist, and it imparted a silky fullness to the sauce. But since shank can be hard to find in American supermarkets, we set it as the benchmark to be matched and made our way through a list of alternatives.

Brisket was tender but dry. Chuck roast and blade steak were tender and rich but required a lot of trimming before going into the pot. In the end, we opted for boneless short ribs, which had enough fat and collagen to cook up moist but required minimal prep before we put them in the pot. True, short ribs didn't produce a sauce with the richness of that made with shank, but we would address that later. On the upside, short ribs cooked in about half the time of shank. After bringing the pot to a simmer, we moved the bulk of the cooking to the oven, where the meat could simmer without constant monitoring. We left the meat in large pieces to make it easier to remove from the pot when it came time to strain out the aromatics and reduce our sauce, and we simply used a pair of forks to pull apart the tender meat into bite-size chunks before we added them to the reduced sauce.

About that blanching step: Briefly cooking the meat in boiling water removes free proteins from the surface, which produces a clearer stock—but since we were reducing the stock to a concentrated, opaque sauce, we realized that this probably wasn't important. One test confirmed that blanching not only made no difference in the appearance of our red-cooked beef but didn't affect its flavor or texture either, so we happily eliminated that step.

And what about browning? In the West we are very influenced by French cooking, which often means browning meat to deepen its flavor. However, we decided that this wasn't necessary here. While browning could provide a moderate boost to the meatiness of the dish, short ribs are plenty beefy, and in the case of red cooking, the complex, potently flavored sauce would—or should—overshadow it. Which brought us to our next task: improving the rather one-dimensional flavor of the sauce.

To balance the saltiness of the soy sauce and impart a subtle sweetness, thus far we had been using white sugar. Brown sugar added a little more depth, but we were still intrigued by recipes that incorporated caramelized sugar. For our next batch, we cooked ¼ cup of sugar with a bit of water until it turned dark brown; then we added the other ingredients to the pot. Its slight bitterness contributed interesting new flavor notes. Could we get the same effect without the extra step? When we tried substituting 2 tablespoons of molasses straight out of the jar for the sugar, we were pleased to find that it provided a similarly bittersweet flavor. Some thick hoisin sauce introduced complementary sweetness and flavor and a bit of body, too.

Now for the spices. Though tasters had loved the versions we had made that called for a slew of whole spices, were the spices really necessary? Some recipes required just one spice—preground five-spice powder. It was here that we suffered a crisis of conscience. We had ditched the blanching step and opted for molasses over caramelized sugar (with, it must be said, no detrimental effect in either case), but surely substituting a ground mixture of spices was going a step too far.

Not at all. In fact, we found that with just 1½ teaspoons of five-spice powder, the flavors in the braise

really came together, shifting from a subtle infusion to a more developed and powerful punch. A bit of heat was the only thing missing, so we added 1 teaspoon of red pepper flakes.

Now the sauce had all the deep, nuanced flavor that we were after, but the consistency was wrong. Because you know what you get when you boil down a water-based stock? Very flavorful water.

We wanted a sauce that would cling to the meat and accompanying rice rather than flow to the bottom of the bowl, and this wasn't it. We tried flour—the most common thickener in recipes for Western-style beef stews—but it produced a gravy rather than the lacquer-like glaze we wanted. Cornstarch wasn't quite right here either: It gave the sauce that slick texture often found in a stir-fry sauce, and it seemed a bit lightweight for this application. What we really wanted was that rich glazelike texture we had gotten when we had braised the beef shanks for 5 hours. When we considered that it was the meat's collagen that really made that version such a success, the answer was obvious: Add gelatin, since collagen converts to gelatin during cooking.

We admit that we went a bit overboard at first: 2 tablespoons of gelatin gave the sauce a tacky consistency. Backing down to 1½ tablespoons, added at the beginning of cooking, and introducing a mere teaspoon of cornstarch at the end produced a sauce that coated the meat nicely without forming a gel.

With its tender meat and satisfying heartiness, this version of red-cooked beef had all the appeal of an American-style stew, but the warmth of the sweet spices and the deep savory flavor made it a welcome change from our usual cool-weather offerings. Best of all, with fussy steps like blanching meat and caramelizing sugar eliminated, this dish had come together with an ease that made it comfort food in every sense.

Chinese Braised Beef

SERVES 6

With its generous amount of soy sauce, this dish is meant to taste salty, so we like to pair it with plain white rice. A simple steamed vegetable like bok choy or broccoli completes the meal. Boneless beef short ribs require little trimming, but you can also use a 4-pound chuck roast. Trim the roast of large pieces of fat and sinew, cut it across the grain into 1-inch-thick slabs, and cut the slabs into 4 by 2-inch pieces.

1½ tablespoons unflavored gelatin
2½ cups plus 1 tablespoon water
½ cup dry sherry
⅓ cup soy sauce
2 tablespoons hoisin sauce
2 tablespoons molasses
3 scallions, white and green parts separated, green parts sliced thin on bias
1 (2-inch) piece ginger, peeled, halved lengthwise, and crushed
4 garlic cloves, peeled and smashed
1½ teaspoons five-spice powder
1 teaspoon red pepper flakes
3 pounds boneless beef short ribs, trimmed and cut into 4-inch lengths
1 teaspoon cornstarch

1. Sprinkle gelatin over 2½ cups water in Dutch oven and let sit until gelatin softens, about 5 minutes. Adjust oven rack to middle position and heat oven to 300 degrees.

2. Heat softened gelatin over medium-high heat, stirring occasionally, until melted, 2 to 3 minutes. Stir in sherry, soy sauce, hoisin, molasses, scallion whites, ginger, garlic, five-spice powder, and pepper flakes. Stir in beef and bring to simmer. Remove pot from heat. Cover tightly with sheet of heavy-duty aluminum foil, then lid. Transfer to oven and cook until beef is tender, 2 to 2½ hours, stirring halfway through cooking.

3. Using slotted spoon, transfer beef to cutting board. Strain sauce through fine-mesh strainer into fat separator. Wipe out pot with paper towels. Let liquid settle for 5 minutes, then return defatted liquid to now-empty pot. Cook liquid over medium-high heat, stirring occasionally, until thickened and reduced to 1 cup, 20 to 25 minutes.

4. While sauce reduces, using 2 forks, break beef into 1½-inch pieces. Whisk cornstarch and remaining 1 tablespoon water together in small bowl.

5. Reduce heat to medium-low, whisk cornstarch mixture into reduced sauce, and cook until sauce is slightly thickened, about 1 minute. Return beef to sauce and stir to coat. Cover and cook, stirring occasionally, until beef is heated through, about 5 minutes. Sprinkle scallion greens over top. Serve.

RATING FIVE-SPICE POWDER

Chinese five-spice powder adds a punch that offsets richness in both sweet and savory recipes. Most blends from China include cinnamon, star anise, cloves, fennel, and Sichuan pepper (American companies usually substitute white or black pepper). We tried the updated version of our former favorite, from Dean & DeLuca, as well as five additional brands in warm sweetened milk and in Chinese Braised Beef. We also had an independent lab test the overall potency of each sample by measuring the total volatile oils. And since the piney licorice notes and tangy heat of star anise make it a key player, we also had the lab analyze levels of anethole, the compound that supplies its flavors and aromas. The winner and runner-up were in the middle range for overall potency and high in anethole; this translated into a complex flavor in which star anise predominated but still allowed other spices to come to the fore. Our favorite, Frontier Natural Products Co-op Five Spice Powder ($4.69 for 1.92 ounces), won for "lots of licorice" plus a "piney" taste with a "nice kick" of heat. Products are listed in order of preference. See AmericasTestKitchen.com for updates and complete tasting results.

RECOMMENDED

FRONTIER NATURAL PRODUCTS CO-OP Five Spice Powder
PRICE: $4.69 for 1.92 oz ($2.44 per oz)
ANETHOLE: 1.43 g in 100 g
INGREDIENTS: Cinnamon, fennel, cloves, star anise, white pepper
VOLATILE OILS: 4.28 ml in 100 g
COMMENTS: Warmed in milk, this blend had a "rounded" "licorice" flavor that was "woodsy," "sweet," and "aromatic." In braised beef, its "harmonious flavor" had a "nice kick" and was "heaviest on anise, but with cinnamon coming through, too."

DYNASTY Chinese Five Spices
PRICE: $2.79 for 2 oz ($1.40 per oz)
ANETHOLE: 1.97 g in 100 g
INGREDIENTS: Cinnamon, star anise, fennel, ginger, cloves, white pepper, licorice root
VOLATILE OILS: 4.56 ml in 100 g
COMMENTS: The "savory" and "slightly woodsy" flavor of this blend—which contains seven spices—also had an "assertively licorice" aspect in the warmed milk. In braised beef, it was "earthy" and "complex," with hints of "allspice" and "star anise."

MCCORMICK GOURMET COLLECTION Chinese Five Spice
PRICE: $6.99 for 1.75 oz ($3.99 per oz)
ANETHOLE: 1.90 g in 100 g
INGREDIENTS: Anise, cinnamon, star anise, cloves, ginger, sulfiting agents
VOLATILE OILS: 5.18 ml in 100 g
COMMENTS: With an "earthy" and "floral" taste in warmed milk, this blend provided "pungency" in braised beef, along with a "woodsy" flavor. But some tasters picked up on an odd "curry" taste. It was the only blend to use sulfites, which preserve spice color and prevent bacterial growth (but impart no flavor).

RECOMMENDED *(cont.)*

DEAN & DELUCA Five Spice Blend
PRICE: $6.50 for 1.4 oz ($4.64 per oz), plus shipping
ANETHOLE: 0.68 g in 100 g
INGREDIENTS: Star anise, cinnamon, clove, fennel, black pepper
VOLATILE OILS: 1.33 ml in 100 g
COMMENTS: This mail-order blend, with the lowest levels of both volatile oils and anethole, seemed "sweet" and "licorice-y" but otherwise "mild" in warmed milk. In braised beef, it "begins sweet [and] ends with a tiny bit of heat." "I'd find myself adding more," one taster said.

MORTON & BASSETT Chinese Five Spice
PRICE: $5.49 for 1.9 oz ($2.89 per oz)
ANETHOLE: 0.86 g in 100 g
INGREDIENTS: Cinnamon, anise seed, cloves, ginger, fennel
VOLATILE OILS: 2.15 ml in 100 g
COMMENTS: Warmed in milk, this "sweet," "anise-y" blend—with the second-lowest levels of volatile oils and anethole—was "too faint" for some tasters. In braised beef it had a "smoky, sweet pungent flavor," though some tasters found it lacking "heat."

RECOMMENDED WITH RESERVATIONS

PENZEYS Chinese Five Spice Powder
PRICE: $7.55 for 2.1 oz ($3.60 per oz), plus shipping
ANETHOLE: 0.91 g in 100 g
INGREDIENTS: Cinnamon, star anise, anise seed, ginger, cloves
VOLATILE OILS: 6.43 ml in 100 g
COMMENTS: The "gingerbread" flavor of this mail-order blend came across as "mostly cinnamon" and "clove" in warmed milk. In braised beef, its "cinnamon" flavor predominated again. Despite having the most volatile oils in the lineup, it had one of the lowest levels of anethole, so that the key flavors of star anise were missing.

Great Grilled Burgers and Sweet Potato Fries

Placing the beef patties in the freezer for 30 minutes helps them hold together on the grill and prevents overcooking, allowing the burgers to pick up extra char.

CHANCES ARE, YOU'VE HAD A REALLY GOOD BURGER BEFORE. MAYBE even a great burger. But until you've tried our Tender, Juicy Grilled Burgers, you haven't experienced the best of this backyard barbecue staple. For our best burger ever, we wanted a moist, flavorful interior and a craggy, perfectly charred crust. We accounted for all the variables—size, texture, seasonings, grilling method—and found that each small change made a big impact on how the burgers turned out. Plus, a secret ingredient made them richer, heartier, and even more flavorful. We've made burgers before, but none of them holds a candle to this one.

And what goes better with a perfect burger than perfect fries? While we love thin, crisp, russet fries, sometimes we like to switch it up and make sweet potato fries. But when cooked, low-starch sweet potatoes don't behave the same way that their white-fleshed, starchy cousins do. We weren't willing to settle for limp, soggy sweet potatoes, so we came up with a solution. And we found our inspiration in a surprising place: frozen commercial fries.

TENDER, JUICY GRILLED BURGERS

TENDER, JUICY GRILLED BURGERS

✓ WHY THIS RECIPE WORKS: Creating a juicy and loosely textured burger that could withstand the rigors of grilling called for a number of tactics. First, we ground our own meat in the food processor, which let us choose the cut (steak tips), grind (coarse), and consistency (loose) of the burger when we shaped it. Incorporating a little salt before shaping added richness, boosted juiciness, and seasoned the burgers throughout. Finally we shaped the burgers (with a dimple in their centers to prevent bulging) and froze them for 30 minutes, which held them together as they cooked and let them stay on the grill a few minutes longer for excellent char and perfect rosy centers. Finally, we developed a few creamy vegetable toppings to perfectly complement the rich meat.

TO US, ONE OF THE BEST THINGS ABOUT SUMMER IS THE chance to eat a really great burger off the grill. By that we mean a burger with an ultracraggy charred crust, a rich beefy taste, and an interior so juicy and tender that it practically falls apart at the slightest pressure.

The problem is, such a burger is actually pretty hard to come by. While the typical specimen may have a nicely browned crust, it's also heavy and dense with a pebbly texture. The reason is no mystery: Most cooks use preground meat from the supermarket, which is usually ground so fine that a certain amount of graininess is inevitable. Furthermore, they tend to shape the meat into tightly packed disks that, while easier to flip on the grill, guarantee dense texture. Forming loose patties produces that prized open texture, but it's a far riskier proposition on a grill than in a skillet or on a griddle. On a flat uniform surface, a loosely packed patty is fully supported, and once that patty forms a crust, carefully sliding a spatula beneath it and gently flipping it over is relatively easy. On the open grate of a grill, however,

that same patty is likely to wind up on the coals before a crust can form to hold it together.

This summer we decided to tackle these issues head on and find an approach to a truly excellent backyard burger. We'd look at every possible variable, from how and when to season the meat, to how best to form the patties and what size to make them, and of course, how to get them on and off the grill in one piece. The perfect burger might take a little more work, but it would definitely be worth it.

It was a given that we'd need to grind our own meat. Besides being ground too fine, commercial burger meat is also manhandled during processing and compressed inside tightly wrapped packages. This overmanipulation draws out a lot of the sticky protein myosin, so even if you form your patties with a gentle hand at home, your results have already been compromised—a denser texture is inevitable. And while chuck (the cut that's often preground for supermarkets) might make a decent burger—we would certainly consider it—we wanted to decide for ourselves which cut would deliver the best flavor.

In the test kitchen, we've found it easy to grind meat ourselves with a food processor. The method we've developed (no matter the cut) calls for trimming gristle and excess fat from the meat, cutting the meat into ½-inch pieces, freezing it for about 30 minutes to firm it up so that the blades cut it cleanly instead of smashing and smearing it (which leads to pasty, dense results), and finally processing it in small batches to ensure an even, precise grind.

We narrowed the cut of meat to three options: chuck, boneless short ribs, and sirloin steak tips (aka flap meat). Each of these choices is relatively inexpensive, decently tender, and contains a sufficient amount of fat to ensure burgers that are reasonably moist and flavorful. Chuck had great flavor and ample marbling, but it contained a lot of sinewy connective tissue that had to be painstakingly removed before grinding (something the mass-market preground versions easily take care of during processing). Deeply marbled short ribs were gloriously fatty and rich—but a bit too rich for several tasters, so they were also out. Somewhat leaner steak tips had great meaty flavor and required virtually no trimming. They came up a bit short in terms of richness, but we had a trick up our sleeves for fixing that.

In another test kitchen burger recipe, we call for tossing the ground meat with melted butter. The burgers don't taste of butter, but they gain deeper flavor and richness. However, pouring melted butter over our near-frozen meat was somewhat problematic; the butter started to solidify on contact, making it tricky to evenly distribute. We realized that there was a way to incorporate the butter that would not only enable even

NOTES FROM THE TEST KITCHEN

MAKE A BURGER THAT GOES SPLAT

Store-bought burger meat can't help but cook up dense and tough. It's ground very fine and then wrapped up tightly for retail—factors that cause too much of the sticky protein myosin to be released, literally gluing the meat together. By grinding meat ourselves, we can keep it coarse and pack it gently into patties that stay fall-apart tender.

A TOUGH SELL
This burger made with preground meat held together even when we dropped a 10-pound Dutch oven on it.

SMASHINGLY TENDER
Meat ground at home delivers a much more tender burger, one that splattered easily under the Dutch oven's weight.

distribution but also be easier: adding it to the food processor when grinding the meat. Cut into ¼-inch cubes and frozen, 4 tablespoons of butter ground perfectly into pieces the same size as the beef and were scattered uniformly throughout the mixture.

Now we were ready to sort out the mechanics of shaping and grilling. We determined that 6 ounces was the ideal portion size: generous but not excessive. A patty that was 4½ inches across would fit perfectly on the average bun once cooked. This gave us patties that were ¾ inch thick, which we figured was just thick enough to allow decent char on the exterior without overcooking at the center (any thicker and they'd be too hard to eat). We also knew from experience that we would need to make a small depression in the center of each patty before grilling to ensure that they finished flat instead of ballooning outward.

But before we could even add those divots, we had to sort out our biggest obstacle: How could we form our burgers so that they wouldn't fall apart on the grate but at the same time achieve that essential open texture? Too much manipulation of ground meat translates to tough burgers, but maybe a little handling of it could work in our favor. If we could draw out just a little sticky myosin, maybe it would help hold the burgers together without making them tough. First we tried kneading the ground meat lightly as if it were dough. Unfortunately, with this approach knowing exactly when to stop was difficult; it was far too easy to under- or overshoot the mark. What if we heavily kneaded only a small portion of the mixture until it was very sticky and then combined that with the remainder? This wasn't much better; it was a challenge to evenly incorporate the sticky, tightly packed portion into the rest without eventually overworking the lot of it.

Salt, like kneading, also draws out myosin. For this reason, we've always avoided adding it to ground meat before shaping, instead seasoning the patties just before putting them on the grill. We wondered if there was a middle ground. It would certainly be easier to control how much salt we added compared with how much we kneaded, so we made batches of burgers containing increasing amounts of salt, from ¼ teaspoon up to

1 teaspoon per pound of meat. Adding the salt and then using a fork to toss the meat allowed us to evenly distribute the salt without overworking the meat. Sadly, small amounts did little to help bind the meat together, and by the time we'd added enough to give them the necessary structure, the resulting burgers were tough and springy.

However, working salt into the interior of the meat did have an upside: It thoroughly seasoned the meat and made it juicier. This made good sense: Just as the salt in a brine helps meat retain moisture as it cooks (salt alters the structure of the proteins to allow them to hold on to water more efficiently), the salt mixed into the ground meat ensured that it stayed juicy and moist on the grill. We just had to be precise, adding only as much salt as we could get away with before adversely affecting the burgers' texture. That turned out to be ½ teaspoon per pound.

We had made great progress, but if we couldn't find a way to keep our burgers intact, it didn't matter how good they tasted. Our loosely formed patties held together pretty well for the first few seconds on the grill, but as soon as the meat lost its chill from the refrigerator, the patties started to fall apart. We needed an approach that would hold the patties together long enough for them to develop a crust (which would then take over the job). When we thought about it that way, the answer became obvious: Freeze them. For our next test, we placed the burgers in the freezer until they were just firm but not frozen solid (which took about 30 minutes) and then headed out to the grill. As we'd hoped, by the time they'd thawed at their centers, they had developed enough crust to ensure that they held together. In fact, because they were cold, we found that they could stay on the grill a few minutes longer per side—gaining even more tasty char and making flipping all the more fail-safe—without going beyond medium-rare.

All that remained were the details of the fire itself. To ensure that the burgers charred on the exterior dramatically and quickly, a hot fire proved best. Since the burgers took up very little real estate on the grate, we corralled a few quarts of charcoal inside a disposable aluminum roasting pan (perforated to let in oxygen so that they would burn) underneath the burgers to guarantee a

cooking space that was plenty hot. (On a gas grill, this translated to setting all the burners to high and preheating the grill for 15 minutes.)

Whether served with the classic fixings like lettuce and tomato or something fancier—we developed three different creamy grilled-vegetable toppings—this was a grilled burger that actually lived up to our ideal.

Tender, Juicy Grilled Burgers
SERVES 4

This recipe requires freezing the meat twice, for a total of 65 to 80 minutes, before grilling. When stirring the salt and pepper into the ground meat and shaping the patties, take care not to overwork the meat or the burgers will become dense. Sirloin steak tips are also sold as flap meat. Serve the burgers with your favorite toppings or one of our grilled-vegetable toppings (recipes follow).

1½ pounds sirloin steak tips, trimmed and cut into
      ½-inch chunks
4   tablespoons unsalted butter, cut into ¼-inch pieces
      Kosher salt and pepper
1   (13 by 9-inch) disposable aluminum pan (if using
      charcoal)
4   hamburger buns

1. Place beef chunks and butter on large plate in single layer. Freeze until meat is very firm and starting to harden around edges but still pliable, about 35 minutes.

2. Place one-quarter of meat and one-quarter of butter cubes in food processor and pulse until finely ground into pieces the size of rice grains (about 1/32 inch), 15 to 20 pulses, stopping and redistributing meat around bowl as necessary to ensure beef is evenly ground. Transfer meat to baking sheet. Repeat grinding with remaining 3 batches of meat and butter. Spread mixture over sheet and inspect carefully, discarding any long strands of gristle or large chunks of hard meat, fat, or butter.

3. Sprinkle 1 teaspoon pepper and 3/4 teaspoon salt over meat and gently toss with fork to combine. Divide meat into 4 balls. Toss each between your hands until uniformly but lightly packed. Gently flatten into patties 3/4 inch thick and about 4 1/2 inches in diameter. Using your thumb, make 1-inch-wide by 1/4-inch-deep depression in center of each patty. Transfer patties to platter and freeze for 30 to 45 minutes.

4A. FOR A CHARCOAL GRILL: Using skewer, poke 12 holes in bottom of disposable pan. Open bottom vent completely and place disposable pan in center of grill. Light large chimney starter filled two-thirds with charcoal briquettes (4 quarts). When top coals are partially covered with ash, pour into disposable pan. Set cooking grate in place, cover, and open lid vent completely. Heat grill until hot, about 5 minutes.

4B. FOR A GAS GRILL: Turn all burners to high, cover, and heat grill until hot, about 15 minutes. Leave all burners on high.

5. Clean and oil cooking grate. Season 1 side of patties liberally with salt and pepper. Using spatula, flip patties and season other side. Grill patties (directly over coals if using charcoal), without moving them, until browned and meat easily releases from grill, 4 to 7 minutes. Flip burgers and continue to grill until browned on second side and meat registers 125 degrees (for medium-rare) or 130 degrees (for medium), 4 to 7 minutes longer.

6. Transfer burgers to plate and let rest for 5 minutes. While burgers rest, lightly toast buns on grill, 1 to 2 minutes. Transfer burgers to buns and serve.

Grilled Scallion Topping

Start grilling the scallions about 5 minutes before the burgers so that the topping will be ready as soon as the burgers come off the grill.

- 2 tablespoons sour cream
- 2 tablespoons mayonnaise
- 2 tablespoons buttermilk
- 1 tablespoon cider vinegar
- 1 tablespoon minced fresh chives
- 2 teaspoons Dijon mustard
- ¼ teaspoon sugar
- Salt and pepper
- 20 scallions
- 2 tablespoons vegetable oil

1. Combine sour cream, mayonnaise, buttermilk, vinegar, chives, mustard, sugar, ½ teaspoon salt, and ⅛ teaspoon pepper in medium bowl. Set aside.

2. Toss scallions with oil in large bowl. Grill scallions over hot fire until lightly charred and softened, 2 to 4 minutes per side. Return to bowl and let cool for 5 minutes. Slice scallions thin, then transfer to bowl with reserved sour cream mixture. Toss to combine and season with salt and pepper to taste.

Grilled Shiitake Mushroom Topping

Start grilling the mushrooms about 5 minutes before the burgers so that the topping will be ready as soon as the burgers come off the grill.

- 2 tablespoons sour cream
- 2 tablespoons mayonnaise
- 2 tablespoons buttermilk
- 1 tablespoon cider vinegar
- 1 tablespoon minced fresh chives
- 2 teaspoons Dijon mustard
- ¼ teaspoon sugar
- Salt and pepper
- 8 ounces shiitake mushrooms, stemmed
- 2 tablespoons vegetable oil

1. Combine sour cream, mayonnaise, buttermilk, vinegar, chives, mustard, sugar, ½ teaspoon salt, and ⅛ teaspoon pepper in medium bowl. Set aside.

2. Toss mushrooms with oil in large bowl. Grill mushrooms over hot fire until lightly charred and softened, 2 to 4 minutes per side. Return to bowl and let cool for 5 minutes. Slice mushrooms thin, then transfer to bowl with reserved sour cream mixture. Toss to combine and season with salt and pepper to taste.

Grilled Napa Cabbage and Radicchio Topping

Start grilling the cabbage and radicchio about 5 minutes before the burgers so that the topping will be ready as soon as the burgers come off the grill.

- 2 tablespoons sour cream
- 2 tablespoons mayonnaise
- 2 tablespoons buttermilk
- 1 tablespoon cider vinegar
- 1 tablespoon minced fresh parsley
- 2 teaspoons Dijon mustard
- ¼ teaspoon sugar
- Salt and pepper
- ¼ small head napa cabbage
- ½ small head radicchio, cut into 2 wedges
- 2 tablespoons vegetable oil

1. Combine sour cream, mayonnaise, buttermilk, vinegar, parsley, mustard, sugar, ½ teaspoon salt, and ⅛ teaspoon pepper in medium bowl. Set aside.

2. Place cabbage and radicchio on rimmed baking sheet and brush with oil. Grill over hot fire until lightly charred and beginning to wilt, 2 to 4 minutes on each cut side. Return to sheet and let cool for 5 minutes. Slice cabbage and radicchio thin, then transfer to bowl with reserved sour cream mixture. Toss to combine and season with salt and pepper to taste.

THICK-CUT SWEET POTATO FRIES

✔ **WHY THIS RECIPE WORKS:** Too often, sweet potato fries simply don't do justice to their namesake vegetable. We wanted thick-cut sweet potato fries with crispy exteriors and creamy, sweet interiors. Taking a cue from commercial frozen fries, which rely on a starchy coating to encourage crispness, we dunked the potato wedges in a slurry of water and cornstarch. Blanching the potatoes with salt and baking soda before dipping them in the slurry helped the coating stick to the potatoes, giving the fries a super-crunchy crust that stayed crispy. To keep the fries from sticking to the pan, we used a nonstick skillet, which had the added benefit of allowing us to use less oil. For a finishing touch to complement the natural sweetness of the fries, we made a spicy Belgian-style dipping sauce.

THOUGH THEY'RE BOTH CALLED POTATOES, WHITE potatoes and sweet potatoes couldn't be more different. Sweet potatoes come from a completely different plant family than white potatoes like russets and contain far less starch, more water, and a lot more sugar. As a result, they cook very differently—a fact that is nowhere more apparent than when making fries: It's very hard to make sweet potato fries that rival classic French fries made from russets.

Sweet potato fries are typically soggy or burnt—and often they hit both marks at once. Occasionally a restaurant manages to deliver crispy sweet potato fries, but they never taste much like the tuber. These fries are usually not even house-made: They're frozen fries purchased from a food processing plant. Furthermore, they're frequently cut too thin for our liking, offering little in the way of a supercreamy, sweet-tasting interior—in our opinion, the biggest selling point of this vegetable. Fueled by a serious hunger for good thick-cut sweet potato fries, we ordered 50 pounds of the orange spuds and got to work.

While commercial frozen sweet potato fries lack flavor, we have to respect their ability to turn (and stay) super-crispy. How do they do it? When we compared the ingredient lists of a few products, we found a common theme: starch. A starchy coating on these frozen fries makes all the difference. This discovery didn't come entirely by surprise. After all, it's the high-starch composition of russet potatoes that makes them so suited to frying, and we use starchy coatings to give all kinds of low-starch foods (like chicken) a crispy fried exterior. Meanwhile, sweet potatoes don't just contain less starch than white potatoes do; a little research informed us that they also contain an enzyme that, when heated, converts some of the starch in the sweet potatoes into sugars. All this translates into a serious handicap in the world of deep frying.

So would adding a starchy coating to our fries be the fix that allowed them to crisp up? We rounded up a group of easy-to-find starches—potato starch, cornstarch, arrowroot, and all-purpose flour (while not a pure starch, it's often used for coating foods when deep-frying)—and ran a test to compare. After heating 2 quarts of vegetable oil in a large Dutch oven to 350 degrees, we dusted four batches of ¾-inch-wide peeled sweet potato wedges (which we'd cut in half crosswise for a more manageable shape) with each type of starch and fried them until tender and, in theory, crispy.

What a disappointment. None of the starches formed anything resembling a crispy crust: They clung meekly to the sweet potatoes as a dry, flaky, dusty coating. It turns out that cut sweet potatoes—unlike, say, chicken—don't exude much moisture. Instead, almost all the water that they contain stays trapped within their cell walls. Why is liquid so important in a coating when frying? In hot oil the food's surface moisture quickly turns into steam, and as the steam escapes the food, the outer starchy coating dries out and crisps. The escaping steam leaves behind small holes, and oil fills those holes, helping create a crispy brown crust. These little holes also break up the texture of the coating so that it's crunchy when bitten into rather than hard or leathery—think of a porous Nestlé Crunch bar versus a dense, hard bar of solid chocolate.

THICK-CUT SWEET POTATO FRIES

Given that, the solution seemed easy: We simply added some water to each of the starches, creating thin slurries that we could dip the wedges into before frying. This was a promising step forward. All the fries emerged with at least a modicum of crust. In the end, cornstarch won out, producing the best crust, with a nicely crisped texture.

But there were still some issues to deal with. For one, our fries looked more like sweet potato tempura—the fried coating was wispy and puffed away from the wedges. In addition, the coating, while crispy right out of the oil, had a tendency to quickly turn soft and soggy. And finally, the interiors of the sweet potatoes were more chalky than smooth, creamy, and sweet.

Thinking that we should switch gears, we turned our focus away from the coating and toward achieving the perfect creamy interior. The cause of the problem was quite clear: The short time that it took to dry and crisp the slurry on the outside wasn't sufficient to cook the thick wedges all the way through.

Our first thought was to go the classic French fry route and treat our uncoated wedges to a quick blanch in lower-temperature (around 250-degree) oil before

dipping them in the slurry and frying them again at the proper higher temperature to crisp the coating. We gave it a try, and while it resulted in a big difference for the interior texture—which turned soft and sweet—the oil slick on the outside of the blanched fries made it hard to get good slurry coverage. So we switched to blanching in water rather than in oil, simmering the wedges in a couple of quarts of salted water until their exteriors were tender but their very centers remained slightly firm. (Blanched any further, our fries tended to break apart when mixed with the slurry.) Then we proceeded with the coating and frying as before. This adjustment made a big difference. Without an oily barrier, the slurry clung evenly to each blanched wedge. Plus, adding the salt created better-tasting interiors. This was the best batch yet.

It was time to return to the issues with the coating—namely, it was too thin (and thus prone to sogginess) and didn't cling to the fries very well. Was there a way to thicken the coating and at the same time make it adhere better to the wedges? In the past, we've found that adding baking soda to the cooking water for white potatoes breaks down their exteriors, turning them pasty and starchy while their interiors remain firm. In many cases this would, of course, be a bad thing, but we wondered if using baking soda here would be a plus, creating a tacky exterior that the slurry would bind to more firmly.

We gave it a shot, adding 1 teaspoon of baking soda to the blanching water. After about 5 minutes of simmering, the water turned orange and the potatoes' exteriors were mushy, just as we'd expected. Once we'd folded these spuds into the slurry, a thick, gloppy orange paste coated the wedges. It looked promising—and it delivered. These wedges had a substantial, crispy coating that clung close to the potatoes, and our fries remained crispy for a long time out of the oil. What's more, they had visual appeal, with great orange color both inside and out. Finally we'd made exactly the fries that we'd been after.

Our last move was to try to simplify and foolproof the frying process. Up to this point we'd been using our standard setup: frying in batches in 2 quarts of oil in a large Dutch oven and keeping the fries warm in a low oven. But our supersticky coating mixture meant that now our fries were pretty likely to stick to one another, as well as to the bottom of the pot. To eliminate the bottom-sticking issue, we opted for nonstick cookware. At first a skillet seemed like an odd choice, but we found that we could drop the oil from 2 quarts to just 3 cups and still keep the wedges fully submerged.

To limit how much the fries stuck to one another, we added them to the pan individually with tongs to ensure that there was good spacing around them—a simple step, considering we were using thick-cut wedges rather than shoestring fries. Any fries that did manage to stick together were easily pried apart with tongs or two forks either during or after frying.

While many restaurants serve ketchup with their sweet potato fries, we always find the combination cloyingly sweet. Instead, we took a cue from the Belgians and whipped up a creamy, spicy mayonnaise-based sauce. Into the mayonnaise base we stirred spicy Asian chili-garlic sauce and white vinegar.

Supercrispy, ultracreamy, and complete with a spicy sauce, these thick-cut sweet potato fries would be the reason we save russets for baking and mashing.

Thick-Cut Sweet Potato Fries

SERVES 4 TO 6

If your sweet potatoes are shorter than 4 inches in length, do not cut the wedges crosswise. We prefer peanut oil for frying, but vegetable oil may be used instead. Leftover frying oil may be saved for further use; strain the cooled oil into an airtight container and store it in a cool, dark place for up to one month or in the freezer for up to two months. We like these fries with our Spicy Fry Sauce (recipe follows), but they are also good served plain.

½   cup cornstarch
    Kosher salt
1   teaspoon baking soda
3   pounds sweet potatoes, peeled and cut into
    ¾-inch-thick wedges, wedges cut in half crosswise
3   cups peanut oil

SWEET POTATO FRIES GONE WRONG

The typical sweet potato fry is cut thin, which means too little creamy sweet potato interior. Cutting our fries into wedges was a good fix, but their shape wasn't the only hurdle. Because sweet potatoes are low in starch, most sweet potato fries end up limp or burnt. Giving our sweet potato fries a starchy coating ensures a crust with a crispy texture.

LIMP, BURNT LOSERS
Low-starch sweet potatoes often burn before they crisp up.

MAKING GOOD ON SWEET POTATO FRIES

Here's how we turned sweet potatoes into impressively crispy fries with perfect creamy interiors.

1. BLANCH: Blanching the wedges helps ensure that their interiors fully cook and turn creamy when fried. Adding baking soda to the water makes them tacky on the outside.

2. COAT: The cornstarch slurry stays put thanks in part to the parcooked wedges' tacky exteriors, and it crisps up beautifully in the hot oil.

3. FRY: Frying the wedges in a nonstick skillet prevents them from sticking to the bottom of the pan. The change in vessel also allows us to use far less oil.

WHY STARCH GETS CRISPY WHEN FRIED

When frying food in hot oil, we often dip it in a starchy coating first. Such coatings provide a few benefits: They help protect the food from moisture loss, and they shield the food from direct contact with the hot frying oil for more gentle cooking. And perhaps most important, these starchy coatings become incredibly crispy when fried. So what exactly is happening that makes starch the key?

Here's what we've learned. First, the starch granules in the coating absorb water, whether from the wet surface of the food or because they are combined with a liquid to make a slurry before coating the food (as we do for our Thick-Cut Sweet Potato Fries). The hydrated granules swell when they are initially heated in the oil, allowing the starch molecules to move about and separate from one another. As water is driven away during the frying process, these starch molecules lock into place, forming a rigid, brittle network with a porous, open structure.

Furthermore, the two types of starch molecules (amylose and amylopectin) form some cross-links with one another at high frying temperatures, further reinforcing the coating's structure. Thus, the molecules in this porous network have room to compress and fracture, providing the sensation of crispiness. Interestingly, cornstarch contains 25 to 28 percent amylose, which is higher than the amount in wheat or potato starch (which are 20 to 22 percent amylose), and this is why cornstarch works the best for making crispy coatings on fried foods.

1. Adjust oven rack to middle position and heat oven to 200 degrees. Set wire rack in rimmed baking sheet. Whisk cornstarch and ½ cup cold water together in large bowl.

2. Bring 2 quarts water, ¼ cup salt, and baking soda to boil in Dutch oven. Add potatoes and return to boil. Reduce heat to simmer and cook until exteriors turn slightly mushy (centers will remain firm), 3 to 5 minutes. Whisk cornstarch slurry to recombine. Using wire skimmer or slotted spoon, transfer potatoes to bowl with slurry.

3. Using rubber spatula, fold potatoes with slurry until slurry turns light orange, thickens to paste, and clings to potatoes.

4. Heat oil in 12-inch nonstick skillet over high heat to 325 degrees. Using tongs, carefully add one third of potatoes to oil, making sure that potatoes aren't touching one another. Fry until crispy and lightly browned, 7 to 10 minutes, using tongs to flip potatoes halfway through frying (adjust heat as necessary to maintain oil temperature between 280 and 300 degrees). Using wire skimmer or slotted spoon, transfer fries to prepared wire rack (fries that stick together can be separated with tongs or forks). Season with salt to taste, and transfer to oven to keep warm. Return oil to 325 degrees and repeat in 2 more batches with remaining potatoes. Serve immediately.

Spicy Fry Sauce

MAKES ABOUT ½ CUP

For a less spicy version, use only 2 teaspoons of Asian chili-garlic sauce. The sauce can be made up to four days in advance and stored, covered, in the refrigerator.

- 6 **tablespoons mayonnaise**
- 1 **tablespoon Asian chili-garlic sauce**
- 2 **teaspoons white vinegar**

Whisk all ingredients together in small bowl.

RATING SWISS CHEESE

A pockmarked wedge of Swiss may be instantly recognizable as the icon of "cheese," but it's rarely celebrated for its flavor—at least here in the United States. But genuine Swiss cheese, also known as Emmentaler, can boast nuanced, nutty flavors. We sampled cheeses from a wide spectrum of price points and presentations (sliced or in wedges) and tasted them plain and in grilled cheese sandwiches. Sampling the cheeses plain at room temperature, tasters preferred the savory flavors of long-aged cheeses over the rubbery, bland younger cheeses. But in grilled cheese sandwiches, the longest-aged wedges were panned for their unpleasant flavors. However, heat improved the younger cheeses: Not only did most of them melt beautifully but several young cheeses suddenly boasted "nutty tang." We recommend shopping for Swiss with a purpose: For heated applications, a younger cheese like Emmi Emmentaler Cheese AOC is an excellent option. For cheese plates, go for aged raw-milk cheeses like Edelweiss Creamery Emmentaler Switzerland Swiss Cheese, our favorite from a Wisconsin-based producer that we think out-Swisses the Swiss. Products are listed in order of preference. See AmericasTestKitchen.com for updates and complete tasting results.

HIGHLY RECOMMENDED FOR CHEESE PLATE ONLY

EDELWEISS CREAMERY Emmentaler Switzerland Swiss Cheese

PRICE: $12.99 for 1¼ lb ($0.65 per oz)   AGED: Up to 12 months
STYLE: Raw milk, American-made   SODIUM: 60 mg per oz
COMMENTS: Wisconsin-based Edelweiss Creamery emulates traditional Swiss methods, including the use of copper vats for flavor development. We think they make a better Swiss cheese than the Swiss—and for a lot less money. This cheese's "grassy" nuttiness makes it worth mail-ordering, but don't melt it. Those flavors turned "funky" in grilled cheese.

EMMI Kaltbach Cave-Aged Emmentaler Switzerland AOC

PRICE: $12.99 for 8 oz ($1.62 per oz)   AGED: 12 to 18 months
STYLE: Raw milk, Swiss import   SODIUM: 50 mg per oz
COMMENTS: The "savory" flavors that make this cave-aged raw-milk Swiss import eminently worthy of a cheese plate also render it unsuitable for melting. It made for an "oily" grilled cheese with a "lingering metallic taste."

RECOMMENDED FOR CHEESE PLATE AND COOKING

EMMI Emmentaler Cheese AOC

PRICE: $18.99 for 1 lb ($1.19 per oz)   AGED: 120 days (4 months)
STYLE: Raw milk, Swiss import   SODIUM: 50 mg per oz
COMMENTS: Thanks to its relative youth and raw-milk base, this Swiss import offered the best of both worlds: a texture that turned "creamy" when melted in a grilled cheese and enough "pleasantly pungent" character for eating out of hand.

RECOMMENDED FOR COOKING ONLY

BOAR'S HEAD Gold Label Switzerland Swiss Cheese

PRICE: $9.75 for 1 lb ($0.61 per oz)   AGED: More than 120 days
STYLE: Pasteurized milk, Swiss import   SODIUM: 60 mg per oz
COMMENTS: Tasters dubbed this product a "generic Swiss" straight out of the package, but it soared to the top of the heap in grilled cheese, where it boasted great taste and a "smooth" texture.

RECOMMENDED FOR COOKING ONLY (cont.)

NORSELAND Jarlsberg

PRICE: $6.99 for 1 lb ($0.44 per oz)   AGED: 60 days
STYLE: Pasteurized milk, Norwegian import   SODIUM: 180 mg per oz
COMMENTS: This Norwegian version of Swiss shared the relatively bland flavor profile of many of the other cheeses in the lineup, but heat drew out its "nicely salty" flavor (Jarlsberg typically contains more sodium than other Swiss-style cheeses) and also turned it pleasantly "gooey."

KERRYGOLD Swiss Cheese

PRICE: $5.99 for 7 oz ($0.86 per oz)   AGED: 90 days or longer
STYLE: Pasteurized milk, Irish import   SODIUM: 110 mg per oz
COMMENTS: As with the Norseland Jarlsberg, relatively high sodium bolstered the flavor of this Irish-made Swiss; some likened it to a mild "cheddar" straight out of the package. Heated in grilled cheese, it gained "nuttiness." Though its texture was "stretchy" to some, it was still "a good melt."

NOT RECOMMENDED

KRAFT Natural Cheese Big Slice Swiss

PRICE: $2.68 for 8 oz ($0.34 per oz)   AGED: 0 days
STYLE: Pasteurized milk, American-made   SODIUM: 49 mg per oz
COMMENTS: Without raw milk or any aging at all, this cheese couldn't help tasting like "bland city." Though it developed "some nutty tang" when melted, its texture was also unappealingly "chewy."

SARGENTO Natural Aged Swiss Deli Style Sliced Swiss Cheese

PRICE: $4.29 for 7 oz ($0.61 per oz)   AGED: 60 days or longer
STYLE: Pasteurized milk, American-made   SODIUM: 55 mg per oz
COMMENTS: "Kids' cheese," "generic," "plasticky"— pick your descriptor. This cheese was downright "bland" when eaten plain. Warming it in grilled cheese made it "extremely melty and oozy," but the flavor was still "blandsville."

Scallops and Shrimp Hot Off the Grill

Pressing the scallop-bacon bundles tightly together on the skewers prevents them from spinning around and makes them easier to flip.

WE'VE ALL HAD GRILLED SCALLOPS OR SHRIMP—USUALLY, THE shellfish are simply skewered and cooked just long enough to pick up some char. But we wanted to step outside our comfort zone by bringing two different recipes to the grill: bacon-wrapped scallops and shrimp burgers.

We love bacon in any context, but it seems to work particularly well with buttery, tender scallops—which probably explains why the bacon-wrapped scallop appetizer is so ubiquitous. We wanted to give this tired hors d'oeuvre a flavor boost and transform it into a grilled entrée. The trouble with grilling bacon, however, is that the grease drips into the fire and causes flare-ups, which can incinerate the scallops (and the wooden skewers). Plus, no one can (or should) eat six slices of bacon for dinner. We solved these problems using a bit of ingenuity—and a common kitchen appliance.

Shrimp burgers? Think crab cakes (minus the hefty price tag) and you're on the right track. Shrimp burgers are popular in the South, where shrimp are abundant. But these pan-fried patties are often weighed down by heavy, bready binders that overwhelm the shrimp's subtle flavor. We wanted to put the shrimp at the fore for our grilled take on this Southern favorite.

GRILLED BACON-WRAPPED SCALLOPS

GRILLED BACON-WRAPPED SCALLOPS

✔ **WHY THIS RECIPE WORKS:** Smoky, salty bacon pairs perfectly with delicate scallops, but snagging one of these treats off of a passing appetizer tray is never enough to satisfy our cravings. We wanted to turn this classic appetizer into a grilled entrée. To prevent the bacon grease from dripping into the grill fire and incinerating our scallops, we microwaved strips of bacon between paper towels (to absorb grease) and weighed them down with a plate to prevent curling. We wrapped each strip of bacon around two scallops for an ideal scallop-to-bacon ratio. Tossing the scallops in melted butter added richness, and pressing the scallops firmly together on the skewers prevented them from spinning when flipped. A two-level fire cooked both scallops and bacon to perfection. A spritz of grilled lemon juice and a sprinkling of chopped chives gave the dish a bright finish.

ANYONE WHO'S EVER BEEN TO A WEDDING RECEPTION or cocktail party knows a thing or two about bacon-wrapped scallops: They're a common passed appetizer at catered functions. It's no secret why they're so popular. The smoky, salty bacon beautifully accents the sweet, succulent scallops. Surely taking it to the grill would make a great thing even better.

Grilling scallops is a straightforward matter. Start with "dry" scallops, which have no chemical additives or excess moisture; toss them with oil or melted butter to keep them from sticking to the grate; skewer them; and sear them over high heat for a minute or two on each side until they're just cooked through. But you can't grill bacon like that. The fat will cause flare-ups that will cover the scallops in soot, and the bacon needs longer, gentler cooking to render and crisp. We knew that parcooking the bacon before skewering and grilling was a must. We were hoping that we could make our lives easier by doing it in the microwave.

We started by microwaving the bacon on a plate between layers of paper towels (to absorb the grease). To make sure we could get a snug fit when wrapping the bacon around the scallops, we weighed down the bacon with a second plate to prevent it from curling. Four minutes produced bacon that had given up a good bit of its fat and would finish crisping up after a few minutes on the grill.

Now we needed to find the best way to wrap and skewer the scallops. In the test kitchen, we've grilled scallops on a single skewer as well as on double skewers (that is, with two parallel skewers running through each scallop). The benefit of double skewers is that the scallops can't spin, making them easier to flip and ensuring that they cook evenly. The downside is the amount of work that it takes to double-skewer scallops while keeping the bacon in position. (Once the bacon is cut to length and wrapped around the scallop, the skewer needs to go through the overlapped bacon ends to hold it in place.) For the sake of ease, we decided on a single skewer, taking care to firmly press each bacon-wrapped scallop into its neighbor on the skewer to minimize spinning. We found that tossing the scallops in melted butter not only helped prevent sticking to the grill and added richness but also made the scallops a little sticky and thus easier to handle and skewer.

After several grilling attempts, though, we were still struggling with dripping bacon fat and the resulting flare-ups. We tried lowering the flame to slow down the cooking. Medium heat worked fine on the bacon—it mitigated the

NOTES FROM THE TEST KITCHEN

WRAP AND GRILL

Here's how to ensure properly cooked Grilled Bacon-Wrapped Scallops.

1. Wrap 1 strip of parcooked bacon around 2 scallops and run skewer through overlapped bacon. Place three 2-scallop bundles on each skewer.

2. Grill on 2 bacon sides over medium heat for 4 minutes each.

3. Finish by grilling 1 scallop side over high heat for 4 minutes.

flare-ups—but it wasn't hot enough to mark the scallops with a tasty sear. So we created a fire with both medium and hot zones and cooked the two bacon sides of the skewers over medium and then just one of the nonbacon sides over high heat. (There was no need to cook the other nonbacon side, as the scallops were now cooked just right.)

Though a few scallops wrapped in bacon are perfect as an appetizer, six scallops wrapped in bacon means you're eating six slices of bacon for dinner—too much, even when we cut the bacon into shorter lengths that would fit comfortably around one scallop. We decided instead to double up the scallops and wrap a single slice of bacon around two of them. Three two-scallop

bundles were a perfect dinner portion. Plus, this meant we didn't have to spend extra time cutting the bacon into single-scallop-size pieces—one slice of bacon fit almost perfectly around two scallops.

As final flourishes, we grilled lemon halves and squeezed the juice over the skewers and scattered chopped chives over the platter. With perfectly cooked scallops and bacon spritzed with the smoky juice of grilled lemons, we had given new life to an old favorite. And we could have this party dish whenever we wanted—without having to stand in line to kiss the bride.

Grilled Bacon-Wrapped Scallops
SERVES 4

Use ordinary bacon, as thick-cut bacon will take too long to crisp on the grill. When wrapping the scallops, the bacon slice should fit around both scallops, overlapping just enough to be skewered through both ends. We recommend buying "dry" scallops, which don't have chemical additives and taste better than "wet." Dry scallops will look ivory or pinkish; wet scallops are bright white. This recipe was developed with large sea scallops (sold 10 to 20 per pound).

12 slices bacon

24 large sea scallops, tendons removed

3 tablespoons unsalted butter, melted

½ teaspoon salt

⅛ teaspoon pepper

2 lemons, halved

¼ cup chopped fresh chives

1. Place 4 layers paper towels on large plate and arrange 6 slices bacon over towels in single layer. Top with 4 more paper towels and remaining 6 slices bacon. Cover with 2 layers of paper towels; place second large plate on top and press gently to flatten. Microwave until fat begins to render but bacon is still pliable, about 4 minutes. Toss scallops, butter, salt, and pepper together in bowl until scallops are thoroughly coated with butter.

2. Press 2 scallops together, side to side, and wrap with 1 slice bacon, trimming excess as necessary. Thread onto skewer through bacon. Repeat with remaining scallops and bacon, threading 3 bundles onto each of 4 skewers.

3A. FOR A CHARCOAL GRILL: Open bottom vent completely. Light large chimney starter filled with charcoal briquettes (6 quarts). When top coals are partially covered with ash, pour two-thirds evenly over half of grill, then pour remaining coals over other half of grill. Set cooking grate in place, cover, and open lid vent completely. Heat grill until hot, about 5 minutes.

3B. FOR A GAS GRILL: Turn all burners to high, cover, and heat grill until hot, about 15 minutes. Leave primary burner on high and turn other burner(s) to medium.

4. Clean and oil cooking grate. Place skewers, bacon side down, and lemon halves, cut side down, on cooler side of grill. Cook (covered, if using gas) until bacon is crispy on first side, about 4 minutes. Flip skewers onto other bacon side and cook until crispy, about 4 minutes longer. Flip skewers scallop side down and move to hot side of grill. Grill until sides of scallops are firm and centers are opaque, about 4 minutes on 1 side only. Transfer skewers to platter, squeeze lemon over, and sprinkle with chives. Serve.

SOUTHERN SHRIMP BURGERS

✔ **WHY THIS RECIPE WORKS:** Great shrimp flavor should be at the center of this regional specialty. Unfortunately, that's not always the case: Tasteless or overly bready patties are frequent pitfalls of shrimp burger recipes. We wanted a flavorful, well-textured shrimp burger with a nice crust from cooking on the grill. Roughly chopping the shrimp in a food processor was the secret to the perfect consistency. As for the binder, we kept the mayonnaise to add richness to the lean shrimp, but cut back on bread crumbs and eliminated the egg. To flavor the patties, we went with additions that complemented the shrimp, rather than overwhelming it—minced scallion, parsley, lemon zest, and just a touch of cayenne pepper.

ALTHOUGH NOT AS WELL KNOWN AS OTHER SOUTHERN favorites such as fried chicken or collard greens, shrimp burgers are a long-standing specialty in coastal towns in South Carolina and Georgia, where seafood is abundant. Beneath their shells, shrimp conceal sweet, briny flesh that lends itself to a wide variety of applications: everything from stir-fries to pasta dishes. We're always on the hunt for new ways to prepare this versatile shellfish, so when we heard about Southern-style shrimp burgers, we knew we had to try them for ourselves. We tracked down some recipes and headed for the kitchen. Although pan-frying is the most common way to cook these burgers, we thought they would be even better on the grill, where they could develop a nice crust.

Although the particulars may vary, a good shrimp burger should be first and foremost about the shrimp. Unfortunately, many of the shrimp burgers we tried were underwhelming at best. Many recipes overcooked or overprocessed the delicate shrimp, turning the patties rubbery or pasty. Others called for so many binder ingredients (almost always some combination of bread crumbs, mayonnaise, and egg) that they ended up more

SOUTHERN SHRIMP BURGERS

like bread balls than shrimp burgers—but those that called for too few binders fell apart on the grill. With these pitfalls in mind, we set out to develop a recipe for our ideal shrimp burger: moist, chunky yet still cohesive, and with seasoning that complements the sweet shrimp flavor but doesn't overpower it.

We started with the shrimp. We typically prefer to buy shell-on shrimp because we find them to be firmer and sweeter than prepeeled ones. Based on our initial tests, we decided we needed a combination of textures—finely chopped shrimp to help bind the burgers, and some larger, bite-size chunks. We peeled and thoroughly dried 1½ pounds of shrimp, tossed half in the food processor until finely minced, then chopped the other half by hand. This worked well, but we wanted to streamline the process. We tried pulsing all of the shrimp in the food processor, which worked perfectly. The inconsistent texture it produced—annoying for some applications—was exactly what we were looking for in this recipe.

As for a binder, we wanted to use as little as possible to ensure the shrimp flavor was at the fore. We tried tinkering with the proportions of mayonnaise, bread crumbs, and egg, but we continually ended up with shrimp swathed in a soggy, unappealing mush. The mayonnaise was adding much-needed fat and moisture (unlike beef, shrimp have little fat of their own), so maybe the egg was at fault—it only made the burgers wet, requiring more bread crumbs. We made a batch of burgers without the egg and decreased the bread crumbs to a single slice of bread, which proved to be just the right amount of binder to keep the patties together without detracting from the flavor. Plus, eliminating the egg also eliminated the rubbery texture, as long as we were careful not to overcook the patties. As a final preparation step, we allowed the burgers to firm up in the refrigerator. Despite the small amount of binder, we were surprised at how well these burgers held together. Even better, they stayed together on the grill, and tasters loved their moist texture and sweet shrimp flavor, with no hint of soggy filling.

For seasonings, there were a lot to choose from, some better than others. Chunky vegetables like celery and bell peppers caused the burgers to break apart during

cooking, so they were out. Tasters agreed that aggressively flavored ingredients like mustard, Old Bay, and hot sauces detracted from the shrimp flavor. Ultimately, tasters preferred simplicity—some minced scallion and parsley, as well as lemon zest, which accentuated the sweetness of the shrimp, and a touch of cayenne pepper. By themselves or on a bun with lettuce and our simple tartar sauce, these burgers are sure to disappear as fast as they come off the grill.

Southern Shrimp Burgers
MAKES 4 BURGERS

Be sure to use raw, not cooked, shrimp here. Dry the shrimp thoroughly before processing, or the burgers will be mushy. If using shrimp with sodium added as a preservative, omit the salt in the recipe. Although we prefer extra-large shrimp, almost any size shrimp will

work in this recipe. Serve with Tartar Sauce (recipe follows) or another flavored mayonnaise.

- 1 **slice hearty white sandwich bread, torn into large pieces**
- 1½ **pounds extra-large shrimp (21 to 25 per pound), peeled, deveined, and patted dry**
- ¼ **cup mayonnaise**
- 2 **scallions, minced**
- 2 **tablespoons minced fresh parsley**
- 2 **teaspoons grated fresh lemon zest**
  Pinch cayenne pepper
- ¼ **teaspoon salt**
- ⅛ **teaspoon pepper**
  Vegetable oil

1. Pulse bread in food processor to fine crumbs, 10 to 15 pulses; transfer to bowl. Pulse shrimp in now-empty food processor until some pieces are finely minced and others are coarsely chopped, about 7 pulses; transfer to separate bowl.

2. Whisk mayonnaise, scallions, parsley, lemon zest, cayenne, salt, and pepper together in large bowl, then gently fold into processed shrimp until combined. Sprinkle bread crumbs over mixture and fold until thoroughly incorporated.

3. Divide shrimp mixture into 4 equal portions and shape each into 1-inch-thick patty. Cover and refrigerate patties for at least 30 minutes or up to 3 hours.

4A. FOR A CHARCOAL GRILL: Open bottom grill vents completely. Light large chimney starter three-quarters filled with charcoal briquettes (4½ quarts). When coals are hot, pour evenly over grill. Set cooking grate in place, cover, and heat grill until hot, about 5 minutes.

4B. FOR A GAS GRILL: Turn all burners to high, cover, and heat grill until hot, about 15 minutes. Turn all burners to medium-high. (Adjust burners as needed to maintain medium-hot fire.)

5. Clean and oil cooking grate. Lightly brush tops of burgers with oil, lay them on grill, oiled side down, and lightly brush other side with oil. Cook burgers, without pressing on them, until lightly browned and register 140 to 145 degrees, 10 to 14 minutes, flipping halfway through cooking. Transfer burgers to platter, tent loosely with aluminum foil, and let rest for 5 minutes before serving.

Tartar Sauce

MAKES ABOUT 1 CUP

- ¾ **cup mayonnaise**
- 1½ **tablespoons minced cornichons (about 3 large) plus 1 teaspoon brine**
- 1 **tablespoon minced scallion**
- 1 **tablespoon minced red onion**
- 1 **tablespoon capers, minced**

Whisk all ingredients together in bowl. Cover and refrigerate until flavors meld, at least 30 minutes. (Sauce can be refrigerated for up to 4 days.)

RATING FROZEN YOGURT

The recent popularity of frozen yogurt drove us to wonder if the hype was warranted, so we scooped up eight of the best-selling national products, both low-fat and nonfat versions, in the most straightforward flavor: vanilla. We looked for a rich, creamy texture and clean, not-too-sweet flavor. The better brands achieved smoothness and creaminess thanks to a few key components. The first: corn syrup, which inhibits iciness by restricting the movement of the water molecules so that they are less likely to link up and form large crystals. Stabilizers also help stave off ice crystal formation and boost the perception of creaminess. Another core, but less obvious, component of the texture of frozen desserts is air. Manufacturers aerate their products to increase the overall volume and to produce a lighter texture. "Overrun" refers to the percentage increase in volume from aeration, and by law it can be as high as 100 percent in frozen desserts. Some overrun is a must in frozen desserts, particularly lean frozen yogurts; without air, they would be rock solid and virtually inedible. And, even in small quantities, cream made a big difference. Besides adding richness, it also boosted vanilla flavor, since vanillin (the flavor compound in vanilla extract) is largely fat-soluble. Though none of our sampled frozen yogurts elicited anything close to the rave reviews of a great ice cream, if you're looking for a low-fat frozen dessert with decent texture and reasonably good flavor, our winning yogurt—TCBY Classic Vanilla Bean Frozen Yogurt—will do the trick. Fat and sugar amounts are per ½-cup serving. Products are listed in order of preference. See AmericasTestKitchen.com for updates and complete tasting results.

RECOMMENDED

TCBY Classic Vanilla Bean Frozen Yogurt
PRICE: $3.95 per 1.5-qt container ($0.08 per oz)
FAT: 2.5 g   SUGAR: 15 g   OVERRUN: 78.4%
INGREDIENTS: Skim milk, sugar, cream, corn syrup, vanilla bean flavoring (vanilla bean specks, natural flavor, xanthan gum), propylene glycol monoesters, mono and diglycerides, guar gum, locust bean gum, carrageenan, probiotic yogurt cultures (*S. thermophilus, L. bulgaricus, L. lactis, B. lactis, L. acidophilus, L. casei, L. rhamnosus*)
COMMENTS: Tasters praised the "balanced sweetness" and "straightforward vanilla flavor" of this product. Its combination of corn syrup, carrageenan, and cream, not to mention its chart-topping overrun percentage, helped it achieve a smooth texture.

BEN & JERRY'S Vanilla Greek Frozen Yogurt
PRICE: $6.50 per 1-pt container ($0.41 per oz)
FAT: 4.5 g   SUGAR: 19 g   OVERRUN: 20.3%
INGREDIENTS: Skim milk, Greek yogurt (cultured skim milk, natural flavor, carrageenan), liquid sugar (sugar, water), cream, water, corn syrup solids, egg yolks, nonfat yogurt powder (cultured nonfat milk), vanilla extract, sugar, locust bean gum
COMMENTS: With a "pleasant tang" and a "natural vanilla flavor," this frozen yogurt (available in Ben & Jerry's shops) was "appealing." Tasters also praised its "smooth," if "a bit runny," texture.

TURKEY HILL DAIRY Vanilla Bean Frozen Yogurt
PRICE: $3.69 per 1.5-qt container ($0.08 per oz)
FAT: 0 g   SUGAR: 14 g   OVERRUN: 54.7%
INGREDIENTS: Nonfat milk, sugar, cultured nonfat milk (contains live active cultures), corn syrup, maltodextrin, calcium carbonate, cellulose gel, cellulose gum, mono and diglycerides, vanilla, vanilla bean, polysorbate 80, carrageenan, vitamin A, vitamin D3
COMMENTS: Lots of stabilizers and emulsifiers created a "smooth" consistency, though some tasters found it "a little thin and icy." It tasted "clean," "appealing," and "sweet."

NOT RECOMMENDED

HÄAGEN-DAZS Vanilla Low Fat Frozen Yogurt
PRICE: $3.99 per 14-oz container ($0.29 per oz)
FAT: 2.5 g   SUGAR: 21 g   OVERRUN: 9.6%
INGREDIENTS: Skim milk (lactose reduced), corn syrup, sugar, egg yolks, cream, vanilla extract, active yogurt cultures
COMMENTS: Because it had no stabilizers, tasters bemoaned this yogurt's chalky texture, which quickly melted. Its high sugar content gave it a "cloying" flavor.

HEALTHY CHOICE Vanilla Bean Greek Frozen Yogurt
PRICE: $3.99 per package of three 4-oz containers ($0.33 per oz)
FAT: 2 g   SUGAR: 11 g   OVERRUN: 75%
INGREDIENTS: Nonfat milk, cultured nonfat milk, sugar, cream, polydextrose, maltodextrin, milk protein concentrate, less than 2% of: vanilla extract, vanilla bean seed powder, gelatin, dextrose, cellulose gel, propylene glycol, monoesters, citric acid, mono and diglycerides, cellulose gum, carrageenan, calcium phosphate
COMMENTS: Tasters found this "Greek" frozen yogurt "sludgy," perhaps due to a lack of corn syrup combined with a high overrun percentage. That texture, paired with "buttermilk" tang, was more reminiscent of "frozen cheesecake" than yogurt.

STONYFIELD Oikos Greek Vanilla Organic Nonfat Frozen Yogurt
PRICE: $4.29 per 1-pt container ($0.27 per oz)
FAT: 0 g   SUGAR: 17 g   OVERRUN: 52%
INGREDIENTS: Cultured pasteurized organic nonfat milk, naturally milled organic sugar, organic whey protein concentrate, organic rice syrup, organic carob bean gum, organic guar gum, organic vanilla extract, organic vanilla bean specks; contains live active cultures (*S. thermophilus, L. bulgaricus, L. acidophilus, bifidus, L. casei*)
COMMENTS: This nonfat yogurt was plagued by a host of off-flavors that summoned comparisons to "spoiled milk." Its "grainy" and "gritty" texture helped secure its spot at the bottom.

Spicing Up the Backyard Barbecue

Crosshatches on our pork tenderloin steaks create more surface area for browning and encourage the meat to absorb more of our flavorful marinade.

BACKYARD BARBECUES ARE A SUMMERTIME MAINSTAY. BUT EVENTUALLY we tire of hamburgers, hot dogs, and potato salad. For a unique and memorable take on summer barbecue fare, we sought out complex flavors with a little bit of finesse. Grab a cold beer—we're doing barbecue right.

Pork tenderloin medallions, although great for picking up lots of char-grilled flavor, are fussy to cook: The small pieces can fall through the grate, and flipping all those pieces means spending a lot of time standing over a hot grill. We wanted all the flavorful browning of medallions, without all the bother. We'll show you how to get the most flavorful, well-browned pork tenderloin ever—you just need a meat pounder.

Quinoa has become wildly popular in recent years, and understandably so: The tiny, crunchy seeds make appealing salads and pilafs, and their nutty flavor lends itself to a variety of ingredient additions. But overcooked, washed-out quinoa pilafs are all too common. Our goal here was twofold: get perfectly cooked, crunchy quinoa, and develop a pilaf that would pair nicely with our garlic-lime marinated pork. Flavor was easy; we simply added boldly flavored, South American–inspired ingredients like chipotle and *queso fresco*. But our biggest discovery? Most people cook quinoa the wrong way. Serve these dishes at your next backyard bash, and we're pretty sure the Joneses will be trying to keep up with you.

GARLIC-LIME GRILLED PORK TENDERLOIN STEAKS

✔ **WHY THIS RECIPE WORKS:** Pork tenderloin is a great fit for the grill: The mild meat benefits from a well-browned crust. We wanted to figure out how to maximize browning while keeping the meat tender. Cutting two tenderloin roasts in half and pounding them to an even thickness created easy-to-grill "steaks." A two-level grill fire, with both hotter and cooler areas, allowed us to sear the steaks on the hotter side and then let them gently finish cooking on the cooler side. A salty oil-based marinade provided seasoning and richness. Lime juice and zest, garlic, fish sauce (which provided a savory boost without tasting fishy), and honey (the sugars in which encouraged browning) rounded out the marinade. Crosshatch marks in the steaks made for extra crispy edges and allowed the steaks to absorb even more marinade. A bit of reserved marinade, whisked with some mayo for body and cilantro for freshness, made a perfect finishing sauce.

ONE OF THE MOST COMMON—AND, IN OUR VIEW, pointless—ways to grill pork tenderloin is to turn it into medallions. You start with an oblong, easy-to-manage roast but cut it into coins that require constant attention lest they overcook or, worse, slip through the grate. That said, we understand why folks do it. Pork tenderloin is a mild cut, so it makes sense to build up as much flavor as possible on the exterior. Cutting the roast into smaller pieces is an obvious way to accomplish that because it creates much more exposed surface area to absorb seasonings or a marinade, not to mention char from the grill.

Our job would be to take the spirit of the medallion approach but find a shape and a technique that reliably delivered a maximum amount of flavorful, nicely browned crust, yet kept this lean cut tender.

Since more surface area was our goal, perhaps what we really needed to do was pound the roast into wider, flatter pieces that would maximize the exterior surface area. So we cut each tenderloin in half to create two shorter cylinders and then pounded the halves into "steaks" that were ¾ inch thick. Those cutting and pounding steps took just minutes and produced—we did some quick calculations—almost 30 percent more surface area.

From there we seasoned the steaks simply, with salt and pepper, and then spread a full chimney of lit coals over half of the kettle to create areas for both direct and indirect cooking. This setup allowed us to sear the steaks (on both sides for maximum browning) over high heat and then pull them across the grate to the cooler side of the grill to cook until they had reached the target 140 degrees, making sure that the wider end of each steak was pointed toward the fire for even cooking.

The good news was that our tasters unanimously preferred this unusual tenderloin treatment to a roast that we'd simply cooked whole and sliced; the pork steaks delivered much more flavorful browned crust per bite. But our tasters' compliments came with constructive feedback, too—specifically, that searing the steaks had turned the exterior on this fat-deficient cut somewhat leathery and tough. They also said that they wanted the pork to taste meatier. Dressing up the flavor of mild-mannered pork tenderloin was a must.

Bold seasonings and fat would help solve flavor and texture problems, so we turned to a treatment that offers both: a marinade. Putting the test kitchen's knowledge into practice, we grabbed marinade must-haves, starting with salt. In addition to seasoning the meat, salt dissolves proteins within the meat, which helps it trap moisture and become more tender. We also included oil, because most of the aromatics, herbs, and spices that we add to marinades are soluble in fat; plus, oil helps the marinade evenly coat the meat. For flavor, we tossed in minced garlic, plus lime juice for brightness, as we've found that the strong flavor of acids in marinades usually comes through in the cooked meat quite well. The final core ingredient was honey, which adds complexity and encourages browning. (We also mixed up marinades

GARLIC-LIME GRILLED PORK TENDERLOIN STEAKS

THE GEOMETRY OF POUNDING PORK

Cylindrical pork tenderloin doesn't have much surface area for browning. Pounding the roast into a flat steak seemed like an obvious way to increase the amount of meat that comes in contact with the grill—and as a result, the flavor in every bite—but we didn't realize how significant the difference actually was until we did the math. Flattening a cylindrical piece of pork tenderloin into a ¾-inch rectangular steak increased its surface area by almost 30 percent.

CYLINDRICAL TENDERLOIN	POUNDED STEAK
Volume: 250 Ml	Volume: 250 Ml
Surface Area: 172.7 Sq Cm	Surface Area: 220 Sq Cm

MAYO MAKES IT A SAUCE

To add a last-minute burst of flavor to our Garlic-Lime Grilled Pork Tenderloin Steaks, we reserve a portion of the garlic-citrus marinade to use as a sauce. But pouring the punchy liquid over the steaks resulted in a too-sharp taste; plus, its consistency was thin and runny. Adding mayonnaise solved both problems. A few teaspoons balanced the marinade's sharp acidity and contributed much-needed body.

Whisk 4 teaspoons mayonnaise into ½ cup reserved marinade until smooth and creamy.

with orange juice and with lemon juice to create a couple of variations.)

After whisking together those ingredients (plus salt and pepper), we marinated the steaks for 30 minutes and then wiped off the excess marinade and proceeded with our two-phase grilling method. But the flavor boost wasn't much. Tasters reported good garlic flavor, but

the lime was faint. Also, while the crust was decently browned, it was still tough.

Thinking that a longer marinade time would help, we let the next batch of pork steaks soak for 45 minutes—still well within the 1-hour limit that the test kitchen sets for marinating meats in acidic liquids. (After that point, acids break down surface proteins and turn meat mushy.) This time, our tasters noticed that the salt had penetrated further into the meat, improving seasoning and tenderness, but the other flavors of the marinade—from the lime in particular—were still barely detectable.

We doubted that extending the marinating time another 15 minutes would bring out much more lime flavor or boost meatiness, so we tried enhancing the citrus presence by adding a tablespoon of grated lime zest—a fairly large amount so that its flavor would come through even after the meat had been cooked. (Unlike juice, citrus zest doesn't boost acidity, nor does it affect the texture of meat.) As for ramping up meaty flavor, we traded a portion of the salt in the marinade for a splash of umami-rich fish sauce, which, in small quantities, heightens savory flavor without making foods taste distinctly Asian or fishy.

Our tasters deemed this batch brighter and meatier but wanted more of those flavors—a request that made us think twice about wiping off the excess marinade. Our only concern was that leaving all that moisture on the meat would thwart our browning efforts. On the contrary: When we gave it a shot, the results were surprisingly good. Not only was the flavor deeper, but the water in the marinade burned off quickly enough that the pork required, at most, an extra 45 seconds to achieve the deep brown color that we were looking for. Leaving excess marinade on the meat had another benefit: Its extra fat and moisture kept the crust from drying out and toughening during cooking.

This simple tweak had been so effective that we wanted to see if we could get even more of the marinade to cling to the meat. With a sharp knife, we cut ⅛-inch-deep crosshatch marks into the steaks—thin channels that trapped more of the marinade, giving the pork bolder flavor. The slits also beefed up the crust, since they created more surface area for browning.

The marinade made the outside of our steaks taste so bright and meaty that we couldn't help but wish that their milder interior did, too. Thinking that this was the perfect job for a sauce, we set aside ½ cup of the marinade before adding the pork to the liquid and poured it over the cooked steaks just before serving. This was a little better—but all that lime juice and raw garlic made the uncooked marinade taste too harsh. Its body was also too thin to function as a sauce. A few teaspoons of mayonnaise fixed both issues, giving the sauce lightly creamy body and balanced flavor. Stirring in some chopped cilantro freshened it up nicely.

We had one last thought: Pouring the sauce over the whole steaks put it in contact with only the exterior. To ensure that its flavor reached the inside of the pork, too, we sliced the steaks before serving, drizzled them with some sauce, and passed the rest at the table. We also sprinkled the meat with flake sea salt (such as Maldon), a small touch that added bursts of crunch and seasoning to each bite.

Our grilled pork tenderloin looks and tastes nothing like most versions—and we couldn't be happier about that.

Garlic-Lime Grilled Pork Tenderloin Steaks
SERVES 4 TO 6

Since marinating is a key step in this recipe, we don't recommend using pork that has been enhanced (injected with a salt solution).

- 2 (1-pound) pork tenderloins, trimmed
- 1 tablespoon grated lime zest plus ¼ cup juice (2 limes)
- 4 garlic cloves, minced
- 4 teaspoons honey
- 2 teaspoons fish sauce
- ¾ teaspoon salt
- ½ teaspoon pepper
- ½ cup vegetable oil
- 4 teaspoons mayonnaise
- 1 tablespoon chopped fresh cilantro
  Flake sea salt (optional)

1. Slice each tenderloin in half crosswise to create 4 steaks total. Pound each half to ¾-inch thickness. Using sharp knife, cut ⅛-inch-deep slits spaced ½ inch apart in crosshatch pattern on both sides of steaks.

2. Whisk lime zest and juice, garlic, honey, fish sauce, salt, and pepper together in large bowl. Whisking constantly, slowly drizzle oil into lime mixture until smooth and slightly thickened. Transfer ½ cup lime mixture to small bowl and whisk in mayonnaise; set aside sauce. Add steaks to bowl with remaining marinade and toss thoroughly to coat; transfer steaks and marinade to large zipper-lock bag, press out as much air as possible, and seal bag. Let steaks sit at room temperature for 45 minutes.

3A. FOR A CHARCOAL GRILL: Open bottom vent completely. Light large chimney starter filled with charcoal briquettes (6 quarts). When top coals are partially covered with ash, pour evenly over half of grill. Set cooking grate in place, cover, and open lid vent completely. Heat grill until hot, about 5 minutes.

3B. FOR A GAS GRILL: Turn all burners to high, cover, and heat grill until hot, about 15 minutes. Leave primary burner on high and turn off other burner(s).

4. Clean and oil cooking grate. Remove steaks from marinade (do not pat dry) and place over hotter part of grill. Cook, uncovered, until well browned on first side,

3 to 4 minutes. Flip steaks and cook until well browned on second side, 3 to 4 minutes. Transfer steaks to cooler part of grill, with wider end of each steak facing hotter part of grill. Cover and cook until meat registers 140 degrees, 3 to 8 minutes longer (remove steaks as they come to temperature). Transfer steaks to cutting board and let rest for 5 minutes.

5. While steaks rest, microwave reserved sauce until warm, 15 to 30 seconds; stir in cilantro. Slice steaks against grain into ½-inch-thick slices. Drizzle with half of sauce; sprinkle with sea salt, if using; and serve, passing remaining sauce separately.

VARIATIONS

Lemon-Thyme Grilled Pork Tenderloin Steaks

Substitute grated lemon zest and juice (2 lemons) for lime zest and juice. Add 1 tablespoon minced fresh thyme to lemon mixture with garlic. Omit cilantro.

Spicy Orange-Ginger Grilled Pork Tenderloin Steaks

Reduce lime zest to 1½ teaspoons and juice to 2 tablespoons. Add 1½ teaspoons grated orange zest plus 2 tablespoons juice, 2 teaspoons grated fresh ginger, and ¼ teaspoon cayenne to lime mixture with garlic.

QUINOA PILAF

☑ WHY THIS RECIPE WORKS: Most recipes for quinoa pilaf turn out woefully overcooked because they call for nearly twice as much liquid as they should. We cut the water back to ensure tender grains with a satisfying bite, and gave it a stir partway through cooking to ensure that the grains cooked evenly. We let the quinoa rest for several minutes before fluffing to help further improve the texture. We also toasted the quinoa in a dry skillet before simmering to develop its natural nutty flavor, and finished our pilaf with a judicious amount of boldly flavored ingredients.

IN THE SPAN OF A DECADE, QUINOA, A SEED WITH humble South American roots, has gone from obscurity to mass consumption in America. We've always assumed that its rapid ascent is mainly due to awareness of its health benefits (it's a nearly complete protein that's rich in fiber). While in theory the cooked grain (almost no one calls quinoa a seed) has an appealingly nutty flavor and crunchy texture, in practice it more often turns into a mushy mess with washed-out flavor and an underlying bitterness.

Pilaf recipes that call for cooking the grain with onion and other flavorings don't help matters. If it's blown out and mushy, quinoa pilaf is no better than the plain boiled grain on its own. We were determined to develop a foolproof approach to quinoa pilaf that we'd want to make not because it was healthy but because it tasted great.

Our first clue as to what might go wrong with the usual quinoa pilaf surfaced as soon as we gathered up recipes to try. All called for softening onion in butter or oil, adding quinoa to the pan and toasting it in the same fat, then pouring in liquid, and simmering covered until the grains were cooked through and the liquid was absorbed. Almost without exception, these recipes used a 2:1 ratio of liquid to quinoa. Could that be the problem?

To find out, we put together a basic working recipe: Soften finely chopped onion in butter in a saucepan,

QUINOA PILAF WITH CHIPOTLE, QUESO FRESCO, AND PEANUTS

THE MANY COLORS OF QUINOA

These tiny seeds are native to South America, and are available in white, red, and black varieties. White quinoa, the largest seeds of the three, has a slightly nutty, vegetal flavor; it also has the softest texture. The medium-size red seeds offer a heartier crunch, thanks to their additional seed coat, and a predominant nuttiness. Black quinoa seeds, the smallest of the three, have the thickest seed coat. They are notably crunchy, but many tasters disliked their slightly sandy texture. Mild-flavored black quinoa has a hint of molasses-like sweetness.

You can use white and red quinoa interchangeably in dishes like our quinoa pilaf, but black quinoa is better saved for recipes tailored to its distinctive texture and flavor.

WHITE
Most commonly available quinoa.

RED
Can be used interchangeably with white quinoa.

BLACK
Use only when specified in recipes.

stir in quinoa and water, cover, and cook until tender. We then tested a range of water-to-quinoa ratios and found that, while 2 to 1 might be the common rule, 1 to 1 was nearly perfect. To allow for evaporation, we tweaked this ratio just slightly, using a bit more water than quinoa (1¾ cups water to 1½ cups quinoa). After about 20 minutes of covered simmering, the quinoa was tender, with a satisfying bite.

Or at least most of it was. There was a ½-inch ring of overcooked seeds around the pot's circumference. The heat of the pot was cooking the outer grains faster than the interior ones. To even things out, our first thought was to stir the quinoa halfway through cooking, but we feared that we would turn our pilaf into a starchy mess, as so easily happens with rice. But we needn't have worried. A few gentle stirs at the midway point gave us perfectly cooked quinoa, with no ill effects. Why? While quinoa is quite starchy—more so than long-grain white rice—it also contains twice the protein of white rice. That protein is key, as it essentially traps the starch in place so you can stir it without creating a gummy mess.

The texture of the quinoa improved further when we let it rest, covered, for 10 minutes before fluffing. This allowed the grains to finish cooking gently and firm up, making them less prone to clump.

It was time to think about the toasting step. While the majority of quinoa on the market has been debittered, some bitter-tasting compounds (called saponins) remain on the exterior. We have found that toasting quinoa in fat can exacerbate this bitterness, so we opted to dry-toast the grains in the pan before sautéing the onion. After about 5 minutes in the pan, the quinoa smelled like popcorn. This batch was nutty and rich-tasting, without any bitterness.

Finally, we turned to seasonings. For a simple take, we finished the quinoa with herbs and lemon juice. Next, we looked to quinoa's birthplace for a combination with chile, *queso fresco*, lime juice, and peanuts. We kept a judicious hand with additions, ensuring that our quinoa stayed in the spotlight—right where it belonged.

Quinoa Pilaf with Herbs and Lemon

SERVES 4 TO 6

If you buy unwashed quinoa, rinse the grains in a fine-mesh strainer, drain them, and then spread them on a rimmed baking sheet lined with a dish towel and let them dry for 15 minutes before proceeding with the recipe. Any soft herbs, such as cilantro, parsley, chives, mint, and tarragon, can be used.

1½ **cups prewashed quinoa**

2 **tablespoons unsalted butter, cut into 2 pieces**

1 **small onion, chopped fine**

¾ **teaspoon salt**

1¾ **cups water**

3 **tablespoons chopped fresh herbs**

1 **tablespoon lemon juice**

1. Toast quinoa in medium saucepan over medium-high heat, stirring frequently, until quinoa is very fragrant and makes continuous popping sound, 5 to 7 minutes. Transfer quinoa to bowl and set aside.

2. Return now-empty pan to medium-low heat and melt butter. Add onion and salt; cook, stirring frequently, until onion is softened and light golden, 5 to 7 minutes.

3. Increase heat to medium-high, stir in water and quinoa, and bring to simmer. Cover, reduce heat to low, and simmer until grains are just tender and liquid is absorbed, 18 to 20 minutes, stirring once halfway through cooking. Remove pan from heat and let sit, covered, for 10 minutes. Fluff quinoa with fork, stir in herbs and lemon juice, and serve.

VARIATION

Quinoa Pilaf with Chipotle, Queso Fresco, and Peanuts

Add 1 teaspoon chipotle chile powder and ¼ teaspoon ground cumin with onion and salt. Substitute ½ cup crumbled queso fresco; ½ cup unsalted roasted peanuts, chopped coarse; and 2 thinly sliced scallions for herbs. Substitute 4 teaspoons lime juice for lemon juice.

EQUIPMENT CORNER

GRILLING TOOLS

A good grill brush can be an invaluable tool for the avid griller, scrubbing even the toughest residue off of grill grates. We rounded up nine brushes in a range of styles and used them to clean barbecue sauce, honey, mustard, and molasses, which we baked onto the grates. What we found: the less complicated the brush, the better. Brushes fitted with multiple scrubbing mechanisms usually meant that one was in the way when we tried to employ the other. Hand position also mattered. Our tested method is to preheat the grill to loosen residue before scrubbing, and brushes with short handles got us too close to the heat. However, excessively long handles subtracted scrubbing leverage and often flexed under pressure. Brushes that wore out quickly also lost major points. We downgraded brushes with bristles that became loose during testing. Our top performers offered good leverage and thorough scrubbing without undue effort, but the **Grill Wizard 18-Inch China Grill Brush**, $31.50, earned top marks for its durable steel pads.

When our grill needs a deeper cleaning than can be achieved with a brush, we turn to a pumice block. Although the short handle of the **GrillStone Value Pack Cleaning Kit by Earthstone International** made it difficult to clean a hot grill, this strong scrubber quickly stripped off all the accumulated gunk even from cold grates. Because each block lasted for only three or four cleanings (replacement blocks cost $4.49), and it generated abundant pumice dust that had to be rinsed off before we could use the grate, at $9.99, we find that it's worth using as a once-per-season grill grate reconditioning tool.

Most ovens can't reach the 700 plus–degree temperatures of commercial ovens. Enter KettlePizza kits, which are designed to turn 18.5- and 22.5-inch kettle-style charcoal grills into wood-fired ovens. All kits include a metal collar that elevates the grill's lid and has a cutout that lets you insert pizzas without losing heat. The **KettlePizza Pro 22 Kit** contains a grate replacement that holds the tombstone-shaped baking stone and features openings in the sides, which made refueling easy. A metal fire basket that holds wood chips alongside the stone helped boost temperatures in the dome to more than 900 degrees. Pizzas had evenly cooked toppings, perfectly charred crusts, and great wood-fired flavor. If you are serious about outdoor pizza, at $299.95, this kit is still far cheaper than a backyard wood-fired oven.

Baguettes at Home

CHAPTER 21

THE RECIPE
Authentic Baguettes at Home

EQUIPMENT CORNER
Baguette Baker's Kit

To mimic the steamy environment created when many baguettes are baked at once (as they are in a professional bakery), we start baking our baguettes under a pair of disposable roasting pans. The result? Loaves as crisp as those from the best Parisian boulangerie.

WE ADMIT IT: WE'VE BEEN BITTEN BY THE ARTISANAL BREAD BUG. Sure, you can buy a decent baguette from a number of bakeries that have popped up all over the country. You may even find one that's pretty darn close to what you could get in Paris, the birthplace of the long, thin loaves. But what about baking a great baguette in your own kitchen? We were itching to give it a try. We wanted shatteringly crisp, perfectly browned crusts and sweetly wheaty, delightfully soft interiors—in short, we wanted perfect baguettes.

Unfortunately, most of the recipes we tried produced subpar results, with pale crusts and tight-crumbed, chewy insides with little to no flavor. For baguettes fit for the French president's table, we started by taking some cues from the masters. But for the average home cook, we made it our goal to break down the process into manageable and approachable steps. Little by little, we uncovered the secrets to baking authentic Parisian-style baguettes with serious depth and complexity of flavor. We even found everyday substitutions for some uncommon tools. Don't get us wrong—the recipe takes some dedication, but these baguettes are worth every step. An excellent homemade meal surely deserves excellent homemade bread to go with it, and what better way to capture the attention of your guests than with a warm, gorgeously bronzed baguette? Just don't be surprised if the bread steals the show.

AUTHENTIC BAGUETTES AT HOME

THE BEST BAGUETTE

✔ **WHY THIS RECIPE WORKS:** Most American baguettes turn out doughy and pale. We wanted a homemade baguette that would rival the best from Parisian boulangeries. For an authentic wheaty flavor, we added a bit of whole-wheat flour (sifted to remove some of the larger pieces of bran that would otherwise add bitterness and make the loaf dense) to the white flour. Starting the dough in a stand mixer and then using a series of gentle folds to develop the dough created the perfect tender, irregular crumb. Next we employed a long, slow rise in the refrigerator, which delivered complex flavor. To shape the loaves perfectly without overworking the dough, we took a multistep approach that gradually transformed them into baguettes. Finally, we ensured a crispy, crackly crust in two ways: First, we moistened the *couche*, the pleated linen cloth that holds the loaves as they proof. We also baked the loaves for the first 10 minutes underneath a pair of upturned disposable roasting pans, which trapped the steam that evaporated from the exterior of the dough.

WE THINK HOME COOKS RARELY MAKE BAGUETTES FOR two reasons: One, they are intimidated, and two, they don't know what they are missing. A great baguette is hard to come by, at least outside France. Those from the supermarket or the average U.S. bakery, with their pale, soft crust and fine crumb, are no comparison to the real thing. The ideal: a moist, wheaty interior punctuated with irregular holes and a deeply browned crust so crisp it shatters into millions of tiny shards (if it isn't messy, *c'est pas bon*). Even if a nearby bakery makes a great baguette, you have to buy one within hours of baking or else it's rock hard. If you want a great baguette, you are better off just making it yourself.

But when we tested some promising recipes, not one produced loaves that attained that ideal. Many had a pale, soft crust and weak flavor; others were dense and

uniform on the inside. We'd need to develop our own recipe—and what better place to begin than by looking to the baguette's home turf?

The best Parisian baguettes have a few things in common. The darker the crust, the deeper the flavor. Excess flour on the exterior will dull flavor and compromise crispness. Irregular interior holes indicate that the dough has been handled gently and thus will have a tender crumb. Almond-shaped slashes that open wide likewise signify tenderness and a fully expanded interior, while color that changes from pale to dark within those cuts is a sign of complex flavor. And finally, a great baguette should have the flavor of sweet wheat, with just a subtle hint of tangy, complex fermented flavor.

The problem with the recipes we had tried wasn't so much what they instructed us to do but how little instruction and explanation they provided. In France, so much of what goes into making a good baguette is in the mechanics of the thing—shaping, proofing, scoring, steaming in the oven—and this wasn't conveyed in recipes. Our role was clear: cull what we could from recipes and then apply what we had learned from the French to create a step-by-step, authentic baguette recipe for the home oven.

The standard baguette ingredient list is simple: flour, water, salt, and yeast. We settled on 1 pound of flour, 1 teaspoon of yeast, 1½ teaspoons of salt, and enough water (12 ounces) for a moderately wet dough. (We also added a teaspoon of diastatic malt powder to help the loaf brown deeply; see page 243 for more information.) As for mixing and kneading, we found that less is more in both cases. Using a stand mixer to do both jobs left the interior crumb too uniform and tight. Mixing by hand and then giving the dough several folds during the initial proofing to develop the structure gave us better results, but it was difficult to evenly combine the ingredients. We settled on a hybrid approach: We mixed the dough in the machine and then folded the dough several times during the initial proofing.

The next detail was fermentation, which is when the yeast consumes sugar and starches in the flour to produce gas and alcohol, giving the loaf both lift and flavor.

The simplest approach is the straight dough process, which calls for doing everything from mixing through baking in a single day, allowing 2 to 3 hours for fermentation. Another option is the sponge or pre-ferment method, in which a portion of the yeast, flour, and water are mixed and proofed for at least a few hours, and often overnight, before proceeding. And finally, there is the slow-rise, or cold-fermentation, method, in which the dough is mixed and then placed in the fridge for a day or more before finishing. The straight dough method resulted in baguettes with little character. Doughs using a pre-ferment had a far better flavor, but the slow-rise baguettes were equally flavorful and offered another benefit: convenience. The dough needed at least 24 hours in the refrigerator, but it could sit for as long as 72 hours. Furthermore, this dough could be portioned out to make baguettes as desired within that window.

Using this method, we got good flavor, but our loaves were missing that critical, sweet wheaty flavor of Parisian baguettes. Suspecting that the flour might be to blame, we contacted French baking scholar James MacGuire for insight. Here's what he told us: The flavor of a baguette's interior comes primarily from yellow carotenoid pigments, which naturally occur in wheat. Some wheat varieties are higher in carotenoids than others. Much of the wheat grown in North America is destined for the Far East, where people want pure white dumplings and noodles, so the growth of wheat varieties high in carotenoids is discouraged. But in France, the best flours are high in carotenoid pigments. To mimic the more intense wheatiness of French flours, James suggested adding a small amount of whole-wheat flour to our recipe.

So we tried substituting ¼ cup of whole-wheat flour for some of the white flour. Tasters welcomed the wheatiness, but they also noted a hint of bitterness and found these baguettes more dense and less crisp. The bran in the wheat flour was adding a bitter flavor and its sharp edges were cutting gluten strands, weakening the structure. Happily, there was a ready solution: Sifting the wheat flour removed large flakes of bran. Subbing in this sifted flour gave us baguettes with the same texture as that of all-white-flour loaves, but with far better flavor.

Now that we had a dough we were happy with, we could focus on shaping. Too often our loaves had a dense, uniform crumb—or they had inappropriately giant holes—instead of a mix of small and large holes. We learned that shaping has a major impact here.

We knew that turning that mass of dough into a baguette shape gradually was critical. If you do it too quickly, you'll either push the dough too hard and overwork it or you won't get the right shape—or both. As we worked out our own step-by-step method, we found that the key was using a gentle touch and avoiding trapping large pockets of air. We settled on a three-stage process—preshape, fold, stretch—and a few key tricks that ensured ideal results. For instance, pressing the dough into a square and then rolling it like a log was the gentlest way to start the shaping process, while moving the semi-formed loaf back and forth at the center until its ends widened, giving it a dog-bone shape, tightened the loaf and also pushed large air bubbles out either end, which we made sure not to seal until the very last moment.

We also learned that to score the loaves properly, we needed to keep the blade at a shallow angle while making the cuts. A *lame,* the traditional baguette scoring tool with a slightly curved blade, made producing slashes that baked up into the right almond-shaped openings easy, and it also created the proper ridge, or "ear" along one side of the slash that baked up deliciously crisp. (Alternatively, we found that a box cutter also works reasonably well.)

It was time to move on to the crust. It was too thick, almost leathery. At bakeries, the shaped loaves are typically proofed in the folds of a piece of heavy linen known as a *couche,* which is floured just enough to prevent sticking. The couche has two core jobs: It helps the baguette retain its shape, and it wicks away moisture from the exterior to encourage a crisp crust. But the thick crusts on our loaves suggested that they might be losing a little too much moisture. Most bakeries make hundreds of baguettes at a time, and as loaves sit side by side on their large couches, the moisture that comes off them saturates the couche and the air around it. With our small batch, the same effect wasn't possible. Misting the back of our couche lightly with water was a step in the right direction, but still the crust wasn't quite right.

Steam within the oven serves three important functions in bread baking. First, it keeps the exterior of the bread moist when it begins to bake, preventing the crust from hardening before the interior has fully expanded. Second, it ensures good color since the enzymes that convert some of the starches to sugars, which in turn lead to browning, need water to function. And finally—and most important for our current concern—steam promotes crispness. The remaining starches on the loaf's surface absorb the steam and cook into a crisp crust (a process known as gelatinization); without it, they simply dry out, leaving the crust dull and raw-tasting.

We had been creating steam using our go-to method: Just before putting the bread into the oven, we poured boiling water into a pan of preheated lava rocks sitting on the bottom shelf. Steam is most important at the start of the baking time, and as we watched a fair amount of it escape when we put baguettes into the oven, we began doubting our technique. With the standard boule, which requires about 45 minutes of baking, there is time to

EQUIPMENT CORNER

BAGUETTE BAKER'S KIT
Baguettes require a few specialty items, though we did find some alternatives.

DIASTATIC MALT POWDER
Because of the long proofing time, nearly all the sugars in baguette dough will be consumed by yeast. Since sugars are responsible for browning, this will leave the crust pale and dull-tasting. Adding diastatic malt powder, a naturally occurring enzyme that converts the starches in flour to sugar, guarantees a supply of sugar at baking time and thus a crust that browns quickly and deeply (it also improves the texture of the loaf). It's not essential, but it makes a difference. Purchase diastatic malt powder (available from Amazon, $7.63 for 1 pound), not plain malt powder or malt syrup.

COUCHE
To proof shaped baguettes, bakers cradle them in the folds of a piece of heavy raw linen called a *couche.* A couche wicks away moisture, helping create a crisp crust, and releases the dough without tugging it out of shape as cotton or synthetic will. Our favorite, the **San Francisco Baking Institute 18" Linen Canvas (Couche)** ($8 for 36 by 18-inch couche), has good body without being too stiff. Alternatively, you can use a double layer of 100 percent linen tea towels that are at least 16 inches long and 12 inches wide.

FLIPPING BOARD
To move baguettes from the couche to the oven, professional bakers use a long narrow piece of wood called a flipping board or transfer peel. While the boards aren't expensive ($12 from breadtopia.com), we found that a homemade substitute, made by taping together two pieces of clean, stiff cardboard (16 inches long by 4 inches wide) with packaging tape, works equally well.

LAME
Baguettes require scores that taper at the ends and open wide at the center, with an edge that peels back into a crisp ridge or "ear" that lends both flavor and texture. To achieve this, you must cut the loaf at a low angle, something much more easily done with the curved blade of a *lame.* Our favorite, the **Breadtopia Bread Lame** ($9.50), scored baguettes perfectly, and its blades are easy to change. Plus, it came with 10 extra blades. Alternatively, an unused box cutter blade will work.

WHY WE FOLD BAGUETTE DOUGH

In our Authentic Baguettes at Home, we interrupt the rising time by folding (or turning) the dough, gently folding the dough over itself several times as it rises. Like kneading, this process builds strength by bringing wayward sheets of gluten, the protein that gives bread structure once flour and water have been combined, into alignment. But folding is a more gentle process than kneading, and it works out large air pockets that can form as the dough rises, giving you a more even dough by the end of the rising time.

Using your fingertips or a bowl scraper, gently lift the edge of the dough and fold it toward the middle. Turn the bowl 45 degrees and repeat.

SLASHING RUSTIC LOAVES

The slashes on rustic loaves, like our Authentic Baguettes at Home, aren't just about aesthetics. Slashes create weak spots in a loaf's surface, which allow the interior crumb to expand fully in the right direction. Without the slashes, the loaf will expand outward wherever it finds a random weak spot, resulting in an oddly shaped loaf and an uneven crumb.

Narrow baguettes and torpedo- or oval-shaped loaves should be scored along their length with long ½-inch-deep slashes made at a shallow, 30-degree angle (almost horizontal to the work surface). For even, smooth cuts, it's important to use a swift, fluid motion. If the blade is held upright or the cut is too deep, it will close up during baking. Scoring of this type is most easily done with a curved-blade *lame* (our favorite is the Breadtopia Bread Lame, $9.50; see page 243 for more information). This blade will produce broad, almond-shaped openings. Since the openings taper at the ends, the ends of each cut should overlap just slightly to ensure that the loaf expands evenly down its length.

recover that steam without much impact, but with a baguette, which requires only 20 minutes or so of oven time, by the time the steam has been replaced, it's too late.

We racked our brains for a solution. We recalled our Almost No-Knead Bread recipe, which starts the bread in a covered pot, steaming the loaf by surrounding it in its own evaporating moisture. Once the bread is fully expanded and the crust set, the bread is uncovered and finished. We wondered if a similar approach would work here. For our next test, we covered our baguettes with a pair of large, overturned disposable roasting pans (doubled up for a better seal against the baking stone). After 10 minutes, we pulled off the pans and continued baking the baguettes. Tearing into a baguette after it had cooled confirmed it—these baguettes were shatteringly crisp. This was a baguette that could sit proudly on anyone's table—French, American, or otherwise.

Authentic Baguettes at Home

MAKES FOUR 15-INCH-LONG BAGUETTES

We recommend using a *couche, lame*, flipping board, and diastatic malt powder for this recipe (see page 243 for more information). You will also need a pizza peel and baking stone. If you can't find King Arthur all-purpose flour, substitute bread flour, not another all-purpose flour. For best results, weigh your ingredients. This recipe makes enough dough for four loaves, which can be baked anytime during the 24- to 72-hour window after placing the dough in the fridge.

¼   **cup (1⅓ ounces) whole-wheat flour**

3   **cups (15 ounces) King Arthur all-purpose flour**

1½ **teaspoons salt**

1   **teaspoon instant or rapid-rise yeast**

1   **teaspoon diastatic malt powder (optional)**

1½ **cups (12 ounces) water**

2   **(16 by 12-inch) disposable aluminum roasting pans**

1. Sift whole-wheat flour through fine-mesh strainer into bowl of stand mixer; discard bran remaining in strainer. Add all-purpose flour, salt, yeast, and malt powder, if using, to mixer bowl. Fit stand mixer with dough hook, add water, and knead on low speed until cohesive dough forms and no dry flour remains, 5 to 7 minutes. Transfer dough to lightly oiled large bowl, cover with plastic wrap, and let rest at room temperature for 30 minutes.

2. Holding edge of dough with your fingertips or using a bowl scraper, fold dough over itself by gently lifting and folding edge of dough toward center. Turn bowl 45 degrees; fold again. Turn bowl and fold dough 6 more times (total of 8 folds). Cover with plastic and let rise for 30 minutes. Repeat folding and rising every 30 minutes, 3 more times. After fourth set of folds, cover bowl tightly with plastic and refrigerate for at least 24 hours or up to 72 hours.

3. Transfer dough to lightly floured counter, pat into 8-inch square (do not deflate), and divide in half. Return 1 piece of dough to container, wrap tightly with plastic, and refrigerate (dough can be shaped and baked anytime within 72-hour window). Divide remaining dough in half crosswise, transfer to lightly floured rimmed baking sheet, and cover loosely with plastic. Let rest for 45 minutes.

4. On lightly floured counter, roll each piece of dough into loose 3- to 4-inch-long cylinder; return to floured baking sheet and cover with plastic. Let rest at room temperature for 30 minutes.

5. Lightly mist underside of couche with water, drape over inverted baking sheet, and dust with flour. Gently press 1 piece of dough into 6 by 4-inch rectangle on lightly floured counter, with long edge facing you. Fold upper quarter of dough toward center and press gently to seal. Rotate dough 180 degrees and repeat folding step to form 8 by 2-inch rectangle.

SHAPING AND BAKING BAGUETTES

Once your dough has gone through the initial rising, folding, and resting stages, it's ready to be shaped. For more information on the *couche, lame*, and flipping board, see page 243.

1. On lightly floured counter, roll each piece of refrigerated and rested dough into loose 3- to 4-inch-long cylinder. Move dough to floured baking sheet and cover with plastic. Let rest at room temperature for 30 minutes.

2. Gently press 1 piece of dough into 6 by 4-inch rectangle with long edge facing you. Fold upper quarter of dough toward center and press to seal. Rotate dough 180 degrees and repeat folding step to form 8 by 2-inch rectangle.

3. Fold dough in half toward you, using thumb of your other hand to create crease along center of dough, sealing with heel of your hand as you work your way along the loaf. Do not seal ends of loaf.

4. Cup your hand over center of dough and roll dough back and forth gently to form dog-bone shape. Working toward ends, gently roll and stretch dough until it measures 15 inches long by 1¼ inches wide.

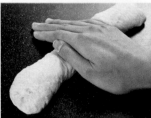

5. Moving your hands in opposite directions, use back-and-forth motion to roll ends of loaf under your palms to form sharp points.

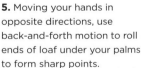

6. Transfer dough to floured couche, seam side up. On either side of loaf, pinch edges of couche into pleat. Cover loosely with large plastic garbage bag.

7. Place second loaf on opposite side of pleat. Fold edges of couche over loaves to cover, then carefully place sheet inside bag, and tie or fold under to enclose. Let rise for 45 minutes to 1 hour. While bread rises, preheat baking stone.

8. Unfold couche. Use flipping board to roll each loaf over so it is seam side down. Hold long edge of flipping board between loaf and couche at 45-degree angle. Lift couche and flip loaf seam side up onto board. Invert loaf onto parchment-lined peel.

9. Holding lame concave side up at 30-degree angle to loaf, make series of three 4-inch-long, ½-inch-deep slashes along length of each loaf, using swift, fluid motion, overlapping each slash slightly.

10. Transfer loaves, on parchment, to baking stone, cover with stacked inverted disposable pans; bake for 5 minutes. Remove pans and bake until loaves are evenly browned, 12 to 15 minutes longer, rotating parchment halfway through baking.

6. Fold dough in half toward you, using thumb of your other hand to create crease along center of dough, sealing with heel of your hand as you work your way along the loaf. Without pressing down on loaf, use heel of your hand to reinforce seal (do not seal ends of loaf).

7. Cup your hand over center of dough and roll dough back and forth gently to tighten (it should form dog-bone shape).

8. Starting at center of dough and working toward ends, gently and evenly roll and stretch dough until it measures 15 inches long by 1¼ inches wide. Moving your hands in opposite directions, use back and forth motion to roll ends of loaf under your palms to form sharp points.

9. Transfer dough to floured couche, seam side up. On either side of loaf, pinch edges of couche into pleat, then cover loosely with large plastic garbage bag.

10. Repeat steps 4 through 9 with second piece of dough and place on opposite side of pleat. Fold edges of couche over loaves to cover completely, then carefully place sheet inside bag, and tie or fold under to enclose.

11. Let stand until loaves have nearly doubled in size and dough springs back minimally when poked gently with your fingertip, 45 minutes to 1 hour. While bread rises, adjust oven rack to middle position, place baking stone on rack, and heat oven to 500 degrees.

12. Line pizza peel with 16 by 12-inch piece of parchment paper with long edge perpendicular to handle. Unfold couche, pulling from ends to remove pleats. Gently pushing with side of flipping board, roll 1 loaf over, away from other loaf, so it is seam side down. Using your hand, hold long edge of flipping board between loaf and couche at 45-degree angle, then lift couche with your other hand and flip loaf seam side up onto board.

13. Invert loaf onto parchment-lined peel, seam side down, about 2 inches from long edge of parchment, then use flipping board to straighten loaf. Repeat with remaining loaf, leaving at least 3 inches between loaves.

14. Holding lame concave side up at 30 degree angle to loaf, make series of three 4-inch-long, ½-inch-deep

slashes along length of loaf, using swift, fluid motion, overlapping each slash slightly. Repeat with second loaf.

15. Transfer loaves, on parchment, to baking stone, cover with stacked inverted disposable pans, and bake for 5 minutes. Carefully remove pans and bake until loaves are evenly browned, 12 to 15 minutes longer, rotating parchment halfway through baking. Transfer to cooling rack and let cool for at least 20 minutes before serving. Consume within 4 hours.

Pizza and Cookies
Go Gluten-Free

*Because almonds don't
release a lot of oil when
heated, using almond flour
in our gluten-free pizza
dough was a good way
to add richness without
making the crust greasy.*

IF YOU OR SOMEONE YOU COOK FOR IS AVOIDING GLUTEN, YOU probably know what a challenge it can be to find gluten-free baked goods worth eating. While naturally gluten-free grains like quinoa and rice can go a long way in getting dinner on the gluten-free table, some dishes are more difficult to make on a gluten-free diet. We set ourselves the daunting challenge of creating gluten-free pizza and chocolate chip cookies that were as tasty as their wheat-flour counterparts. We started by developing a gluten-free flour blend, a hurdle in and of itself. But with that formula nailed down, our work was still only half done.

For a gluten-free pizza crust with a crispy exterior and a tender, airy interior, we couldn't just substitute our flour blend in a basic pizza dough recipe. After many rounds of testing, we discovered that the key to the best texture lay in the simplest ingredient of all: water.

Everyone loves a good chocolate chip cookie, but most gluten-free versions of these bake sale darlings are gritty, crumbly, and just not worth eating. Our work was cut out for us: create a cookie with a chewy center and crispy edges, and eliminate the unpleasant sandy texture that plagues so many gluten-free cookies. To achieve our goal, we had to throw most of what we knew about making cookies out the window and develop a new method from the ground up. With gluten-free pizza and cookies this good, you won't even miss the wheat.

THE BEST GLUTEN-FREE PIZZA

✓ **WHY THIS RECIPE WORKS:** Achieving a crispy crust and a tender interior on a gluten-free pizza was no easy feat. First, we developed a gluten-free flour blend that mimicked many of the properties of wheat flour: white rice flour for starch, brown rice flour for wheaty flavor, potato starch for tenderness, tapioca starch for spring and stretch, and milk powder for browning and structure. To mimic the gluten in wheat flour, we used a small amount of ground psyllium husk. To create a tender, airy, open crumb, we significantly increased the water in the dough and then gently parbaked the crusts to drive off the excess moisture once it had served its purpose. Finally, we added a small amount of ground almond flour to introduce richness and increase crispiness without leaving the crust greasy.

WE'VE ALWAYS EMBRACED GLUTEN AS THE MAGIC ingredient in bread. It's the source of its structure and, as a result, much of its texture. Which is, perhaps, why gluten-free baked goods are so hard to get right. We set ourselves the challenging goal of developing a gluten-free pizza crust that everyone would want to eat, whether they were avoiding gluten or not.

Our first forays into the world of gluten-free pizza were, in an odd way, encouraging. We sought out every pizza joint that sold a gluten-free pie, and every crust was awful. Some were rubbery and dense. Others were stiff and flavorless. And none bore any resemblance to the real thing, which needs to be—at the very least—crispy on the underside and airy and tender within. We also tried a handful of recipes from various gluten-free cookbooks and websites; the results were no better.

Clearly, the world of gluten-free pizza was so dismal that almost any improvement would be welcome. But

we didn't want to settle for just passable. We wanted to make a crust with an airy texture and good chew, a crust that could hold its own against the wheat-flour versions.

The first thing we needed was a substitute for the wheat flour. This isn't an easy swap since there isn't a single wheat-free flour that can supply the same characteristics as wheat flour's makeup of protein, starch, and fat. A blend was a must. Fortunately, we had recently developed just such a blend for the test kitchen's new gluten-free cookbook. With the substitute on hand, we got down to business.

Given the numerous flaws that we'd encountered in those early samples, we decided to start from the ground up. For two 12-inch pizzas, we figured that roughly 3 cups of the flour blend would be right. To this we added a teaspoon of instant yeast, 2 teaspoons of salt, and a teaspoon of xanthan gum.

Why xanthan gum? The gluten-free flour blend's protein network is weak in comparison with the gluten network of wheat flour, and xanthan gum (made by fermenting simple sugars using the microorganism *Xanthomonas campestris*) behaves like glue in many gluten-free baked goods, strengthening the weak network and improving elasticity. That's exactly what our gluten-free dough would need. Without such reinforcement, the carbon dioxide produced by the yeast would simply escape from the dough and the resulting crust would be tough, dense, and squat. If xanthan gum is so effective at holding gluten-free baked goods together, you might wonder why we didn't include it in the test kitchen's flour blend. We left it out because not all recipes need it, and those that do require varying amounts.

We placed our dry ingredients in the bowl of a stand mixer fitted with a dough hook and poured in 1½ cups of water and ¼ cup of oil (typical amounts for standard pizza dough). We let the machine work the dough until it started to pull away from the sides of the bowl—the signal that there was decent structural development. (In a wheat-based dough you'd say "gluten development,"

THE BEST GLUTEN-FREE PIZZA

but we were obviously dealing with a different protein network.) Then we put our dough in a lightly oiled bowl, covered it with plastic wrap, and waited for it to proof.

And waited. Even after 90 minutes, the dough showed no signs of expanding. When we cut into it, we found a network of tiny bubbles, but hardly the airy holes that we'd hoped for. But we forged ahead anyway, rolling out the dough (even with the xanthan gum, the dough was still too fragile to stretch like wheat-based pizza dough), topping the rounds with sauce and cheese, and baking them in a hot oven. The result? A crust that was dense and flat, with a tough underside and gummy interior. This was far from passable.

The obvious question to address was why the dough didn't rise. In traditional yeasted doughs, the rise and the yeast tend to go hand in hand since yeast produces gas

(as well as flavor compounds) as it ferments. So we tried adding more yeast in increasing amounts. But no matter how much we added, the dough refused to budge. In fact, the only noticeable difference was that in high amounts, the yeast gave the dough a sour, overproofed flavor.

Maybe the dough lacked the structure necessary to contain the gases; that pointed to the xanthan gum. For the next few tests, we added increasing amounts of xanthan gum, from 1½ teaspoons up to 3 tablespoons. While the greater amount increased the dough's ability to expand, it also gave the dough an unappealing rubbery consistency.

Could it be that xanthan gum wasn't the best choice? Maybe we should have been using one of the other two structural-reinforcement options that we'd seen called for: guar gum (produced by grinding the endosperm of Indian guar plant seeds) or powdered psyllium seed husks (most commonly used as a dietary fiber). The guar gum performed no better than the xanthan gum, and it also contributed an off-flavor. However, psyllium husk was a definite improvement. One and a half tablespoons delivered a dough that rose visibly during proofing and a final crust that had a more open crumb. Our science editor explained that psyllium husk is far more effective at attracting and holding on to water molecules than the gums are, which allows it to create a thick gel. This gel, combined with psyllium husk's insoluble fiber and protein, was providing incredibly strong structural reinforcement for our dough's protein network, making it capable of trapping lots of gas during proofing as well as steam during baking. Nevertheless, the crust was far from the light and airy crust that we'd set our sights on.

But we'd been noticing something. While the dough now rose well during proofing, when we rolled it out to shape the crust, much of the gas was expelled. The dough never recovered like a wheat-flour dough, even when we tried letting it rise a second time post-shaping. If the crust couldn't hold on to gas as well as we needed it to, maybe we could give it a little boost. To this end we turned to an ingredient used in countless baked goods, though less often in yeasted ones: baking powder. Sure enough, a couple of teaspoons of the leavener, activated by the heat of the oven, gave the dough a bit more of the lift that it had been missing.

Still, it wasn't enough. Many traditional wheat-based pizza doughs can be rather stiff right after mixing yet end up open and airy after proofing, making them easy to stretch. This elasticity also translates into a dough that can puff up with steam in the oven, and thus a crust that bakes up light and airy. But in the case of our gluten-free dough, the dough started out stiff and stayed stiff. Thinking about how, in the past, we've gotten some unworkably stiff wheat-based doughs to stretch more, we landed on water. Increasing the water in a wheat-based dough allows the protein network to be more fluid and thus more flexible and stretchable. Would the same rule apply to the network in our gluten-free pizza dough? To find out, we made a series of doughs using increasing amounts of water.

Even before we topped the pizzas with tomato sauce, Parmesan cheese, and mozzarella cheese and baked them off, we could tell that we were onto something: The more water the dough contained the more it rose during proofing. As it happened, our dough seemed to benefit from the additional water far more than we'd expected: The most tender crust and open crumb came when we'd added so much water that it went from being a dough to more of a thick batter.

Of course, this added liquid created some new problems. For one, mixing the dough with the dough hook was now ineffective: The dough was so wet that the hook just spun around. Switching to the paddle attachment was an easy fix. Second, the additional water made shaping the crust with a rolling pin, as we had been doing, impossible. Instead, we spread it out on a baking sheet with a rubber spatula into an 8-inch circle, much like spreading frosting on a cake, and then misted the dough with vegetable oil spray, covered it with a piece of plastic wrap, and pressed it into an even, large round with a properly thick edge around the perimeter. Last, and most

BUILDING OUR OWN GLUTEN-FREE FLOUR BLEND

When developing our gluten-free pizza and cookie recipes, we wanted a wheat-free substitute for all-purpose flour that would work in both applications (as well as other gluten-free recipes). We found that store-bought gluten-free blends perform inconsistently; one product might deliver great cookies but subpar pizza crust. For that reason, we decided to create our own.

To start, we reviewed how wheat flour works. When hydrated, starch granules in the flour swell, and with the help of mixing or kneading (or sufficient time), the proteins in the flour link up to form long elastic strands called gluten. These strands surround the gelled starch granules, creating a network that enables rise and a sturdy structure. Since no single gluten-free flour or starch performs in this way, a blend was necessary. We found that two flours—white rice flour and brown rice flour—provided the right baseline of protein, starch, and flavor. And since different starches absorb water, swell, and gel at different temperatures and to different degrees, we enlisted two kinds—potato starch and tapioca starch—to create the right amount of chew and structure. Finally, the proteins and sugars in milk powder ensure that baked goods brown properly.

Be aware: A gluten-free flour blend is a complicated mixture, and thus brands aren't easily interchangeable. It's best to work with recipes that have been developed around a particular blend.

WHITE RICE FLOUR

Provides a neutral-tasting, refined protein/starch base.

BROWN RICE FLOUR

Supplies proteins that, along with those in the white rice flour, create a network that mimics gluten. Also provides a nutty, wheaty flavor.

POTATO STARCH

Contributes large starch granules that gel at higher temperatures and set to a more extensive, open network when cool, thus providing tenderness.

TAPIOCA STARCH

Provides smaller granules that gel at lower temperatures, forming a more compact network when cool, thus providing chew and elasticity.

MILK POWDER

Contributes proteins that help improve structure and, along with its sugars, undergo the Maillard browning reaction, which leads to more complex flavor.

important, while the final crust had the perfect tender texture and open, airy crumb around the outer edge, the added water had made it gummy toward the center.

To remove the excess water, we tried parbaking the rounds without any toppings in a hot oven just until they'd started to brown. This produced crusts that looked nice and dry on the exterior, but they were still gummy inside. To drive off enough water without overbaking the exterior, we tested incrementally lower oven temperatures and increased baking times. We finally got it just right when we started the crust in a cold oven, set the temperature to 325 degrees, and let it cook through slowly for about 45 minutes. We then sauced the parbaked crust, sprinkled it with mozzarella and a little Parmesan, and put it back in a 500-degree oven briefly to melt the cheese and finish browning the crust.

Now that we had a pizza crust with a light and airy (but not gummy) interior, there was only one obstacle: The underside of the crust was more tough than crispy. No problem, we thought: Adding more oil to the dough would get it to fry up a bit. Alas, while this did help it crisp, it also left the pizza greasy. Gluten-free flours, we learned, don't absorb fats as readily as wheat flour does, and clearly we'd gone over the maximum.

The solution turned out to be almond flour. Adding just 2½ ounces to the dough boosted the overall fat content and gave our crust the crispness that it needed without causing any noticeable change in flavor. And because almonds (and nuts in general) don't shed all their oil when heated, the crust wasn't greasy.

As for the toppings, we liked keeping it simple with just cheese and sauce, but we did find that additional toppings were fine as long as we limited them to no more than 6 ounces of vegetables and 4 ounces of meat per pie. (We thinly sliced hearty vegetables, such as peppers and onions, and sautéed them before using, and precooked meats like pepperoni to drain them of fat.) Finally, we had a gluten-free pizza crust that we could serve proudly, even to those who didn't have to avoid gluten.

The Best Gluten-Free Pizza
MAKES TWO 12-INCH PIZZAS

If you don't have almond flour, you can process 2½ ounces of blanched almonds in a food processor until finely ground, about 30 seconds. You can substitute 16 ounces (2⅔ cups plus ¼ cup) King Arthur Gluten-Free Multi-Purpose Flour or 16 ounces (2⅔ cups plus ½ cup) Bob's Red Mill GF All-Purpose Baking Flour for our flour blend. Crust made with King Arthur will be slightly denser and not as chewy, and crust made with Bob's Red Mill will be thicker and more airy and will have a distinct bean flavor.

CRUST

16 ounces (3⅓ cups plus ¼ cup) America's Test Kitchen Gluten-Free Flour Blend (recipe follows)
2½ ounces (½ cup plus 1 tablespoon) almond flour
1½ tablespoons powdered psyllium husk
2½ teaspoons baking powder
2 teaspoons salt
1 teaspoon instant or rapid-rise yeast
2½ cups warm water (100 degrees)
¼ cup vegetable oil
Vegetable oil spray

SAUCE

1 (28-ounce) can whole peeled tomatoes, drained
1 tablespoon extra-virgin olive oil
1 teaspoon red wine vinegar
1 garlic clove, minced
1 teaspoon dried oregano
½ teaspoon salt
¼ teaspoon pepper

1 ounce Parmesan cheese, grated fine (½ cup)
8 ounces whole-milk mozzarella cheese, shredded (2 cups)

1. FOR THE CRUST: Using stand mixer fitted with paddle, mix flour blend, almond flour, psyllium, baking powder, salt, and yeast on low speed until combined.

Slowly add warm water and oil in steady stream until incorporated. Increase speed to medium and beat until dough is sticky and uniform, about 6 minutes. (Dough will resemble thick batter.)

2. Remove bowl from mixer, cover with plastic wrap, and let stand until inside of dough is bubbly (use spoon to peer inside dough), about 1½ hours. (Dough will puff slightly but will not rise.)

3. Adjust oven racks to middle and lower positions. Line 2 rimmed baking sheets with parchment paper and spray liberally with oil spray. Transfer half of dough to center of 1 prepared sheet. Using oil-sprayed rubber spatula, spread dough into 8-inch circle. Spray top of dough with oil spray, cover with large sheet of plastic, and, using your hands, press out dough to 11½-inch round, about ¼ inch thick, leaving outer ¼ inch slightly thicker than center; discard plastic. Repeat with remaining dough and second prepared sheet.

4. Place prepared sheets in oven and heat oven to 325 degrees. Bake dough until firm to touch, golden brown on underside, and just beginning to brown on top, 45 to 50 minutes, switching and rotating sheets halfway through baking. Transfer crusts to wire rack and let cool.

5. FOR THE SAUCE: Process all ingredients in food processor until smooth, about 30 seconds. Transfer to bowl and refrigerate until ready to use.

6. One hour before baking pizza, adjust oven rack to upper-middle position, set baking stone on rack, and heat oven to 500 degrees.

7. Transfer 1 parbaked crust to pizza peel. Using back of spoon or ladle, spread ½ cup tomato sauce in thin layer over surface of crust, leaving ¼-inch border around edge. Sprinkle ¼ cup Parmesan evenly over sauce, followed by 1 cup mozzarella. Carefully slide crust onto stone and bake until crust is well browned and cheese

FORGET PIZZA DOUGH: MAKE A BATTER INSTEAD

Because our gluten-free pizza dough has a higher-than-normal hydration level, it can't be shaped like traditional dough.

1. Drop batter onto parchment-lined baking sheet, then spread it into rough circle with rubber spatula. Spritz dough with vegetable oil spray.

2. Cover with plastic wrap and press into even round with raised edge. To avoid gummy results, prebake crust, then top and bake to finish.

A GLUTEN-FREE CRUST THAT DOESN'T FALL FLAT

With psyllium husk and plenty of water, our dough has the structure and elasticity that others lack.

OUR CRUST
Airy and tender

TYPICAL GLUTEN-FREE CRUST
Dense and rubbery

is bubbly and beginning to brown, 10 to 12 minutes. Transfer pizza to wire rack and let cool for 5 minutes before slicing and serving. Repeat with second crust, ½ cup tomato sauce (you will have extra sauce), remaining ¼ cup Parmesan, and remaining 1 cup mozzarella.

TO MAKE AHEAD: Extra sauce can be refrigerated for up to 1 week or frozen for up to 1 month. Parbaked and cooled crusts can sit at room temperature for up to 4 hours. Completely cooled crusts can be wrapped with plastic wrap and then aluminum foil and frozen for up to 2 weeks. Frozen crusts can be topped and baked as directed without thawing.

The America's Test Kitchen Gluten-Free Flour Blend

MAKES 42 OUNCES (ABOUT 9⅓ CUPS)

Be sure to use potato starch, not potato flour, with this recipe. Tapioca starch is also sold as tapioca flour; they are interchangeable. We strongly recommend that you use Bob's Red Mill white and brown rice flours. We also recommend that you weigh your ingredients; if you measure by volume, spoon each ingredient into the measuring cup (do not pack or tap) and scrape off the excess.

24   ounces (4½ cups plus ⅓ cup) white rice flour
7½   ounces (1⅔ cups) brown rice flour
7   ounces (1⅓ cups) potato starch
3   ounces (¾ cup) tapioca starch
¾   ounce (¼ cup) nonfat dry milk powder

Whisk all ingredients in large bowl until well combined. Transfer to airtight container and refrigerate for up to 3 months.

GLUTEN-FREE CHOCOLATE CHIP COOKIES

☑ WHY THIS RECIPE WORKS: Chocolate chip cookies are a classic favorite, but most gluten-free versions turn out crumbly, gritty, and greasy. Using the test kitchen's gluten-free flour blend, we set out to create a gluten-free cookie that would be as good as the original version. Cutting back on butter helped to minimize greasiness. Melting the butter, rather than creaming (as called for in traditional recipes), gave the cookies a chewier texture. Some xanthan gum helped give the cookies structure, allowing them to hold together. To alleviate grittiness, we added more liquid in the form of milk and let the dough rest for 30 minutes so that the starches had time to hydrate and soften. Upping the ratio of brown sugar to granulated sugar made our cookies crisp on the edges and chewy in the center, and also gave the cookies more complex, toffee-like flavor.

WHEN IT COMES TO COOKIES, CHOCOLATE CHIP RANKS high on the list of universal favorites. But even with the abundance of gluten-free baked goods available now, we had yet to come across a gluten-free chocolate chip cookie that came anywhere close to the classic original. The gluten-free versions we had tried were too cakey or had an odd, gritty texture. We wanted to make a gluten-free chocolate chip cookie with the toffee-like flavor, crisp exterior, and tender interior of a cookie made with wheat flour.

We set to work, mixing up a batch of the gluten-free flour blend that the test kitchen had just developed (see more information on page 253). To start our cookie recipe, we simply swapped in the blend for the all-purpose flour in a standard Toll House cookie recipe.

Unsurprisingly, these cookies had problems: They were flat, sandy, greasy, and nothing like what a chocolate chip cookie should be.

First, we decided to address the structural issues. Because starches are liquid when hot and don't set up until cool, and because the bonds between the proteins in gluten-free flour blends are weak and few in number, gluten-free cookies don't have the ability to hold their shape like traditional cookies. To prevent the cookies from spreading all over the baking sheet, we needed to add something to reinforce the weak structure of our gluten-free flour. Just a small amount of xanthan gum did the trick.

Next, we worked on the greasiness problem. We knew from colleagues' testing of other gluten-free recipes that gluten-free flours behave differently than wheat flour. Our gluten-free flour blend contains more starch and less protein than all-purpose flour, and it's the proteins that are compatible with fat. The 12 tablespoons of butter found in traditional chocolate chip cookie recipes weren't being properly absorbed by the gluten-free blend, making the cookies greasy. We made several more batches, decreasing the butter by a tablespoon each time. We found that 8 tablespoons of butter was the most that the cookies could manage.

GLUTEN-FREE CHOCOLATE CHIP COOKIES

We also realized that creaming the butter and sugar was aerating the butter, which made the cookies too cakey. Melting the butter got us closer to the texture we were after.

But because we had decreased the amount of butter, the dough now had very little liquid to hydrate the flour (butter is about 18 percent water) and the cookies were noticeably gritty. To solve this problem, we added a small amount of liquid in the form of milk. We also knew that a brief rest would give the starches enough time to absorb the liquid. Two tablespoons of milk and a 30-minute rest hydrated the dough just enough to eliminate grittiness. Resting the dough also helped stiffen it, which further improved structure and prevented spread.

Finally, we moved on to texture and flavor. We wanted a cookie that was chewy in the center and slightly crisp on the outside. The Toll House cookie recipe calls for equal amounts of granulated sugar and brown sugar. Granulated sugar contributes to a caramelized, crisp texture and provides structure, while brown sugar adds moisture and rich caramel notes. We decided to increase the brown sugar and decrease the granulated sugar to achieve a perfectly chewy center with crisp edges. Using more brown sugar than white also had the added benefit of enhancing the rich, toffee-like flavor that we expect in a cookie like this.

We baked up a final batch and called in our tasters. When our non-gluten-free colleagues started reaching for seconds, we knew we had done something right.

Gluten-Free Chocolate Chip Cookies
MAKES ABOUT 24 COOKIES

Not all brands of chocolate chips are processed in a gluten-free facility, so read labels carefully. We highly recommend you weigh the ingredients for this recipe, rather than rely on cup measurements. You can substitute 8 ounces (¾ cup plus ⅔ cup) King Arthur Gluten-Free Multi-Purpose Flour or 8 ounces (1½ cups plus 2 tablespoons) Bob's Red Mill GF All-Purpose Baking Flour

TRICKS TO GREAT GLUTEN-FREE COOKIES
Gluten-free cookies are often overly cakey or gritty. We used a few tricks to make our cookies as good as traditional versions.

1. ADD XANTHAN GUM: To prevent the cookies from spreading all over the baking sheet, we add a small amount of xanthan gum to reinforce the weak structure of our gluten-free flour.

2. HYDRATE THE DOUGH: Because this dough contains a relatively small amount of butter, the flour did not hydrate properly (butter is about 18 percent water). We add milk and let the dough rest to give the starches time to absorb the liquid.

COOLING AND STORING GLUTEN-FREE COOKIES

Like their traditional counterparts, gluten-free cookies need to briefly cool on the baking sheet when they come out of the oven and are then moved to a wire rack to finish cooling.

But you don't want to let them sit out for an extended time. These cookies have a shorter shelf life than cookies made with all-purpose flour. Gluten-free flour blends have a higher starch content, and that starch absorbs the moisture in the cookies over time, making them taste drier and crumble more easily. Consequently, they are best eaten the day they are made.

However, if you do want to store leftover baked cookies, they will keep acceptably well in an airtight container for a day or two at room temperature. We recommend using a container instead of a zipper-lock bag, and stacking them in as few layers as possible, using parchment in between each layer, since the cookies become more delicate over time and fare better with sturdier protection.

FREEZING COOKIE DOUGH

Given the fact gluten-free cookies don't store all that well—and that a fresh cookie, gluten-free or traditional, is better than an old one—we have found that freezing the cookie dough is a good option for our Gluten-Free Chocolate Chip Cookies. You can freeze portioned and shaped cookie dough as directed in the recipe, then bake the cookies straight from the freezer as you want them.

To bake frozen cookie dough, arrange the dough balls (do not thaw) on parchment-lined baking sheet and bake as directed, increasing baking time by 2 to 5 minutes.

1. After portioning and shaping dough according to recipe, arrange unbaked cookies on baking sheet. Place sheet in freezer.

2. Freeze dough until completely firm, 2 to 3 hours, then transfer to zipper-lock freezer bag and freeze for up to 2 weeks.

for our flour blend. Note that cookies made with King Arthur will spread more and be more delicate, while cookies made with Bob's Red Mill will spread more and have a distinct bean flavor.

8	ounces (1¾ cups) America's Test Kitchen Gluten-Free Flour Blend (page 256)
1	teaspoon baking soda
¾	teaspoon xanthan gum
½	teaspoon salt
8	tablespoons unsalted butter, melted
5¼	ounces (¾ cup packed) light brown sugar
2⅓	ounces (⅓ cup) granulated sugar
1	large egg
2	tablespoons milk
1	tablespoon vanilla extract
7½	ounces (1¼ cups) semisweet chocolate chips

1. Whisk flour blend, baking soda, xanthan gum, and salt together in medium bowl; set aside. Whisk melted butter, brown sugar, and granulated sugar together in large bowl until well combined and smooth. Whisk in egg, milk, and vanilla and continue to whisk until smooth. Stir in flour mixture with rubber spatula and mix until soft, homogeneous dough forms. Fold in chocolate chips. Cover bowl with plastic wrap and let dough rest for 30 minutes. (Dough will be sticky and soft.)

2. Adjust oven rack to middle position and heat oven to 350 degrees. Line 2 baking sheets with parchment paper. Using 2 soupspoons and working with about 1½ tablespoons of dough at a time, portion dough and space 2 inches apart on prepared sheets. Bake cookies, 1 sheet at a time, until golden brown and edges have begun to set but centers are still soft, 11 to 13 minutes, rotating sheet halfway through baking.

3. Let cookies cool on sheet for 5 minutes, then transfer to wire rack. Serve warm or at room temperature. (Cookies are best eaten on day they are baked, but they can be cooled and placed immediately in airtight container and stored at room temperature for up to 1 day.)

RATING GLUTEN-FREE SPAGHETTI

The challenge for gluten-free pasta manufacturers is to achieve both structure and chew without the help of gluten. We tasted eight products made variously with rice, corn, and quinoa, first tossed with olive oil and then with tomato sauce. Most samples were "mushy" and "gritty," absolutely failing to meet our spaghetti standards. In terms of both flavor and texture, our preferred gluten-free pastas were made from rice flour—brown rice flour in particular. Thanks to its bran content, the brown rice flour pasta contained a relatively high combined total of fiber and protein (the combined total matters more than the amount of either fiber or protein alone). Protein and fiber keep the noodles intact during cooking, forming a barrier around the starch molecules, which prevents them from escaping and leaving the cooked pasta sticky and soft. We also thought that the flavor of brown rice pasta came closest to that of the wheat-based kind. Our top choice, Jovial Gluten Free Brown Rice Pasta, Spaghetti, is dried for a long time at a low temperature, which helps preserve flavor and ensures that the proteins coagulate and provide structure for the starch. Its flavor and texture were fairly close to that of spaghetti made with wheat flour, which made it our favorite by a long shot. Fiber and protein amounts are per 57-gram serving. Products are listed in order of preference. See AmericasTestKitchen.com for updates and complete tasting results.

RECOMMENDED

JOVIAL Gluten Free Brown Rice Pasta, Spaghetti
PRICE: $3.99 for 12 oz ($0.33 per oz)
FIBER: 2 g PROTEIN: 5 g
INGREDIENTS: Organic brown rice flour, water
DRYING TIME AND TEMPERATURE: 12 to 14 hours at 70 degrees
COMMENTS: Thanks to a relatively high combined total of fiber and protein and a low, slow drying process, these "delicate and thin" brown rice strands were "springy" and "clean" tasting with none of the gumminess or off-flavors that plagued other brands.

RECOMMENDED WITH RESERVATIONS

ANDEAN DREAM Gluten & Corn Free Quinoa Pasta, Spaghetti
PRICE: $4.39 for 8 oz ($0.55 per oz)
FIBER: 3 g PROTEIN: 6 g
INGREDIENTS: Organic rice flour, organic quinoa flour
DRYING TIME AND TEMPERATURE: Proprietary
COMMENTS: Several tasters noted that this "slightly translucent," "plastic"-looking rice and quinoa pasta was "rubbery," like "plastic" or "Twizzlers," and a few noted that its generally "neutral," "bland" flavor took on a "fishy," "ashy" aftertaste when eaten plain. At least tomato sauce camouflaged some of those off-flavors.

NOT RECOMMENDED

BIONATURAE Organic Gluten Free Spaghetti
PRICE: $3.99 for 12 oz ($0.33 per oz)
FIBER: 2 g PROTEIN: 5 g
INGREDIENTS: Organic rice flour, organic rice starch, organic potato starch, organic soy flour
DRYING TIME AND TEMPERATURE: 15 hours at 160 degrees
COMMENTS: "Soft" and "super-mushy," this pasta was also "utterly bland," a flaw that was only moderately helped by adding sauce.

NOT RECOMMENDED *(cont.)*

ANCIENT HARVEST Quinoa Pasta, Gluten Free, Spaghetti-Style
PRICE: $3.29 for 8 oz ($0.41 per oz)
FIBER: 4 g PROTEIN: 4 g
INGREDIENTS: Organic corn flour, organic quinoa flour
DRYING TIME AND TEMPERATURE: 7 to 8 hours, mostly at 120 to 125 degrees, then the temperature is briefly raised to 140 to 160 degrees
COMMENTS: This so-called quinoa spaghetti actually contains more corn than quinoa—so much so that its color is "neon yellow" and one taster likened it to eating a "boiled corn muffin." Tasters also universally panned its texture; the "gritty," "gummy" strands "dissolve and break apart," they complained.

RUSTICHELLA D'ABRUZZO Gluten Free Spaghetti, 100% Corn
PRICE: $8.80 for 8.8 oz ($1 per oz)
FIBER: 1 g PROTEIN: 3 g
INGREDIENTS: Organic corn flour, water
DRYING TIME AND TEMPERATURE: 10 hours; average temperature is 140 degrees, but for a short time the temperature is raised to 167 degrees
COMMENTS: These strands tasted like "raw corn flour," one taster complained, while another found them "gritty" and even "gluey," perhaps as a result of the high-temperature drying process. Plus, their "abnormally yellow" color was "alarming."

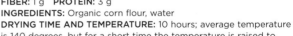

DEBOLES Gluten Free Rice Spaghetti Style Pasta
PRICE: $3.99 for 8 oz ($0.50 per oz)
FIBER: <1 g PROTEIN: 4 g
INGREDIENTS: Rice flour, rice bran extract
DRYING TIME AND TEMPERATURE: 10 to 12 hours at 105 degrees
COMMENTS: "Gummy," "mushy," and "gluey" were the watchwords for this rice-based pasta that contained almost no fiber. Tasters also complained about a "weird, bitter wet paper flavor" that gave way to an "awful aftertaste." Its "ugly gray color" made it even less appealing. In sum: "This is not pasta."

Let's Make Bread

*Squeezing excess water
from our shredded zucchini
before incorporating it into
the batter ensures a moist,
not dense, bread.*

YOU'VE GOT TWO CHOICES WHEN IT COMES TO MAKING BREAD: yeasted breads and quick breads. Yeasted breads are often perceived by home cooks as difficult, taking nearly a day to complete. And quick breads, while the process is speedy, aren't all that special. Our goals were to make an easier sandwich bread and a zucchini quick bread worth a bit of extra effort.

Batter bread recipes are all over the Internet, claiming all the goodness of yeasted loaves in far less time. Unfortunately, the ones we tried both looked and tasted unimpressive—barely worth even the small amount of effort they required. But the concept of a quick yeasted bread was too good to pass up, so we made it our goal to produce an attractive domed loaf with a soft, uniform interior. The key turned out not to be in the ingredients themselves, but the order in which we added them.

Zucchini bread was invented as a health food in the '60s, but the oil-laden recipes we found hardly seemed healthy—or appealing. For our version, we cut back on oil and focused our energy in a seemingly obvious place: the zucchini. With these recipes, you'll have all the goodness of homemade bread whenever you want it.

EASY SANDWICH BREAD

EASY SANDWICH BREAD

✔ **WHY THIS RECIPE WORKS:** Hastily made yeast breads can often lack the structure necessary for a satisfactory domed top, and their interiors are often wet and bland. Our goal was to make a soft, well-risen, even-crumbed loaf of bread in less than 2 hours. To encourage a strong gluten structure, we used plenty of warm water, and used high-protein bread flour instead of all-purpose flour. We also added some whole-wheat flour for nutty flavor. A small amount of honey added extra complexity and promoted browning. We withheld the salt until the second mix, which gave our bread more time to develop spring and lift. Switching our mixer's dough hook for the paddle attachment and increasing the speed to medium not only shortened our mixing time but also gave our dough enough structure to rise into a high dome. To give our bread some presentation-worthy appeal, we painted on a shiny egg wash before baking and then brushed the baked loaf with a thin coat of melted butter.

A FRESHLY BAKED LOAF OF BREAD IS ONE OF LIFE'S great pleasures. But these days, most people don't have 4 hours to devote to mixing dough, waiting for it to rise for an hour or so—twice—plus kneading (even if it's the stand mixer approach of most recipes today), shaping, and baking. While we appreciate the classic bread-making process, we wondered: Could we find a way to make a yeasted loaf of bread in about half of the time? Furthermore, could we possibly avoid, or at least shortcut, some of the work?

We began by scouring cookbooks and websites for clever bread-making tricks and came across an old-fashioned type of loaf: batter bread. As its name implies, the yeasted loaf begins with a fluid batter (not a thick dough) that's made of all-purpose flour, yeast, salt, sugar, and quite a bit of water. Since its hydration level is so high (80 to 85 percent), the batter is beaten with a paddle instead of a dough hook (usually for about 5 minutes) and is transferred straight from the mixing bowl to a prepared loaf pan, no shaping required. And some recipes call for only one rise rather than the two needed to make most traditional loaves. They all promised tender loaves with great flavor—homemade sandwich bread without all the work. Was it too good to be true?

Well, yes and no. The few batter bread recipes we tried featured quick and easy aspects—less time being kneaded in the mixer (some even relied on just a wooden spoon and bowl), abbreviated or fewer proofs, and no shaping—that met our requirements. But that speed and simplicity came at a price. The loaves were generally squat and dumpy-looking, with bumpy, sunken tops instead of smooth, tender domes. Slicing revealed damp, fragile interiors that were exceedingly yeasty but otherwise bland. We wanted great-tasting bread with a soft, uniform crumb sturdy enough to support sandwich fillings. To get a loaf that justified even a modest effort, we'd have to make some serious modifications.

We decided to solve the easiest problem first: that single-note yeast flavor. For quick rising, all the batter bread recipes that we found rely on more than twice as much yeast as traditional artisanal loaf recipes do: 2¼ teaspoons versus 1 teaspoon. But all that yeast was giving the breads an overly yeasty, not "bready," flavor. Nevertheless, we were committed to sticking with the large amount since it made such a huge time savings.

Our elementary but effective strategy was to cover up part of the yeastiness by working in some more flavorful ingredients. Adding a few tablespoons of melted butter was a good start toward a tastier loaf, and substituting whole-wheat flour for a portion of the all-purpose flour provided nutty, wheaty depth. We also traded the sugar for 1 tablespoon of honey, which was a twofer: It contributed complexity, and because heat causes honey to break down into simple sugars that encourage browning, it also gave the crust a bit more color.

Next up: building that complexity. In traditional bread, complexity develops by way of fermentation, which happens during the first and second rises. In these two proofing stages (each of which takes about an hour) the yeast consumes the sugars that are created as the

starches in the flour break down, producing the gases essential for making the dough rise. Along the way, a multitude of flavorful by-products are generated: sugars, acids, and alcohol. Knowing this, we decided that there was no way that we could get by with just one rise. Two 20-minute proofs—one after mixing the batter and one after transferring it to the pan—would allow for at least some flavor development.

The bread, which was coming together in about 90 minutes, now had quite a bit more depth, and the yeast flavor was much less noticeable than in previous versions. But it still wasn't winning points for its damp, fragile texture or sunken appearance.

Yeasted breads derive their light, airy structure from gluten, a stretchy protein network that forms only when wheat flour is combined with water. That network traps the gases given off by the yeast, inflating the dough and causing it to rise. (If the gluten structure is weak, the network can't hold enough gas and the bread will collapse in the heat of the oven.) When a dough is initially mixed, the proteins that form the network are weak and disorganized. They need to align in order to link up and acquire strength. Given enough time, they will line up

on their own, or they can be physically encouraged to do so by kneading.

You'd think that our bread would have had a mighty strong gluten network since we had been beating the batter in the mixer for 5 minutes. Yet the loaf's inadequate volume, sunken top, and fragile crumb suggested otherwise.

Before launching an in-depth investigation into the disappointing structure and crumb, we made a quick adjustment: We swapped the all-purpose flour for higher-protein bread flour. More gluten-forming proteins in the bread-flour dough would surely result in a more robust structure. This switch was a step in the right direction, but our loaf still had a long way to go.

The batter had so much water in it that the loaf was damp. Maybe that was too much liquid? We knew that the hydration level of a dough (or batter, in this case) affects gluten strength: Generally, the more water, the stronger and more extensible the gluten strands are and the better able they are to provide support. That translates into a sturdier, airier bread. But there's a tipping point: Unless you are planning on a long fermentation—which we weren't—too much water can actually inhibit the formation of gluten. We had been using 1¾ cups of warm water (using warm, rather than room-temperature, water helps jump-start the yeast's activity, ensuring a faster rise). Guessing that the existing batter was too wet, we reduced the water in the next batch to 1¼ cups. We hoped that the resulting loaf would have a slightly drier crumb and that the gluten framework would be sturdier.

We attached the paddle to the mixer, beat the batter for 5 minutes on medium speed, and then set it aside to rise. (The hydration level was still notably high—the dough was still pourable.) After 20 minutes, we transferred the mixture to a greased loaf pan, smoothed the top with a spatula, and let it rise again briefly before baking it for 40 minutes. After the loaf cooled, we evaluated it for signs of improvement. It had a better top: not quite domed, but at least it wasn't lumpy or sunken. When we sliced it, we found a crumb that was not as damp as those of our earlier versions, but it was still fragile. We had made modest progress but not enough.

We thought back to other test kitchen bread recipes in which we have waited to add the salt until later in the mixing process. Why? Salt inhibits both the ability of flour to absorb water and the activity of the enzymes that break down proteins to begin the process of forming gluten. By delaying the addition of salt, we hoped that our bread would be able to develop a stronger gluten network. We mixed the flours, yeast, honey, water, and butter until everything was evenly combined and let the batter rise for 20 minutes. Then we added the salt (dissolved in 2 tablespoons of water for even distribution) and proceeded with mixing, rising, and so on.

At last we had a complete success. The resulting loaf was crowned with a rounded top, and the crumb was more resilient and no longer wet. We had a flavorful sandwich bread that could be made start to finish in about 90 minutes. But we had to admit that its parched surface was not really showcasing our success. To highlight our crowning achievement, we brushed the risen loaf with a shine-enhancing egg wash before baking. As a finishing touch, we brushed the warm loaf with melted butter after turning it out on the cooling rack, which augmented the sheen and made the thin crust even more tender and delicious.

This bread is so easy and quick that fitting it into your weekly schedule will be no problem. But considering how quickly it disappears, you might need to make it twice a week.

Easy Sandwich Bread

MAKES 1 LOAF

The test kitchen's preferred loaf pan measures 8½ by 4½ inches; if using a 9 by 5-inch pan, check for doneness 5 minutes early. To prevent the loaf from deflating as it rises, do not let the batter come in contact with the plastic wrap. This loaf is best eaten the day it is made, but leftovers may be wrapped in plastic wrap and stored for up to two days at room temperature or frozen for up to one month.

THREE WAYS WE SPEED UP SANDWICH BREAD

For our take on batter bread, we wanted an easy-to-work-with dough that would rise much more quickly than a typical yeasted loaf. Here's how we made it happen.

MORE YEAST

WHY IT HELPS: Lots of yeast means a faster rise—20 minutes versus up to 2 hours for a standard loaf.

HIGHER HYDRATION

WHY IT HELPS: More water in the dough (up to a point) enhances gluten structure without requiring as much kneading; it also results in pourable dough that doesn't need shaping.

PADDLE ATTACHMENT

WHY IT HELPS: Using a paddle (more typically used to beat heavy cookie dough) instead of a dough hook allows for more aggressive, faster kneading.

DEVELOPING FLAVOR FAST

One downside of cutting back on rising time is a sacrifice in flavor, since the trademark taste of a classic loaf develops as fermentation occurs during two slow rises. We compensate for this by adding butter and honey to the batter as well as a bit of nutty whole-wheat flour.

POURABLE DOUGH

The dough for this sandwich bread is so wet that it is actually more like a batter. After a brief first rise, you simply pour it straight from the mixer bowl into the loaf pan—you couldn't shape it even if you tried.

2 cups (11 ounces) bread flour

6 tablespoons (2 ounces) whole-wheat flour

2¼ teaspoons instant or rapid-rise yeast

1¼ cups plus 2 tablespoons warm water (120 degrees)

3 tablespoons unsalted butter, melted

1 tablespoon honey

¾ teaspoon salt

1 large egg, lightly beaten with 1 teaspoon water and pinch salt

1. In bowl of stand mixer, whisk bread flour, whole-wheat flour, and yeast together. Add 1¼ cups warm water, 2 tablespoons melted butter, and honey. Fit stand mixer with paddle and mix on low speed for 1 minute. Increase speed to medium and mix for 2 minutes. Scrape down bowl and paddle with greased rubber spatula. Continue to mix 2 minutes longer. Remove bowl and paddle from mixer. Scrape down bowl and paddle, leaving paddle in batter. Cover with plastic wrap and let batter rise in warm place until doubled in size, about 20 minutes.

2. Adjust oven rack to lower-middle position and heat oven to 375 degrees. Spray 8½ by 4½-inch loaf pan with vegetable oil spray. Dissolve salt in remaining 2 tablespoons warm water. When batter has doubled, attach bowl and paddle to mixer. Add salt-water mixture and mix on low speed until water is mostly incorporated, about 40 seconds. Increase speed to medium and mix until thoroughly combined, about 1 minute, scraping down paddle if necessary. Transfer batter to prepared pan and smooth surface with greased rubber spatula. Cover and leave in warm place until batter reaches ½ inch below edge of pan, 15 to 20 minutes. Uncover and let rise until center of batter is level with edge of pan, 5 to 10 minutes longer.

3. Gently brush top of risen loaf with egg mixture. Bake until deep golden brown and loaf registers 208 to 210 degrees, 40 to 45 minutes. Using dish towels, carefully invert bread onto wire rack. Reinvert loaf and brush top and sides with remaining 1 tablespoon melted butter. Let cool completely before slicing.

ZUCCHINI BREAD

✔ **WHY THIS RECIPE WORKS:** For a zucchini bread that did justice to its namesake vegetable, we coarsely grated a full 1½ pounds of zucchini. Squeezing out the zucchini's excess water had multiple benefits: It eliminated gumminess, and it got rid of out-of-place vegetal flavors. Whole-wheat flour added to the all-purpose flour helped to absorb more moisture. Replacing white sugar with brown sugar made for a loaf with deeper, more molasses-y flavor, and increasing the amount of cinnamon and adding nutmeg and vanilla made for the most flavorful zucchini bread yet.

IN THE HEALTH FOOD–CRAZED 1960S AND '70S, RECIPES FOR zucchini bread popped up everywhere. With bits of healthy green vegetable speckling the crumb, the bread was a sweet treat you could not only enjoy but also feel virtuous about eating. Even now, zucchini bread remains hugely popular, and it's easy to see why: The high water content of the vegetable makes it ideal for producing the soft, moist crumb that is the hallmark of a great quick bread.

But zucchini can also be a liability, as too much leads to a soggy loaf. That's why, in spite of the oft-stated goal of using up surplus squash, most recipes top out at a mere 10 to 12 ounces. And funnily enough, despite being associated with a health-food movement, the recipes tend to call for copious amounts of oil that turn the loaf greasy and overly rich.

We hoped that packing more zucchini into the bread would pave the way for scaling back the ½ to ¾ cup of oil that most recipes call for, so we set a goal of doubling the usual amount of squash. Simply folding coarsely grated zucchini shreds into the batter is common, but wringing them out in a towel first seemed like a better approach: The drier the zucchini was, the more we could squeeze into a loaf without sogging it out. Sure enough, a full ½ cup of pale green liquid dripped out of 1½ pounds of squash. Encouraged, we ran a few more zucchini along the fine holes of the grater before wringing them out,

ZUCCHINI BREAD

reasoning that the increased surface area of the smaller pieces would help expel more liquid. Indeed, we got ¾ cup of juice from this batch.

We used each type (both wrung out), as well as 1½ pounds of unsqueezed coarse shreds as a control, in a typical zucchini bread recipe minus most of the fat: all-purpose flour, generous amounts of baking soda and powder for lift, sugar, touches of salt and cinnamon, eggs, a handful of toasted walnuts, and just ¼ cup of oil. We scraped the batters into greased loaf pans before putting them into 325-degree ovens. The bread made with unsqueezed shreds emerged predictably wet and gummy, and the finely shredded loaf was just as dense— the thin shreds had clumped together, compressing the crumb. Fortunately, the coarsely grated squeezed squash produced a crumb that was supermoist, more open, and significantly less gummy. Plus, it wasn't greasy at all. We'd stick with the squeezed coarse shreds.

Now what about this loaf's flavor? Here we were pleasantly surprised. As low-key as zucchini may be, we had feared that an overload would give the bread a vegetal taste. But despite the significant amount, the bread had a sweet, mildly earthy taste; mineral or strong vegetal flavors were absent. It turns out that by removing much of the moisture, we had also removed some of the key compounds, called Amadori compounds, responsible for zucchini's vegetal flavor, which are concentrated in the juice, not the flesh.

We just needed to get rid of a remaining trace of gumminess. We swapped a portion of the all-purpose flour for whole-wheat flour, since the bran and germ in whole-wheat flour allow it to absorb more moisture than the all-purpose kind. We were gratified to find that not only was this latest loaf no longer sticky but it also boasted a nice coarseness from the whole wheat. It just needed some complexity. No problem: we simply switched from granulated sugar to molasses-y brown sugar, increased the cinnamon to 1 tablespoon, and added nutmeg and vanilla.

With its light, moist crumb that's low on oil and chock-full of zucchini (and even boasts a whole-grain element), this bread might even pass as a "health" food. We just consider it the best zucchini bread we've ever tasted.

Zucchini Bread

MAKES 1 LOAF

Use the large holes of a box grater to shred the zucchini. The test kitchen's preferred loaf pan measures 8½ by 4½ inches; if you use a 9 by 5-inch loaf pan, start checking for doneness 5 minutes early.

- 1½ pounds zucchini, shredded
- 1¼ cups packed (8¾ ounces) brown sugar
- ¼ cup vegetable oil
- 2 large eggs
- 1 teaspoon vanilla extract
- 1½ cups (7½ ounces) all-purpose flour
- ½ cup (2¾ ounces) whole-wheat flour
- 1 tablespoon ground cinnamon
- 1½ teaspoons salt
- 1 teaspoon baking powder
- 1 teaspoon baking soda
- ½ teaspoon ground nutmeg
- ¾ cup walnuts, toasted and chopped (optional)
- 1 tablespoon granulated sugar

1. Adjust oven rack to middle position and heat oven to 325 degrees. Grease 8½ by 4½-inch loaf pan.

2. Place zucchini in center of dish towel. Gather ends together and twist tightly to drain as much liquid as possible, discarding liquid (you should have ½ to ⅔ cup liquid). Whisk brown sugar, oil, eggs, and vanilla together in medium bowl. Fold in zucchini.

3. Whisk all-purpose flour, whole-wheat flour, cinnamon, salt, baking powder, baking soda, and nutmeg together in large bowl. Fold in zucchini mixture until just incorporated. Fold in walnuts, if using. Pour batter into prepared pan and sprinkle with granulated sugar.

4. Bake until top bounces back when gently pressed and toothpick inserted in center comes out with a few moist crumbs attached, 65 to 75 minutes. Let bread cool in pan on wire rack for 30 minutes. Remove bread from pan and let cool completely on wire rack. Serve.

VARIATION

Zucchini Bread with Walnuts and Dried Cherries
Substitute cocoa powder for cinnamon and ground cloves for nutmeg. Prepare bread with walnuts and add ¾ cup dried cherries, chopped, to batter with walnuts.

NOTES FROM THE TEST KITCHEN

REMOVING MOISTURE FROM SHREDDED ZUCCHINI
Zucchini is more than 95 percent water, so it's no wonder that zucchini bread is notoriously soggy. This technique rids the zucchini of much of its moisture and eliminates unpleasant "vegetal" flavors at the same time.

1. Grate zucchini on large holes of box grater.

2. Place grated zucchini in clean dish towel and wring out as much liquid as possible.

RATING ARTISANAL CREAM CHEESE

To find out if a small-batch approach could take this supermarket staple to the next level, we mail-ordered three tubs of handmade cream cheese, from Vermont, Michigan, and Virginia. When tasted plain, all three won over tasters, who singled out strong notes of herbs, fresh milk, radishes, and butter. When it came to smearing the cream cheese on bagels, two of the small-batch samples were favored over the familiar tacky, dense texture of our supermarket favorite for their lighter consistency. In baked applications, the lack of stabilizers was problematic when the cream cheese was the primary ingredient. Excess moisture sank to the bottom of cheesecake, while cream cheese frosting looked curdled. However, as a secondary ingredient in our Cream Cheese Brownies (page 59), all three artisanal cream cheeses excelled, even beating out our favorite supermarket brand. Products are listed in order of preference. See AmericasTestKitchen.com for updates and complete tasting results.

HIGHLY RECOMMENDED

ZINGERMAN'S CREAMERY Fresh Cream Cheese
PRICE: $15 for 1-lb tub ($0.94 per oz), plus shipping
COMMENTS: Made at a creamery founded by the Ann Arbor delicatessen of the same name, this cheese won top marks for being supercreamy and smooth, with "impressive depth of flavor." The saltiest cheese in the lineup, it also boasted "floral" and "herbal" notes, with hints of "lavender" and "radish."

RECOMMENDED

NIGHT SKY FARM Fresh Cream Cheese
PRICE: $13.50 for two 8-oz packages ($0.84 per oz), plus shipping
COMMENTS: We found this cream cheese from a Virginia farm to be "moist" and "light," with a "very smooth, pleasant texture." Its tangy, "lemony" brightness reminded tasters of sour cream and crème fraîche. They also noted appealing "earthy undertones" when the cream cheese was sampled on its own. These flavors were harder to detect when the cream cheese was spread on a bagel.

CHAMPLAIN VALLEY CREAMERY Old Fashioned Organic Cream Cheese
PRICE: $4.50 for 8-oz tub ($0.56 per oz), plus shipping
COMMENTS: The least like supermarket cream cheese, this Vermont offering had a drier, more crumbly texture that tasters likened to fresh goat cheese. While some tasters found this "off-putting," others described it as "enjoyable." This cream cheese's flavor was the most "subtle" of the lineup. Though still "tangy" and "tart," it was the "buttery" and "milky" notes of dairy and "fresh cream" that stood out most to tasters.

Almond Cake
and British Scones

Starting our scones in a hot oven and then reducing the temperature maximizes their initial lift and creates beautifully risen, fluffy scones.

WHEN IT COMES TO BAKED GOODS, OUR NEIGHBORS ACROSS THE Atlantic have much to offer. But not every European recipe is perfectly suited to our tastes. We set out to give almond cake and classic British scones American makeovers, test kitchen style.

Almond cake is represented in a number of European cuisines. But while the European standard is a heavy, dense, and fudge-like cake, we craved something a bit lighter and cakier. Without losing the incredible nutty flavor of the original, we set out to create an almond cake that could function as an after-dinner treat as well as a rich accompaniment to tea. In the end, our food processor did most of the work—we just reaped the benefits.

Unlike their sometimes over-the-top American counterparts, British scones are restrained: soft, tender, almost cakey, and only lightly sweet. And frankly, the English teatime tradition of butter and jam–smeared scones was too tempting to pass up. We made a few adjustments for our American palates (and grocery stores), but we're pretty sure these scones would be just as at home in Buckingham Palace as they would on your breakfast table. But please—no fake accents.

BEST ALMOND CAKE

BEST ALMOND CAKE

☑ **WHY THIS RECIPE WORKS:** Simple, rich almond cake makes a sophisticated dessert, but traditional European versions can be heavy and dense. For a slightly cakier version with plenty of nutty flavor, we swapped out traditional almond paste for toasted blanched sliced almonds and added a bit of almond extract for extra depth. Lemon zest in the batter provided citrusy brightness. For a lighter crumb, we increased the flour slightly and added baking powder. Making the batter in a food processor ensured that the cake had just the right amount of structure. We swapped some butter for oil and lowered the oven temperature to produce an evenly baked, moist cake. For a crunchy finishing touch, we topped the cake with sliced almonds and a sprinkle of lemon zest–infused sugar.

ALMOND CAKE IS ELEGANTLY SIMPLE, CONSISTING OF A single layer so rich in flavor that it requires no frosting. That nearly every European country has a version of the cake—from Sweden's visiting cake to Italy's *torta di mandorle* to Spain's *tarta de Santiago* (which dates back to the Middle Ages)—is a testament to its appeal.

In addition to its great taste, a reason for the cake's popularity in Europe may be that it's almost impossible to screw up. Putting one together is a straightforward matter. First you cream almond paste or ground almonds with sugar and then butter. Eggs go into the bowl next, followed by a small amount of flour, a bit of salt, and perhaps some almond extract. The batter is poured into a prepared pan and baked, and the dessert is ready to eat as soon as it's cool.

Since recipes for almond cake typically call for little flour and rarely include a leavening agent, the texture of the cake is usually quite dense—the opposite of a fluffy American yellow cake. And when almond paste is used instead of ground almonds, the cake becomes even more solid, bearing a particularly smooth, almost fudge-like consistency. While this is exactly what European cooks intend, we've always found this style a bit too heavy to nibble with tea or to enjoy after a rich dinner. We didn't want an ultrafluffy crumb, but we did want a dessert that was more cake than confection—without sacrificing the trademark rich almond flavor and simplicity of the original.

Our first decision was to nix the almond paste. Store-bought almond paste is usually made up of a 1:1 ratio of ground almonds to sugar, along with a binding agent, such as glucose syrup. But its high sugar content is at least partially responsible for the candy-like texture that we wanted to eliminate. That said, commercial almond paste does have one thing going for it: great nutty flavor. Could we replace the almond paste without losing that?

Using a basic recipe calling for 1¼ cups of sugar, 10 tablespoons of butter, four eggs, and ½ cup of flour, we tried the most convenient substitute first: store-bought almond flour (which is just very finely ground blanched almonds), which we added to the batter with the other dry ingredients. Unfortunately, almond flour's only benefit was accessibility: The cake that it produced had weak almond flavor; plus, the flour was so finely milled that the crumb was still quite dense. Since nuts are commonly toasted to improve their taste, we whipped up one more cake using almond flour that we'd browned in a skillet, but it was tricky to get the small particles to toast evenly, and the browning did nothing to help the textural issue.

Next up: toasted whole almonds ground in a food processor. The flavor of this cake was miles ahead of the almond-flour cake, but the pulverized skins of the nuts looked unappealing and tasted somewhat bitter, so we switched to blanched almonds. For depth, we stirred in a drizzle of almond extract. These changes did the trick. This cake had the concentrated almond flavor of an almond-paste cake, and though it was still rather dense, the cake was now dotted with tiny nut particles that at least broke up the crumb a little. With the almonds settled, we went on to find other ways to lighten the cake.

We considered the flour first. When butter and sugar are creamed, the airy mixture can help give a cake

dry ingredients, poured the batter into a prepared pan, and slid the pan into a 325-degree oven. Sure enough, the cake that came out of the oven was the tallest yet. In fact, it was even loftier than we had intended: Now it was on the high end of the fluffiness spectrum, with the domed top and superlight, aerated crumb typical of an American layer cake. Using fewer eggs wasn't the answer; a two-egg cake was squat and dense.

Feeling as though we were at the end of our rope, we decided to take a break from ingredient testing to consider the equipment. Given that this was a cake known for its simplicity, we weren't happy calling for two large kitchen appliances—a food processor and a stand mixer. The food processor was a must, as there was no way our stand mixer was going to grind almonds. But what would happen if we tried to whip our ingredients in the food processor instead of in the mixer?

We cracked our eggs into the food processor, added the sugar, and hit the on button. We were excited to see the mixture turn pale and gain some height in the bowl. But when we turned off the machine, the foam partially deflated. Still, we pressed on, adding the melted butter and finally the flour, ground almonds, salt, and baking powder to the food processor bowl. We put the cake in the oven, worried that we'd wasted our time and ingredients. But when we pulled out the finished cake, things were looking up. The unwanted doming hadn't happened, leaving the nicely level top that we were looking for. Once the cake had cooled, we eagerly took a taste. The crumb was no longer reminiscent of an American layer cake. Instead, it was rich and rustic—neither too fluffy nor too dense. Even better, we had used only one appliance to make the cake.

It turns out that a mixer gently unfolds the protein strands of eggs, creating a strong foam that holds on to air. The sharp blade of a food processor is more damaging to protein strands, so the foam that it creates is less sturdy. Lucky for us, this meant that we got exactly the moderately risen crumb and elegant level top that we were looking for.

Now for a few tweaks. The perimeter of the cake was baking through before the middle was set, resulting in

lift—but only if the batter contains enough gluten to support air pockets. Our cake had so little flour (and therefore so little gluten development) that it was unable to hold on to air, hence its short, dense form. We tried substituting higher-protein bread flour for all-purpose flour, hoping that we could stick with ½ cup and still produce a cake with a strong structure. The bread flour created structure all right—so much that the crumb turned tough and chewy. The best option turned out to be a simple one: adding an extra ¼ cup of all-purpose flour (for a total of ¾ cup), which helped our cake rise a bit higher. Another obvious consideration was leavener, so we stirred a bit of baking powder into our next batch. Just ¼ teaspoon helped inflate the air pockets, resulting in a taller rise. But the cake needed even more lift.

We knew that whipped eggs can give a cake—particularly a low-flour cake like this one—great structure since their protein network can trap air, so we gave it a shot. Using a stand mixer, we whipped the four eggs and 1¼ cups of sugar for 2 minutes. We lit up when the pale yellow mixture nearly tripled in volume. With high hopes, we added the butter (melted this time so it would be easy to incorporate) and then the remaining slightly dry edges. Knocking down the oven temperature by 25 degrees and substituting vegetable oil for half of the butter solved the problem. The lower oven temperature allowed the cake to bake more slowly, so it cooked more evenly, and since oil, unlike butter, contains no water that evaporates during baking, it produced a moister crumb.

But the lower oven temperature created a new problem. Now the cake wasn't browning as well, emerging pale instead of golden brown. Once again, a seemingly small change had a dramatic impact. Just ⅛ teaspoon of baking soda, which encourages browning reactions, brought back the color without noticeably altering the crumb.

Finally, we wanted to create a crunchy, flavorful topping with a hint of citrus to play off of the great almond flavor. In keeping with the nearly effortless adornment of traditional almond cakes (usually just a dusting of confectioners' sugar), we decided on a sprinkling of sliced almonds and lemon-infused granulated sugar. To echo the lemony flavor of our topping, we also added some lemon zest to the cake batter itself. These easy additions produced a delicate crunch and a pop of citrus flavor. And for those who really want to dress up the dessert, we also developed an orange-spiked crème fraîche.

With its rich taste, lighter texture, and lovely flat top, our almond cake had all the great flavor of the European version with a texture more suited to our American palates.

Best Almond Cake

SERVES 8 TO 10

If you can't find blanched sliced almonds, grind slivered almonds for the batter and use unblanched sliced almonds for the topping. Serve plain or with Orange Crème Fraîche (recipe follows).

1½ cups plus ⅓ cup blanched sliced almonds, toasted
¾ cup (3¾ ounces) all-purpose flour
¾ teaspoon salt
¼ teaspoon baking powder
⅛ teaspoon baking soda
4 large eggs
1¼ cups (8¾ ounces) plus 2 tablespoons sugar

NOTES FROM THE TEST KITCHEN

HOW WE GOT THE BEST ALMOND FLAVOR—AND CAKE TEXTURE

For a rich, nutty taste and a consistency that's not too dense, we toast blanched almonds (we dislike the slight bitterness imparted by skin-on almonds) to deepen their flavor. Then we grind them in the food processor. The ground nuts give the crumb an open, rustic texture.

START WITH BLANCHED ALMONDS

TOAST UNTIL GOLDEN BROWN

GRIND WITH FLOUR, SALT, AND LEAVENERS

1 tablespoon plus ½ teaspoon grated lemon zest (2 lemons)
¾ teaspoon almond extract
5 tablespoons unsalted butter, melted
⅓ cup vegetable oil

1. Adjust oven rack to middle position and heat oven to 300 degrees. Grease 9-inch round cake pan and line with parchment paper. Pulse 1½ cups almonds, flour, salt, baking powder, and baking soda in food processor

until almonds are finely ground, 5 to 10 pulses. Transfer almond mixture to bowl.

2. Process eggs, 1¼ cups sugar, 1 tablespoon lemon zest, and almond extract in now-empty processor until very pale yellow, about 2 minutes. With processor running, add melted butter and oil in steady stream, until incorporated. Add almond mixture and pulse to combine, 4 to 5 pulses. Transfer batter to prepared pan.

3. Using your fingers, combine remaining 2 tablespoons sugar and remaining ½ teaspoon lemon zest in small bowl until fragrant, 5 to 10 seconds. Sprinkle top of cake evenly with remaining ⅓ cup almonds followed by sugar-zest mixture.

4. Bake until center of cake is set and bounces back when gently pressed and toothpick inserted in center comes out clean, 55 minutes to 1 hour 5 minutes, rotating pan after 40 minutes. Let cake cool in pan on wire rack for 15 minutes. Run paring knife around sides of pan. Invert cake onto greased wire rack, discard parchment, and reinvert cake onto second wire rack. Let cake cool, about 2 hours. Cut into wedges and serve. (Store cake in plastic wrap at room temperature for up to 3 days.)

NOTES FROM THE TEST KITCHEN

EGG FOAMS: MIXER VERSUS FOOD PROCESSOR

The goal when mixing most cake batters is to incorporate a lot of air into the eggs so that the cake will bake up light and tall, and a mixer is usually the best tool to get the job done. For our Best Almond Cake, however, we wanted a flat, level top; just a moderate rise; and a texture that was neither too fluffy nor too dense. Ditching the mixer in favor of a food processor did the trick. Here's why: When eggs and sugar are whipped in a mixer, the whisk gently unfolds the protein strands in the eggs while incorporating lots of air, producing a foam with a strong network that holds on to that air. The outcome? A tall, well-risen, domed cake. A food processor, with its high rpm and very sharp blade, similarly unravels the eggs' protein strands and incorporates air, but it also damages some strands along the way. The result is just what we were after: a flatter, slightly denser cake.

MIXER: TALL AND DOMED

FOOD PROCESSOR: PERFECTLY FLAT

Orange Crème Fraîche
MAKES ABOUT 2 CUPS

- **2** oranges
- **1** cup crème fraîche
- **2** tablespoons sugar
- **⅛** teaspoon salt

Remove 1 teaspoon zest from 1 orange. Cut away peel and pith from oranges. Slice between membranes to release segments and cut segments into ¼-inch pieces. Combine orange pieces and zest, crème fraîche, sugar, and salt in bowl and mix well. Refrigerate for 1 hour before serving.

BRITISH-STYLE CURRANT SCONES

✓ **WHY THIS RECIPE WORKS:** Compared to American scones, British scones are lighter, fluffier, and less sweet; perfect for serving with butter and jam. Rather than leaving pieces of cold butter in the dry ingredients as we would with American scones, we thoroughly worked in softened butter until it was fully integrated. This protected some of the flour granules from moisture, which in turn limited gluten development and kept the crumb tender and cakey. For a higher rise, we added more than the usual amount of leavening and started the scones in a 500-degree oven to boost their lift before turning the temperature down. We brushed some reserved milk and egg on top for enhanced browning, and added currants for tiny bursts of fruit flavor throughout.

AMERICAN SCONES AND BRITISH SCONES ARE LIKE cousins who have grown up in very different environments. Though they share the same name and a lot of the same DNA, they are, as the Brits might say, as different as chalk and cheese.

Proper British scones are round and tall, with a light, cake-like crumb and a soft, tender crust. They're not as sweet or as rich as American scones, but that's because they're usually split in half, lavishly spread with butter or clotted cream, and piled high with jam at teatime.

While we love American-style scones, that cozy British teatime ritual holds tremendous appeal. And because rich, buttery American scones would be a bit over the top in that context, we resolved to develop a recipe for light, fluffy scones, suitable for serving in the British style.

Here's how we make American scones: We combine all-purpose flour, sugar, baking powder, and salt in a bowl; then we rub in a very generous amount of cold butter until it is distributed throughout the dry ingredients in thin, broad flakes. We whisk together milk and eggs and gently stir that mixture into our dry ingredients

to form a shaggy dough. At that point we add some flavorings (fresh or dried fruit, nuts, chocolate chips, spices, maple syrup—the sky's the limit), and then, working gently and quickly, we form the dough into disks, which we cut into wedges. A bit of egg wash, maybe a sprinkling of coarse sugar, and the scones go into the oven. They emerge somewhat crumbly, squat, and whimsical in shape, but they have a certain buttery charm.

The recipes that we collected for British scones featured the same basic ingredients as ours, minus all the add-ins and with two key differences. First, British recipes call for self-raising flour, which is like American all-purpose flour with a leavening agent already added. (Don't confuse it with American self-rising flour, which is lower in protein and has added salt.) It's ubiquitous in the United Kingdom but harder to find here. For authenticity's sake, we tracked down a couple of bags locally, knowing that we would devise a substitution later.

The second difference was more clear-cut: British recipes call for about one-third of the amount of butter that our recipe requires. So we lowered the butter content in our recipe, and we also cut back on the sugar to make our scones more jam-compatible. We followed our trusty mixing method, but instead of forming the dough into wedges, we used a cookie cutter to make round scones. No egg wash, no sugar—just straight into a 425-degree oven. The result looked familiar. In fact, here in America we have a special name for such a thing: a biscuit.

A few bites confirmed our suspicions: These scones tasted great, but they lacked the tender, cake-like crumb of British scones. Strange: They were made with the same ingredients and in the same ratios. How had we ended up with a bready biscuit?

Realizing that the difference had to be in the methods, we compared them closely to see what didn't line up: dry ingredients combined—check; dairy and egg whisked—check; butter worked into the dry ingredients—aye, there's the rub, so to speak.

We were still working the cold, hard fat quickly into the dry ingredients, leaving noticeable bits of butter in the mixture per the usual approach with American scones. But a close reading of traditional British scone

BRITISH-STYLE CURRANT SCONES

recipes reveals a significant difference in technique: The butter is rubbed into the dry ingredients so completely that it is no longer visible—no lumps, no flakes. In fact, British cooks often use soft, room-temperature butter to make the process even easier, quicker, and more thorough. This approach promises a finer, more even crumb because the structure is not disrupted by those large pieces of fat. It also produces a crumb that is more tender. Why? Because with more of the flour particles coated with fat, and thus protected from the wet ingredients, a lot of the proteins in the flour are prevented from linking up to form gluten. The result is a fine-textured and tender scone, much more cake-like than biscuit-like.

So we made up another batch, this time thoroughly working softened butter into the dry ingredients before mixing the dough lightly. (We also switched to using a food processor to blend in the butter, which many cooks prefer to using their hands.) And indeed, this subtle change in tactics was enough to give us the cake-like texture we were after.

This discovery led to another equally compelling one. Our method called for rolling out the dough once, cutting eight scones from it, and then rerolling the scraps to make four more scones. We noticed that the scones from the second roll consistently rose a bit higher in the oven than those from the first roll, which seems counterintuitive when you consider all those dire warnings about overmixing that are so often a feature of baking recipes. The fear in those cases is that the gluten network will overdevelop and become tighter if it is overworked when it comes in contact with moisture, leading to tougher texture and a hampered rise. But in this case, so much of the flour was coated in fat that it was effectively waterproofed, making it harder for gluten bonds to form. This meant that working the dough a bit more was actually beneficial since it offered those proteins still available (i.e., from any uncoated flour) a chance to link together, giving the scones a little more structure to support more lift. With this in mind, we upped the number of times that we kneaded the dough from a dozen to 25 to 30 for maximum lift and rerolled the scraps with no qualms.

We were encouraged by our progress, but our scones still lacked the impressive height of those that we had enjoyed in Britain. We knew that we could do better.

It was time to find a substitute for that self-raising flour. We had seen recommendations for adding anywhere from 1 to 2 teaspoons of baking powder per cup of all-purpose flour to approximate the lift of self-raising, and the issue was further complicated because most British scone recipes go on to boost the lift even more with additional baking powder, which varied in amount from recipe to recipe as well. We had to start somewhere, so we added 3 tablespoons of baking powder to our 3 cups of flour. In doing so, we seriously overshot the mark. Though the scones were indeed light and tall, they

NOTES FROM THE TEST KITCHEN

A TALE OF TWO SCONES
While rich, dense American scones are no-holds-barred pastries, cake-like British scones show restraint.

THE AMERICAN		THE BRIT
1½ cups, chilled	BUTTER	½ cup, softened
1 tablespoon of baking powder	LEAVENER	2 tablespoons of baking powder
The more the better	ADD-INS	A smattering of currants
Egg wash and lots of coarse sugar	TOPPING	Light milk-and-egg wash

SCONES ROLLED FROM SCRAPS WON'T BE SECOND BEST WITH OUR RECIPE
For many baked goods that require rolling out the dough (biscuits, pie dough), rerolling scraps produces a tougher, more squat result. This is because just as with kneading, the action of rolling creates a stronger, tighter gluten network—and too much gluten can negatively influence texture and rise. But our British-style scones offer more leeway. The butter is worked into the flour so thoroughly that it prevents many of the proteins from ever linking up to form gluten in the first place. Far from being a hazard, rerolling the second batch of dough merely encourages a little more of the proteins to link together, leading to a bit more structure and more lift in the oven.

also had that telltale flavor of excess leavening, which some tasters described as soapy and others metallic.

In search of maximum lift and no leavening flavor, we made four more batches, decreasing the baking powder by 1 teaspoon per batch and tracking scone height and negative flavor comments. We found our sweet (or at least nonsoapy) spot at 2 tablespoons.

Aspiring to even greater heights, we considered the oven temperature. Yeast-leavened breads often start in an extremely hot oven to maximize "oven spring," the growth spurt that happens when water vaporizes into steam and the air in the dough heats up and expands. Then the heat is lowered to ensure that the crust does not burn before the interior is cooked through. Would this approach work with chemically leavened scones? It did. When we preheated our oven to 500 degrees and then turned it down to 425 degrees after putting in the scones, we got the lightest, fluffiest batch yet.

A couple more tweaks brought our scones up several notches. We added currants rather than raisins because their smaller size meant better distribution within each scone, and they seemed more appropriate. And we reserved a small amount of the milk and egg mixture to brush on top of the scones before baking. It made the dough a little less soft so it was easier to handle, and it helped the scones brown a bit more. It also gave our scones the soft, tender crust that we wanted.

The words "stately" and "fluffy" are rarely used together, but they both described our scones perfectly. And while they looked quite impressive piled on a plate, they really came into their own when split and topped with plenty of butter—or clotted cream—and jam, served alongside a mug of tea. We're confident that these scones will please everyone, English and American.

British-Style Currant Scones
MAKES 12 SCONES

We prefer whole milk in this recipe, but low-fat milk can be used. The dough will be quite soft and wet; dust your work surface and your hands liberally with flour. For a tall, even rise, use a sharp-edged biscuit cutter and push straight down; do not twist the cutter. These scones are best served fresh, but leftover scones may be stored in the freezer and reheated in a 300-degree oven for 15 minutes before serving. Serve these scones with jam as well as salted butter or clotted cream.

3 cups (15 ounces) all-purpose flour

⅓ cup (2⅓ ounces) sugar

2 tablespoons baking powder

½ teaspoon salt

8 tablespoons unsalted butter, cut into ½-inch pieces and softened

¾ cup dried currants

1 cup whole milk

2 large eggs

1. Adjust oven rack to upper-middle position and heat oven to 500 degrees. Line rimmed baking sheet with parchment paper. Pulse flour, sugar, baking powder, and salt in food processor until combined, about 5 pulses. Add butter and pulse until fully incorporated and mixture looks like very fine crumbs with no visible butter, about 20 pulses. Transfer mixture to large bowl and stir in currants.

2. Whisk milk and eggs together in second bowl. Set aside 2 tablespoons milk mixture. Add remaining milk mixture to flour mixture and, using rubber spatula, fold together until almost no dry bits of flour remain.

3. Transfer dough to well-floured counter and gather into ball. With floured hands, knead until surface is smooth and free of cracks, 25 to 30 times. Press gently to form disk. Using floured rolling pin, roll disk into 9-inch round, about 1 inch thick. Using floured 2½-inch round cutter, stamp out 8 rounds, recoating cutter with flour if it begins to stick. Arrange scones on prepared sheet. Gather dough scraps, form into ball, and knead gently until surface is smooth. Roll dough to 1-inch thickness and stamp out 4 rounds. Discard remaining dough.

4. Brush tops of scones with reserved milk mixture. Reduce oven temperature to 425 degrees and bake scones until risen and golden brown, 10 to 12 minutes, rotating sheet halfway through baking. Transfer scones to wire rack and let cool for at least 10 minutes. Serve scones warm or at room temperature.

RATING ORANGE JUICE

Orange juice is America's most popular juice, a breakfast staple with a sunny, wholesome image. Package labels tempt us with phrases like "fresh squeezed" and "grove to glass," but can the contents live up to the promises on the cartons? To find out, we built a tasting lineup consisting of five nationally available refrigerated orange juices, two frozen concentrates, and two lower-calorie juices. The juices were evaluated for freshness, flavor, texture, and overall appeal. Fresh flavor was of top importance to our tasters. Our top juice was minimally processed, while the juices that ranked just below our favorite used relatively high quantities of ethyl butyrate, a compound that occurs naturally in oranges and that is added back to most commercial orange juice to make its flavor seem fresher. Juices are listed in order of preference. See AmericasTestKitchen.com for updates and complete tasting results.

RECOMMENDED

NATALIE'S 100% Florida Orange Juice, Gourmet Pasteurized
PRICE: $5.99 for 64 oz ($0.09 per fl oz)
ETHYL BUTYRATE: 1.01 mg per liter
COMMENTS: Natalie's squeezes its juice within 24 hours of shipping it and doesn't manipulate its flavor. The juice tasted "superfresh."

SIMPLY ORANGE Not from Concentrate 100% Pure Squeezed Pasteurized Orange Juice, Medium Pulp
PRICE: $3.99 for 59 oz ($0.07 per fl oz)
ETHYL BUTYRATE: 3.22 mg per liter
COMMENTS: A generous amount of ethyl butyrate helped this juice taste "fresh squeezed."

RECOMMENDED WITH RESERVATIONS

TROPICANA Pure Premium Orange Juice, Homestyle
PRICE: $3.99 for 59 oz ($0.07 per fl oz)
ETHYL BUTYRATE: 1.71 mg per liter
COMMENTS: Tropicana's flagship juice (and our previous winner) tasted "slightly sweet" and "reasonably fresh" but comparatively acidic.

NOT RECOMMENDED

TROPICANA Trop50 Orange Juice Beverage
PRICE: $3.99 for 59 oz ($0.07 per fl oz)
ETHYL BUTYRATE: None detected
COMMENTS: A "sugar bomb," this stevia-sweetened low-calorie juice was "abrasively sweet," and "artificial." It was also "watery" and "thin."

Springtime Sweets

We use lemon zest to infuse the milk and cream in our pudding cake with lemon flavor, then discard the zest so its texture doesn't mar the silkiness of the pudding.

IN BETWEEN THE WARM-SPICED, DECADENT DESSERTS OF THE HOLIDAY season and the juicy, bubbling pies of summer lies a dessert limbo. As the weather begins to warm, we crave fresher foods. But without much fruit yet in season here in New England, we've learned how to work with what we do have. Grab a spoon and dig in to two delectable springtime treats: lemon pudding cake and strawberry mousse.

Lemon pudding cake isn't exactly a new idea: These bi-layer desserts have been around for centuries. But in the recipes we found, neither pudding nor cake was turning out the way it should. We wanted creamy pudding and tender cake that magically separated into two perfectly cooked layers. Want to know how we did it? We'll give you a hint: The secret's in the water bath.

Strawberry mousse is often doomed from the start: Overly juicy, ripe strawberries make for flavorful but soupy mousse, while out-of-season fruit makes—you guessed it—creamy but wan-tasting mousse. To get the best of both worlds, we created a foolproof method to get the most out of any strawberries, even frozen ones. These desserts are so good, you'll want to make them year-round—and we've designed them so you can.

LEMON PUDDING CAKES

✔ **WHY THIS RECIPE WORKS:** Despite the appeal of a single batter that produces two texturally distinct layers, lemon pudding cake can be unpredictable, sporting underbaked cake or grainy pudding. We wanted lots of lemon flavor, tender cake, and rich, creamy pudding. Whipping the egg whites to soft peaks and decreasing the amount of flour gave us the best ratio of pudding to cake. Baking powder gave the cake layer some lift, while also producing a bronzed top. Using a cold water bath in a large roasting pan prevented the pudding from curdling while still allowing the cake to cook through. By infusing the milk and cream with lemon zest, we achieved maximum lemon flavor without a disruption in the smooth texture of the dessert. We finished off the cakes with a sweet, fruity blueberry compote to complement the tart lemon flavor.

PUDDING CAKES HAVE BEEN AROUND, IN ONE FORM OR another, since the 1700s. Part of the dessert's appeal is its seemingly magical transformation during baking: A single batter goes into the oven but comes out as a twofer—an airy, soufflé-like cake resting on top of a silky lemon pudding. Of course, that's assuming it's executed correctly. The reality is that most of the lemon pudding cakes we've sampled have been subpar, often featuring wet, underbaked cake or grainy, curdled pudding, or both. What would it take to fix the problems associated with this dessert?

We got our bearings by preparing a fairly typical recipe, whisking together ¾ cup of sugar, two egg yolks, fresh lemon juice and zest, and ½ cup of flour. Next we stirred in 1 cup of whole milk plus ½ cup of cream for richness and then gradually folded in four egg whites whipped with a bit more sugar. Finally, we poured the batter into six ramekins. (Baking the pudding in a single dish is more typical, but we thought individual ramekins would be more elegant.) This dessert always bakes in a water bath,

which helps insulate the pudding layer from the heat of the oven and prevents it from curdling. Following the test kitchen's approach, we arranged a folded dish towel in the bottom of a roasting pan as an anchor and then nestled the ramekins into the towel. We poured boiling water into the pan and transferred the assembly to a 350-degree oven. Once baked, the batter separated into distinct tiers of cake and pudding. So what causes the batter to do its trademark split? The answer is surprisingly straightforward: The whipped egg whites are less dense than the other ingredients and thus rise to the top of the dessert during baking, taking some of the flour with them. The egg white proteins coagulate and set to a "solid" cake-like structure, while the denser ingredients settle to the bottom of the baking dish, where they thicken into a pudding.

Simple enough, but we wanted to better understand the role that the egg whites play. We made two desserts, one in which we whipped our egg whites only very slightly and another in which we beat them to firm, dry peaks that stood up on our whisks. As it turned out, the quantity of air incorporated into the whites affected the end result quite a bit. Though the pudding layers were unsurprisingly nearly identical, the cake layers had stark differences. The barely whipped whites produced a dense, rubbery cake that was less than ¼ inch tall. The stiff whites, on the other hand, produced a firm, almost tough layer that rose higher than an inch. We wanted a tender cake with moderate lift, so we would whip our whites to the midway point between loose and stiff: soft, glossy peaks.

Next up: the flour. Since pudding cakes contain so little flour, we wondered if adjusting the quantity might shed even more light on the mechanics of this dessert. Sure enough, when we doubled the amount of flour to 1 cup, the pudding disappeared entirely and the dessert baked into a single clay-like mass. On the other hand, when we tried ¼ cup of flour instead of the ½ cup we had been using, we got a 1:4 pudding-to-cake ratio that our tasters thought was ideal.

We now had a better understanding of the nuts and bolts of the dessert, and we were ready to make some other improvements. There were two big problems. First,

LEMON PUDDING CAKES

top, since it made the acidic batter slightly more alkaline, and an alkaline cake browns better than an acidic one.

Now what could we do to prevent the pudding layer from cooking more quickly than the cake and curdling? Reducing the oven temperature from 350 to 325 degrees helped a little bit, but not enough.

Would it help to alter the water bath? In most recipes that use the technique, including those for lemon pudding cake, the water added to the pan is typically boiling. We wondered if we could slow things down with a cool bath instead of a hot one. We baked pudding cakes in pans filled with cold water, ice water, and (as a control) boiling water. We made sure to pour the water only one-third of the way up the sides of the ramekins, so the water insulated only the pudding portion, giving the slow-baking cake a little extra exposure to the heat. As it had been doing, the pudding in the boiling-water bath continued to curdle, even at the lower oven temperature. However, the desserts baked in cold and ice water boasted smooth pudding. Since it took longer to bake, the cake layer could now fully cook without risk of overdone pudding. Because cold and ice water produced nearly identical results, we chose to use cold since it baked the desserts a little faster.

The size of the water bath also made a difference. By using probes to record the temperatures of the baths, we learned that the cake layers in a smaller bath baked in 40 minutes (at which point the water was 186 degrees), but the puddings curdled. The cakes in a larger pan required 53 minutes of baking and their puddings were as silky as could be. We checked the final temperature of this water bath: 179 degrees. Going back to our data, we found that the smaller water bath had reached the same temperature a whole half-hour earlier, at 23 minutes. The bigger bath was better, delivering a gentler cooking environment so that the layers finished in tandem.

With the consistency of the dessert right where we wanted it, we were ready to focus on the lemon flavor. After some tinkering, we determined that ½ cup of lemon juice and 3 tablespoons of zest struck just the right balance. The only problem was that the zest ruined

our recipe was producing cake that lacked structure. Second, the pudding cooked faster than the cake, and even with the water bath, it was still curdling when we baked the dessert until the cake was done.

We decided to tackle the texture of the cake first. Though somewhat unconventional for lemon pudding cake, using baking powder to create and expand gas pockets might give the top layer a little more lift and make it seem more cake-like. When we added various amounts to our batter, tasters agreed that ½ teaspoon of baking powder did the trick. As an added bonus, the baking powder also helped produce a gorgeous golden the texture of the silky pudding, riddling it with tiny, gritty threads.

Seeking to capture the flavor of the zest but not its abrasive texture, we tried infusing it into the warmed milk/cream mixture for 15 minutes and then straining out the solids. And because we thought that lots of fat might be necessary to extract flavor, we also steeped some zest in a small amount of warm melted butter (we figured that we could incorporate this into the cake if necessary). In a side-by-side taste test, the tart, floral notes were more present in the milk/cream mixture than in the infused butter. After a little research, this result made total sense.

Lemon peel contains numerous flavor compounds. Some are water-soluble and others are fat-soluble. Butter has such a low water content that the zest's water-soluble compounds could not be effectively extracted in it. In contrast, the more hydrated (but still fatty) milk and cream mixture was able to extract a better balance of the fat-soluble and water-soluble flavor compounds.

Our last move was to embellish the dessert with a colorful, flavorful garnish. Taking a classic, simple approach, we whipped up a quick blueberry compote that meshed well with the dessert's tart notes.

With a few tweaks, we'd turned a rather humble classic into a dessert that consistently delivered a smooth, silky pudding and a light cake every time.

Lemon Pudding Cakes
SERVES 6

To take the temperature of the pudding layer, touch the tip of an instant-read thermometer to the bottom of the ramekin and pull it up ¼ inch. The batter can also be baked in an 8-inch square glass baking dish. We like this dessert served at room temperature, but it can also be served chilled (the texture will be firmer). Spoon Blueberry Compote (recipe follows) over the top of each ramekin or simply dust with confectioners' sugar.

1   cup whole milk
½   cup heavy cream

3   tablespoons grated lemon zest plus
    ½ cup juice (3 lemons)
1   cup (7 ounces) sugar
¼   cup (1¼ ounces) all-purpose flour
½   teaspoon baking powder
⅛   teaspoon salt
2   large eggs, separated, plus 2 large whites
½   teaspoon vanilla extract

1. Adjust oven rack to middle position and heat oven to 325 degrees. Bring milk and cream to simmer in medium saucepan over medium-high heat. Remove pan from heat, whisk in lemon zest, cover pan, and let stand for 15 minutes. Meanwhile, fold dish towel in half and place in bottom of large roasting pan. Place six 6-ounce ramekins on top of towel and set aside pan.

2. Strain milk mixture through fine-mesh strainer into bowl, pressing on lemon zest to extract liquid; discard lemon zest. Whisk ¾ cup sugar, flour, baking powder, and salt in second bowl until combined. Add egg yolks, vanilla, lemon juice, and milk mixture and whisk until combined. (Batter will have consistency of milk.)

3. Using stand mixer fitted with whisk, whip egg whites on medium-low speed until foamy, about 1 minute. Increase speed to medium-high and whip whites to soft, billowy mounds, about 1 minute. Gradually add remaining ¼ cup sugar and whip until glossy, soft peaks form, 1 to 2 minutes.

4. Whisk one-quarter of whites into batter to lighten. With rubber spatula, gently fold in remaining whites until no clumps or streaks remain. Ladle batter into ramekins (ramekins should be nearly full). Pour enough cold water into pan to come one-third of way up sides of ramekins. Bake until cake is set and pale golden brown and pudding layer registers 172 to 175 degrees at center, 50 to 55 minutes.

5. Remove pan from oven and let ramekins stand in water bath for 10 minutes. Transfer ramekins to wire rack and let cool completely. Serve.

Blueberry Compote

MAKES ABOUT 1 CUP

To use fresh blueberries, crush one-third of them against the side of the saucepan with a wooden spoon after adding them to the butter and then proceed as directed.

  1 **tablespoon unsalted butter**
 10 **ounces (2 cups) frozen blueberries**
  2 **tablespoons sugar, plus extra for seasoning**
      Pinch salt
 ½ **teaspoon lemon juice**

Melt butter in small saucepan over medium heat. Add blueberries, 2 tablespoons sugar, and salt; bring to boil. Lower heat and simmer, stirring occasionally, until thickened and about one-quarter of juice remains, 8 to 10 minutes. Remove pan from heat and stir in lemon juice. Season with extra sugar to taste.

SCIENCE DESK

MAXIMIZING CITRUS FLAVOR
To produce bold citrus flavor in our pudding without marring its silky-smooth texture with pieces of lemon zest, we steep the zest in liquid and then strain it out. Some of the flavor compounds in the zest are fat-soluble, such as d-limonene. Others, like citric acid, are water soluble. To extract the most flavor, we infuse the zest into a mixture of two liquids that we use in our batter—milk and heavy cream—that together contain goodly amounts of both water and fat.

FRESH STRAWBERRY MOUSSE

✓ WHY THIS RECIPE WORKS: There's a good reason that strawberry mousse recipes aren't very prevalent: The berries contain lots of juice that can easily ruin the texture of a mousse, which should be creamy and rich. Plus, the fruit flavor produced by most strawberry mousse recipes is too subtle. To achieve a creamy yet firm texture without losing the strawberry flavor, we replaced some of the cream with cream cheese. We processed the berries into small pieces and macerated them with sugar and a little salt to draw out their juice. We then reduced the released liquid to a syrup before adding it to the mousse, which standardized the amount of moisture in the dessert and also concentrated the berry flavor. Fully pureeing the juiced berries contributed bright, fresh berry flavor. A dollop of lemon whipped cream made for a tangy finish.

WHEN IT COMES TO MOUSSE DESSERTS, RECIPES FOR the chocolate kind—or even citrus versions—abound. But it's not often that you see recipes for mousses that feature strawberries—which, as we see it, is a sad omission. The berry's bright, sweet flavor could surely make a light and refreshing variation. Plus, mousse is great for warm-weather entertaining: It doesn't require turning on the oven, it looks elegant once it's dressed up with a simple garnish, and it's entirely make-ahead.

With a little digging, we found a few recipes for strawberry mousse. Most followed the same simple steps: Puree fresh berries, strain the mixture, add sugar and a stabilizer (most often gelatin), and then fold the puree into whipped cream and allow it to set in the refrigerator. But once we tried these recipes, we realized why this type of mousse isn't more common: Not one of the resulting mousses tasted much like strawberries. The reason wasn't hard to determine. Even in season, the average supermarket strawberry is watery and just doesn't have

FRESH STRAWBERRY MOUSSE

NOTES FROM THE TEST KITCHEN

GETTING THE MOST OUT OF SUPERMARKET STRAWBERRIES

Supermarket strawberries rarely deliver the bright flavor and concentrated sweetness that you find in farmers' market specimens. By macerating the finely chopped berries and then using both fresh and cooked forms of the fruit, we were able to capture the bright, deep strawberry flavor that we wanted.

A LOT OF FRESH PUREE

Pureeing and straining the macerated chopped berries yields about 1⅔ cups of puree—enough for a punch of bright, fresh berry flavor.

A LITTLE CONCENTRATED JUICE

By reducing the shed berry juice (about ⅔ cup) to just 3 tablespoons, we're able to deepen its flavor and control the amount of liquid we add to the mousse.

CREAM CHEESE FOR CONSISTENCY

In addition to using whipped cream and gelatin, we fortify our Fresh Strawberry Mousse with an unusual ingredient: cream cheese. The rich, soft-but-dense texture of the cultured dairy lends the mousse just enough body and a bit of subtle tang.

BODY BUILDER

Cream cheese gives mousse a thick, creamy texture without turning it dense.

a lot of flavor. Cooking the berries to drive off some of their moisture and concentrate flavor, as a few recipes suggest, wasn't the answer. While these mousses had more discernible strawberry flavor, they also lacked the fresh taste of a berry eaten out of hand. Meanwhile, those recipes that didn't call for cooking down the fruit also suffered textural problems: The large amount of juice given up by the berries made these desserts loose and runny.

A strawberry mousse that lived up to the name would need to have a lush yet light texture and the sweet flavor of the best fresh summer berries. Our strategy would be to get the flavor of the mousse tasting genuinely like fresh strawberries and then figure out how to deal with what would inevitably be an overly wet, soft texture.

Because we were developing this recipe during strawberry season, we ran one test with the best farmers' market berries we could find. While this batch did taste brighter and sweeter, it was still problematic: Besides the high price and limited availability of the fruit, the superjuicy berries turned the dessert into something more akin to melted ice cream than mousse.

We went back to supermarket berries, figuring we'd ramp up the amount of puree until we had something that tasted sufficiently fruity. We started by softening 1¾ teaspoons of gelatin in a few tablespoons of water. Then we pulsed 2 pounds of strawberries—nearly twice the amount called for in most recipes—to create about 2 cups of puree. We strained out the seeds and added the softened gelatin and ½ cup of sugar. We folded the fruit mixture into 1 cup of heavy cream that we'd whipped to stiff peaks, portioned it into serving bowls, and let the mousse chill for about 4 hours to set up.

Frustratingly, this puree-heavy mousse wanted for still more concentrated fruit flavor. And the texture was worse than we thought—so loose that it practically dribbled off the spoon.

Putting the flavor issue on hold, we reviewed our options for tightening up the texture. Adding more gelatin only made the mousse so overly set that it jiggled like Jell-O. We tried other common mousse stabilizers: pectin, whipped egg whites, and even white chocolate, none of which was quite right.

What if we replaced some of the whipped cream with another dairy product that contributed thicker body? Sour cream, mascarpone, and cream cheese came to mind, and after another round of tests, we settled on the latter. The soft but dense cream cheese (we swapped in 4 ounces for ½ cup of heavy cream) was a big step in the right direction. It firmed up the mousse's texture and didn't mask strawberry flavor.

And yet the mousse was still softer than we liked. It also lacked depth—an important part of great strawberry flavor. Cooking the berries would only destroy that brightness, but there was an approach that could allow us to keep the fresh berry taste while still concentrating its flavor: macerating the berries and then reducing their shed liquid to a fixed amount. This would also allow us to limit the amount of juice going into the mousse without wasting it.

Instead of immediately pureeing the berries for our next batch, we pulsed them just a bit (to produce small pieces with lots of surface area) and then tossed them with sugar and a pinch of salt. After 45 minutes, we strained them, which left us with an impressive ⅔ cup of juice. We then pureed the drained berries and strained the resulting pulp to get rid of the seeds. From there we reduced the juice until it measured about 3 tablespoons—we'd essentially made a berry syrup—and then we whisked in the softened gelatin until it was dissolved, followed by the softened cream cheese and the berry puree. We folded the enriched fruit puree into the whipped cream and chilled it.

This batch was wonderfully rich and creamy and not runny in the least, and the strawberry flavor was the best yet. Thanks to the tandem effect of the berry syrup and the fresh puree, our mousse tasted both bright and concentrated (but not "cooked"). Happily, the results were just as good when we made the mousse with frozen berries, which turned this into a year-round dessert. (Frozen berries actually offer a perk of their own: Freezing causes them to naturally exude quite a bit of moisture, so the macerating step is unnecessary.)

We made just two more adjustments. Instead of softening the gelatin in water, we dissolved it in a little of the drained strawberry juice—a tweak that enhanced the berry flavor a bit more. (We still reduced the remaining liquid to 3 tablespoons.) Replacing berry juice with strawberry (or raspberry) liqueur was a great option for when we wanted more-complex berry flavor.

The other adjustment addressed a lingering complaint from our tasters: The mousse had always been a bit streaky—that is, folding the fruit mixture into the cream with a spatula didn't thoroughly marry the two components. Using a whisk to more thoroughly combine the cream with the puree–cream cheese mixture gave the mousse uniform flavor and color.

Finally, to make this dessert more elegant and give it one more boost of fresh berry flavor, we scattered extra diced fresh strawberries over the top. And since frozen strawberries don't make for a pretty garnish, we also came up with a topping that would work whether you're using fresh or frozen fruit: a lemon-zest-and-juice-spiked whipped cream, which underscored the bright, lightly tangy flavor in the berries.

Fresh Strawberry Mousse
SERVES 4 TO 6

This recipe works well with supermarket strawberries and farmers' market strawberries. In step 1, be careful not to overprocess the berries. If you like, substitute 1½ pounds (5¼ cups) of thawed frozen strawberries for fresh strawberries. If using frozen strawberries skip step 1 (do not process berries). Proceed with the recipe, adding the ½ cup of sugar and the salt to the whipped cream in step 4. For more complex berry flavor, replace the 3 tablespoons of raw strawberry juice in step 2 with strawberry or raspberry liqueur. In addition to the diced berries, or if you're using frozen strawberries, you can serve the mousse with Lemon Whipped Cream (recipe follows).

2 **pounds strawberries, hulled (6½ cups)**
½ **cup (3½ ounces) sugar**
   Pinch salt
1¾ **teaspoons unflavored gelatin**
4 **ounces cream cheese, cut into 8 pieces and softened**
½ **cup heavy cream, chilled**

1. Cut enough strawberries into ¼-inch dice to measure 1 cup; refrigerate until ready to garnish. Pulse remaining strawberries in food processor in 2 batches until most pieces are ¼ to ½ inch thick (some larger pieces are fine), 6 to 10 pulses. Transfer strawberries to bowl and toss with ¼ cup sugar and salt. (Do not clean processor.) Cover bowl and let strawberries stand for 45 minutes, stirring occasionally.

2. Strain processed strawberries through fine-mesh strainer into bowl (you should have about ⅔ cup juice).

Measure out 3 tablespoons juice into small bowl, sprinkle gelatin over juice, and let sit until gelatin softens, about 5 minutes. Place remaining juice in small saucepan and cook over medium-high heat until reduced to 3 tablespoons, about 10 minutes. Remove pan from heat, add softened gelatin mixture, and stir until gelatin has dissolved. Add cream cheese and whisk until smooth. Transfer mixture to large bowl.

3. While juice is reducing, return strawberries to now-empty processor and process until smooth, 15 to 20 seconds. Strain puree through fine-mesh strainer into medium bowl, pressing on solids to remove seeds and pulp (you should have about 1⅔ cups puree). Discard any solids in strainer. Add strawberry puree to juice-gelatin mixture and whisk until incorporated.

4. Using stand mixer fitted with whisk, whip cream on medium-low speed until foamy, about 1 minute. Increase speed to high and whip until soft peaks form, 1 to 3 minutes. Gradually add remaining ¼ cup sugar and whip until stiff peaks form, 1 to 2 minutes. Whisk whipped cream into strawberry mixture until no white streaks remain. Portion into dessert dishes and chill for at least 4 hours or up to 2 days. (If chilled longer than 6 hours, let mousse sit at room temperature for 15 minutes before serving.) Serve, garnishing with reserved diced strawberries.

Lemon Whipped Cream
MAKES ABOUT 1 CUP

If preferred, you can replace the lemon with lime.

½ **cup heavy cream**
2 **tablespoons sugar**
1 **teaspoon finely grated lemon zest plus 1 tablespoon juice**

Using stand mixer fitted with whisk, whip cream on medium-low speed until foamy, about 1 minute. Add sugar and lemon zest and juice, increase speed to medium-high, and whip until soft peaks form, 1 to 3 minutes.

RATING STAND MIXERS

A stand mixer can be a worthwhile investment—if you shop carefully. To find the best mixer, we ordered nine models, ranging in price from about $230 to a whopping $849. We put each machine through a battery of tests, whipping egg whites, kneading pizza and bagel dough, and creaming butter and sugar. We measured each mixer bowl's usable capacity—the volume of the space between the top of the attachment and the bottom of the bowl—and discovered that no model actually made use of its bowl's total volume. The highest marks went to the machines that could quickly and easily handle all tasks, and were intuitive to set up, use, and clean. Some machines lost points for attachments that did not reach the entire surface of the bowl. We found that the torque, or rotational force, of each machine mattered more than horsepower. Our winner, the KitchenAid Pro Line Series 7-Qt Bowl Lift Stand Mixer, performed perfectly on every task. Products are listed in order of preference. See AmericasTestKitchen.com for updates and complete testing results.

RECOMMENDED

KITCHENAID Pro Line Series 7-Qt Bowl Lift Stand Mixer
MODEL: KSM7586P **PRICE:** $549.95 **STYLE:** Bowl-lift
STATED CAPACITY: 7 qt **USABLE CAPACITY:** 5¾ qt
WEIGHT: 27 lb **HORSEPOWER:** 1.3
COMMENTS: This powerful, smartly designed machine made quick work of large and small volumes of food. The whisk fit the bowl's shape perfectly, and the model handled batches of stiff dough without flinching. Testers liked the bowl-lift design and large vertical bowl handle.

KITCHENAID Classic Plus Series 4.5-Quart Tilt-Head Stand Mixer
MODEL: KSM75WH **PRICE:** $229.99 **STYLE:** Tilt-head
STATED CAPACITY: 4½ qt **USABLE CAPACITY:** 3¼ qt
WEIGHT: 21.5 lb **HORSEPOWER:** 0.37
COMMENTS: This basic, compact, heavy machine's across-the-board performance knocked out many competitors that were bigger and much more costly. We wish that its bowl had a handle, and a bowl-lift design would have been nice, but those are small concessions given its affordable price.

KITCHENAID Professional 600 Series 6-Quart Bowl-Lift Stand Mixer
MODEL: KP26M1X **PRICE:** $449.95 **STYLE:** Bowl-lift
STATED CAPACITY: 6 qt **USABLE CAPACITY:** 5¼ qt
WEIGHT: 25.4 lb **HORSEPOWER:** 0.8
COMMENTS: Runny egg whites didn't turn into stiff peaks until we cranked the speed to create a vortex. This model was also noisy, and jerked slightly on tough kneading tasks. But the results were nonetheless excellent.

RECOMMENDED WITH RESERVATIONS

WARING Commercial Professional 7-Quart Stand Mixer
MODEL: WSM7Q **PRICE:** $564.65 **STYLE:** Tilt-head
STATED CAPACITY: 7 qt **USABLE CAPACITY:** 4½ qt
WEIGHT: 19.25 lb **HORSEPOWER:** 1.07
COMMENTS: This powerful machine performed well when kneading, but its tilt head flew up during mixing unless we were extra careful to secure it. Its horizontal handles were unwieldy for pouring batter into cake pans.

RECOMMENDED WITH RESERVATIONS (cont.)

CUISINART 5.5 Quart Stand Mixer
MODEL: SM-55 **PRICE:** $349 **STYLE:** Tilt-head
STATED CAPACITY: 5½ qt **USABLE CAPACITY:** 3 qt
WEIGHT: 17.8 lb **HORSEPOWER:** 1.07
COMMENTS: This model's loose speed dial made it hard to pinpoint settings; the jumpy timer raced past the numbers we wanted; and its small, horizontal bowl handles made pouring awkward. It produced fine dough, but whipping cream and egg whites took extra time.

NOT RECOMMENDED

VOLLRATH 7-Quart Countertop Commercial Mixer
MODEL: 40755 **PRICE:** $849 **STYLE:** Bowl-lift
STATED CAPACITY: 7 qt **USABLE CAPACITY:** 5¼ qt
WEIGHT: 43.9 lb **HORSEPOWER:** 0.87
COMMENTS: We struggled to move this 43.9-pound behemoth, and its 19.5-inch-tall body didn't fit under our cupboards. Cake batter and larger volumes of cream and egg whites were no problem, but the ill-designed bowl and attachments meant that it struggled with smaller amounts of food.

CUISINART 7.0 Quart 12-Speed Stand Mixer
MODEL: SM-70 **PRICE:** $449.90 **STYLE:** Tilt-head
STATED CAPACITY: 7 qt **USABLE CAPACITY:** 4½ qt
WEIGHT: 19.25 lb **HORSEPOWER:** 1.3
COMMENTS: This mixer's deep, narrow bowl limited testers' view of mixing progress and let cream and egg whites pool out of reach of the whisk. Its motor was loud and shrill. When kneading bagel dough, the dough hook separated from a bolt at its base and had to be rethreaded.

BREVILLE Scraper Mixer Pro
MODEL: BEM800XL **PRICE:** $280.95 **STYLE:** Tilt-head
STATED CAPACITY: 5 qt **USABLE CAPACITY:** 3¾ qt
WEIGHT: 16.5 lb **HORSEPOWER:** 0.74
COMMENTS: This model's fast, quiet whipping and creaming and user-friendly features (scraper paddle and timer) advanced it to the lead—until it utterly choked during kneading. A second copy also failed.

Sweet on Custard and Cookies

Unsweetened chocolate and cocoa powder deliver potent flavor in our chocolate crinkle cookies, and instant espresso powder intensifies their chocolate flavor even more.

NEVER UNDERESTIMATE THE POWER OF DESSERT. AND WE'RE NOT just talking about its ability to wow your friends. Some desserts seem to have a mind of their own—they can outsmart even experienced bakers. Take baked custards, for example. They never seem to turn out quite the way you think they will. And chocolate crinkle cookies often suffer from a lack of crinkles (not to mention chocolate flavor). We hope you saved room for dessert, because you won't want to miss out on our foolproof recipes for rich, creamy flan and the ultimate chocolate crinkle cookies.

Making flan can be a gamble. Sometimes it bakes up too loose and breaks as you flip it onto the serving platter. Other times, it's overcooked and rubbery. Plus, most of the caramel sauce sticks irretrievably to the pan. We made it our goal to develop a Latin American–style flan that solves all of these problems.

Cookies can be somewhat difficult—the slightest variation in technique or ingredients can lead to disaster, and chocolate crinkle cookies are a prime example. The inside is often too wet, the crinkles on top disappear, and they're cloyingly sweet. We wanted chocolate crinkle cookies that lived up to their name—superbly chocolaty, with a striking, crackled exterior. To do this, we had to rethink what sugar we used—and how we used it. Don't let your dessert get the best of you—make it the best part of your meal.

LATIN AMERICAN–STYLE FLAN

✔ WHY THIS RECIPE WORKS: At its best, Latin American–style flan is a rich, creamy dessert with deep, toffee-like flavor and a uniformly silky texture. But many of the recipes we found produced overly heavy custards with unpleasantly thick "skins," and much of the caramel layer ended up stuck to the bottom of the pan. Although most recipes call for dairy only in the form of canned evaporated and sweetened condensed milks, we added fresh milk to ensure a creamy, rich (but not heavy) texture. Reducing the oven temperature and wrapping the pan in aluminum foil helped the flan bake evenly and prevented a skin from forming. Swapping out the typical shallow round cake pan for a loaf pan made a sturdier flan. Adding a bit of water to our caramel made it softer, which meant that our finished flan was topped with a thick, decadent layer of caramel.

SPAIN IS KNOWN FOR FLAN THAT IS CREAMY AND lightly set—almost indistinguishable from French crème caramel—but we've always had a soft spot for the versions served in Mexican and Cuban restaurants. Though they share the same layer of caramelized sugar glistening on top and pooling at the bottom, the Latin style of this baked custard isn't light and quivering like its European counterparts. It is far richer and more densely creamy, with a texture somewhere between pudding and cheesecake. It also boasts a more deeply caramelized, toffee-like flavor.

Paging through flan recipes claiming a Latin heritage, we got our first clue as to how the custard gets its thick, luxurious texture: In place of fresh dairy, all such recipes called for canned milk—evaporated as well as sweetened condensed. The cooking process that concentrates canned milks also causes their sugars and proteins to brown, which accounts for the light tan color and toffee flavor they lend to this style of the dessert.

We made a few recipes, cooking sugar with a little water on the stove to create a caramel that we poured into a mold (typically a round cake pan), adding eggs whisked together with the canned milks, baking the custard in a water bath, and inverting it onto a platter when chilled. The first things we noticed: Even more so than with crème caramel, much of the caramel stuck to the bottom of the pan. And often the custard was so dense that it was borderline stiff, with even thicker skin where the flan had been exposed to the direct heat of the oven.

Needless to say, this was not the dessert we had in mind, so we got to work on a version that was as dense and rich-tasting as it was creamy.

We homed in on the best-tasting recipe we'd made: three whole eggs and five yolks whisked together with one can each of evaporated and sweetened condensed milk (plus a touch of vanilla and salt for flavor) and baked in a water bath at 350 degrees for about an hour. It tasted appropriately rich and sweet, if overly eggy. The bigger issue was its texture, which was not only stiff but also uneven; while the exterior was rubbery, the core was pudding-like.

A review of how custards work seemed in order. At their most basic, all custards are cooked mixtures of eggs and dairy in which the eggs are largely the source of proteins and the dairy largely the source of water. When the proteins are heated, they link up and form a matrix that traps the water, giving the custard structure. The exact texture of a custard mainly depends on the ratio of eggs to dairy: The more the proteins are diluted with water (from the dairy), the looser the custard's consistency will be.

But in Latin flan, we had a hunch that the dairy was playing a different role. Since canned milks contain less water than fresh milk, they obviously had less to contribute to the custard. Not only that, but these concentrated forms of milk were without a doubt contributing far more protein to the custard than fresh milk does—though we didn't realize just how much more until we took a look at their nutrition labels. Both products, in fact, contain at least twice as much protein per ounce as fresh milk.

Knowing that an overload of protein was making our flan too stiff, we tried removing one whole egg. We knew we were on the right track when the next batch of flan

PERFECT LATIN FLAN

custard where it was exposed to heat, but we had fixes in mind. We wrapped the cake pan in aluminum foil before baking, which prevented that pesky skin. As for the undercooked center, we cooked the custard to a slightly higher temperature than we had been (180 degrees instead of 175 degrees) while also reducing the oven temperature to 300 degrees to ensure that the custard cooked evenly from edge to center.

Now our flan tasted great—but unfortunately, it wasn't looking so hot. When we unmolded the more-fragile custard, a crack inevitably developed on the surface.

It occurred to us that the cake pan we'd been using was not helping the problem, as it produced a wide, shallow flan that was clearly inclined to crack. Looking through the test kitchen's arsenal of baking vessels, we wondered if the deeper walls and narrower surface area of a loaf pan might produce a sturdier flan. That it did. Even better, this taller flan was more statuesque—a presentation bonus.

Now back to that caramel-sticking problem. We suspected that the lack of water in this style of flan was partly to blame, since the caramel relies on moisture from the custard to keep it fluid. Up until now, we'd been resting the flan for about 4 hours—enough time for it to thoroughly chill. But resting it longer would surely allow more of the custard's moisture to seep into the caramel, so we let the next batch sit overnight before we unmolded it. The longer rest was worth it, as the liquid did indeed dilute the caramel, so that more caramel traveled with the custard this time. This approach also put our flan squarely in the make-ahead dessert category, which we considered a plus.

And yet we wanted even more of the caramel to release with the custard, so we decided to address the issue more directly. After cooking one more batch of caramel, we swirled 2 tablespoons of water (warm—to prevent the caramel from seizing) into the sugar just as it turned reddish-amber and then poured it into the pan and proceeded as before. When we turned out the next flan and saw that it was covered with a substantial layer of runny caramel, we knew we'd hit the mark. Plus, the small amount of caramel left in the pan was soft enough to scrape out with a spatula.

turned out noticeably creamier (albeit still uneven from edge to center). Even better, this quick fix did away with the custard's distinct eggy flavor. But ideally the custard would still be a tad looser.

Removing another egg was the obvious next step, but the test backfired. In exchange for the more-velvety texture we wanted, we were left with a custard that lacked richness. So we stuck with the two whole eggs and considered our alternatives. Cutting back on either the sweetened condensed or evaporated milk was one option, but we quickly dismissed it, realizing that this would not only reduce the volume of the custard but also leave us with a small amount of canned milk we would surely waste.

The other option would be to add some liquid to the mixture, and fresh milk was the obvious choice; in essence, we'd be merging the European and Latin versions of this dessert. Of course, we didn't want to dilute the protein network so much that the custard would buckle when we unmolded it, so we went with what we hoped was a judicious ½ cup of fresh milk, whisking it into the egg-and-canned-milk mixture and proceeding with the recipe as before.

This was the texture we had in mind: dense, but not stiff, and luxuriously creamy. The core was still gooey and there was still a thin skin on the very edge of the

Now that our version was a reliable showpiece that we'd want to make often, we created a few easy flavor variations by infusing the custard with orange and cardamom, as well as with typically Latin flavors: coffee and almond extract. That made four rich, densely creamy, make-ahead desserts—a profile that may have permanently stolen our allegiance from French custards.

Perfect Latin Flan
SERVES 8 TO 10

This recipe should be made at least one day before serving. We recommend an 8½ by 4½-inch loaf pan for this recipe. If your pan is 9 by 5 inches, begin checking for doneness at 1 hour and 15 minutes. You may substitute 2 percent milk for the whole milk, but do not use skim milk. Serve the flan on a platter with a raised rim to contain the liquid caramel.

- ⅔ cup (4⅔ ounces) sugar
- 2 large eggs plus 5 large yolks
- 1 (14-ounce) can sweetened condensed milk
- 1 (12-ounce) can evaporated milk
- ½ cup whole milk
- 1½ tablespoons vanilla extract
- ½ teaspoon salt

1. Stir together sugar and ¼ cup water in medium heavy saucepan until sugar is completely moistened. Bring to boil over medium-high heat, 3 to 5 minutes, and cook, without stirring, until mixture begins to turn golden, another 1 to 2 minutes. Gently swirling pan, continue to cook until sugar is color of peanut butter, 1 to 2 minutes. Remove from heat and swirl pan until sugar is reddish-amber and fragrant, 15 to 20 seconds. Carefully swirl in 2 tablespoons warm tap water until incorporated; mixture will bubble and steam. Pour caramel into 8½ by 4½-inch loaf pan; do not scrape out saucepan. Set loaf pan aside.

2. Adjust oven rack to middle position and heat oven to 300 degrees. Line bottom of 13 by 9-inch baking pan

NOTES FROM THE TEST KITCHEN

WHEN GOODNESS COMES (MAINLY) FROM A CAN
The advent of canned milk in Latin America in the late 1800s helped make flan, which was introduced by Spanish conquistadores 300 years earlier, even more popular. When refrigeration became widespread and shelf-stable milk was no longer as necessary, the practice of using the canned stuff stuck. And with good reason: Evaporated and sweetened condensed milks give flan a distinctively thick, luxurious texture and caramelized notes. (In some Latin American countries, this texture has given rise to the alternate name *quesillo*, or little cheesecake). But these milks can also have a negative effect, contributing to a stiff, almost rubbery consistency. This is because, compared with an equivalent amount of fresh dairy, they have about twice as much protein, which, when combined with egg proteins in the custard, can create an overly tight structure. Our solution? Add ½ cup of fresh milk, which loosens the texture without adding much protein of its own or diluting dairy flavor.

EVAPORATED
This canned milk is made by heating pasteurized fresh milk in two stages to drive off nearly half of its water, which also triggers some Maillard browning. Once sealed in a can, the milk is sterilized to become shelf-stable, a process that triggers more browning and the creation of subtle caramel flavors.

SWEETENED CONDENSED
Adding sucrose or glucose syrups to milk that's been evaporated (and undergone Maillard browning) results in this canned milk. In combination with the lactose naturally present in the milk, these added sugars make up more than 50 percent of its weight, rendering sterilization unnecessary.

with dish towel, folding towel to fit smoothly, and set aside. Bring 2 quarts water to boil.

3. Whisk eggs and yolks in large bowl until combined. Add sweetened condensed milk, evaporated milk, whole milk, vanilla, and salt, and whisk until incorporated. Strain mixture through fine-mesh strainer into prepared loaf pan.

4. Cover loaf pan tightly with aluminum foil and place in prepared baking pan. Place baking pan in oven and

DON'T LET THE CARAMEL STICK TO THE PAN

The rich layer of caramel on top of flan is the best part of the dessert—except when most of it sticks to the pan like glue. Adding a couple of tablespoons of warm water to the syrup after it's caramelized will dissolve some of the sugar and keep it runny. In addition, resting the flan overnight allows moisture from the custard to dissolve more of the sugar, ensuring that most of the caramel will release from the pan (and that what's left in the pan is soft and easy to remove).

CLINGY CARAMEL
To prevent the caramel from sticking to the pan,
we add a little warm water.

SEPARATING EGGS

To separate eggs, use either the broken shell halves or your hand.

A. To use broken shell halves, gently transfer egg yolk from one shell half to other, so white will drip into bowl and leave intact yolk behind.

B. To use your hand (make sure it's very clean), cup your hand over small bowl, transfer egg into your palm, and slowly allow white to slide through fingers, leaving yolk intact.

carefully pour all of boiling water into pan. Bake until center of custard jiggles slightly when shaken and custard registers 180 degrees, 1¼ to 1½ hours. Remove foil and leave custard in water bath until loaf pan has cooled completely. Wrap loaf pan tightly with plastic wrap and chill overnight or up to 4 days.

5. To unmold, slide paring knife around edges of pan. Invert serving platter on top of pan and turn pan and platter over. When flan is released, remove loaf pan. Using rubber spatula, scrape residual caramel onto flan. Slice and serve. Leftover flan may be covered loosely and refrigerated for up to 4 days.

VARIATIONS

Almond Latin Flan

Reduce vanilla to 1 tablespoon and whisk 1 teaspoon almond extract into the egg-milk mixture.

Coffee Latin Flan

Whisk 4 teaspoons of instant espresso powder into the egg-milk mixture until dissolved.

Orange-Cardamom Latin Flan

Whisk 2 tablespoons orange zest and ¼ teaspoon ground cardamom into the egg-milk mixture before straining.

CHOCOLATE CRINKLE COOKIES

✔ **WHY THIS RECIPE WORKS:** Chocolate crinkle cookies are usually tooth-achingly sweet, with just a couple of gaping fissures instead of a crackly surface. We wanted cookies that lived up to their name. For a deep, rich chocolate flavor, we used a combination of unsweetened chocolate and cocoa powder (with a boost from espresso powder). Using brown sugar instead of granulated lent a more complex, tempered sweetness with a molasses-y edge that complemented the chocolate. Using both baking powder and baking soda gave the cookies just the right amount of lift and spread, helping produce a nicely textured surface. But the real key was rolling the cookies in granulated sugar before rolling them in powdered sugar. This helped produce the perfect crackly exterior by creating a "shell" that broke into numerous fine fissures as the cookies rose and spread, and kept the powdered sugar coating in place.

THE NAME SAYS IT ALL—THESE COOKIES ARE AS MUCH about looks as they are about flavor. Rolled in powdered sugar before going in the oven, chocolate crinkle cookies (aka earthquakes) form dark chocolaty fissures that break through the bright white surface during baking. They have an eye-catching appearance, with an irresistible deep chocolaty richness to back it up.

Or at least, that's how they should be. These cookies are often a little too sweet, the chocolate flavor is underwhelming, and the cracks are more like gaping chasms than fissures. And because the confectioners' sugar coating usually all but vanishes in the oven, those few cracks aren't even that noticeable. We wanted a cookie with deep chocolate flavor and only enough sweetness to balance the chocolate's bitterness; a moist and tender—but not gooey—interior; and plenty of small irregular crinkly fissures breaking through a bright-white surface.

We started by trying a handful of published recipes, limiting ourselves to those that called for preparing the dough by hand—no stand mixer required—since the melted chocolate and melted butter should make this a loose, easy-to-stir dough. The ingredient lists we saw were surprisingly varied in both the types of chocolate and the amounts of sugar they called for. And yet, the results were all strikingly similar. Because every recipe used either sweetened varieties of chocolate or large amounts of sugar, they were all too sweet, with muted chocolate flavor. Furthermore, they all had cracks that were too wide and few in number.

The most promising recipe of the bunch achieved decent chocolate flavor from 3 ounces of unsweetened chocolate, 3 ounces of bittersweet bar chocolate, and ¼ cup of cocoa powder. Since these cookies were still too sweet, our first decision was to drop the bittersweet chocolate since it contains added sugar. In its place, we upped the unsweetened chocolate to 4 ounces and the cocoa powder to ½ cup. We decided to see how these changes fared and left the sugar alone, at 1¾ cups.

While we didn't go into sugar shock on this first attempt, the cookies were still a bit cloying and not chocolaty enough; plus, they were too wet. Dropping the sugar down to 1½ cups not only helped bring the chocolate flavor to the fore and keep the sweetness in check but also helped to make the cookies less gooey. This is because sugar is hygroscopic, meaning that it holds on to water. Less sugar in the dough meant that more moisture was able to evaporate during baking—resulting in a cookie that was appropriately moist but not overly gooey.

The cookies were impressively chocolaty now, but we felt that they could taste even better. Taking a cue from one of the recipes we'd tested, we substituted brown sugar for the granulated, since it would lend a more complex sweetness, with a molasses undertone that would complement the chocolate. After we added some espresso powder, which helps heighten chocolate flavor, our cookies really hit the mark for bold chocolate taste. It was time to move on to issues of appearance.

Just as we'd seen in the initial recipe tests, the cracks on the cookies were too few and too wide and the cookies weren't spreading enough—they looked a bit humped. In the past, we've found that leaveners not only contribute

CHOCOLATE CRINKLE COOKIES

to rise and spread in cookies but also help create a more crackly, fissured surface. Before a cookie sets in the oven, bubbles produced by the leavener rise to the surface and burst, leaving fissures. In a past recipe for gingersnaps, we found that baking soda alone was most effective, while sugar cookies benefited from both baking powder and baking soda. We'd started our testing with baking powder since it was the most commonly used leavener in the recipes we'd seen, but baking soda, which requires an acidic ingredient to work, was also an option for us since our recipe now included brown sugar and espresso powder.

Cookies made with baking soda alone weren't impressive. Using ¼ teaspoon didn't provide enough leavening power, and ½ teaspoon gave the cookies a metallic aftertaste. Baking powder, as we already knew, did a decent job by itself, but a combination of baking powder and baking soda proved to be the winner. These cookies spread nicely, without any hump, and they had a more crackly surface than anything we'd produced thus far. However, the cracks still gaped and were fewer in number than we had hoped.

We wondered if the temperature of the dough was playing a role. Because it was too fluid to work with right after we mixed it, we had been refrigerating it overnight before portioning the cookies and baking them. This is a common crinkle cookie step, but maybe it was causing more harm than good. To find out, we baked two more batches—one after refrigerating the dough for 4 hours and another after letting the dough sit at room temperature until the melted chocolate and butter cooled just enough to make the dough workable, which took only 10 minutes—and compared these with our current recipe that had the refrigerated overnight rest. Our hunch was right. The cookies made after the 10-minute rest were the best of the group, with finer and more numerous cracks than the other two batches (and it didn't hurt that we didn't have to wait as long to enjoy them either).

The cookies made with refrigerated dough were cold toward the center and thus hadn't spread much by the time the heat of the oven had dried out their exteriors. This meant that these cookies did almost all their spreading after that dried exterior had formed, forcing cracks to

open wide as the cookies spread. Meanwhile the room-temperature dough had already spread somewhat by the time the exterior dried in the oven. Minimal spreading once the exterior had dried meant smaller, more numerous cracks. Though we wondered if the cracks could be even more fine and numerous, they were looking pretty

good, certainly the best yet, so we decided to turn our attention to the coating.

The coating of confectioners' sugar on our cookies was faded. We recalled that some of the recipes in our early tests, flawed as they were, produced cookies with a picture-perfect bright-white exterior. We realized that they all called for rolling the cookies in granulated sugar before the powdered sugar. When we added this step, not only did the powdered sugar stay put, but the cracking actually improved. These cookies had ideal fine cracks all over the surface.

What was happening? The heavy coating of granulated sugar was creating a barrier that kept the fine-grained confectioners' sugar from soaking into the dough, ensuring a bright-white appearance. As for the improved crackly appearance, our science editor explained that before the cookies finished expanding in the oven, granulated sugar in the coating was melting and then recrystallizing into a very dry "shell" on the cookies' surface. As the cookies spread, numerous fine cracks broke through all over the sugary shell. These were the best crinkly, crackly cookies yet. Combined with their deep chocolaty flavor, we finally had chocolate crinkle cookies that were all they were cracked up to be.

Chocolate Crinkle Cookies

MAKES 22 COOKIES

Both natural and Dutch-processed cocoa will work in this recipe. Our favorite natural cocoa is Hershey's Natural Cocoa Unsweetened; our favorite Dutch-processed cocoa is Droste Cocoa.

- 1 cup (5 ounces) all-purpose flour
- ½ cup (1½ ounces) unsweetened cocoa powder
- 1 teaspoon baking powder
- ¼ teaspoon baking soda
- ½ teaspoon salt
- 1½ cups packed (10½ ounces) brown sugar
- 3 large eggs
- 4 teaspoons instant espresso powder (optional)
- 1 teaspoon vanilla extract

- 4 ounces unsweetened chocolate, chopped
- 4 tablespoons unsalted butter
- ½ cup (3½ ounces) granulated sugar
- ½ cup (2 ounces) confectioners' sugar

1. Adjust oven rack to middle position and heat oven to 325 degrees. Line 2 baking sheets with parchment. Whisk flour, cocoa, baking powder, baking soda, and salt together in bowl.

2. Whisk brown sugar; eggs; espresso powder, if using; and vanilla together in large bowl. Combine chocolate and butter in bowl and microwave at 50 percent power, stirring occasionally, until melted, 2 to 3 minutes.

3. Whisk chocolate mixture into egg mixture until combined. Fold in flour mixture until no dry streaks remain. Let dough sit at room temperature for 10 minutes.

4. Place granulated sugar and confectioners' sugar in separate shallow dishes. Working with 2 tablespoons dough at a time, roll into balls (or use #30 scoop). Drop dough balls directly into granulated sugar and roll to coat. Transfer dough balls to confectioners' sugar and roll to coat. Evenly space dough balls on prepared sheets, 11 per sheet.

5. Bake cookies, 1 sheet at a time, until puffed and cracked and edges have begun to set but centers are still soft (cookies will look raw between cracks and seem underdone), about 12 minutes, rotating sheet halfway through baking. Let cool completely on sheet before serving.

RATING COOKIE PRESSES

A cookie press works like a dough "gun": You put a perforated disk for the desired cookie shape at the bottom of the barrel, fill the tube with cookie dough, and screw on a handle at the top. You place the press on the cookie sheet and squeeze the trigger to release a spritz of dough. When they work well, cookie presses can produce dozens of uniform spritz cookies in a flash. We tested five models priced from around $13 to nearly $30. After forming and baking multiple batches of buttery cookies, we rated each press on how easy it was to fill, use, and clean, taking into account how appealing the cookies it produced turned out. In testing, while our top three presses all rapidly and comfortably pumped out good cookies most of the time, only the OXO Good Grips Cookie Press with Disk Storage Case made crisp, consistent shapes with every one of its dozen disks. Products are listed in order of preference. See AmericasTestKitchen.com for updates and complete testing results.

RECOMMENDED

OXO Good Grips Cookie Press with Disk Storage Case
CLEANUP: ★★   EASE OF USE: ★★★
COOKIE SHAPE: ★★★   PRICE: $29.99
COMMENTS: This press created consistent cookies every time, with a nonslip base to keep it steady while dispensing. A button releases the plunger so that there is no need to engage and disengage the ratcheting mechanism. Straightforward and comfortable to use, this model comes apart completely for cleaning. The only downside is that occasionally dough gets trapped behind the plunger. We like the handy ventilated storage case for its disks.

WILTON Cookie Pro Ultra II
CLEANUP: ★★★   EASE OF USE: ★★★
COOKIE SHAPE: ★★   PRICE: $24.99
COMMENTS: This press was quick, simple, and comfortable to use. The knob at the top of the center rod indicates whether the ratcheting mechanism is engaged. The nonslip base provides stability when pressing and the plunger creates a tight seal, leaving the barrel clean of any dough at the end of pressing. Its flaw was that not every one of the disks produced the advertised shape.

WILTON Comfort Grip Cookie Press
CLEANUP: ★★★   EASE OF USE: ★★
COOKIE SHAPE: ★★   PRICE: $12.99
COMMENTS: Our previous winning press still performed well and was comfortable and easy to use and clean. It pumped out dough quickly and produced good-looking cookies with almost every disk in the set. It was missing two features that help with foolproof cookies: a nonslip base and an indicator for when the ratcheting mechanism is engaged.

NOT RECOMMENDED

NORPRO Cookie/Icing Press
CLEANUP: ★★   EASE OF USE: ★½
COOKIE SHAPE: ★   PRICE: $20.00
COMMENTS: This press uses a lever to pump out cookies and features a regulator that allows you to choose between small and large cookies. Unfortunately, the small cookies were really tiny and often irregular in shape, and the large cookies turned into amorphous blobs after they were baked. Also, the stainless-steel barrel has sharp edges that cut one of our testers when she cleaned it.

NORDIC WARE Spritz Cookie Press
CLEANUP: ★★   EASE OF USE: ½
COOKIE SHAPE: ½   PRICE: $26.50
COMMENTS: Assembly and cleanup were easy; getting anything that resembled a properly formed cookie out of this gadget was the hard part. Despite following instructions to the letter and trying multiple times, we simply could not get a full tray of whole, good-looking cookies from this press.

CONVERSIONS AND EQUIVALENCIES

SOME SAY COOKING IS A SCIENCE AND AN ART. WE would say that geography has a hand in it, too. Flour milled in the United Kingdom and elsewhere will feel and taste different from flour milled in the United States. So, while we cannot promise that the loaf of bread you bake in Canada or England will taste the same as a loaf baked in the States, we can offer guidelines for converting weights and measures. We also recommend that you rely on your instincts when making our recipes. Refer to the visual cues provided. If the bread dough hasn't "come together in a ball," as described, you may need to add more flour—even if the recipe doesn't tell you so. You be the judge.

The recipes in this book were developed using standard U.S. measures following U.S. government guidelines. The charts below offer equivalents for U.S., metric, and imperial (U.K.) measures. All conversions are approximate and have been rounded up or down to the nearest whole number. For example:

1 teaspoon = 4.929 milliliters, rounded up to 5 milliliters
1 ounce = 28.349 grams, rounded down to 28 grams

VOLUME CONVERSIONS

U.S.	METRIC
1 teaspoon	5 milliliters
2 teaspoons	10 milliliters
1 tablespoon	15 milliliters
2 tablespoons	30 milliliters
¼ cup	59 milliliters
⅓ cup	79 milliliters
½ cup	118 milliliters
¾ cup	177 milliliters
1 cup	237 milliliters
1¼ cups	296 milliliters
1½ cups	355 milliliters
2 cups	473 milliliters
2½ cups	591 milliliters
3 cups	710 milliliters
4 cups (1 quart)	0.946 liter
1.06 quarts	1 liter
4 quarts (1 gallon)	3.8 liters

WEIGHT CONVERSIONS

OUNCES	GRAMS
½	14
¾	21
1	28
1½	43
2	57
2½	71
3	85
3½	99
4	113
4½	128
5	142
6	170
7	198
8	227
9	255
10	283
12	340
16 (1 pound)	454

CONVERSIONS FOR INGREDIENTS COMMONLY USED IN BAKING

Baking is an exacting science. Because measuring by weight is far more accurate than measuring by volume, and thus more likely to achieve reliable results, in our recipes we provide ounce measures in addition to cup measures for many ingredients. Refer to the chart below to convert these measures into grams.

INGREDIENT	OUNCES	GRAMS
Flour		
1 cup all-purpose flour*	5	142
1 cup cake flour	4	113
1 cup whole-wheat flour	5½	156
Sugar		
1 cup granulated (white) sugar	7	198
1 cup packed brown sugar (light or dark)	7	198
1 cup confectioners' sugar	4	113
Cocoa Powder		
1 cup cocoa powder	3	85
Butter†		
4 tablespoons (½ stick, or ¼ cup)	2	57
8 tablespoons (1 stick, or ½ cup)	4	113
16 tablespoons (2 sticks, or 1 cup)	8	227

* U.S. all-purpose flour, the most frequently used flour in this book, does not contain leaveners, as some European flours do. These leavened flours are called self-rising or self-raising. If you are using self-rising flour, take this into consideration before adding leavening to a recipe.

† In the United States, butter is sold both salted and unsalted. We generally recommend unsalted butter. If you are using salted butter, take this into consideration before adding salt to a recipe.

OVEN TEMPERATURES

FAHRENHEIT	CELSIUS	GAS MARK (imperial)
225	105	¼
250	120	½
275	135	1
300	150	2
325	165	3
350	180	4
375	190	5
400	200	6
425	220	7
450	230	8
475	245	9

CONVERTING TEMPERATURES FROM AN INSTANT-READ THERMOMETER

We include doneness temperatures in many of our recipes, such as those for poultry, meat, and bread. We recommend an instant-read thermometer for the job. Refer to the table above to convert Fahrenheit degrees to Celsius. Or, for temperatures not represented in the chart, use this simple formula:

Subtract 32 degrees from the Fahrenheit reading, then divide the result by 1.8 to find the Celsius reading.

EXAMPLE:

"Roast until chicken thigh registers 175 degrees."
To convert:

175° F − 32 = 143°
143° ÷ 1.8 = 79.44°C, rounded down to 79°C

INDEX

Curry

powder, mild versus Madras, 191

Thai, by color and spice, 196

D

Desserts

Best Almond Cake, *274*, 275–78

Chocolate Crinkle Cookies, 303–6, *304*

Cream Cheese Brownies, 56–60, *58*

French Apple Tart, 79–84, *80*

Fresh Strawberry Mousse, 290–94, *291*

Gluten-Free Chocolate Chip Cookies, 257–60, *258*

Lemon Pudding Cakes, 286–90, *287*

Perfect Latin Flan, 298–302, *299*

Almond, 302

Coffee, 302

Orange-Cardamom, 302

Diastatic malt powders, ratings of, 243

E

Easy Sandwich Bread, *264*, **265–68**

Eggplant Involtini, 146–51, *147*

Eggs

Cheese Soufflé, 8–13, *11*

Pasta Frittata with Broccoli Rabe, 8

Pasta Frittata with Sausage and Hot Peppers, *4*, 5–8

separating yolks from whites, 302

Singapore Noodles, 188–91, *189*

Equipment, ratings of

bench scrapers, 123

bread lame, 243

colanders, 20

cookie presses, 307

couche, 243

diastatic malt powder, 243

flipping board, 243

freezer storage bags, 111

French presses, 85

Equipment, ratings of *(cont.)*

grill brushes, 237

grill cleaning kits, 237

grilling tools, 237

KettlePizza kits, 237

mandolines, 31

mixing bowls, 167

soufflé dishes, 13

stand mixers, 295

tablet stands and covers, 71

13 by 9-inch metal baking pans, 61

wine savers, 99

F

Feta and Tahini, Roasted Butternut Squash with, 110

Fish

Cioppino, 126–30, *127*

reheating, 122

Sesame-Crusted Salmon with Lemon and Ginger, 119–22, *121*

Sesame-Crusted Salmon with Lime and Coriander, 122

Sesame-Crusted Salmon with Orange and Chili Powder, 122

Tacos, Grilled, *114*, 115–18

Five-spice powder, taste tests on, 203

Flan, Latin, Perfect, 298–302, *299*

Almond, 302

Coffee, 302

Orange-Cardamom, 302

Flipping boards, ratings of, 243

Flour Blend, The America's Test Kitchen Gluten-Free, 256

Fond, creating flavor with, 55

Freezer storage bags, ratings of, 111

French Apple Tart, 79–84, *80*

French presses, ratings of, 85

Fresh Strawberry Mousse, 290–94, *291*

Fried foods, starch for, 216

Fries, Thick-Cut Sweet Potato, 212–16, *213*
Frittata, Pasta
   with Broccoli Rabe, 8
   with Sausage and Hot Peppers, *4*, 5–8
Frozen yogurt, taste tests on, 227
Fruit. *See* Berries; *specific fruits*
Fry Sauce, Spicy, 216
Fusilli with Ricotta and Spinach, 151–54, *152*

G

Game Hens, Cornish
   Roasted, 74–79, *75*
   Roasted, Cumin-Coriander, 79
   Roasted, Herb-, 79
   Roasted, Oregano-Anise, 79
   taste tests on, 77
Garlic
   and Almond Soup, Spanish Chilled, 141–43, *142*
   -Lime Grilled Pork Tenderloin Steaks, 230–34, *231*
Ginger
   -Carrot Soup, 28–30, *29*
   and Lemon, Sesame-Crusted Salmon with, 119–22, *121*
   -Orange Grilled Pork Tenderloin Steaks, Spicy, 234
   Rice and Pasta Pilaf with Pomegranate and Walnuts, 42
   Thai Chicken Curry with Potatoes and Peanuts, 194–98, *195*
   -Tomato Vinaigrette, Warm, *32*, 37
Gluten-Free Chocolate Chip Cookies, 257–60, *258*
Gluten-Free Flour Blend, The America's Test Kitchen, 256
Gluten-Free Pizza, The Best, 250-256, *251*
Gluten-free spaghetti, taste tests on, 261
Goat Cheese, Pecans, and Maple, Roasted Butternut Squash with, 110
Grains
   jasmine rice, taste tests on, 49
   quinoa, varieties of, 236

Grains *(cont.)*
   Quinoa Pilaf with Chipotle, Queso Fresco, and Peanuts, *235*, 237
   Quinoa Pilaf with Herbs and Lemon, 234–37
   Rice and Lentils with Crispy Onions (Mujaddara), 93–98, *95*
   Rice and Pasta Pilaf, 41–42
   Rice and Pasta Pilaf, Herbed, 42
   Rice and Pasta Pilaf with Golden Raisins and Almonds, *40*, 42
   Rice and Pasta Pilaf with Pomegranate and Walnuts, 42
   Tabbouleh, 163–66, *164*
Grapes
   Spanish Chilled Almond and Garlic Soup, 141–43, *142*
Green Beans, Pesto, and Potatoes, Pasta with, 21–24, *22*
Green curries, about, 196
Greens
   Caldo Verde, *138*, 139–40
   Fusilli with Ricotta and Spinach, 151–54, *152*
   Grilled Fish Tacos, *114*, 115–18
   Grilled Napa Cabbage and Radicchio Topping, 211
   Roasted Butternut Squash with Radicchio and Parmesan, 110
Grilled dishes
   Garlic-Lime Grilled Pork Tenderloin Steaks, 230–34, *231*
   Grilled Bacon-Wrapped Scallops, *220*, 221–23
   Grilled Chicken Souvlaki, *158*, 159–63
   Grilled Fish Tacos, *114*, 115–18
   Grilled Napa Cabbage and Radicchio Topping, 211
   Grilled Scallion Topping, 211
   Grilled Shiitake Mushroom Topping, 211
   Lemon-Thyme Grilled Pork Tenderloin Steaks, 234
   Mexican-Style Grilled Steak (Carne Asada), 170–74, *171*
   Spicy Orange-Ginger Grilled Pork Tenderloin Steaks, 234
   Tender, Juicy Grilled Burgers, *206*, 207–11